The Best American Travel Writing 2010

The Best American Travel Writing™ 2010

Edited and with an Introduction
by **Bill Buford**

Jason Wilson, Series Editor

A Mariner Original
HOUGHTON MIFFLIN HARCOURT
BOSTON · NEW YORK 2010

www.hmhbooks.com

ISSN 1530-1516
ISBN 978-0-547-33335-9

Printed in the United States of America

DOC 10 9 8 7 6 5 4 3 2 1

Contents

Foreword

"YOU CAN'T DRIVE NATURE," the Amarone producer said. "Nature drives you." She was talking about the wine, the way her family is able to release vintages from certain vineyards only in certain years, and how the grapes determine this, as well as if the wine will be aged for two or three or four years, and whether that aging will happen in large barrels or small. "We never know what Nature gives us." Of course, I hear some version of this trope every time I visit a winery, no matter where it is. But on this day, the idea that Nature drives the world took on special meaning.

That's because, at that point, I'd been stranded in Italy for three days. As you surely know, a volcano in Iceland with the unpronounceable name Eyjafjallajokull had been spewing a bit of ash this year, causing havoc with air travel. Many, in fact, have called Eyjafjallajokull the worst disruption in the history of transportation. My trip was supposed to be a four-day jaunt to visit wineries in the Veneto, focusing on Prosecco. The plan: jet in; visit a dozen wineries in four days; jet out; return home; write article. Like millions of others during April's shutdown of European airspace, I hadn't factored a volcano into my plans. So the airline canceled my Sunday morning flight from Venice, with the earliest possibility of return on Thursday.

Ha-ha. That's your comment on my plight, right? Stuck for four extra days in Italy! As you can imagine, there was very little sympathy forthcoming from family, friends, and coworkers when I texted them the news. "Awwww," texted my wife. "It must be *such* a struggle to be stranded in that boutique hotel featured in *Architectural Digest!*"

"You can always get a boat home," texted my friend Pete, an Italian American pasta maker. "That's how my family got over to the States."

When I let one friend know of my predicament, she simply texted, "You suck."

Indeed, folks, life can be a struggle. But perhaps this was not one of them. On Sunday, the first day of my exile, I accompanied a young winemaker to lunch at the restaurant his family just opened on an island off Venice. It was a warm, sunny day. There were these delicious soft-shell crabs you can only eat in Venice. And also lots of Prosecco.

"Everything OK?" my mother texted.

"Yes," I wrote back. "All is fine. I'm just boarding the vaporetto back from lunch, and Matteo is going to give me a tour of Venice's wine bars."

No further reply or concern from Mom.

At a certain point, I felt like the overprivileged son of a deposed dictator, one who lives in the lap of luxury and yet will never go back to his homeland. The night before my flight was canceled, I'd had dinner in the beautiful hill town of Asolo. A famous exile, Caterina Cornaro, the queen of Cyprus from 1474 to 1489, was sent to Asolo after she may or may not have poisoned her husband. (Perhaps he'd also been waylaid by volcanic ash?) During her exile, the Italian verb *asolare*—meaning "to pass time in a delightful but meaningless way"—came into usage. Perhaps that's how I can sum up my brief stranding in Italy. I visited some more wineries. Made some more friends. *Ho asolato.*

I'd love to tell you of a single hardship. That I paid a thousand dollars for a taxi to take me to an open airport, where I had to sleep on a cot. That my boss was really upset with me. That my children forgot who I was. But no. Basically, I just spent four more days drinking wine and eating in Italy.

After I visited the Amarone producer, I had another sunny lunch at a restaurant facing Lago di Garda. This is the same region that D. H. Lawrence wrote about in his classic travel book *Twilight in Italy*, a series of sketches about his stay from the fall of 1912 to the spring of 1913. Lawrence uses the slow peasant existence of Lago di Garda as a metaphor for all that is good and pure in the world, setting it against what he calls the "purpose stinking in it all, the mechanising, the perfect mechanising of human life."

"Yet what should become of the world?" Lawrence writes. ". . . The industrial countries spreading like a blackness over all the world, horrible, in the end destructive. And the Garda was so lovely under the sky of sunshine, it was intolerable."

I was actually reading *Twilight in Italy* during my stranding. Lawrence's book is strange—as is all great travel writing. But *Twilight in Italy* is also something else that all great travel writing seems to be: prescient. On the surface, Lawrence's account is about lemon houses or ancient churches or old women spinning wool. But at the same time, it's undeniably about war, the collapse of the old order, the coming fascism. Lawrence left Lago di Garda only slightly more than a year before Archduke Franz Ferdinand was assassinated in Sarajevo, leading swiftly to the outbreak of World War I. *Twilight in Italy*, published in 1916, predated Mussolini's rise to power by only six years.

"Events ought to prove the worth of the travel book," wrote Paul Theroux in an essay called "Travel Writing: The Point of It." According to Theroux, "The job of the travel writer is to go far and wide, make voluminous notes, and tell the truth. There is immense drudgery in the job. But the book ought to live, and if it is truthful, it ought to be prescient without making predictions."

As I relaxed in the warm Garda sunshine, I wondered whether Eyjafjallajokull marked a new turning point in travel. Nearly a hundred years after *Twilight in Italy*, what would Lawrence have to say about this? Here was a case where an ancient geological structure completely halted—for a brief time, anyway—the "mechanising of human life" he so disdained. What new, exciting, and frightening epoch were we about to enter?

I still don't know what Lawrence would say, but this is what I told myself: Relax, dude. You're in Italy. Try to find a little enjoyment. Great travel writing is about that, too.

The stories included here are, as always, selected from among hundreds of pieces in hundreds of diverse publications—from mainstream and specialty magazines to Sunday newspaper travel sections to literary journals to travel Web sites. I've done my best to be fair and representative, and in my opinion the best travel stories from 2009 were forwarded to Bill Buford, who made our final selections.

I now begin anew by reading the hundreds of stories published in 2010. I am once again asking editors and writers to submit the best of whatever it is they define as travel writing. These submissions must be nonfiction, published in the United States during the 2010 calendar year. They must not be reprints or excerpts from published books. They must include the author's name, date of publication, and publication name, and they must be tear sheets, the complete publication, or a clear photocopy of the piece as it originally appeared. I must receive all submissions by January 1, 2011, in order to ensure full consideration for the next collection.

Further, publications that want to make certain that their contributions will be considered for the next edition should make sure to include this anthology on their subscription list. Submissions or subscriptions should be sent to Jason Wilson, The Best American Travel Writing, P.O. Box 260, Haddonfield, NJ 08033.

I truly enjoyed working with Bill Buford, one of my literary heroes as both writer and editor, and I very much envy his current project, investigating whether French cuisine is all that it's cracked up to be. I am also grateful to Nicole Angeloro and Jesse Smith for their help on this, our eleventh edition of *The Best American Travel Writing*.

JASON WILSON

Introduction

FIVE YEARS AGO, I was introduced to a book that includes what may be the first example of modern travel writing. It was written in Latin and describes a trip to the British Isles made in 1435 by a Tuscan emissary of the Church in Rome. The emissary, from a village south of Siena and between the towns of Montalcino and Montepulciano, was born to a farming family, the eldest of eighteen children, and, from early on, appears to have had a literary gift. He found his first job, at twenty-six, writing speeches. He wrote many more, mainly for the various cardinals who employed him, plus an obscene play (now lost), poetry (most of it lost), a universal history of everything (incomplete), an erotic novel (widely circulated among monasteries in Europe), and an autobiographical journal, his *Commentaries,* that were discovered a hundred years after his death and published in 1584, after the saltier passages had been excised. The author is Aeneas Piccolomini, and in his name are many of the contradictions that would surface in his life. In "Aeneas," he seemed to have been born the wanderer he became. But in "Piccolomini," he had a surname so Tuscan and geographically specific that it calls to mind the wet smells of the region's hilly dark dirt, as if the author's fate had always been to bear a bit of home wherever he went. The name has lived on in a wine made by his family for the past five centuries. It seems fitting that I learned about him from someone who is both a Renaissance scholar and an oenologist.

Aeneas (as the author refers to himself, always in the third person) begins his journey in Arras, a cathedral town north of Paris, where, in July 1435, he joined a summer-long congress convened to end the Hundred Years' War between the British and the French. The war resumed, but the congress succeeded in repairing some of the damage that had been done to France. The country was a rump version of itself. It had lost western and northern provinces to the English. It had lost eastern and other northern provinces to Philip III, the powerful Duke of Burgundy—in effect, one of its own. Even the town of Arras was under the control of the duke, who, in a historically flamboyant act, had abjured his oath to the French king and sworn an allegiance to the English. But the "Good Duke," as he became known, also attending the congress, was subjected to weeks and weeks of cajoling and flattery. He was brought round. On September 15, 1435, he renounced his Englishness and once again became French. (The Good Duke was an accomplished practitioner of serial fidelity in his home as well—where he fathered eighteen illegitimate children, by twenty-one mistresses, in addition to the three legitimate children born from three marriages.) Aeneas celebrated the reconciliation by writing a poem, which he presented to the pragmatic nobleman, and then, on or around the autumnal equinox, he set off for Scotland. He had a diplomatic mission involving a disgraced prelate.

At Calais, Aeneas was suspected by the city's English overseers of being a sympathizer of the now "traitorous Duke" (the poem, surely, gave him away) and was imprisoned. Once he was released, he crossed the English Channel, reached Dover, and then traveled, probably on foot, to London for a Royal Passport to guarantee his safe passage to Edinburgh. It was denied (the poem again). Aeneas was ordered back across the Channel, a stressful business, not least because he had been to sea only once before, sailing up the Tuscan coast a hundred miles, hugging the shore, land always in view, utterly straightforward—until a wind blew his ship off course: first Elba, then Corsica, then across the Mediterranean to Africa.

Once back in Calais, Aeneas briskly headed north, walking through the Netherlands, to Sluis, then an inland port near Bruges, and, welcomed by a young Flemish captain, set sail for Scotland. That night, just after reaching the English Channel, they were caught in a storm—a fourteen-hour horror, everyone on board believing the ship was going to capsize and sink. The wind died down; the weather improved. Then another storm struck, its hurricane-force winds so much more severe than the first storm's that the ship, its hull rupturing and taking on water, was tossed into the Norwegian Arctic. When the sky cleared, the stars were unknown to the Flemish captain and his crew. Aeneas prayed to be saved. When they reached Scotland—the trip took nearly two weeks—he vowed to walk barefoot to the nearest shrine and give thanks, not knowing that, unlike in Italy, Scotland's places of worship were far apart (it was ten miles), the weather was severe (it was December), and no one, no matter how grateful, hiked without his shoes on ground covered by ice. Carried by others (his feet frostbit), Aeneas arrived in Edinburgh on or around the winter solstice. The city must have been incomprehensible to him, but he was animated by its foreignness—the strange short days (he counted four hours of light), the strange short men, the strangely uninhibited women—and once his diplomatic mission was completed, he didn't want to leave, even though the Flemish captain, a fiancée waiting to marry him back home, had saved a berth for him. Did Aeneas watch as the ship pulled away, relishing the complex emotions of being left behind? The text is unclear. Others did watch, however, as the vessel sank, the Scottish weather rising up again without warning. Four survivors clung to floating detritus, but everyone else drowned, including the betrothed captain. Aeneas doesn't say how much longer he remained in Scotland, or even why, satisfying a writer's curiosity, no doubt, and for other reasons, perhaps, including an uninhibited Scottish woman who, unblemished by the weakest ray of sun, had a ghostly pallor that the tawny Tuscan appears to have found otherworldly and difficult to resist. At least one illegitimate child was left behind.

The Aeneas Piccolomini story is illuminating in several ways, including the most elementary, being an example of the salty sailor's yarn: someone travels to a place where no one else from home has been and returns with an account of what he has witnessed. In Piccolomini's case, that includes dinner (never a small concern for an Italian, even then). Crossing the Scottish-English border near the River Tweed, he stops for shelter and is served a hearty meal of chickens, geese, and savory pies (stuffed with game birds, probably)—a primitive feast of grunting and grease, bounteous in quantity but not in kind (no vegetable, little starch), a hunter's knife the likely utensil. Bemused but grateful, Aeneas shares his wine and bread. His hosts have never seen either item. They regard them as miraculous. All night, pregnant women and their husbands touch the bread and sniff the wine, perplexed and excited. In the detail is narrative writing at its most basic — I saw, you didn't, I can't wait to tell you — and it is a refreshing characteristic of good travel writing, akin, say, to figurative painting in art (what is more basic than the human body?) or a melody in music (what is more basic than a tune you can whistle?). It is old-fashioned; it works. The Polish journalist Ryszard Kapuscinski (*The Emperor, Shah of Shahs*), who died in 2007, was the greatest travel writer among our contemporaries, and I wonder if his storytelling urgency owes something to the perverse anachronisms of his early life — the Neanderthals of the Communist state colluding with postwar poverty to keep his Polish compatriots in a cultural stone age, where the exotic and the faraway were no more exotic and no farther away than some spot too far to walk to. Kapuscinski became Poland's foreign correspondent, famously witnessing nineteen revolutions and coups. But he became a writer by describing for his readers back home Indian tigers with stripes and Chinese eating with chopsticks.

Every piece in this volume is informed by this basic "I saw, you didn't" travel writer's axiom (or by its sometimes comic variation: "I saw, you didn't, you should be glad"). Matthew Power learns that two men are walking the length of the Amazon, four thousand miles, starting in Peru. By the time he joins up, a year into the journey, the team has been reduced to one. (The horror! You are glad not to be there.) Not far away, Ted Genoways and his father enter a rainforest in Suriname, looking for a species of bat that lives, if it still lives, in trees untouched by humans. (Grumpy father, grumpy son, grumpy prospect. Glad not to be there.) The steaks of Argentina are the best on the planet; Steven Rinella travels there to eat one. The food of Emilia-Romagna is unearthly; Patrick Symmes seeks out its unearthliness. (I tasted, you haven't.) For twenty-seven years, Simon Winchester has visited, or tried to visit, an island that few people go to (we are glad not to be among them): the barren Tristan da Cunha, a minuscule volcanic hump off the coast of South Africa, settled mainly by British émigrés who refuse to leave. (Principal activity: home knitting. Principal industry: home knitting. Principal export: home knitting.)

Piccolomini's story is modern, however, in a different way. It is one of the first accounts in which the traveler is as important as the tale. These were early days. The press, with movable type, that would ultimately print Piccolomini's *Commentaries* after his death hadn't been invented. Neither had the audience to whom the press would introduce authors, nor, for that matter, travel writing itself. Daniel Defoe's story of his journey around the British Isles, regarded by many as the first travel book in English, wouldn't be published for three hundred years. The Atlantic had yet to be crossed—no Spanish or Italian sea captain or warring conqueror had an exotic New World yarn to tell—and readers were spared, for another four centuries, the bigoted, self-important "literature" occasioned by an English grand tour. There were chronicles, but the model was ecclesiastic or historic (the Gallic wars, the North African wars, the Alexandrine wars). Piccolomini, by making himself a character in his own story—Aeneas did this, Aeneas saw that—renders the person on the journey as important as what he observes. With considerably more contrivance, Norman Mailer would use the same technique more than five hundred years later in *The Armies of the Night:* Mailer went, Mailer saw, Mailer now knows. The effect of both efforts is the same: a narrative in the third person ("he") has the force of the first ("I"). The adventures we read have been made by the authors themselves. We know that.

All travel writing is, without exception, told in the first person—I go, I see, I tell you what I saw—even if it's disguised or buried. That point is rarely made, probably because it's obvious, but it illustrates what one hopes to find in writing of this kind. Not tips about hotels or restaurants. For that, you go to a newspaper or log on to TripAdvisor.com. Not even, necessarily, a sense of the place visited. Yes, the place matters, in varying degrees—sometimes a lot, sometimes hardly at all. In Peter LaSalle's elegant, almost overwhelmingly first-person account of walking, place is replaceable. It could be Paris. It could be Rio de Janeiro. It could be anywhere but home: someplace, anyplace, disorienting enough to make him notice what he wouldn't otherwise see. (The medicinal benefits of disorientation can never be overestimated.) Place defines us more than our habits allow us to know. In this is the appeal of Aeneas's story. He was changed by his trip to the British Isles. "I was changed," I want a writer to concede, believing that if I am going to read about a journey that I am unable to take, I want it to be a journey that scrambles the writer's brain.

"Everybody I knew," Peter Hessler writes in "Strange Stones," describing the people he had met in the Peace Corps, "had been changed forever by the experience." Every one of them, including Hessler and the other midwestern refugees from American normalcy, who had signed on not knowing what they were going to find, except that it wasn't going to be what they had left behind, now think differently. "The days I spent with the Hadza," Michael Finkel writes, describing two weeks in the company of Tanzanian hunter-gatherers, "altered my perception of the world." He slept with them, joined a nighttime hunt, shared its bounty: a baboon's campfire-roasted cranium; hot, burning the fingers he slurped the contents up with. In the members of the tribe, he glimpsed something. "They made me feel calmer, more attuned to the moment, more self-sufficient . . . I don't care if this sounds maudlin: my time with the Hadza made me happier."

The change isn't always theatrical. Tom Bissell's trip to Jerusalem is less like travel writing than a monologue about the nature of betrayal. He spends an uncompromisingly intense afternoon in the Hinnom Valley, where Judas may have hanged himself. Nothing happens, but, in effect, everything has happened and continues to happen. The result is a very internalized piece of writing, closer in tone and ambition to fiction than journalism. (This was the first writing I'd read by Bissell, when I was alone at home, on a Saturday afternoon. I stopped halfway through and hurled his piece to the ground in awe and respect, shouting to an empty room: "Who is this guy? He is a terrific writer!") Susan Orlean wasn't changed by her most recent trip to Morocco, but she was by an earlier one, haunted by a vision of a donkey, work animal of prehistory, bearing all of Wal-Mart on its back. Then there is Ian Frazier.

Some writers find stories on the extreme verges of human behavior. They get shot at, beaten. They go to Afghanistan (very in vogue if you're in the Graham Greene wannabe school): mountains, bandits, illegal drugs, illegal guns, illegal everything, bad guys, our guys, stories in every direction. I picture Ian Frazier at his desk, surveying the world. Afghanistan, the Amazon, the Sudan: Nah, too easy. He thinks: Flat. Why jump from an airplane, join guerrillas, tag along with heroin smugglers, when, instead, you could have . . . monotony? Setting the bar high, he thinks: Boredom and unrelieved tedium. Then the dare of all dares. He thinks: I will make claustrophobia funny. He decides he will drive very slowly across Siberia. No, that's too easy. He will get someone else to drive him very slowly, in a very bad car.

Four years ago, I was asked to introduce readings by two authors, Ian Frazier and Steve Martin, at a theater on New York's Lower East Side. A privilege, obviously. Beforehand, we met in the greenroom. Steve Martin was effortlessly present: groomed, his silver hair bright like electricity, wearing a lightweight blue suit, casual but respectful. He stood, aware of every millimeter of his body and how it occupied space. He had a presence, an aura. Ian Frazier sat hunched in a plastic chair, one leg crossed over the other, his shoulders rolled forward. He looked like a tired question mark in repose. He had shabby flops of hair, half-covering his ears, jagged, poking this way and that. Three months earlier, he must have looked in the mirror and thought: It's time for a haircut. And then: Who knows? His shirttail billowed and came loose when he stood up, and he would, or would not, tuck it back in. His skin looked like Diet Coke. He addressed Steve Martin.

"Who should go first?"

Martin didn't understand.

"Out there. I was wondering if you'd thought about who should go first."

We hadn't discussed this. Frazier is talented and funny—on the page. He's a writer. He works in a small room. Martin has done years of standup comedy. He is a performer. He works in theaters and on household television sets across the country. Who wants to follow Steve Martin?

Frazier's worry seemed genuine. "You know, I've been doing this for a long time."

Steve Martin chuckled. The chuckle was involuntary. It embarrassed him. He didn't want to be patronizing. But Steve Martin is America's funniest funnyman. I found myself studying Frazier's mouth. What would come out next?

"It's just that people don't know what it's like to come second.

After me, that is. They're not prepared for it, because I don't do this sort of thing very much, and so they don't know. I wanted to warn you. I'm really good."

Steve Martin smiled.

"I don't want you to be surprised."

There is often a difference between the author you know from reading his writing and the one you happen to meet in person. Writing is lonely. I had an ungenerous thought: Is Frazier a loony narcissist?

Frazier would go first. I did my introduction. My wife was in the audience. I took a seat. Frazier read.

Within a minute — maybe it was thirty seconds — the entire audience was laughing. In another two minutes, I heard, from three people at once, that shrieking hysteria that I associate with being fourteen and unable to stop my root beer from pouring back out through my nose: the laughter that doesn't stop, high-pitched, beyond controlling, embarrassing but infectious, a little like sex in public, and just an emotional degree lower than crying. Then there was that: crying. My wife cried. Some guy next to me cried. I cried, my cheek sopping with streaky tears. I was the introducer. Where was my dignity? Then I fell out of my chair.

Steve Martin followed. He didn't have a chance. DOA.

As you read Ian Frazier's account of driving across Siberia, you may want to consider his gift for understatement. (You will never read a more understated piece of writing. Consider the tedium that goes into one of the simple lines describing it. We read it in ten seconds. It was written in ten minutes. But the actual real-time experience? Days, a spring poking into Frazier's butt, a driver who won't stop at any of the places on Frazier's list, the food, the indigestion, the smell of that indigestion, and then every time Frazier looks out the window, he sees exactly what he saw the last time: nothing. Beckett? A chatterbox.) Next: Imagine a shaggy-haired, badly dressed man reading it to you. He will be droll. His timing will be impeccable. He will be very, very funny. Then, once you've finished imagining, pause. Good writing has a quality of being self-erasing. There is nothing wrong, so you don't notice how good it is. Hold the moment — it is so evanescent — and recognize that it will be a long, long time before you read anything better.

*

It took Aeneas a long, long time to reach Edinburgh. It took him longer to return. The question was this: how was he going to get back? He refused to sail from Scotland, not surprisingly. The alternative, crossing from Dover, was shorter and safer—and in England. England, for Aeneas, was not safe. His entry had been barred by the king himself, young Henry VI. Without a Royal Passport, Aeneas would not be allowed to board a ship, if he got that far. The solution? Clandestine travel. Aeneas dressed as a merchant, a fugitive, and found refuge here and there, mainly in the cathedral towns (Newcastle, Durham, York) and, possibly—who knows? —among women, whose pale charms he had such difficulty resisting. (Another illegitimate child was born of an English woman.) Then, on reaching Dover, he discovered that the keepers of the port were happy to overlook the king's passport laws: for a price, of course, one he was prepared to pay.

Aeneas had been away for a year. He continued to work for the Church, but he wasn't of it, and he didn't take his orders until 1449, thirteen years later. The following year he was made a bishop; nine years later, a cardinal; two years after that, in 1458, pope, when, now Pius II, he returned to the village of his birth, evidently for the first time in four decades, hoping to find boyhood friends. He was disappointed. They were ill. Most were dead. Pius II departed, vowing to leave a memorial to his birthplace, which he renamed Pienza, after himself, and rebuilt it into a masterpiece of Renaissance humanist architecture. He died four years later.

Jessica Green is the Renaissance scholar and oenologist who introduced me to Aeneas's *Commentaries,* reading me hilarious extracts not long after they appeared in a new edition six years ago. Pienza combined her interests like a metaphor: the uniquely coherent monument to Renaissance humanism; the Piccolomini Palace, undisturbed because it had been lived in until 1961, when the last family member died in an airplane crash; the Piccolomini family wine, a one-of-a-kind Brunello. Jessica Green is my wife. In May 2005, we visited Pienza. The weather was awful, the town was nervous and mean, and the curator of the family palace guarded his treasures as though they were his own, jealously, suspicious of outsiders, more interested in keeping what he had than sharing any of it. For my wife and me, it was a turning point. She was five months pregnant with what would turn out to be outsize twin boys. We left discouraged. When would we return to Italy? Or Europe? The Pienza project looked doubtful.

Piccolomini's trip came back to me in Simon Winchester's account of the inhabitants of the miserable Tristan da Cunha, off South America. In 1961, when the volcano on their stump hump of an island had become active, they were evacuated to Hampshire, England. For a temperament hardened by foul-weather island life, Hampshire was far too nice. It was outright cushy. So most of them returned. It was the return that puzzled me. The British, or their islander descendants, actually like a miserable island in miserable weather. On balance, they really like misery. And I thought of puzzled Aeneas trying to figure out why anyone would want to live in a place with four hours of light and no trees. The Winchester piece comes to mind now because he describes a dilemma faced by most writers, especially travel writers, who go out into the world looking for stories. They are scavengers, my wife pointed out. They steal. I had just told her that I'd found a way of using Piccolomini's writing. Why, I now wonder, did I think this news would make her happy?

Our world had changed, and I hadn't noticed. In some curious way, reading these pieces, admiring their authors' gifts, projecting myself (or not) into the trips they took, I fell into a kind of armchair traveler's lull, regretting that our new life, with twin four-year-old boys, prevented us from being travelers, prepared to change our circumstances in order to risk, well, everything. Then I remembered: I'm reading this piece in an apartment that overlooks the River Saône. We live in a place that has been occupied for four millennia. I moved my long-suffering family to Lyon and never realized the implications. We are living the very phenomenon described in these pieces. Maybe it's time we returned to Pienza.

BILL BUFORD

The Best American
Travel Writing 2010

HENRY ALFORD

Appointment in Istanbul

FROM *New York Times Magazine*

SOMETIMES WHAT YOU GET is not what you thought you wanted. I had just broken up with my boyfriend of ten years back in New York, and had flown to Istanbul to try to sightsee my heartbreak away. But then here, unexpectedly, was this very handsome Istanbul native sitting in the placid park just outside the Hagia Sophia: we'd been staring at each other admiringly from our respective park benches. After our glances grew less furtive, he waved me over. I feigned surprise, introduced myself, and sat down. His name was Zia, he said, and he had been studying English for three years. He proudly pulled a Turkish-English phrase book from his pocket. His slightly awkward manner seemed situational—but I couldn't tell whether the situation was that his English was halting, or that he was Muslim and flirting with a man, or that he was Muslim and flirting with a man in front of such a historic mosque.

We stumbled through a conversation. He invited me to dinner at a nearby restaurant. We ordered beer and some mezes. Our eye contact was intermittent but potent. When I asked Zia if he had a job, he didn't understand, so I looked up "job" in his phrase book, which it wrongly translated as "cog." I asked, "Do you have a cog?" He said, "I am doing with shoes." He'd even made the shoes he was wearing; I looked, and complimented him: "Nice cog."

Next we discussed music; Zia said he liked blues, Barbra "Strayand," Céline Dion, the Rolling Stones. "But my favorite is Céline Dion." The combination of footwear professional and homely-songbird worship made me think that I was definitely going to get lucky. Then he asked me if I was free the following day, and I said yes, and that I was interested in the cinema and swimming. Zia said he knew of a beautiful pool that is never mentioned in guidebooks.

When we left the restaurant, I gently leaned my body against his, our only physical contact since shaking hands in the park. He murmured in the affirmative, looking down at the ground. I asked him if he wanted to come to my hotel room, and he said, "I live with my mother and family." I nodded my head sympathetically. He said it would take him almost an hour to get home. I asked if he would travel by bus or subway, and he said, "On camel." Then: "I make joke."

We made a plan to meet on the park bench the next day at 10 A.M., and outside my hotel he shook my hand good night. We met on the park bench the next morning, all smiles and sheepishness. I'd folded up my bathing suit and put it in the pocket of my cargo pants; Zia smiled when I showed it to him, but then changed the topic: "Also to say about my guidance wages."

I felt a pang in my heart and mumbled, "How much?" He said, "Normally it is one hundred dollars for the day but for you sixty dollars." I looked down at the ground, hurt. I said, "When I saw you here yesterday, I thought you were very handsome. I was not looking for a guide." He lighted a thoughtful cigarette. I added: "I like men. Do you?" He said, "That is difficult to answer," pronouncing the *w*. He added, "It is complicated for me."

I waited for a minute, letting the feelings from my breakup carry over to this rejection. Then I stood up abruptly, reached into my pocket, and handed out a fistful of Turkish lira, which I computed as being about forty-five dollars. "That's for yesterday," I said huffily, before turning and walking away as fast and as purposefully as possible. I took pains to stay in his line of vision, in case he wanted to come after me. He did not. But I ran into him in the park three hours later. I put on my best face and lorded over him the details of my visit to Topkapi Palace; he looked at me as if to say, "I could have shown you that."

Gradually an air of détente settled over us. We trudged around Istanbul for about four hours—time infused with a sodden, emotionally humid quality, as if we were walking through hot broth. Once outside my hotel, it was clear that we were saying goodbye to each other for the last time. I dreaded him asking me for guidance wages for the day, and had decided that if he did, I would ask for the location of the pool.

He smiled at me knowingly and started to say something. I thought, Here it comes. When he stumbled on his words, I asked, "Yes?" He said, "And also thanks for the practice of language." I said, "And thanks for helping me forget about my breakup." I reached out to shake his hand, but realized that I wanted to hug him, so I did.

TOM BISSELL

Looking for Judas

FROM *Virginia Quarterly Review*

WE HAD BEEN LOOKING for Hakeldama for close to an hour, wandering through deep, desertic, geological gouges stubbled with little merkins of shrubbery and low gray trees that look squashed and drained of chlorophyll. The sun did strange things to the land- scape here, vivifying the dominating grays and sands, weakening the greens, and walling off thousands of hilltop and hillside houses behind shimmering heat-haze force fields. To walk along the Hin- nom Valley in a certain frame of mind, for a long enough time, is to become lonely and thirsty and vaguely alarmed, forgetful that above, on the upper slopes of the valley, a fifteen-minute walk away, is the walled Old City of Jerusalem. That this remote, unfriable, tactically worthless city, many miles from the nearest meaningful river or harbor, has become the Finland Station of monotheism is one of history's more enigmatic accidents. God would never have chosen Jerusalem and so Jerusalem chose God.

Jay suggested we try yet another path, one lined by a shin-high wall of pale-brown stones. This was his first visit to Jerusalem, too, but Jay was a historian, so I followed him. Some of the paths we had explored previously were blacktopped; this one was not. The path's gravel was still loose and crunchy: not many feet had been this way. To the left was the base of Mount Zion, the southern face of which was bare and undeveloped. To the right were rocky cliffs and, above them, sandstone apartment buildings (some quite tony) that could not be seen at present due to the steepness of the cliff walls. There was not much grass and what grass there was looked hayish. Nor was there much trash. What we did see along the path were many caves; most of them were barred but a few of the shallower ones could be explored. We passed some apparent dig sites fenced off with thin wire barriers. These little excavations all had an ongoing, archaeological neatness to them, but there were no archaeologists working here this afternoon who could help us find Hakeldama.

It was strange that, in a city where even the alleys had sites of world-changing historical consequence (not to mention several dozen motormouth freelance "tour guides" who would happily leave you alone for only a twenty-dollar bribe), we found ourselves nearing one of the few places whose present-day location scholars are reasonably sure is the same place mentioned by the New Testament—and yet there were no plaques, no signs, no people, no obvious paths; just caves, mud, and bushes. From where we now stood we could see at least ten pathways through the Valley of Hinnom. All of them were empty.

According to a fairly obscure verse in 2 Kings, in the Hinnom Valley children were burned alive as offerings to stubbornly enduring Canaanite gods. Jeremiah goes further, quoting the Lord's fulmination against those who spill the "blood of the innocent" in this "valley of Slaughter" and recording his dreadful promise of divine wrath: "I will make this city a horror, a thing to be hissed at; everyone who passes by it will be horrified and will hiss because of all its disasters." Later the valley was used as a place to dump things considered unclean (a rather overarching category for ancient Jews), whereupon all such refuse, including unclean corpses, was burned. The Hinnom Valley is thought to have spent a considerable span of time more or less continuously on fire. These fires' greasy soot and smoke, some of it redolent of barbecued human flesh, likely blew through the streets of Jerusalem, dirtying cloaks and staining buildings. Evidently, it became a social irritant of such magnitude that its only future lay in metaphor.

In Greek, *Hinnom* becomes *Gehenna,* a word employed several times in the New Testament. In the Gospel according to Matthew, Jesus claims it as a place the "scribes and Pharisees" will be unable to escape, while in the Gospel according to Mark, Jesus refers to its "unquenchable fire." By the first century c.e. the Valley of Hinnom was no longer used as an open-air furnace; certain associations, however, proved difficult for it to molt. Here was the rare religious tradition whose point mutations could be tracked virtually step-by-step. A site of child sacrifice, municipal incineration, and generally fell associations found at the base of a city becomes a fiery transdimensional prison imagined for some strange reason as being located *beneath* the physical world. In a pleasing swap of the usual semantics, in the Valley of Hinnom one could literally, rather than figuratively, walk through hell.

The valley was home to another site of profound but ambiguous importance to early Christianity, though its precise location was becoming increasingly difficult to verify. Jay, far ahead of me now, jumped off a small ledge onto another exceedingly thin path that led muddily toward a new clearing. Finally, Hakeldama. A dead tree, a rampike as gray and hard as concrete, stood near the middle of the clearing, all of its naked branches pushed one way, as though arranged by millennia of wind. Exposed, unfriendly stones the shape of mandibular canines stuck up out of the weedy grass. A Palestinian woman in a white headscarf and carrying a plastic shopping bag was walking along the ridge above us. A rooster called from the vicinity of Silwan, a nearby neighborhood.

Very little of the Old City could be seen from Hakeldama. We could see the Mount of Olives, from whence Jesus is said to have ascended to heaven, and which was now crowned with a glittering salt-white diadem of over 150,000 Jewish tombstones. Parts of the Mount's slope were striped with tall shaggy spears of cedar and blotted with shorter, rounder olive trees, but large portions of the Mount were bare. The Romans had cut down nearly every tree in the final years of the First Jewish War (66–73 C.E.) and the Mount had apparently never fully recovered. Jesus was arrested somewhere on or at the base of the Mount of Olives, in the Garden of Gethsemane, the present location of which is at best an informed guess. Judas Iscariot, one of Jesus' own disciples, guided the arresting party to Gethsemane, and Hakeldama is traditionally believed to be the place where that betrayer met his end.

In the various ancient copies of the New Testament texts that mention it, Hakeldama goes by many names: Akeldama, Acheldemach, Akeldaimach, Haceldama. It is a transliteration of an Aramaic word that means "field of blood." Two thousand years later, we stood in the middle of a place that had a reasonably valid claim to being that field. Here, many believed, a mysterious and calamitous fate laid its word across the most despised betrayer in human history. Yet once the initial frisson of its notoriety had passed, Hakeldama was not only lonely but unendurably dull.

Indeed, the Jerusalem Jay and I had thus far encountered could only be described as a series of disappointments in the face of history revealed. The zonated nature of the city—the source of its many ionized tensions—is, for the first-time visitor, its most overriding feature. No one is allowed entrance to as much as a coffee shop without being passed over by a security guard's explosive-detecting wand. This is expected, of course. Less expected are the church doors hung with signs that read: ABSOLUTELY NO FIRE-ARMS. The city's surreal variety of faiths and people, meanwhile, lives in something short of obvious amity. Jerusalem's crowded streets had the tight, phobic, elbowy feeling of a convention no one was particularly happy to be attending. Greek Orthodox priests in black robes and rope belts sullenly ate ice cream beside glum Franciscan priests in sunglasses and floppy hats. Hasids and headscarfed Arab women hurried through the streets as though being pursued by modernity. On David Street, vendors stepped out into the passing crowd, found someone with whom to make eye contact, offered unbidden directions, then demanded as a reciprocal favor that their new friend look inside their stores. The markets themselves were largely a gallows of shoddy merchandise: bowls of beads, body stockings, stuffed camels, plastic toy sniper rifles, pirated Arab-language copies of *Toy Story*. At one corner an Evangelical tour group led by a man with a thick Tennessee accent argued over the opening line of the Twenty-third Psalm while a few feet away a Roman Catholic tour group led by a young, sunburned priest stopped at one of the stations of the Via Dolorosa, which was essentially invented by Franciscans in the 1600s, while M16-bearing Israeli soldiers looked upon them all with unmistakable irritation. A little farther down the street, mouthy Palestinian schoolkids shouted down insults from atop the wall of the Aqsa school. Nearby, tourists gawked at the gargantuan crown of thorns around the dome of the Church of the Flagellation while others posed for photos beneath its freestanding, photo-op cross. Elsewhere, young Palestinian men manned T-shirt stands that sold "Free Palestine!" shirts alongside shirts emblazoned with "For the sake of Zion—I WILL NOT BE SILENT!"

Before our search for Hakeldama began, Jay and I had stopped for an early lunch in what had become our favorite falafel restaurant. Near the end of our meal, three dozen pilgrims from New Ulm, Minnesota, invaded the otherwise empty restaurant, though their Palestinian guide remained outside, pensively smoking. All thirty ordered hamburgers. A large, Santa Claus–like man with a thick white nicotined beard and intensely merry eyes sat next to Jay; his short-haired, penologically thin, and nervously smiling wife sat next to me. Both were eager to chat with what they were delighted to learn were fellow Americans. They had been in Israel six days. What had they seen? Bethlehem, of course. Galilee, where they had gazed upon the very place where Jesus once trod upon water. This morning had brought them to the shore of yet another amazement: the dungeon in which Jesus had been beaten. And us? Well, as it happened, today we were planning on finding Hakeldama, which Judas supposedly purchased with the money he had earned by betraying Jesus. Husband and wife shifted, then looked at each other as carefully as bridge partners. What kind of Americans were these? Jay explained, to their noticeable relief, that he was a professional historian. And what kind of history did Jay study? His area was the Crusades, generally, but his particular specialty was the study of how Jerusalem was perceived by, and propagandized on behalf of, those who had never been there. He described how nearly all of the first travel guides about Jerusalem were written by Crusade-era scribes who routinely failed—to the frustration of modern historians—to take note of the contemporaneous reality of the city around them and instead focused on imagining they had found the exact spot where Jesus saved the adulterous woman from stoning. Jay had not said this pointedly, or snidely, or rudely, or dismissively. In fact, he had spoken with considerable sympathy. Our new friends nodded politely and for a while did not speak. Finally, the man looked up and asked, "Why the heck would you want to see where Judas killed himself?"

"The figure of Judas Iscariot," one Christian has written, "is the most tragic in all the Bible." Another writes, "He committed the most horrible, heinous act of any individual, ever." Yet another writes that Judas "is the greatest failure the world has ever known." The name Judas has become an electromagnet for the negatively categorical.

Who Judas was, what he did, why he did it, and what he ultimately means have been debated within Christianity since its first
decades. In the centuries since, many—believers and nonbelievers
alike—have attempted to discern in his few scriptural appearances
a personality complicated and large enough to merit the crime for
which he is condemned. These myriad attempts have resulted in
almost as many Judases as attempts. We have been presented with a
Judas who is tormented and penitent, a Judas possessed by devils, a
Judas possessed by the Devil, a Judas who is diseased, a Judas who is
loyal, a Judas who does what he has to do, a Judas who wants Jesus
to act against Rome, a Judas who is confused, a Judas who is loving,
a Judas who loves women, a Judas who kills his own father, a Judas
who works as a double agent, a Judas who does not understand
what he has done, a Judas who kills himself, a Judas who lives to old
age, a Judas who loves Jesus "as cold loves flame," a Judas who is the
agent of salvation itself.

Later writers who set out to imagine their own Judas were merely
following the evangelists' necessarily abbreviated lead. The greatest failure the world has ever known is mentioned a mere twenty-
two times in the New Testament. The Gospel according to John
mentions him the most; the Gospel according to Mark, which was
probably the first Gospel to have been written, mentions him the
least. In Mark, Judas is little more than plot spot-welded to a
name.

Mark's story of Judas's betrayal begins with Jesus and the disciples in Bethany at the home of Simon the leper. An unnamed
woman opens "an alabaster jar of very costly ointment," which she
proceeds to pour over Jesus' head. According to Mark, "some who
were there" grow angry and ask, "Why was the ointment wasted in
this way?" These unnamed people begin to scold the woman. Jesus
tells them to leave her alone, because she "has performed a good
service for me. For you always have the poor with you . . . but you
will not always have me." Immediately after this, "Judas Iscariot,
who was one of the Twelve, went to the chief priests in order to
betray him to them." Mark writes that the chief priests were very
pleased, and "promised to give [Judas] money." Judas then begins
"to look for an opportunity to betray him." Shortly thereafter, Jesus
announces at the Last Supper that "one of you will betray me, one
who is eating with me," though he does not name Judas. Jesus then
takes the disciples to the Mount of Olives, where, "deeply grieved,"

he prays alone at Gethsemane and asks his father to "remove this cup" from him. When he returns from his prayer and finds the disciples sleeping, he upbraids them ("Enough!"), before suddenly announcing, "See, my betrayer is at hand." And so Judas arrives, along with "a crowd with swords and clubs, from the chief priests, the scribes, and the elders." Judas has told the chief priests that he will identify Jesus with a kiss, which he does while fulsomely calling Jesus "Rabbi!" With this, Mark's haunting, skeletal account of Judas's betrayal ends.

Mark leaves a number of things unclear. Why did the chief priests need Judas's help, exactly? How did Judas know the chief priests wanted Jesus dead? At what point did Judas leave the Last Supper? How did Judas know where to find Jesus? Why, if they were so eager to capture him, did the chief priests not know what Jesus looked like? The questions about Mark's portrayal of Judas are in many ways codicils to larger questions about the Gospel itself. Most scholars believe that an oral tradition concerning Jesus existed before Mark. Does Mark's Gospel indicate a break with that oral tradition, or is it its recorded consummation? Did Mark invent key aspects of the Jesus story or merely preserve them? Was Mark the first to join two separate strands of Jesus material (a "words" strand and a "deeds" strand) into what is called a Gospel? Did Mark *invent* the Gospel form by combining these two strands? In the words of one scholar, is Mark an "evolutionary document" or a "revolutionary document"?

These questions are so difficult to answer in no small part because we cannot be sure if Mark's was the first Gospel. Papias, a second-century Christian bishop and writer who was privy to an expanded form of Judas's death, famously noted that he preferred hearing stories about Jesus to reading them. In that case, what, exactly, was Papias hearing? Was he talking about the familiar Gospels, now lost Gospels, or an earlier oral tradition, upon which Mark may have based his Gospel? If an oral tradition concerning Jesus carried on into the second century, how different from the Gospels might it have been? Given that Papias knew of an expanded version of Judas's death, we can assume it may have been quite different. Papias was by no means alone. Works by Clement of Rome, Clement of Alexandria, and Polycarp, all of whom lived around the same time as Papias, refer to sayings they attribute to

Jesus that have no precise parallel in our versions of the Gospels—
a literary form to which these early Christian leaders make no reference. (Papias refers twice to "sayings," documents that he attributes to Matthew and Mark, but he never calls them Gospels.) The
first oral stage of the Jesus story is also its most potentially reveal-
ing, and we have, at best, oblique access to it.

The Gospel according to Matthew leans heavily on Mark
throughout but includes material that is not found in Mark. Did
Matthew get this information from an oral tradition, a written document, or some source of purported eyewitness? Or are these de-
partures proof of a detectable mind, wherein the author is not
working off outside material at all but writing in the way we today
understand that word? Whatever the case, Matthew had access to a
repository of unique Judas material, and he used it.

Like Mark, Matthew begins the story of Judas's betrayal in Bethany. Again a woman pours ointment over Jesus' head. This time,
however, it is "the disciples" who grow angry. Once more, Jesus attempts to abate their anger with instruction similar to that in Mark,
after which Judas goes to the chief priests and asks them, "What
will you give me if I betray him to you?" The chief priests provide
Judas his answer: thirty pieces of silver. Already the picture is more
complicated than in Mark, for Matthew has made money Judas's
motivation rather than his reward. But was Judas adequately paid?

There is some evidence that thirty silver *shekels*—Matthew does
not specify the coinage of Judas's payment—was, in ancient times,
shorthand for the ransom to be paid for a socially insignificant
victim of kidnapping. It was also, according to Exodus 21:32, the
amount required to repay the owner of an injured slave. It is not
clear Matthew had either imbursement in mind, given that Jesus,
during the Last Supper, tells the Twelve that they will abandon
him, quoting lines from Zechariah ("I will strike the shepherd / and
the sheep of the flock will be scattered") to establish the prophetic nature of his announcement. The passage of Zechariah to
which Matthew has Jesus refer is apparently intended as a broad-
side against the priestly community then leading ancient Israel.
In this passage, one of these priestly "shepherds" narrates his own
disgraceful payment of thirty shekels of silver for abandoning his
flock, money he is then ordered by the Lord to throw "to the potter" or perhaps into the Temple treasury. Matthew, more than any

other Gospel writer, worked with various pieces of Hebrew scripture flattened out next to him, extracting from them as much exe-
getical serum as possible.

Like Mark, Matthew includes Jesus' Last Supper proclamation to
the Twelve that one of them will betray him, but expands it to indicate that Jesus is aware of the identity of his betrayer—something
Mark does not explicitly do—and that the betrayer himself knows
he has been discovered. Several early critics of Christianity pointed
to Jesus' betrayal as a powerful indictment of his divinity: "No good
general and leader of great multitudes was ever betrayed," one
wrote. Mark provided no protection from this criticism. Matthew
seems to want to show that Jesus was not surprised by the betrayal,
thereby shielding him from accusations of fallibility. Unlike Mark,
however, Matthew's Judas speaks up after Jesus' announcement:
"Surely not I, Rabbi?" (*Rabbi* is not a term the other members of
the Twelve use to refer to Jesus.) Jesus answers Judas measuredly:
"You have said so."

When Jesus is brought before Caiaphas, the high priest asks him
if he is the Messiah. Once again, Jesus answers, "You have said so."
Jesus has the same answer for Pilate. In this way, as scholar Kim
Paffenroth notes, Judas is placed among Jesus' enemies. Matthew
also has Jesus address Judas during the betrayal: "Friend, do what
you are here to do." After witnessing Jesus' condemnation, Matthew writes, Judas "repented" to such a degree that he returned
his payment to the chief priests. "I have sinned by betraying innocent blood," Judas tells them, and, in a move reminiscent of the
wicked shepherd of Zechariah, casts his money into the Temple.
He then departs and hangs himself. Does Matthew view Judas's re-
pentance as genuine? Is Jesus sincere when he calls Judas "friend"?
This much is clear: Matthew's Judas publicly and unambiguously
acknowledges his sin, attempts to repudiate those with whom he
collaborated, and doles out to himself the most extreme possible
penalty. This is not Mark's cipher, or a placard of evil, but a human
being whose actions Matthew has at least attempted to comprehend.

Luke apparently struggled hardest with the notion of a betrayer
existing among the Twelve. To account for this unfathomable turn
of events, Luke opted for an explanation that would long affect
Christian thinking: Judas betrayed Jesus because of Satan. This

vastly expanded the reach, efficacy, and anthropological interest of
Satan, hitherto an infrequently glimpsed enigma in human consciousness. Luke, like Matthew, was in all likelihood trying to counter the potent question of how the Messiah could have been betrayed by one of his own. Luke abandons the Bethany portion of
the betrayal narrative, and merely notes that, as Passover in Jerusalem begins, "Satan entered into Judas called Iscariot, who was one
of the Twelve." As in Mark, Judas confers with the authorities (now
expanded beyond the chief priests to include "the temple police"),
and once again is paid for his services. His motivation, however,
remains demonic; money is a worldly afterthought. At the Last
Supper, Jesus tells the Twelve that "the one who betrays is with me."
As in Matthew, Luke's Jesus makes clear that he knows he must be
betrayed to fulfill scripture but wishes a woe, similar to that of
Mark, on the one who will give him over. Judas, though, is not
named. Nor does Judas, when he leads the authorities to his master, get to kiss Jesus. Instead, Jesus stops him short with these words:
"Judas, is it with a kiss that you are betraying the Son of Man?" This
is the only time in the Gospel tradition that Jesus addresses Judas
by name and it could be read to signal some kind of forgiveness or
consolation on the part of Jesus. But why would Jesus want to con-
sole the one who allowed Satan to possess him? Or *did* Judas allow
Satan to possess him? Here, Luke is no help.

In the opening words of the Gospel according to John we learn
that Jesus has existed from the beginning of time—a parsec leap
beyond the claims made by the other evangelists. In fact, in John,
all things exist *because* of Jesus. Jesus is the light, the world is the
darkness, and those who believe in Jesus "are not condemned,"
while those who do not believe in Jesus "are condemned already,
because they have not believed in the name of the only Son of
God." In John, Judas is no different from any other person who
does not believe in Jesus and therefore merits no special punishment. He does, however, merit special consideration. While John
contains no list-of-the-Twelve tradition, which allows the other
evangelists to instantly mark Judas as the traitor, John does manage
to condemn Judas upon his inaugural mention.

This occurs shortly after Jesus has informed his disciples that
"unless you eat the flesh of the Son of Man and drink his blood,
you have no life in you," and as a result has been abandoned by

a number of horrified followers. Jesus asks the remaining Twelve, "Did I not choose you, the Twelve? Yet one of you is a devil." This devil, John tells us, is "Judas son of Simon Iscariot, for he, though one of the Twelve, was going to betray him." Judas is next mentioned during Jesus' trip to Bethany, though the home to which Jesus pays a visit belongs not to Simon the leper but Lazarus, who lives there with his sisters Mary and Martha. The unnamed woman in Mark and Matthew here becomes Mary, who takes "a pound of costly perfume made of pure nard" and applies it to Jesus' feet with her hair. In an additional touch of verisimilitude, the house soon fills "with the fragrance of the perfume." The scene is similar enough to Mark's to warrant the possibility that John knew Mark, but dissimilar enough that a more likely explanation might be that the Bethany anointing was an early oral tradition that Mark and John knew in distinct forms. John also provides a crucial extra detail. In Mark, unnamed people get upset at this profligate use of expensive fragrance. In Matthew, it is the disciples. In John, Judas complains, "Why was this perfume not sold for three hundred denarii and the money given to the poor?" Is this a man of conscience? No. John writes, "Judas said this not because he cared about the poor, but because he was a thief." John's Judas has in fact been stealing from the common purse since Jesus' ministry began — and yet, interestingly, money will have no place in John's version of Judas's betrayal.

Then there is John's rendering of the betrayal itself, which is, of all the Gospels, the most dramatically compelling. As Passover begins, we learn that "the devil" has "already" entered "into the heart of Judas son of Simon Iscariot." Jesus knows this, for "the Father had given all things into his hands." As he sits down for the Last Supper, Judas's heart roils with devilry. John's Last Supper, which lacks the Eucharistic tradition found in the other Gospels, mainly consists of Jesus talking, and one of the first things he says is, "Very truly, I tell you, one of you will betray me." The alarmed apostles look about the table and ask who it might be. Jesus answers, "It is the one to whom I give this piece of bread when I have dipped it in the dish." Jesus gives the bread to Judas. The rest of the passage deserves full citation:

After [Judas] received the piece of bread, Satan entered into him. Jesus said to him, "Do quickly what you are going to do." Now no one at the table knew why he said this to him. Some thought that, because Judas had the common purse, Jesus was telling him, "Buy what we need for the festival"; or, that he should give something to the poor. So, after receiving the piece of bread, he immediately went out. And it was night.

It is a scene of spooky, inarguable power and scalp-clawing mystification. How is it that the disciples do not understand Jesus' words to Judas when he has plainly identified him as his betrayer? What is the difference between the earlier devil that "already" entered Judas and the "Satan" that doubly penetrates him here? John doesn't say. And he is content during the betrayal scene to leave Judas "standing with" the authorities in silence. John has a "detachment" of Roman soldiers there to do the arresting, though none of the other Gospels mentions Roman soldiers. John, turning his back on the unlovely spectacle, never mentions Judas again.

Which leaves the matter of Hakeldama, the Field of Blood, itself. In Matthew, after Judas has thrown his money into the Temple, the chief priests gather it up out of the belief that it is "not lawful" for such money to be placed in the treasury. To cleanse the sum, they use it "to buy the potter's field as a place to bury foreigners." Matthew writes that this "fulfilled what had been spoken through the prophet Jeremiah." The prophecy's fulfillment does not, in fact, exist in any surviving form of Jeremiah. Matthew appears to be mixing various bits of Hebrew scripture, some of it perhaps from Zechariah. That Matthew cites language that has not existed in the Hebrew Bible since the second century has long baffled Christian commentators. Many early copies of Matthew saw the citation of Jeremiah either stricken or changed by attentive scribes.

Luke's run at the prophetic fulfillment of the Field of Blood is no less puzzling. It is contained not in his Gospel but in Acts of the Apostles, and comes through the voice of Peter, who stands "up among the believers" and tells them, "Friends, the scripture had to be fulfilled, which the Holy Spirit through David foretold concerning Judas, who became a guide for those who arrested Jesus—for he was numbered among us and was allotted his share in this ministry." Then Luke tells us that Judas "acquired a field with the reward of his wickedness." When Peter is quoted in the English translation as speaking again, he says, "For it is written in the book of Psalms, 'Let his homestead become desolate, / and let there be no one to live in it.'"

Luke was citing scripture he believed fulfilled prophecy—apparently Psalms 69:25, which also no longer contains the words Peter cites—but he may as well have been forecasting Hakeldama's future himself. Desolate? Lunar. Let there be no one to live in it? Neither Jay nor I had seen anyone for hours. It was the sort of hot, quiet day during which one could almost hear the faint sizzle of solar combustion. While Jay sat on a stone and read a book I filled my notepad with doodles of the hilltop Old City's skyline. We were as mutually oblivious and silently occupied as castaways who had long given up hope of rescue. I had planned to ask all those we encountered at Hakeldama what moved them to come here. Morbid curiosity or historical inquisitiveness? Spiritual openness or angry righteousness? Sadness expressed or vengefulness savored? I imagined that some who sought out Hakeldama might be the Christian equivalent of women who, having confused pity for affection, write long, keening letters to convicted felons. As it happened, my only visitor thus far had been a small gray lizard. It approached, stopped next to my shoe, and locked into the pose of alert stillness unique to reptiles. The moment I lifted my foot the lizard shot away, a living bullet.

Our next visitors arrived a while later. Deep into my doodles —the gold-plated bowler that was the Dome of the Rock turned out to be particularly pleasing to draw—I did not notice these visitors until Jay said my name and told me to look up. On the ridge above Hakeldama, standing behind a barbed-wire fence, three sheep stared down at us with dull, domesticated half interest. Their heads were wonderfully hybrid: the almost piscine placement of their eyes, batlike ears, and proud leonine snouts. The sheep had approached along the same path earlier used by the Palestinian woman, who remained the only human being we had seen in the immediate area. One of the sheep was adobe brown and wore a bright, many-colored collar. The other two were collarless and white, or approximately white: pendulous clumps of dirt and dung dangled from their thick wool coats. A man came up behind the sheep, speaking to them in Arabic. It appeared that he was their shepherd, an occupation that came with certain sartorial expectations, all of which he atomized. He wore dusty jeans and a green and black Windbreaker with a prominent tear on one sleeve. He said nothing; neither did we. Two small children came up behind the shepherd, both carrying long wooden switches. One of the children began to apply his switch, harmlessly but repeatedly, to the backside of the brown sheep, which somehow seemed to sigh.

The shepherd appeared neither friendly nor unfriendly and I debated whether or not to say hello. Jay had already returned to his book. Without saying anything I returned to my doodles. A few minutes later, I looked up again. The shepherd, his small flock, and the children were still standing there, the cloudless sky behind them a wall of brilliant, wet-paint blue. I wondered if this man regarded us as trespassers. Was this perhaps his land? Did his children play here? Did his sheep graze here? All seemed remote possibilities. The land could have belonged to the nearby monastery, if anyone. While the children's Muslim faith likely divorced them from any sense of this place's infamy, the only game I could imagine being played at Hakeldama was who could run away from it the fastest. As for the sheep, there did not seem much to eat other than a few tussocks of grass, a good deal of moss, and some tiny yellow flowers. Everything else was a study in gray.

Below us, on the road that snaked along the bottom of the Hinnom Valley, a hip-hop-blaring white sedan motored toward Silwan. A historically Arab neighborhood adjacent to the Old City, Silwan had lately become the site of a considerable settling effort by Jewish Israelis. (One large Jewish development in Silwan is named for Jonathan Pollard, the convicted and still-imprisoned spy who gave U.S. military secrets to Israel.) The sedan disappeared behind a hill. When the dust raised by its passage had settled, I again reminded myself that what I was looking at was not rural Albania but the southern edge of the historic center of one of the world's most storied cities.

The watchful shepherd was still there, and now it was my turn to say Jay's name. When he looked over I made what I hoped was a clandestine, signifying gesture toward the shepherd. Jay nodded, closed his book, and stood. I looked up at the shepherd and waved. To my surprise he smiled and waved back. I made another, more complicated gesture that involved pointing at myself, performing a two-fingered walking pantomime, and then pointing at him. Once he figured out what I was trying to suggest (admittedly, this took a moment), he nodded and waved us up. We circled our way toward the ridge, stepping over what had to be the most halfhearted barbed-wire fence in all of Israel. It was as though whoever placed the fence here had done so as a token action, confident that obstructions more powerful than metal thorns kept visitors from Hakeldama.

From the top of the ridge we could see more of Silwan. I had read that parts of this neighborhood, which filled a valley and swept handsomely up its hillsides, were lovely, but that many of its muddy and squatly woeful facing buildings resembled nothing so much as a charmless San Francisco. We could see something far worse than charmless, however: a section of what the Israelis call the Separation Barrier and the Palestinians call the Racial Segregation or Apartheid Wall. In the early 1990s, during the first Intifada, the Israeli government proposed a limited barrier to separate Jewish Israelis from Palestinians. Construction on a barrier between the Gaza Strip and Tel Aviv began in 1994, but when Israeli-Palestinian relations worsened and finally ruptured in 2000 with the beginning of the Second Intifada (which killed more than eight hundred people), the Israeli government called for a far more comprehensive barrier. The proposed and repeatedly revised trajectory of the barrier would cover 436 miles. Many have argued that the barrier's ostensibly defensive purpose is in fact calculatedly offensive. In many places the proposed path of the barrier would effectively isolate many Palestinian villages, towns, and neighborhoods from any outside contact. Phase C of the larger barrier's construction, approved in 2003, is called the Jerusalem Defense Plan. Its thirty-two-mile-long path is the most busily wending and spaghetti-like of any section of the barrier and will enclose three parts of the city. It has been met with numerous legal challenges, and while construction continues on some portions of the permanent Jerusalem barrier, other portions have seen work stoppages or the erection of temporary barriers while Israeli courts ponder the permanent barrier's legality.

The majority of the barrier is found in rural areas, and in those places it was, for the most part, a militarized chain-link fence. In urban areas, however, the barrier took the form of an eight-foot-high concrete wall, which was purportedly intended to frustrate snipers.

The portion of the barrier we now looked upon was of the concrete wall variety and lay close to Silwan's southern edge. It was nearly finished. (Another proposed portion of the barrier would brush the edge of the neighborhood of Givat Hananya or Abu Tor, which is found directly to the south of Hakeldama and has the distinction of being one of Jerusalem's only mixed Jewish-Arab neighborhoods. As far as I could figure from the barrier's currently planned coordinates, Hakeldama would be hemmed in on at least two sides but would not fall inside it. On one older, outdated map the barrier's proposed path seemed purposely altered to avoid enclosing Hakeldama—a place, it appeared, no one had any wish to claim.) However effective the barrier had been in decreasing terrorism (and it inarguably had), and however inclined one's sympathies, the barrier possessed the hideous gray inelegance of a supermax prison. This was, no doubt, the barrier's intended emotional effect, but then most prisons do not leave the question of who is the prisoner and who is being imprisoned quite so ambiguous.

The shepherd welcomed Jay and then me to the ridge with a handshake each, his left hand placed over his heart. His name was Nazar and he claimed to be thirty-four years old. If he had said his shoes were thirty-four years old, I might have believed him. Nazar looked at least fifty and seemed unwell in the purest diagnostic sense of the word. One of his eyes had the cloudy opaqueness of a mood ring, his widow's peak was receding as we stood there, and his mouth was filled with the stained and broken teeth of a fairytale goblin. Most Palestinians were not in Nazar's condition, certainly, but there was no question that the vast majority had access to a health-care system and social services that, when compared to those that served Jewish Israelis, barely qualified as substandard. Every society is afflicted by some measure of inequality and the poor will always be with us. But the omnipresent discrepancies between Jewish and Arab Jerusalem seemed beyond the accounting of poverty. It seemed purposeful, systemic, and its effects were apparent down to Jerusalem's daily microscopiae. I had ordered a Diet Coke in a moderately expensive Palestinian restaurant, for instance, and the dirty, dented can I was eventually presented with looked as though it had been interrogated. For virtually every available good and service, Palestinians were at the end of an immensely long begging line. It was not as if I were shocked by this or had not expected it. And it was not as if I believed that Israeli concerns were invalid or that the Palestinians had arrived at the doorstep of their misery through innocent ambulation. But human beings as existence-ravaged as Nazar were better met in orphanages, leper colonies, war zones, and other locales of human collapse, not in a city in which I could have turned around, walked for ten minutes, and had my pick of salves and delights.

Nazar spoke halting English. I asked him if the children with him were his. They were not. He did not know whose they were. Sometimes, he said, they walked with him while he grazed his sheep. I looked at the children. They were ten or eleven, black-haired, brown-eyed, their faces just beginning to shift from youthful roundness to preteen angularity. I said hello. One smiled, but neither responded. The smiling boy was wearing a Darth Maul T-shirt and had a large half-moon scar under his eye. The other boy shifted his gaze from me to Jay and back again in the sad way of someone who had come to take his invisibility for granted.

When I asked Nazar if many people came to Hakeldama, he did not seem to know what I was talking about. I pointed down toward the field. Hakeldama. The Field of Blood. Suddenly he was nodding. I asked, "Do you know the story of this place?"

"I know the story," he said. "Yes."

"Judas?"

"Yehuda. Yes. I know the story." To prove it, he jerked an imaginary noose around his neck, then smiled. "Yehuda."

"Do many people visit Yehuda's field?"

"Yes, some America, some Britannia. Not many people. One day, people come. Two day, no people."

"What do you think of the field?"

Nazar thought for a moment, though it was clear he regarded this question as odd. He looked back at me. "Nothing."

"Nothing?"

"Yes. Nothing."

"Do these children know the story of the field?"

He spoke to them in Arabic. The children emphatically shook their heads. "They don't know."

It seemed apt that of the three people I encountered at Hakeldama, one did not care two figs about its associations and the others knew nothing about it. Nazar's brown sheep bleated irritably.

One of the children hit the brown sheep on its rump with his switch. The sheep trundled along down the ridge, stopped, and bleated again. "These are your sheep?" I asked.

"Yes," he said. But I already knew that, because Nazar had already told me.

Our conversational oscillograph was flatlining. Out of this straining awkwardness, Nazar suddenly pulled a question. "How big is your stay?"

"A few days."

"Yes? Good."

More questions followed. Where we were from. What we did. Did we like Jerusalem.

"And how about you?" I asked him. "Do you live nearby?"

"Yes, I live." He swept his hand toward Silwan, into which a lone red motorcycle with an unhelmeted driver was flying up a path. The low rock wall along the path hid the motorcycle's wheels, which lent the driver's movement a smooth naval swiftness.

"Can you see your house from here?"

Nazar did not answer. Instead he turned and pointed to the southwest, where the keg-like King Solomon Hotel rose up from the horizon. "You live?"

"No," I said, pointing to the west. "Over there. Yemin Moshe." This was a tiered residential complex of apartment buildings, all of them architecture-school elegant and well tended. It was, needless to say, a Jewish neighborhood.

Nazar nodded glumly, and seemed to weigh the advisability of bringing up something else he wished to address. I waited. "Before," he said finally, "I live two houses." He was vaguely aggrieved now and began to speak faster; his grammar quickly became a casualty. These two houses were also in Silwan, but neither was a house he currently lived in. Apparently, a Britannia had wanted to help him with one of his homes, his home, which is under the ground, on the other side, which big shot came to help, help, help, but he come now away, and no help. And three hundred, which is three hundred? One zero zero, which is this? Three hundred. Yes, Britannia help three hundred, he try but no help. And then Israelis take his home. I stood there, nodding in a careful, piecing-it-together way. (Jay and I would spend the next four days exchanging theories as to the precise nature of these described machinations.) Once again, Nazar pointed off into the distance, this time toward what he no doubt knew as the Apartheid Wall (which suddenly looked to me less like a wall and more like a dam, which, I supposed, it was). He began to say something about the barrier but did not have the words. His hand dropped. He shook his head and looked at the ground. He had said as much as he could.

"What is this fence for?" I asked him, placing my hand atop one of the barbed-wire fence's wooden stakes.

Nazar looked up. "For small people and animal not come here. No fence, maybe big fall."

I thanked Nazar for his time. "No problem," he said, and again, fumblingly, we shook hands. As Jay and I started away the muezzins of Jerusalem's many mosques began the Adhan, or call to prayer. They did not begin simultaneously. At first there were four distinct voices, at least one of which did not sound prerecorded, but they were soon joined by others, and then more after that. I had heard the Adhan in many cities of the world and had never found it anything other than an ideal of sonic beauty. The call to prayer made mornings less lonely, late afternoons more melancholy, and filled the evening with strange, silvery omens. But I had never heard a call to prayer quite like this growing gale of sound. The voices—another had just joined—lost their lovely spirals of individuality and overlapped into a formless meteorological whole, something everywhere at once but nowhere specifically. I was not sure if this sensation was due to the acoustics of the valley or the sheer number of voices or was simply caused by my knowledge of the hostility these calls to prayer both provoked and gave voice to. For a moment, it felt as though the Hinnom Valley's every ghost had turned banshee in anger and now sang and swirled around us. Then they stopped. When we looked back at Nazar, he was using a large, flat rock to drive the fence stake I had touched deeper into the ground.

COLBY BUZZELL

Down & Out in Fresno and San Francisco

FROM *Esquire*

ON THE EDGE of downtown Fresno, California, seven in the evening. The guy tells me that he is the spokesperson for this tent city, as well as a Pisces. He's sticking his chest out and says, "I kind of run shit here." And he tells me I don't have permission to be here. Never mind that he doesn't have permission to be here, either. Or that his whole Pisces rap is just confusing. I decide to ask permission.

"Can I have your permission?"

"No sir, you can't."

The self-declared mayor of this miserable cluster of tents hard by an overpass in Fresno is a proud man, and he'll run his camp the way he sees fit. Better than totally giving up and giving in to these hard times, I guess. Just makes it hard to find a place to sleep is all.

Earlier in the day, I had come upon a string of dingy old hotels on the edge of town. They were old-school and looked like they were all built in the fifties, and they had these cool retro neon signs, and as I made my way to see if there was a vacancy, I stopped to snap a picture of one of the signs. It was then that I came across a man out walking his dog, not on a leash, but with the dog seated in a wheelchair, being pushed along. The dog looked happy, as did the man, and I said hello to him. He and his wife were staying at the hotel, he said, $300 for two weeks, and he was excited because next week they were going to move to a swankier place. This place was getting crowded.

I then walked into the hotel lobby and asked the lady, who looked like she'd been chain-smoking for quite a while, if they had any vacancies. She looked at me like I was crazy and told me that they did have a room available. "Was that you taking a picture?" she asked me. I told her that it was, that I liked how the sign looked, and just then a guy with knotty prison muscles strutted into the lobby wearing a wifebeater. He had his back turned to me as he was talking to the lady in a low voice, and I noticed that he had WHITE tattooed in Old English font down the back of one arm and POWER tattooed down the back of the other. He then turned to me and asked me if I was the guy taking pictures. This was a situation. I said, "Yeah, I'm the guy." And he sized me up and down in a way that I can tell that he's figuring out where he's going to stab me with the prison shank he's got stashed in his back pocket, and he took a step toward me, and I was getting ready, and then he stopped and in a soft voice said, "No pictures."

So I got out of there. And now, after being evicted from one tent city, I come upon another, a few dozen tents, and I see a guy who's about my age, in his early thirties, sitting Indian-style in front of his tent with nothing to shade him from the harsh sun, but he seems happy, and he greets me with a friendly smile and asks if I want to trade some of his food—he has several shopping bags of food that he got off some Christians—for a grill or a cooking pot. When I tell him that I don't have a cooking pot, he asks me if I want to trade a couple smokes for some food. This I can do, so I hand him a couple smokes, and then he offers to rent out his spare living space, a one-person tent located right next to his.

"How much?"

"I could give it to you for ten dollars a month," he says. He senses me debating his proposal with myself and quickly adds, "And I'll throw in a weapon!"

"What kind of weapon?"

"Hammer. Free of charge."

Deal. But I don't have ten dollars on me, so I tell him I'll be back later on that night with the rent money. He tells me that's no problem at all, and he calls me neighbor as we shake hands on it.

Cool. I got a place to live. Maybe Fresno really is "The Best Little City in the U.S.A.," as is advertised on the Welcome to Fresno archway as you roll into town.

But later on that night, when I go to move into my tent, there's somebody already inside it. What the fuck? I wake up the guy who rented me the tent, who is in his tent sleeping. He apologizes, says that the guy was gone for a couple days and he didn't think he was going to come back. I'm guessing that the tent was never his to rent, and while I'm wondering what the hell I am going to do now, he tells me not to worry. He crawls into his tent and drags out a couple old military blankets and hands them to me.

"For the night, free of charge," he says. And what's this? Oh, the hammer. Thanks.

So I lay out a spot next to his tent and go to sleep. Or try to. The railroad tracks are so close, and every fifteen minutes a train thrashes by, the thundering locomotive barely perceptible in the pitch black. And every fifteen minutes when the train rolls, the whole encampment stirs, farts, turns over, and tries to fall back asleep.

Not to be rude, but these are collapsed lives. Some have lived this way for a long time, and some told me they are stunned to find themselves here by present circumstance, that when the economy collapsed, their lives went with it. And I lay there in the dark wondering how close I am to living like this. And then I think: I can answer that question. I live in the Tenderloin.

The Tenderloin is the pot of shit at the end of the rainbow, and most of the people who live here have pretty much lived their entire lives in a recession. If you want to know where the TL is, go to the California sex-offender Web site, pull up San Francisco, and it's that area of the city where there's a huge concentration of those blue squares all stacked right on top of one another. That's where I live. It's the part of town that most tourist guides tell you not to go to.

Not long ago, on her deathbed, my mother told my sister that when she died she wanted her to look out for my father—make sure he's OK, hang out with him, go on walks with him, eat dinner with him, etc. I'm assuming my mom didn't ask me to do this because she knew that I could barely look out for myself, let alone someone else. So when she passed away, without even hesitating for a split second, my sister dropped everything—quit her job, broke up with her boyfriend, packed her bags, and left Orange County to move back to the Bay Area to be near our father.

She needed work, and as she was looking around San Francisco,

I asked if there were jobs out there, and she thought about that for a second, and then she told me that there were some, not a lot, and that offices were taking three jobs, rolling them into one, *and* reducing the salary. "They're all paying a ridiculously low amount of money," she said. "Like, ten or fifteen dollars an hour for administrative work."

I asked her if that was enough to live on, and felt stupid when she laughed out loud. She's in property management for rentals, and she says the company is doing well because "people are losing their homes and they have to rent a house—everyone needs somewhere to live."

Which reminded me, I was planning on being out of town for a while in the near future, and during this time my apartment would be vacant. So I offered her the keys to my place, told her she could easily walk to work, no prob, and because she's family: rent-free.

"Hell, no."

"Why not?"

"You live in the fucking ghetto."

I respectfully disagree.

I wake up late one morning to my friend Cesar calling me, telling me that he is outside my apartment, and for me to come out so we can go grab breakfast.

Cesar used to work at a popular bar here called Whiskey Thieves, an establishment I used to go to nightly partly because the bar allowed smoking. When I bitched to my father, a nonsmoker, how the city no longer allowed smoking in my favorite bar, he muttered, "San Francisco liberals."

Anyway, Cesar was just as popular as Whiskey Thieves. It's impossible to walk around with him here in the TL without somebody giving him a hug, honking their car horn and waving at him as they drive by, or shaking his hand on the street. It's like walking around with a celebrity—everybody here seems to know him, which is understandable, since he's a very likable guy and being a hustling bartender, he always says hello back, asks what they're up to, and invites them to his new bar. "Yo, I'm working tonight, you should stop by." A good bartender works even when he's not working.

But being a career bartender isn't really what Cesar wants to do. His dream is to one day open up a business here in the TL, be his own boss, and the vision that he has right now is of an old-school barbershop, with the red-and-white pole spinning outside the door, where men show up to talk about the weather and just hang out reading the newspaper or shooting the shit with the barber, who's wearing a white apron and sweeping the floor with a wooden broom. Sometimes when he's walking around the neighborhood, between greeting people he'll keep his eyes open for locations. But first he has to get through barber school, which doesn't cost a little money, and then save up on the side for the shop.

On our way over to a nearby diner for some cheap breakfast, I ask him how business is. "Not good," he says. "I think people are drinking at home nowadays instead of dumping a bunch of cash at the bar."

And he's noticed that when people order drinks now, they order them all at once and tip a dollar a round. "So typically when they buy a beer, they tip you a dollar or two. Now they're going to buy three beers at once and give you one dollar, you know? I'm still getting tipped, but I'm not getting tipped accordingly." We slip into a booth and order coffees. I look at Cesar, and he looks beat, maybe even depressed. I'm not used to seeing him this way. He studies the menu, folds it, puts it on the table.

"I'm lucky if I make a hundred a shift now," he says. "And that sucks, because for the first time ever I'm delinquent on my bills, I'm constantly getting overdraft fees, and I'm just playing catch-up now because people aren't drinking as much. Everybody's scared now. I'm able to make rent, but I'm always stressing: *Am* I going to make rent? And this is the first time in my life when I haven't paid my bills on time."

Cesar's looking more defeated by the minute. "I'm at the point where I don't care. I don't care if I'm late anymore. You'll get your money when you get it—you know? I'll go three months without paying the electricity until I get that final notice."

After breakfast we decide to grab some mid-afternoon drinks, and so we walk over to the Geary Club, a total dive where the front door has four nonsmoking stickers on it, each in a different language—English, Mexican, Vietnamese, and Chinese. Once seated, I ask for an ashtray, which is made out of tinfoil, and light up a smoke. We start off by ordering two Coronas and two shots of Maker's. "You know when I knew things had changed?" Cesar asks me. "A couple months ago, for the first time in my life I saw a black guy and a white guy standing with a bunch of Mexicans looking for work! And that's when I knew that shit had changed."

Just then Adam shows up. Adam's an artist who moved here from southern California. While attending the Academy of Art, he also works at a local gallery and tends bar where Cesar works to help make ends meet.

Andy Warhol once said that an artist is someone who produces things that people don't need. And even when the economy is good, it's hard for an artist, but right now, Adam says, "people just aren't buying art. It's a luxury, something to decorate your house with."

He works at a gallery in kind of a shitty part of the TL, where they show lowbrow outsider-art kind of stuff, which attracts a lot of *Juxtapoz* subscribers and hipsters who like to rebel by drinking Pabst in an alley. The joint is across the street from a seedy strip club that advertises $5.00 amateur nights every Sunday. Liquor stores and massage parlors fill out the neighborhood, and the whole thing just screams *edgy* and *cool* to those kinds of people.

Adam graduates from the Academy of Art in a couple weeks, and his student loans for that are six digits, and when I ask him if he's worried about that, he says, "I don't have a check coming in every week, so I just tell them, I don't have the money, I'm broke, I'm getting a bachelor's in fine arts—I can't pay you right now, you know?"

We're joined by another friend. This guy lives in one of the many residential hotels, and his room is small. After a night at the bar, we drop by his place. He locks the door, and as we take a seat at the folding table in the middle of the room, he pulls out a glass pipe that's wrapped in toilet paper. "What the hell are you doing?" I ask.

"If you're going to write about the Tenderloin, you're going to have to smoke some crack," he says.

"No way," I say—I see what that drug does to the people here in the TL on a daily basis. I've seen people here crawling on all fours on the concrete sidewalk looking for a microscopic speck of rock that somebody may have accidentally dropped. I've seen people completely lose their mind on that drug. And then again he says, "How are you going to truly write about the TL if you don't smoke crack?"

No. That's retarded. That's like saying . . . shit. I had several shots of whiskey at the bar, and I think it's the whiskey that allows me to do absolutely nothing as I watch him put a couple rocks into the pipe, and absolutely nothing as he hands it to me and says, "You truly enjoy smoking crack the most when you're going through pain." I think of my beloved mother, who recently passed away, and then how she would roar back from the dead and violently kick my ass if she knew what I was about to do. He holds the lighter as he tells me to hold the pipe at a forty-five-degree angle, bring it down slowly, hold it in for three seconds, and slowly exhale.

What the fuck am I doing? Have I gone completely mad?

"What do you think?" he asks.

I exhale. "Not bad," I say.

I feel numb, mellow, and no pain whatsoever, and I can see why people are hooked on this shit, because after the high, which doesn't last long, you go from feeling good directly to *Give me more.* I'm writing down the way crack feels and my new insight into why half the TL is addicted to it when he tells me to put my pen down, which I do, and he grabs it and my journal and writes, "To feel like they are loved."

I thank him for the crack and leave.

On my way home, a police car pulls up alongside of me as I am walking. I look over and nod, as if to say, "Evening, gentlemen . . ." They are stone-faced, and of course my dumb ass is not only high on crack but I'm drinking a beer. I quickly set the open container on the ground as they continue to drive and stare, long and hard. I quickly tell them that I live right around the corner and had a really rough night and I am just going to go home and sleep it off. They stare at me for a couple more seconds, not saying a word, and then they slowly pull away. At that, I go home, turn the computer on, take an online "Which *Sex and the City* Character Are You?" quiz, find out that I am Miranda, which is kind of a shock, and go to sleep.

I was surprised that I could sleep so easily on crack. I thought for sure I'd be up all night cleaning the apartment, but instead I drifted away immediately, sleeping the sleep of the stupid.

The next morning I wake up with the taste of crack in my mouth. I have to get rid of that. I decide to walk over to a nearby Vietnamese restaurant down on Larkin and order a bowl of *pho*. As I dump a bunch of that spicy red stuff into the soup to make sure the crack will not linger, I notice that the joint has increased the price on every menu item by a full dollar. The *bánh mì* sandwich shop down the street I notice has also jacked up their prices a bit as well. After that I decide to walk around and check out some of the businesses in the neighborhood.

On my way back to the apartment, after passing a tranny who looked just like Troy Polamalu of the Steelers, I step into Mirex to pick up a pack of smokes. I used to live across the street from this place back when it was all boarded up and vacant and it was nothing but a gathering place for crackheads. I immediately notice that Miro, the owner, doesn't have one of those WE RESERVE THE RIGHT TO REFUSE SERVICE TO ANYONE signs that are ubiquitous in the TL posted anywhere in or around his store. And that's because he caters to the down-and-out, gladly and without prejudice. And what a store he gives them. Groceries, produce, lottery tickets, phone cards, cigarettes, an assortment of canned foods, junk food, cleaning supplies—every inch of his tiny business has something to purchase, and it's all neatly laid out, well lit, without a speck of dust or filth anywhere.

Miro, who is tall and skinny and from Yugoslavia, is seated in a chair eating while his wife works the register. They've been married twenty-three years and have a son, who's twenty-two. During the war in Yugoslavia, they escaped to Germany, where Miro stayed for five years before coming to America. In San Francisco he first worked hard cleaning rooms at all the upscale hotels. With great pride he tells me that he was really good at that job, cleaned all his rooms perfectly because he had an eye for detail. He worked in hotels for about eight years, and then he decided to open up this shop, and every single day I see him working there bright and early in the morning until way late at night, eighteen hours or so a day.

Up on the wall is a certificate that shows that Mirex received a perfect 100 score on a recent health inspection, which I've never seen achieved before, and when I ask Miro how's business been lately, he tells me, "Business is good. Most of these people are not working and they have plenty of time," which you would instantly think would be the worst possible place for you to open up a business, but he goes on to tell me, "But they have plenty of time to spend their money. You see, a businessperson, they're busy working, so they don't have time to spend their money. These people are not working, they have plenty of time to come here, shopping, shopping, every single day."

His wife is ringing up a customer purchasing a bag of Doritos and a ninety-nine-cent Arizona tea. She tells me that a lot of them get money from the government.

"The economy really doesn't affect me much, because any person can always find five or ten dollars to shop for their food, because you have to buy your food. Clothes, furniture, you can go a while without purchasing those items, but you can't say, Tomorrow I buy nothing to eat."

I look around his shop; the walls are filled from floor to ceiling with inventory. "This is a small space, only five hundred square feet. If I'm just selling soup and bread, a customer who needs something else has to go to another store. That's why I need to provide so many things, so that if you stop here, you completely fill up your bag and go back home. I don't want my customers thinking, Oh, I cannot find these things, I have to go next door.

"It doesn't matter who it is, if it's homeless buying from me, and if they buy only ten cents, I say, 'Thank you, may I see you again.'"

Miro's not worried. "If something happens, I can survive. Nothing can be worse than war. Nothing."

There's a Vietnamese guy named Hoi in the neighborhood who works for food. I see him all the time hanging out with his bucket of cleaning supplies—soap, towel, squirt bottle, squeegee—and he goes around to all the businesses and asks to wash their windows, expecting only food in return. Every time I see him, he's eating takeout and seems happy.

On O'Farrell Street, I run into a guy wearing an SF ball hat, Giants T-shirt, and jeans, has some scruff on his face, like he hasn't shaved in a couple days, and I notice that a great portion of his skin is decorated in prison-style tattoos. He lives in one of the residential hotels with no bathroom. He does the same thing as Hoi. Earlier I saw him helping out at a corner store, and when I ask him about that he tells me that he doesn't get paid for what he does, and he doesn't seem to mind at all. He tells me that San Francisco's minimum wage is $9.79, and a lot of the small businesses can't afford that, so he works for them in exchange for food.

"It helps him and it helps me," he tells me. "I keep the store clean, I stock the shelves, help price stuff, and fill my stomach."

Between that and the money he gets from the government every month—which he says was recently lowered—he gets by. "I'm in a hotel with no bathroom for $550 a month. Most of these hotels are more expensive."

When my mother passed away, I actually moved into one of the residential hotels for a week, just so I could drink by myself for a bit, and the going rate I saw was about $200 to $250 a week.

He has lived in the TL for thirty years, and when I ask him how he ended up here, he simply says to me, "I got in trouble." Which happens to the best of us. And he tells me, "It's getting worse," the changes he's seen over the years. "Once crack showed up here, it really went to hell. Used to be, when people would steal something, they'd sell it for one-third what it was worth, right? Now a crackhead will steal something that's worth one thousand dollars and sell it for ten or fifteen dollars. But crack's cheap. You can get rocks for five or ten bucks. You'd be surprised who does it."

"Yeah, no shit. It is pretty amazing who smokes that stuff."

Before parting ways I ask him if he ever sees himself leaving the Loin. He smiles ear to ear in a way that tells me no, and he says, "I'm stuck."

In the street I run into Armand, a friend of mine whom I know from the bars. He's standing outside Whiskey Thieves, and I ask him what he's up to tonight, and he says the electricity went out at his apartment thanks to his roommate who hasn't paid the bill in months, so instead of hanging out in his dark apartment, he decided to go out. But first he had to run over to a friend's house to put some chicken that he just bought in the fridge so it wouldn't rot. Armand's broke and has taken to eating just one meal a day, mostly rice, and chicken maybe twice a week.

Across the street from where we're talking is a Goodwill, which is always busy, and just then two members of the "Creatures of the Loin" moped "gang" thunder past at thirty miles an hour on their tiny mopeds. The "Creatures of the Loin" is like the TL's version of the Hells Angels, if the Hells Angels were all five-five, a hundred pounds, and armed with, like, art-school degrees.

I wish Armand well and come across a sign for a play, *Night at the Black Hawk,* which is being put on by something called the San

Francisco Recovery Theatre. The poster features a photograph of the front sign of the Black Hawk, which was a famous jazz club here in the Tenderloin that I've heard many stories about, and when I look to see when the play is showing, I see that they're having a performance tonight. As I'm standing there, an old weathered black guy who walks with a limp comes over to see what I'm looking at, and I hear him say, "Wow, I remember that place."

His name, he tells me, is Black, he came out here in 1957, and he's been here off and on ever since. "Have you ever been to the Black Hawk?" I ask, indicating the old picture.

"*Have* I?" he says, and he goes on and on, listing off to me the many jazz greats he's seen there, and when he mentions Miles, I ask what it was like to see him live. "Miles Davis, he was the guy who had to have total silence, otherwise he wouldn't play. He was bad, that muthafucker, he was superbad, yeah."

We get to talking, and he tells me that he ended up here in the TL after "doing a little prison gig," he says with a laugh.

"The Loin's always had a lot of prostitution going on here, because San Francisco is a port town, so a lot of seamen and sailors used to come to patronize the whores," Black says. "But all around here at one point there used to be clubs, too, and people would get all dressed up and come down here. That's all changed, and now it's a disaster. Because at one time this place was so gorgeous."

And he tells me that a lot of these ratty residential hotels are infested with all kinds of bugs, and a lot of bugs they don't even know what the hell they are, and in his opinion it's better to just sleep on the streets, because at least on the streets you know what you're dealing with.

When I ask him how he gets by out here, he tells me that he just does, and "You know, one man's junk is another man's riches."

I walk over to the corner of Turk and Hyde, where the old Black Hawk jazz club used to be, which is now a parking lot with a metal fence all around it, and during the day this street corner looks like the place to go after your luggage goes missing at SFO. For some reason, every day when I walk past this corner, there's always a couple guys there with what looks to be somebody's airport luggage, and they're selling the contents for next to nothing, as well as other random stuff they've found in the garbage.

I pause and stare at the parking lot as an elderly Chinese lady crushes a beer can on the ground with her foot while holding two plastic bags full of crushed cans, and a couple looking to score some crack walks by me asking people if they have any. *You carrying?*

Sad that the Black Hawk is no longer there, I decide to walk over to the corner store to pick up a bottle of wine—merlot, $2.99 a bottle—and a day-old loaf of bread, 75 cents, and I bring that back to my apartment, crack open the bottle of wine, and turn on the record player. I pull out the copy of *Saturday Night Miles Davis in Person at the Blackhawk, San Francisco,* the twelve-inch vinyl record that I bought years ago at a flea market in Hollywood for a couple bucks, and I listen to that as I drink wine and smoke a cigarette in the comfort of my own apartment, while outside I can hear somebody yelling, calling somebody else a motherfucker.

This is about as close as I think anybody is going to get to reliving the experience of seeing Miles at the Black Hawk, which is two blocks from where I live now. While listening to the record, I take a look at the record jacket, which has a cool photo of Miles lighting up a smoke on the front, and on the back a long write-up about the club. "I've worked and slaved for years to keep this place a sewer," the original owner is quoted as saying. "Despite admission price, a standard $1, no musician was ever turned away, and the customers, no matter how eccentric they may be, are uniformly treated with kindness and tolerance."

I step outside the front door to my building and see that the police have the street corner all taped off, and I ask one of the police officers what happened, and he tells me, "Stabbing."

"Is he dead?"

"No. He's living."

"Well, that's good."

There's a coffee shop right outside the door to the building where I live, and if I wake up before 2 P.M., which is the time they close up shop, I'll walk over and purchase a cup of coffee. I have a Cuisinart coffeemaker, which I could use to make a fresh pot myself, but half the time I'm too tired (hungover) and lazy to do so, so I just step next door, pick up a cup, and take it out with me to the wooden bench they have set up outside. There's a tree on the sidewalk in front of the shop that of course has a huge pile of dog shit surrounding it at all times, since there's assholes out there who don't police their pets after they take a dump, and while I'm drinking my coffee, people on their way to work walk past, as well as people who have the crack hunger, in search of.

I'm sitting there thinking about how Frank, the owner of the 21 Club, which is one of the great bars, says that the bad times will actually revitalize the TL, maybe give it sort of a "soul district" feel. As evidence, he points to the theaters and galleries and music venues that are opening up. For its part, the 21 Club is starting up a poetry night soon. I'm thinking about all this as I watch a couple electricians standing around outside the coffee shop drinking coffee and smoking cigarettes. One of them asks the other if there's any more jobs for them to do that day. "A couple," his partner answers. I notice that the box of lightbulbs they have with them are the energy-efficient kind, and their job is to go into buildings and replace all the non-energy-efficient bulbs with those. So even the Tenderloin is going green, and to celebrate this fact the hookers are out and about looking for work. There's always some cause for celebration, and the street in front of my building is a popular spot for them; always they're there, walking back and forth, all day and all night.

She's heavily made up, wears a black miniskirt with high heels, and a guy in an old Cadillac spots her and pulls up and she walks over, opens the door, and steps in, and the two of them drive off as I sit there on the bench with my sunglasses on, drinking my coffee, and then I hear a guy commenting to his girl as they're walking by just how nice a day out it is today, which it is, the sun is out and it's perfect T-shirt–and–shorts weather, and with a sweet smile she says back to him, "They say it'll get better tomorrow."

"Will it?"

"Yeah."

AVI DAVIS

The Undead Travel

FROM *The Believer*

IN APRIL 2006, after suffering for months from a feeling of ex-
haustion that often attacks me when I have spent too long in one
of those cities immortalized in novels and films, I boarded a train
departing from the Paris Est station with the hope that a trip would
revitalize me. I could not help but reflect as I lay down in the narrow frame of my sleeper cabin that I was headed for a place I knew
nothing about, seduced by some fantasy of eastern innocence derived from an out-of-date guidebook. After a short stay in Vienna,
I arrived in Sighişoara, Romania, a tiny town in the foothills of
the Carpathian Mountains. My first impression was of reaching
a place that had dropped out of the stream of history some decades back, forgotten by Europe's progress and decay. The platform
I descended to from the train was little more than a few cement
blocks strewn alongside the tracks, while an unattended wooden
booth nearby constituted what I supposed to be the station. Before
leaving Paris I had made a reservation with the Elen Villa Hostel
on Libertăţii Street—a simple house a few blocks from the station—but I was profoundly relieved to find that the old couple
who ran the establishment not only spoke virtually no French or
English, but were unaware of my reservation, though the hostel's
complete vacancy made this point irrelevant. In any case, I was prepared for this kind of deficiency. An article in a guidebook to eastern Europe from 1998—the source of my original attraction to
Sighişoara—had warned that the area would lack the usual trap-
pings of tourist destinations. Transylvania, it read, that region in
Romania of which Sighişoara is a principal attraction, offers the

traveler dark, mist-shrouded hills and startlingly preserved medieval towns, but is also characterized by unreliable transportation, rampant inflation, and occasional danger from rabid dogs. As I walked on that first morning through the town, whose cobblestone streets were lined by low, squat houses with tiled roofs, while horse-drawn carts creaked by me as often as coughing Soviet-era cars, and crowds of youths lounged against the lower walls of the citadel at the heart of the town, sporting spiked hair and tracksuits emblazoned with the insignias of exotic sports teams, while the dark spires of a medieval clock tower loomed above us all, awaiting the turning of the hour, when its miniature, painted wooden figurines would execute a tiny, lifeless dance, it was easy to imagine that I was the only foreigner in Sighișoara. At least those were my thoughts as I climbed the winding stone steps into the heights of the citadel. Looking down from a window of the clock tower at the comings and goings of the town, which seemed so free of the unnatural animation common to more famous cities, I found it almost impossible to comprehend that just three days earlier I had been in Paris, driven almost to distraction by swarms of foreigners, whom I had begun to imagine lurked with burning eyes and strange appetites in the shadows of every street corner.

Indeed, gazing from that height, at which cars disappeared and only the outlines of the streets and houses and the curve of the Târnava River remained, it was easy to imagine I was seeing Sighișoara much as it must have appeared when its most famous inhabitant, Vlad Țepeș, was born, sometime in the 1430s, in a house that still stands in the citadel today (though it has since been rebuilt). Vlad's father, also named Vlad, was stationed in Sighișoara as a military commander assigned to police the border between Transylvania, at the time a part of the Kingdom of Hungary, and Wallachia, its neighboring principality and a permanent battle zone between Hungary and the Ottoman Empire. It was most likely in Sighișoara that young Vlad received an education that was common to the son of an army officer — Italian, some French, and Romanian, the language of the army; the Cyrillic alphabet; Latin, the language of diplomacy; and the current political theory, which prepared him for his later career. In 1436, the elder Vlad, who a few years earlier had been invested into the chivalric Order of the Dragon by King

Sigismund of Hungary and, as a result, had adopted the surname Dracul, expelled Wallachia's former prince and was appointed prince by the country's landowning boyars. Perhaps as a guarantee of subservience from their father, in 1444 Vlad the younger and his brother Radu were taken hostage by the Turkish sultan, who viewed Dracul as a threat to the Turkish Empire's expanding power in the region. Young Vlad could not have been older than thirteen at the time. For years after their capture, the Wallachian prince assumed his sons had been killed. So when he was finally informed by the sultan that his sons had been spared, it must have appeared to Dracul that young Vlad had returned from the dead. Vlad the younger took the Wallachian throne in 1448 following his father's murder. It may have been around this time that he began to occasionally use the name Dracula, meaning "son of Dracul."

Stepping out of the clock tower, I was surprised to find a small crowd of vendors had assembled at its foot, selling T-shirts and pictures and postcards; a nearby poster advertised, in English, pony rides into the surrounding hills. Avoiding these offers, I made my way among the citadel's narrow, cobblestone arteries, and soon wandered into a building on the Piaţa Cetăţii called the Café International, where a group of Spaniards was arguing with the girl behind the counter about a drink. They had no obligation to speak any language other than Spanish, they told her threateningly, since their country was the first to colonize other nations. I hurried away from the coffee shop and tried to find my way out of the citadel. Every block of perfectly preserved, palely painted buildings seemed to host a small hotel or Internet café, and each one had an English name like Culture Club, Burg Hotel, Hotel Rex, or Club B. Returning to my own hostel, I found a family of French backpackers had lodged themselves there. It would be best, I decided, to explore the outskirts of the town. But I had barely passed the last house when I was startled by an enormous billboard advertising a nearby attraction. It read: MOTEL RESTAURANT DRACULA.

I hastened back to the town and soon found myself again walking the citadel's narrow streets. In the center of a small gravel square that looked down the steep side of the hill, I found a bust of Vlad Ţepeş atop a stone-and-cement pedestal. A black plaque near its base displayed the dates of his life: 1431–1476. The features represented in the bust are the same as those found in several portraits painted soon after Vlad's death: a long nose, a drooping mustache, shoulder-length hair, and wide, dark eyes that contain almost a hint of sadness.

When, sitting in the public library of the small seaside town of Whitby sometime in the 1890s, Bram Stoker came across the name Dracula in the old travelogue of an Englishman in Wallachia and Moldavia, he could not have read of Sighişoara. Although Stoker had originally intended to set the vampire novel he was then work-ing on in Styria, the locale of Joseph Le Fanu's earlier, influential vampire story *Carmilla,* he later relocated his tale to Transylvania. He never visited the region, and what he knew of the medieval Ro-manian prince remains unclear. Stoker perhaps knew that while Vlad was alive, and for decades after his mysterious and violent death, in 1476, ballads, pamphlets, and books circulated in the German-speaking world that portrayed the prince as a psycho-pathic lover of torture. Chief among these tales was an epic poem read to the Holy Roman Emperor Frederick III during Vlad's life-time, called *The Story of a Bloodthirsty Madman Called Dracula of Wal-lachia.* Stoker may also have known that this literary craze origi-nated with stories, likely exaggerated, told by Saxons who had visited Transylvania under Vlad's rule and drawn the ire of the prince, who saw the Western foreigners as parasites on the local economy. Stoker may also have known that the word "Dracula," usually translated as "son of Dracul," can also be read as "son of the Devil," but he may not have been aware that in Romania Vlad was more commonly known by his other nickname, Ţepeş, or "the Im-paler." But whatever Stoker knew about the life of the historical Dracula, he kept only the name and the setting for his novel, and buried the history. The author made his Dracula an aristocratic vampire, a seducer, and a predator, with eyes set on a foreign city.

On my first night in Sighişoara I ate tripe soup—a local specialty recommended by my guidebook—at an open-air restaurant at the foot of the citadel. In the middle of dinner, the radio playing in the restaurant's kitchen ratcheted a notch higher and the song "When a Man Loves a Woman" flapped out into the night. It was not the 1960s soul version of the song—which, strangely enough, I had heard earlier that same day while sitting in a café—but the slick, chart-topping, white-boy cover version from the early 1990s. American R & B in a Sighişoara café had struck me as a bit out of place, but something about hearing that cover version, that adult contemporary hit, bouncing off the ancient walls around me felt ominous, like the sudden appearance of a bat in a bedroom at night.

Feeling somewhat engorged after the heavy meal, I wandered up into the citadel once again, to check train schedules at one of the bars that doubled as an Internet café—I think it was the Culture Club, whose name inevitably brought to mind that English singer, popular in the 1980s, who now paints his face white and his lips into a great red grin. "I think you should get me a drink," someone said to me in accented English, almost as soon as I had walked into the bar, which was located in the brick-walled cellar of the building. When I turned to look at the speaker I saw a pale, pudgy young man in his twenties, wearing a Cannibal Corpse T-shirt and a bright-red baseball cap. His name was Petre, he told me, and he could tell right away from my clothes and my hair that I was a foreigner. He worked as a marketing director for a high-end hotel nearby, and had lived in Sighişoara his entire life. When he found out I was from New York, he said he'd like to go there for just one year, and even though he didn't know anyone, in one year he would be the boss because he didn't give a fuck about anybody and fuck my fucking city.

I got Petre a drink, and he talked a lot. For a while I was somewhat mesmerized by his weird stories and idiosyncratic mastery of English, a brew of strange metaphors and violent declarations that he said he had gained entirely from watching American movies. "You have been to the Sighişoara cemetery?" he asked me. I had; it clings to the back of the citadel hill, smothered in ivy, its tombstones tilting in a frozen fall. At one end stands a squat, turreted church, the house of worship for some of those Saxon travelers, hated by Vlad Ţepeş, who came to Transylvania in the late fifteenth and sixteenth centuries. In that cemetery, said Petre, I made a girl from Albuquerque, New Mexico, run around naked. I chased after her, and when I caught her, I fucked her.

Petre introduced me to his younger brother, who spoke less. He had a narrow face, hair that drooped to his shoulders, a thin mustache, and an expression about his eyes that I can only describe as weariness or melancholy. We have a fight club, Petre said, like the movie. My brother is small, but he is quick—he is a fighting champion, Petre told me as he pulled a chain out of his pocket and then wrapped it around his fist. He explained that it was for hitting people, and put the metal ring at one end over his middle finger. I tried putting it on. Like this you will break your hand, said his brother, and showed me how to wrap it correctly. He told me about a kind of fighting they have in Romania where guys use the chains from chain saws to tear one another. That wasn't real fighting, he said. The only kind he did was just two guys, in a ring, and nothing else. This is my brother, Petre said. For him, I would kill.

His brother said he was sick of this bullshit, always talking about fighting. They fought because they needed the money it brought. Their mother had cancer and their father had died when they were young. We continued drinking, and at one point Petre argued with a bespectacled man he knew at the bar—a middle-aged history professor from Italy, who, as chance would have it, once lived in Brooklyn—about whether Romania should have stayed with the Germans in World War II. If I could, Petre declared, I would start a national party to get rid of the Gypsies. His brother disagreed. He said in Romania they had a problem because everyone was poor, and everyone stole, not just the Gypsies.

After a long time and many drinks, we all left the bar and I headed to the hostel to sleep. Come back to Culture Club tomorrow night, said Petre's brother. We are there every night.

"Everywhere has vampires," I overheard a man in the citadel say the next day, in English—so he must have been a foreigner, or speaking to a foreigner. "French vampires, German vampires, Russian vampires . . ." The vampire once inhabited the folklore of nearly every European culture, and could be found even in India and China. But this vampire was little more than a reanimated corpse—bloated, discolored, and foul-smelling, with bright-red blood oozing from the mouth, nose, and ears. He never left his home village, and was swiftly exterminated by a stake through the heart, or by beheading, or burning, or being turned over in his coffin, or some combination of these methods. A series of vampire scares plagued villages in eastern Europe from the 1670s to the 1750s. When the hysteria in one village near Belgrade in Austrian Serbia became so great that the imperial government was forced to send a military team to investigate, the resulting account of unearthed graves and swollen cadavers quickly spawned bestsellers in Leipzig, Versailles, and London. In 1816, a very different vampire appeared in the fictional character of Clarence de Ruthven, Lord Glenarvon, widely recognized at the time as a satirical portrait of George Gordon, Lord Byron, who had earlier seduced and then snubbed the vampire's authoress, Lady Caroline Lamb. Byron himself, having developed a taste for the exotic several years prior during a grand tour through Portugal, Spain, Malta, Albania, Greece, and Turkey, was visiting Switzerland with Percy Shelley and Mary Wollstonecraft at the time Lamb published *Glenarvon*. It was during this same Swiss vacation that Byron's traveling physician, John Polidori, produced "The Vampyre," a story whose villain, another Byronic aristocrat named Ruthven, is discovered during a trip to Rome and Athens. A swarm of translations and imitations followed on the continent.

By 1820, stories of the touring Byron, who enjoyed writing his age as one hundred in hotel registers and who retained valets, a sparring partner, a zoo with a peacock, a dog, and a monkey, dining quarters, sleeping quarters, and a library on his journeys, had passed into a strange undying territory, where his figure exemplified the seductive traveling noble, even as Byron the man rotted and bloated in the shadows of Genoa. Shelley for his part continued to wander Europe, though at the time of his uncanny death, in 1822, the poet had wearied of the trinket sellers, *aubergistes,* and guides who beset him at every turn, and indeed of the entire population of the continent, who, he wrote, subsisted like an army of leeches on weakened travelers.

In September of 1845, British readers were first introduced to Sir Francis Varney in the initial installment of *Varney the Vampyre: or, The Feast of Blood,* which soon became one of England's more luridly popular "penny dreadfuls." On August 4 of that very same year, three hundred people had taken a day trip by rail from Leicester to Liverpool at a special price of fourteen shillings per head. It was the first instance of a commercially successful packaged tour, and the second project of Thomas Cook, a temperance campaigner from Derbyshire who began dabbling in arranged travel four years earlier, when he coordinated an outing from Leicester to Loughborough for 570 fellow campaigners. By 1846, while Sir Francis Varney embarked on an episodic tour of Bath, Venice, Naples, and Pompeii in search of prey, Cook was leading English travelers on sightseeing excursions in Scotland. Within fifteen years, Cook's tours had extended their reach to France, Switzerland, Italy, America, Egypt, and the Holy Land. As the regulated railroad, invented in England in the first decades of the century, rapidly formed new arteries across the body of the continent, international travel ceased to be the exclusive domain of aristocrats, scholars, and artists, and fell into the grasp of the working classes. These new travelers, mostly British, though with an increasing number of Americans, found in packaged tours like Cook's everything to take the mind off itself, as one contemporary guidebook put it, everything to end self-reflection and free oneself from the keen memory of the past.

A collection of Indian tales called *Vikram and the Vampire* was published in 1870. It had been translated into English by the famous explorer and orientalist Sir Richard Francis Burton, perhaps England's most noted traveler, who, according to his acquaintance Bram Stoker, had a strange habit when he laughed of lifting his upper lip to expose a sharp canine tooth. Two years later, Joseph Le Fanu's *Carmilla*, the story of a female vampire in Styria, was published in an English magazine, and Thomas Cook & Son, Inc., organized its first round-the-world tour.

In 1897, the British vampire novel reached its climax with the publication of *Dracula*. Thomas Cook did not live to read it. He had died five years earlier, but had already passed into that deathless realm of household names. Cook's company remained the leader in an industry he had invented, leaving an indelible mark on the world. A poster for Cook's tours from the end of the nineteenth century pictures a mustachioed, pointy-eared, devil-horned man carrying a group of British tourists on his back as he flies over an exotic landscape of steep mountains and turreted castles on a pair of enormous bat wings.

The more I saw of Sighişoara, the more I saw everywhere the twin marks of seduction and predation, with little of the innocence and vitality I had originally looked for in the town—a town that, only forty years ago, seemed immune to the enticements of the very few tourists who visited it. At that time, Jeanne Youngson recently told me, none of Sighişoara's current dozen hotels had yet opened and there were no restaurants at which to eat out; buildings were lit by bare forty-watt bulbs, and almost every business closed after dark, as if to ensure that any foreigners looking for a nightlife would stay indoors. Jeanne, who founded the Count Dracula Fan Club, lives alone in a penthouse on the top floor of a century-old building overlooking Washington Square, where the bookshelves are filled with Dracula- and vampire-related books, and every other available space is covered with portraits and busts and tiny statues and ashtrays depicting Bram Stoker, Vlad Ţepeş, and Bela Lugosi, all of which Jeanne has been collecting since her first visit to Romania, in 1965. Back then, she said, Sighişoara looked very primitive to me, like it existed forever at some point in the 1920s. My husband, Jeanne explained, was a movie producer who frequently traveled to California for work, and since I hated visiting Hollywood he had promised me tickets to anywhere in the world. First I went to Germany. But I found such a suffocating horde of tourists there that I signed up for a small tour of Romania as soon as I got the chance. An Australian man and I were the only English-speakers on the trip.

Our German guides took us to Sighişoara to see the medieval architecture. The town was more or less inhospitable to people like us, so we stayed close to our tour guides. They of course never once mentioned vampires. The bust of Vlad Ţepeş that now stands in the citadel had not yet been built. The plaque that marks Dracul's house, where Vlad was probably born, was not put up until later, and for many years no one went into that building aside from the old men who sat in the front room to drink tea and talk. Today, of course, there is a big electric vending machine outside the building that sells sodas, and inside is a modern tearoom where tourists go for lunch. But in 1965 Sighişoara had nothing for foreigners. At one point on that first trip I went into a toy store to buy a souvenir for my nephew and found the light from the single bulb so dim that it was difficult to see the items on the shelves. The Australian, who like so many of his countrymen seemed to have spent a significant portion of his life visiting the obscure places of the globe, was the only one to bring up vampires on that trip. You know, he said on the bus ride to Sighişoara, this is the birthplace of Dracula—the real Dracula. Only after he had spoken at length about Bram Stoker and Vlad Ţepeş did I realize that he had been lured to Sighişoara by a conviction that the Victorian novelist had based his fictional predator exactingly on the biography of the medieval Romanian prince.

The next time I visited was in 1974, Jeanne continued. By then, the Count Dracula Fan Club had become very active, and for this trip we were able to hire a Romanian tour guide who has since become quite successful. Even then, when he was young—probably only in his twenties—and retained an air of innocence, there was something unpleasant about him. Today he decks himself out in Savile Row suits and drives an extravagant car and sports an expensive haircut and diamond-studded cuff links, but in 1974 he was a frumpy little man in cheap glasses, and when I first saw him I couldn't help but be reminded of a rat. Each time one of us mentioned Bram Stoker he would say we must not speak of such things, and would refuse to discuss them. The Romanian regime did not want its country associated with a British novel of fantasy, and this guide was an agent of that regime, which drained the country for decades and would not allow foreigners, especially Americans, to travel without an approved escort. To this day, our guide, who now runs one of Romania's biggest tour companies, has always made sure to keep in the good graces of whatever government is in power. Indeed, he lives off them just as much as he lives off the tourists.

That was my last visit to Transylvania before all of this began to attach itself to the scene, Jeanne said, and passed her hand over a table in her apartment covered with snapshots of souvenir vendors in Sighişoara selling little portraits of Vlad Ţepeş, some with fangs added; of the Dracula Bazaar at the foot of Bran Castle, where locals hock miniature dolls in black or red capes, Vlad Ţepeş coasters, ashtrays, stuffed heads with fangs, Dracula wine, and postcards depicting a hook-nosed, sharp-toothed old man peering at the body of a sleeping woman whose bare skin is lit by a crescent moon, with the words THINKING OF YOU . . . FROM ROMANIA inscribed in deep-red letters beneath; of Dracula T-shirts of every conceivable variety; of a whole menagerie of vampiric treats, Drac Snax, Vamp-Bites, Candy Fangs and Candy Bats, Count Crunch, Dracula Piller and Pez, Buncula—endless souvenirs, accumulating like feeding flies.

On my second day in Sighişoara, after another dip into the citadel, I was forced by bad weather to take shelter in the Café International, which I found mercifully free of conquering Spanish visitors. For a while I sat and flipped through an Evangelical Christian magazine, the shop's only English reading material, and then went to the coffee house's Internet café. I had been there only a few minutes when a small boy came in and sat next to me. I recognized him from the day before, when he had followed me around the citadel square, demanding money in barely intelligible English. I had given him a euro to buy some bread. When he reappeared five minutes later I told him I was going to the train station. I'll take you there for a hundred thousand lei, he said. Then he said he was joking and told me to give him some lei for a sandwich. Today, in the café, the boy was accompanied by a middle-aged Romanian man carrying a laptop computer. We started talking, and when the man learned I had come from Paris he told me he had once worked in the labs at the Louvre, studying art preservation. He told me the boy's name was Simion, and that he was trying to help Simion become a tour guide in Sighişoara. I told the boy, the man continued, that he needs to give tourists his e-mail address so that they can contact him, but then he told me he couldn't read or write. He is improving, though, added the man. Now at least he knows that he has to work, and then he can get money, and that he can't simply demand it from visitors.

The rain had stopped and I took my leave of Simion and his mentor and made my way out of the citadel to the lower, newer part of town where most Sighişoarans live. I soon happened upon a market set up in an empty lot. On long cement tables that carried an air of half-buried oppression, farmers and Gypsies from the surrounding area had set up their wares of apples and potatoes, vegetables, beans, seeds, and unrecognizable liquids in glass jars. One man was selling cheese, another wooden spoons. There was a woman with handmade brooms, and one with wicker baskets and painted wooden eggs. A farmer opened the trunk of his car and produced two sheep, picking them up by their bound feet and depositing them for sale on the sidewalk. I walked past each table, hoping to find some charming or authentic article that I could bring home to remind me of this moment. But everything was merely practical. Here I had no doubt I was the only foreigner. Each object—the cement tables, the farmers' wares, the old bills and the new bills changing hands—seemed to link with the next to form a current that extended in front of and behind that moment but that did not connect to me, and that I could not access.

That night as I sat down to dinner I opened my guidebook to a page I had previously neglected. A note on vampires, it read: Vlad Țepeș has been confounded with Bram Stoker's Count Dracula by Westerners since 1897, and more recently by the Romanian tourism industry. Stoker never visited Transylvania, and wrote the bulk of his *Dracula* during vacations in Aberdeenshire, Scotland. Stoker's decision to locate the count's castle in the Borgo Pass of the Carpathian Mountains is slightly baffling, since there has never been a castle there. The faux-medieval Hotel Castle Dracula, now a popular tourist destination, was built on the site in 1983. Although *Dracula* was translated into dozens of languages in the years after its publication, the guidebook continued, the novel was not available in Romanian until 1990. In the meantime, Transylvanians have been living with vampire Draculas since 1931, when Hollywood's loose adaptations of Stoker's novel first became popular thanks to the performance of Bela Lugosi, a Hungarian, as the count. But, the guidebook concluded, for decades the steadily increasing number of vampire films (so many of which made use of Transylvania and the name Dracula) somewhat perplexed Romanians, since without a vernacular translation of Stoker's novel the fictional origins of the Dracula-vampire connection remained invisible to them.

Although hundreds of Dracula-inspired movies and plays have sprung up since Stoker's novel was published, no decade was more infested with vampire-inspired media than the 1970s. In the first two years of the decade alone, Hammer Films released *The Vampire Lovers, Taste the Blood of Dracula, Lust for a Vampire, Countess Dracula,* and *Scars of Dracula.* The floodgates were open and could not be shut. Andy Warhol's *Dracula, Dracula A.D. 1972, Vampiros Lesbos, Blacula, Son of Dracula* (which employed the tagline "The First Rock-and-Roll Dracula Movie!"), *Nachts, wenn Dracula erwacht,* and Werner Herzog's *Nosferatu, Deafula, Old Dracula, Doctor Dracula*—these were only a few of the films to cast their shadows across that long decade. Onstage, Frank Langella played Dracula in 1977 (in a production with sets by Edward Gorey), followed by Jeremy Brett as Dracula in 1978, and David Dukes as Dracula in 1979. Anne Rice's *Interview with the Vampire* appeared in 1976. *Varney the Vampyre,* which had been out of print since the 1850s, was republished in 1970. For a new generation of culture consumers, the initial point of contact with the figure of Dracula was no longer the novel *Dracula,* or even its early Hollywood adaptations. The elements of the Stoker narrative—Transylvania, the undead, the Dracula name, seduction, and bloodsucking—began to resemble an organic, free-floating mythology instead of simply a single novel's plot. Indeed, "the Dracula myth" is exactly the phrase now used by tour guides and travel books to refer to a whole constellation of concepts—Vlad Țepeș, Bram Stoker's novel, folkloric vampires—that are factually incompatible.

Raymond McNally was a young professor of Russian studies at Boston College when, in the late 1960s, he was inspired by a love of late-night vampire movies to read Bram Stoker's novel. He then became convinced that there was a historical background to the novel. I had always thought, he later wrote, that Transylvania was an imaginary region, so I was quite surprised to find it really existed. In 1972, McNally and his Romanian colleague Radu Florescu published *In Search of Dracula: A True History of Dracula and Vampire Legends,* in which the pair describe their travels among Transylvania's dark hills and evocative castles. It was here, writes McNally, in this region of colorful peasants and crumbling ruins whose very stones long to tell the traveler their bloody stories, that we discovered Vlad the Impaler, the original Dracula—the authentic, bloodthirsty prototype for Bram Stoker's count. For readers who wanted to follow the trail of his scholarship, McNally included in an appendix to the book a travel guide to Dracula- and Vlad Țepeș–related sites.

The next year, 1973, marked the publication of *Across Asia on the Cheap,* a hand-typed, hand-stapled guidebook that two transplanted Britons named Tony and Maureen Wheeler wrote at their kitchen table in Sydney, Australia. That guidebook was the first publication of Lonely Planet, one of the world's largest producers of travel guides. In a world dominated by the aristocratic, Victorian format of the Michelin and Baedeker guides, the Wheelers' first shoestring-budget books slaked the thirst of a new kind of tourist, one who was not satisfied merely to tick off items on a list of museums and cathedrals, but who wanted to embed himself deep in the country he visited. For these tourists, a destination was no longer just a place to see but a host whose every aspect could feed their imaginations. Today, the Lonely Planet guides are seen as such an authority that many successful novelists draw on them in order to inject their stories' settings with the proper details. That first Lonely Planet book sold eighty-five hundred copies in Australia, and as the 1970s progressed the Wheelers' reach extended across the rest of Asia, into Africa, and eventually into eastern Europe. Other series tried to fill the same niche—Moon Publications also launched in Australia in 1973, while the first Insight Guide had been published three years before—but none was as successful. Handwritten signs in English began appearing in the shadows of remote hotels and inns: TONY WHEELER SLEPT HERE. By the 1980s, stories circulated among travelers that Tony Wheeler had been killed in a bus or motorcycle accident, or by a bout of malaria, or at the hands of a local terrorist group, so that when the next edition of the guidebook arrived, written by Tony Wheeler, it must have seemed to readers that its author had returned from the dead.

It was also about thirty years ago that a new type of visitor was first seen in Romania. Beginning in the 1970s, the travel agent Eduard Popescu told me recently, large numbers of American tourists traveled to Romania searching for the Dracula from those vampire movies that were everywhere in their country. Eduard, who has worked in Romania's travel industry for decades, wrote to me from the Bucharest office of Medieval Tours, his custom tour company. For most of the twentieth century, Eduard explained, the word "Dracula" had held little significance for Romanians. Prince Vlad was always called Vlad Țepeș or Vlad III, and in addition to banning Bram Stoker's book and its many offspring, Nicolae Ceaușescu's regime touted Țepeș as a national hero. But when those first tourists came to Bran, a small village in the Carpathians, it was because the castle there seemed to fit the description in the Dracula novels they read. So they began to call it "Castle Dracula," even though Vlad Țepeș never lived there, and soon both travelers and tour guides referred to it by that name. The real castle of Vlad Țepeș, located hundreds of miles away from Bran, in Romania's Poienari region, is now a pile of ruins. "Today," Eduard writes, "nearly half a million people visit Bran annually, especially Americans around Halloween, a holiday we do not celebrate in Romania."

Indeed, Dracula has done more to promote Romanian tourism

than any tour company or travel bureau. Today, millions of international tourists come to Transylvania, most of them entranced by a fiction. They become like so many Jonathan Harkers, whose journal-entry descriptions of Transylvania at the beginning of *Dracula* are lifted directly from the Romania guidebooks of Stoker's day. Travel literature was as popular a genre as the Gothic narrative in Victorian England, so it is no wonder that Stoker would unite the two. But never having visited Romania himself, he depended entirely on the accounts of other authors, and Harker's journals reflect it. He writes as if hopeful that someone will follow his trail, which is precisely what happens in the novel, and continues to happen today. Like many tourists, Harker jumbles his history and muddles his geography. Everything he sees is a picture. He peoples the picturesque landscape with picturesque Székelys, Germans, Saxons, and Slovaks, but erases the ethnic group that would have actually inhabited Transylvania—the ordinary Romanians. The locals have no religion, Harker writes, only superstitions. After Harker is welcomed to Castle Dracula by his new host, the two discuss at length the count's upcoming trip to England, and the count bemoans his dilemma—the tourist's eternal dilemma: though someday he would be master, Dracula will be a stranger in the strange land of England, unable to participate in the whirl and rush of humanity, the keen current of change. To know England is to love her, says Dracula in his idiosyncratic English, but his love, like his language, is derived entirely from books. From this moment, the vampire (who will soon become a tourist) and the tourist (who soon comes very close to turning into a vampire) are united in their relation to history. The tourist cannot participate in history; the vampire has been cut loose from it. Both are freed from the sickening flow of time and stand outside it, unreflecting. A particular year or a particular life scarcely appears more significant to them than the next, taken altogether in the jumble of humanity.

For a time I thought that whenever a tour guide had to explain to an American or a Brit or a Spaniard that they won't find the thing they're looking for in Romania because what they're looking for is a fiction, something very real was lost, something vital dripped out of the country's national heritage. But it may be that every tourist is a traveler visiting a place for something that isn't really there. The Sighişoarans seem to have figured this out, and appear fine with the arrangement. Now it seems to me that the Romanian guides are seducing the tourists just as much as the tourists seduce them. Both draw on the same body of famous dates and famous names, of unnaturally preserved attractions, of misconceptions and manufactured myths. It may be that, after the pallor of cultural immortality falls on their town, the locals—the ones who are not tour guides or souvenir sellers or hotel owners—get to keep something even more real for themselves, something a tourist can never touch. Because if the tourist, like the vampire, stands outside history, then he also has no access to history. And that is what saves the locals: the knowledge that they can feed the tourist this false, undead body of attractions, monuments, and sites, and keep the living flow of history for themselves.

MICHAEL FINKEL

The Hadza

FROM *National Geographic*

"I'M HUNGRY," says Onwas, squatting by his fire, blinking plac-idly through the smoke. The men beside him murmur in assent. It's late at night, deep in the East African bush. Some singing, a rhythmic chant, drifts over from the women's camp. Onwas men-tions a tree he spotted during his daytime travels. The men around the fire push closer. It is in a difficult spot, Onwas explains, at the summit of one of the steep, boulder-capped hills that rise from the grassy plain. But the tree, he adds, spreading his arms wide like branches, is heavy with baboons. There are more murmurs. Em-bers rise to a sky infinite with stars. And then it is agreed. Everyone stands and grabs his hunting bow.

Onwas is an old man, perhaps over sixty—years are not a unit of time he uses—but thin and fit in the Hadza way. He's maybe five feet tall. Across his arms and chest are the hieroglyphs of a lifetime in the bush: scars from hunts, scars from snakebites, scars from ar-rows and knives and scorpions and thorns. Scars from falling out of a baobab tree. Scars from a leopard attack. Half his teeth remain. He is wearing tire-tread sandals and tattered brown shorts. A hunt-ing knife is strapped to his hip, in a sheath made of dik-dik hide. He's removed his shirt, as have most of the other men, because he wants to blend into the night.

Onwas looks at me and speaks for a few moments in his native language, Hadzane. To my ear it sounds strangely bipolar—lilting and gentle for a phrase or two, then jarring and percussive, with tongue clicks and glottic pops. It's a language not closely related to any other that still exists: to use the linguists' term, an isolate.

I have arrived in the Hadza homeland in northern Tanzania with an interpreter, a Hadza woman named Mariamu, who married a man from a neighboring tribe and left the bush. She is Onwas's niece. She attended school for eleven years and is one of only a handful of people in the world who can speak both English and Hadzane. She translates Onwas's words: do I want to come?

Merely getting this far, to a traditional Hadza encampment, is not an easy task. Years aren't the only unit of time the Hadza do not keep close track of—they also ignore hours and days and weeks and months. The Hadza language doesn't have words for numbers past four. Making an appointment can be a tricky matter. But I had contacted the owner of a tourist camp not far outside the Hadza territory to see if he could arrange for me to spend time with a remote Hadza group. While on a camping trip in the bush, the owner came across Onwas and asked him, in Swahili, if I might visit. The Hadza tend to be gregarious people, and Onwas readily agreed. He said I'd be the first foreigner ever to live in his camp. He promised to send his son to a particular tree at the edge of the bush to meet me when I was scheduled to arrive, in three weeks.

Sure enough, three weeks later, when my interpreter and I arrived by Land Rover in the bush, there was Onwas's son Ngaola waiting for us. Apparently, Onwas had noted the stages of the moon, and when he felt enough time had passed, he sent his son to the tree. I asked Ngaola if he'd waited a long time for me. "No," he said. "Only a few days."

At first, it was clear that everyone in camp—about two dozen Hadza, ranging from infants to grandparents—felt uncomfortable with my presence. There was a lot of staring, some nervous laughs. I'd brought along a photo album, and passing it around helped mitigate the awkwardness. Onwas was interested in a picture of my cat. "How does it taste?" he asked. One photo captured everyone's attention. It was of me participating in a New Year's Day polar bear swim, leaping into a hole cut in a frozen lake. Hadza hunters can seem fearless; Onwas regularly sneaks up on leopards and races after giraffes. But the idea of winter weather terrified him. He ran around camp with the picture, telling everyone I was a brave man, and this helped greatly with my acceptance. A man who can leap into ice, Onwas must have figured, is certainly a man who'd have no trouble facing a wild baboon. So on the third night of my stay, he asks if I want to join the hunting trip.

I do. I leave my shirt on—my skin does not blend well with the night—and I follow Onwas and ten other hunters and two younger boys out of camp in a single-file line. Walking through Hadza country in the dark is challenging; thornbushes and spiked acacia trees dominate the terrain, and even during the day there is no way to avoid being jabbed and scratched and punctured. A long trek in the Hadza bush can feel like receiving a gradual full-body tattoo. The Hadza spend a significant portion of their rest time digging thorns out of one another with the tips of their knives.

At night the thorns are all but invisible, and navigation seems impossible. There are no trails and few landmarks. To walk confidently in the bush, in the dark, without a flashlight, requires the sort of familiarity one has with, say, one's own bedroom. Except this is a thousand-square-mile bedroom, with lions and leopards and hyenas prowling in the shadows.

For Onwas such navigation is no problem. He has lived all his life in the bush. He can start a fire, twirling a stick between his palms, in less than thirty seconds. He can converse with a honeyguide bird, whistling back and forth, and be led directly to a teeming beehive. He knows everything there is to know about the bush and virtually nothing of the land beyond. One time I showed Onwas a map of the world. I spread it open on the dirt and anchored the corners with stones. A crowd gathered. Onwas stared. I pointed out the continent of Africa, then the country of Tanzania, then the region where he lived. I showed him the United States.

I asked him what he knew about America—the name of the president, the capital city. He said he knew nothing. He could not name the leader of his own country. I asked him, as politely as possible, if he knew anything about any country. He paused for a moment, evidently deep in thought, then suddenly shouted, "London!" He couldn't say precisely what London was. He just knew it was someplace not in the bush.

About a thousand Hadza live in their traditional homeland, a broad plain encompassing shallow, salty Lake Eyasi and sheltered by the ramparts of the Great Rift Valley. Some have moved close to villages and taken jobs as farmhands or tour guides. But approximately one-quarter of all Hadza, including those in Onwas's camp, remain true hunter-gatherers. They have no crops, no livestock, no permanent shelters. They live just south of the area where some of the oldest fossil evidence of early humans has been found. Genetic testing indicates that they may represent one of the primary roots of the human family tree—perhaps more than 100,000 years old.

What the Hadza appear to offer—and why they are of great interest to anthropologists—is a glimpse of what life may have been like before the birth of agriculture ten thousand years ago. Anthropologists are wary of viewing contemporary hunter-gatherers as "living fossils," says Frank Marlowe, a Florida State University professor of anthropology who has spent the past fifteen years studying the Hadza. Time has not stood still for them. But they have maintained their foraging lifestyle in spite of long exposure to surrounding agriculturalist groups, and, says Marlowe, it's possible that their lives have changed very little over the ages.

For more than 99 percent of the time since the genus *Homo* arose two million years ago, everyone lived as hunter-gatherers. Then, once plants and animals were domesticated, the discovery sparked a complete reorganization of the globe. Food production marched in lockstep with greater population densities, which allowed farm-based societies to displace or destroy hunter-gatherer groups. Villages were formed, then cities, then nations. And in a relatively brief period, the hunter-gatherer lifestyle was all but extinguished. Today only a handful of scattered peoples—some in the Amazon, a couple in the Arctic, a few in Papua New Guinea, and a tiny number of African groups—maintain a primarily hunter-gatherer existence. Agriculture's sudden rise, however, came with a price. It introduced infectious-disease epidemics, social stratification, intermittent famines, and large-scale war. Jared Diamond, the UCLA professor and writer, has called the adoption of agriculture nothing less than "the worst mistake in human history"—a mistake, he suggests, from which we have never recovered.

The Hadza do not engage in warfare. They've never lived densely enough to be seriously threatened by an infectious outbreak. They have no known history of famine; rather, there is evidence of people from a farming group coming to live with them during a time of crop failure. The Hadza diet remains even today more stable and varied than that of most of the world's citizens. They enjoy an extraordinary amount of leisure time. Anthropologists have estimated that they "work"—actively pursue food—four to six hours a day. And over all these thousands of years, they've left hardly more than a footprint on the land.

Traditional Hadza, like Onwas and his camp mates, live almost entirely free of possessions. The things they own—a cooking pot, a water container, an ax—can be wrapped in a blanket and carried over a shoulder. Hadza women gather berries and baobab fruit and dig edible tubers. Men collect honey and hunt. Nighttime baboon stalking is a group affair, conducted only a handful of times each year; typically, hunting is a solo pursuit. They will eat almost anything they can kill, from birds to wildebeest to zebras to buffalo. They dine on warthog and bush pig and hyrax. They love baboon; Onwas told me that a Hadza man cannot marry until he has killed five baboons. The chief exception is snakes. The Hadza hate snakes.

The poison the men smear on their arrowheads, made of the boiled sap of the desert rose, is powerful enough to bring down a giraffe. But it cannot kill a full-grown elephant. If hunters come across a recently dead elephant, they will crawl inside and cut out meat and organs and fat and cook them over a fire. Sometimes, rather than drag a large animal back to camp, the entire camp will move to the carcass.

Hadza camps are loose affiliations of relatives and in-laws and friends. Each camp has a few core members—Onwas's two sons, Giga and Ngaola, are often with him—but most others come and go as they please. The Hadza recognize no official leaders. Camps are traditionally named after a senior male (hence, Onwas's camp), but this honor does not confer any particular power. Individual autonomy is the hallmark of the Hadza. No Hadza adult has authority over any other. None has more wealth; or, rather, they all have no wealth. There are few social obligations—no birthdays, no religious holidays, no anniversaries.

People sleep whenever they want. Some stay up much of the night and doze during the heat of the day. Dawn and dusk are the prime hunting times; otherwise, the men often hang out in camp, straightening arrow shafts, whittling bows, making bowstrings out of the ligaments of giraffes or impalas, hammering nails into arrowheads. They trade honey for the nails and for secondhand clothing and for colorful plastic and glass beads that the women fashion into necklaces. If a man receives one as a gift, it's a good sign he has a female admirer.

There are no wedding ceremonies. A couple that sleeps at the same fire for a while may eventually refer to themselves as married. Most of the Hadza I met, men and women alike, were serial monogamists, changing spouses every few years. Onwas is an exception; he and his wife, Mille, have been with each other all their adult lives, and they have seven living children and several grandchildren. There was a bevy of children in the camp, with the resident grandmother, a tiny, cheerful lady named Nsalu, running a sort of day care while the adults were in the bush. Except for breastfeeding infants, it was hard to determine which kids belonged to which parents.

Gender roles are distinct, but for women there is none of the forced subservience knit into many other cultures. A significant number of Hadza women who marry out of the group soon return, unwilling to accept bullying treatment. Among the Hadza, women are frequently the ones who initiate a breakup—woe to the man who proves himself an incompetent hunter or treats his wife poorly. In Onwas's camp, some of the loudest, brashest members were women. One in particular, Nduku, appointed herself my language teacher and spent a good percentage of every lesson teasing me mercilessly, often rolling around in laughter as I failed miserably at reproducing the distinct, tongue-tricky clicks.

Onwas knows of about twenty Hadza groups roaming the bush in his area, constantly swapping members, like a giant square dance. Most conflicts are resolved by the feuding parties simply separating into different camps. If a hunter brings home a kill, it is shared by everyone in his camp. This is why the camp size is usually no more than thirty people—that's the largest number who can share a good-size game animal or two and feel decently sated.

I was there during the six-month dry season, May through October, when the Hadza sleep in the open, wrapped in a thin blanket beside a campfire—two to six people at each hearth, eight or nine fires spread in a wide semicircle fronting a brush-swept common area. The sleep groupings were various: families, single men, young women (with an older woman as minder), couples. During the rainy season, they construct little domed shelters made of interwoven twigs and long grasses: basically, upside-down bird's nests. To build one takes no more than an hour. They move camp roughly once a month, when the berries run low or the hunting becomes tough or there's a severe sickness or death.

No one sleeps alone in Onwas's camp. He assigned his son Ngaola, the one who had waited a few days by the tree, to stay with me, and Ngaola recruited his friend Maduru to join us. The three of us slept in a triangle, head to toe to head around our fire, though when the mosquitoes were fierce, I retreated to my tent.

Ngaola is quiet and introspective and a really poor hunter. He's about thirty years old and still unmarried; bedeviled, perhaps, by the five-baboon rule. It pains him that his older brother, Giga, is probably the most skilled archer in camp. Maduru is a solid outdoorsman, an especially good honey finder, but something of a Hadza misfit. When a natural snakebite remedy was passed around camp, Maduru was left out of the distribution. This upset him greatly, and Onwas had to spend an hour beside him, an arm slung avuncularly over his shoulder, calming him down.

Maduru is the one who assumes responsibility for me during the nighttime baboon quest. As we move through the bush, he snaps off eye-level acacia branches with thorns the size of toothpicks and repeatedly checks to make sure I'm keeping pace. Onwas leads us to the hill where he'd seen the tree full of baboons.

Here we stop. There are hand signals, some clipped chatter. I'm unsure of what is going on — my translator has remained back at camp. The hunt is only for men. But Maduru taps me on the shoulder and motions for me to follow. The other hunters begin fanning out around the base of the hill, and I tail Maduru as he plunges into the brush and starts to climb. The slope seems practically vertical — hands are required to haul yourself up — and the thickets are as dense as Brillo pads. Thorns slice into my hands, my face. A trickle of blood oozes into my eye. We climb. I follow Maduru closely; I do not want to become separated.

Finally, I understand. We are climbing up, from all sides, toward the baboons. We are trying to startle them, to make them run.

From the baboons' perch atop the hill, there is no place to go but down. The Hadza have encircled the hill; therefore, the baboons will be running toward the hunters. Possibly toward Maduru and me.

Have you ever seen a baboon up close? They have teeth designed for ripping flesh. An adult male can weigh more than eighty pounds. And here we are, marching upward, purposely trying to provoke them. The Hadza are armed with bows and arrows. I have a pocketknife.

We move higher. Maduru and I break out of the undergrowth and onto the rocks. I feel as though I've emerged from beneath a blanket. There is a sickle of moon, a breeze. We are near the summit — the top is just over a stack of boulders, maybe twenty feet above our heads. The baboon tree is up there, barely out of eyesight.

Then I hear it — a crazed screeching sound. The baboons are aware that something is amiss. The sound is piercing, panicked. I do not speak baboon, but it is not difficult to interpret. *Go away! Do not come closer!* But Maduru clambers farther, up onto a flat rock. I follow. The baboons are surrounded, and they seem to sense it.

Abruptly, there's a new sound. The crack of branches snapping overhead. The baboons are descending, shrieking. Maduru freezes, drops to one knee, slides an arrow into position, pulls back the bowstring. He is ready. I'm hiding behind him. I hope, I fervently hope, that no baboons run at us. I reach into my pocket, pull out my knife, unfold it. The blade is maybe two inches long. It feels ridiculous, but that is what I do.

The screeching intensifies. And then, directly over us, in stark silhouette against the backdrop of stars, is a baboon. Scrambling. Moving along the rock's lip. Maduru stands, takes aim, tracking the baboon from left to right, the arrow slotted, the bowstring at maximum stretch. Every muscle in my body tenses. My head pulses with panic. I grip my knife.

If you ask Onwas how long the Hadza have been hunting baboons, using this same style, among these same hills, he will wrinkle his forehead and affix you with a funny look and say that the Hadza have always hunted this way. His father, Duwau, hunted this way. His father's father, Washema, hunted this way. His father's father's

father, Buluku, hunted this way. And so on, until the beginning of
time.

The chief reason the Hadza have been able to maintain their
lifestyle so long is that their homeland has never been an inviting
place. The soil is briny; fresh water is scarce; the bugs can be intolerable. For tens of thousands of years, it seems, no one else wanted
to live here. So the Hadza were left alone. Recently, however, esca-
lating population pressures have brought a flood of people into
Hadza lands. The fact that the Hadza are such gentle stewards of
the land has, in a way, hurt them—the region has generally been
viewed by outsiders as empty and unused, a place sorely in need
of development. The Hadza, who by nature are not a combative
people, have almost always moved away rather than fight. But now
there is nowhere to retreat.

There are currently cattle herders in the Hadza bush, and goat
herders, and onion farmers, and corn growers, and sport hunters,
and game poachers. Water holes are fouled by cow excrement.
Vegetation is trampled beneath cattle's hooves. Brush is cleared to
make way for crops; scarce water is used to irrigate them. Game animals have migrated to national parks, where the Hadza can't follow. Berry groves and trees that attract bees have been destroyed.
Over the past century, the Hadza have lost exclusive possession of
as much as 90 percent of their homeland.

None of the other ethnic groups living in the area—the Datoga,
the Iraqw, the Isanzu, the Sukuma, the Iramba—are hunter-
gatherers. They live in mud huts, often surrounded by livestock en-
closures. Many of them look down on the Hadza and view them
with a mix of pity and disgust: the untouchables of Tanzania. I once
watched as a Datoga tribesman prevented several Hadza women
from approaching a communal water hole until his cows had finished drinking.

Dirt roads are now carved into the edges of the Hadza bush.
A paved road is within a four-day walk. From many high points
there is decent cell-phone reception. Most Hadza, including Onwas, have learned to speak some Swahili, in order to communicate
with other groups. I was asked by a few of the younger Hadza hunters if I could give them a gun, to make it easier to harvest game.
Onwas himself, though he's scarcely ventured beyond the periph-
ery of the bush, senses that profound changes are coming. This

does not appear to bother him. Onwas, as he repeatedly told me, doesn't worry about the future. He doesn't worry about anything. No Hadza I met, in fact, seemed prone to worry. It was a mind-set that astounded me, for the Hadza, to my way of thinking, have very legitimate worries. *Will I eat tomorrow? Will something eat me tomorrow?* Yet they live a remarkably present-tense existence.

This may be one reason farming has never appealed to the Hadza—growing crops requires planning; seeds are sown now for plants that won't be edible for months. Domestic animals must be fed and protected long before they're ready to butcher. To a Hadza, this makes no sense. Why grow food or rear animals when it's being done for you, naturally, in the bush? When they want berries, they walk to a berry shrub. When they desire baobab fruit, they visit a baobab tree. Honey waits for them in wild hives. And they keep their meat in the biggest storehouse in the world—their land. All that's required is a bit of stalking and a well-shot arrow.

There are other people, however, who do ponder the Hadza's future. Officials in the Tanzanian government, for starters. Tanzania is a future-oriented nation, anxious to merge into the slipstream of the global economy. Baboon-hunting bushmen is not an image many of the country's leaders wish to project. One minister has referred to the Hadza as backward. Tanzania's president, Jakaya Kikwete, has said that the Hadza "have to be transformed." The government wants them schooled and housed and set to work at proper jobs.

Even the one Hadza who has become the group's de facto spokesperson, a man named Richard Baalow, generally agrees with the government's aims. Baalow, who adopted a non-Hadza first name, was one of the first Hadza to attend school. In the 1960s his family lived in government-built housing—an attempt at settling the Hadza that soon failed. Baalow, who says he's fifty-three years old, speaks excellent English. He wants the Hadza to become politically active, to fight for legal protection of their land, and to seek jobs as hunting guides or park rangers. He encourages Hadza children to attend the regional primary school that provides room and board to Hadza students during the academic year, then escorts them back to the bush when school is out.

The school-age kids I spoke with in Onwas's group all said they had no interest in sitting in a classroom. If they went to school, many told me, they'd never master the skills needed for survival. They'd be outcasts among their own people. And if they tried their luck in the modern world—what then? The women, perhaps, could become maids; the men, menial laborers. It's far better, they said, to be free and fed in the bush than destitute and hungry in the city.

More Hadza have moved to the ancestral Hadza area of Mangola, at the edge of the bush, where, in exchange for money, they demonstrate their hunting skills to tourists. These Hadza have proved that their culture is of significant interest to outsiders and a potential source of income. Yet among the Hadza of Mangola there has also been a surge in alcoholism, an outbreak of tuberculosis, and a distressing rise in domestic violence, including at least one report of a Hadza man who beat his wife to death.

Though the youngsters in Onwas's group show little interest in the outside world, the world is coming to them. After two million years, the age of the hunter-gatherer is over. The Hadza may hold on to their language; they may demonstrate their abilities to tourists. But it's only a matter of time before there are no more traditional Hadza scrambling in the hills with their bows and arrows, stalking baboons.

Up on the hill Onwas has led us to, clutching my knife, I crouch behind Maduru as the baboon moves along a fin of rock. And then, abruptly, the baboon stops. He swivels his head. He is so close we could reach out to each other and make contact. I stare into his eyes, too frightened to even blink. This lasts maybe a second. Maduru doesn't shoot, possibly because the animal is too close and could attack us if wounded—it's often the poison, not the arrow, that kills. An instant later the baboon leaps away into the bushes.

There is silence for a couple of heartbeats. Then I hear frantic yelping and crashing. It's coming from the far side of the rock, and I can't tell if it is human or baboon. It's both. Maduru darts off, and I race after him. We thrash through bushes, half-tumbling, half-running, until we reach a clearing amid a copse of acacias.

And there it is: the baboon. On his back, mouth open, limbs splayed; an adult male. Shot by Giga. A nudge with a toe confirms it—dead. Maduru whistles and shouts, and soon the other hunters arrive. No other baboon has been killed; the rest of the troop managed to evade the hunters. Onwas kneels and pulls the arrow out of the baboon's shoulder and hands it back to Giga. The men stand around the baboon in a circle, examining the kill. There is no ceremony. The Hadza are not big on ritual. There is not much room in their lives, it seems, for mysticism, for spirits, for pondering the unknown. There is no specific belief in an afterlife—every Hadza I spoke with said he had no idea what might happen after he died. There are no Hadza priests or shamans or medicine men. Missionaries have produced few converts. I once asked Onwas to tell me about God, and he said that God was blindingly bright, extremely powerful, and essential for all life. God, he told me, was the sun.

The most important Hadza ritual is the *epeme* dance, which takes place on moonless nights. Men and women divide into separate groups. The women sing while the men, one at a time, don a feathered headdress and tie bells around their ankles and strut about, stomping their right foot in time with the singing. Supposedly, on epeme nights, ancestors emerge from the bush and join the dancing. One night when I watched the epeme, I spotted a teenage boy, Mataiyo, sneak into the bush with a young woman. Other men fell asleep after their turn dancing. Like almost every aspect of Hadza life, the ceremony was informal, with a strictly individual choice of how deeply to participate.

With the Hadza god not due to rise for several hours, Giga grabs the baboon by a rear paw and drags the animal through the bush back to camp. The baboon is deposited by Onwas's fire, while Giga sits quietly aside with the other men. It is Hadza custom that the hunter who's made the kill does not show off. There is a good deal of luck in hunting, and even the best archers will occasionally face a long dry spell. This is why the Hadza share their meat communally.

Onwas's wife, Mille, is the first to wake. She's wearing her only set of clothes, a sleeveless T-shirt and a flower-patterned cloth wrapped about her like a toga. She sees the baboon, and with the merest sign of pleasure, a brief nod of her chin, she stokes the fire. It's time to cook. The rest of camp is soon awake—everyone is hungry—and Ngaola skins the baboon and stakes out the pelt with sharpened twigs. The skin will be dry in a few days and will make a fine sleeping mat. A couple of men butcher the animal, and cuts of meat are distributed. Onwas, as camp elder, is handed the greatest delicacy: the head.

The Hadza cooking style is simple—the meat is placed directly on the fire. No grill, no pan. Hadza mealtime is not an occasion for politeness. Personal space is generally not recognized; no matter how packed it is around a fire, there's always room for one more, even if you end up on someone's lap. Once a cut of meat has finished cooking, anyone can grab a bite.

And I mean grab. When the meat is ready, knives are unsheathed and the frenzy begins. There is grasping and slicing and chewing and pulling. The idea is to tug at a hunk of meat with your teeth, then use your knife to slice away your share. Elbowing and shoving is standard behavior. Bones are smashed with rocks and the marrow sucked out. Grease is rubbed on the skin as a sort of moisturizer. No one speaks a word, but the smacking of lips and gnashing of teeth is almost comically loud.

I'm ravenous, so I dive into the scrum and snatch up some meat. Baboon steak, I have to say, isn't terrible—a touch gamy, but it's been a few days since I've eaten protein, and I can feel my body perking up with every bite. Pure fat, rather than meat, is what the Hadza crave, though most coveted are the baboon's paw pads. I snag a bit of one and pop it in my mouth, but it's like trying to swallow a pencil eraser. When I spit the gob of paw pad out, a young boy instantly picks it up and swallows it.

Onwas, with the baboon's head, is comfortably above the fray. He sits cross-legged at his fire and eats the cheeks, the eyeballs, the neck meat, and the forehead skin, using the soles of his sandals as a cutting board. He gnaws the skull clean to the bone, then plunges it into the fire and calls me and the hunters over for a smoke.

It is impossible to overstate just how much Onwas—and most Hadza—love to smoke. The four possessions every Hadza man owns are a bow, some arrows, a knife, and a pipe, made from a hollowed-out, soft stone. The smoking material, tobacco or cannabis, is acquired from a neighboring group, usually the Datoga, in exchange for honey. Onwas has a small amount of tobacco, which is tied into a ball inside his shirttail. He retrieves it, stuffs it all into his pipe, and then, holding the pipe vertically, plucks an ember from the fire—Onwas, like every Hadza, seems to have heat-impervious fingertips—and places it atop his pipe. Pulsing his cheeks in and out like a bellows, he inhales the greatest quantity of smoke he possibly can. He passes the pipe to Giga.

Then the fun begins. Onwas starts to cough, slowly at first, then rapidly, then uncontrollably with tears bursting from his eyes, then with palms pushing against his head, and then, finally, rolling onto his back, spitting and gasping for air. In the meantime, Giga has begun a similar hacking session and has passed the pipe to Maduru, who then passes the pipe to me. Soon, all of us, the whole circle of men, are hacking and crying and rolling on our backs. The smoke session ends when the last man sits up, grinning, and brushes the dirt from his hair.

With the baboon skull still in the fire, Onwas rises to his feet and claps his hands and begins to speak. It's a giraffe-hunting story —Onwas's favorite kind. I know this even though Mariamu, my translator, is not next to me. I know because Onwas, like many Hadza, is a story performer. There are no televisions or board games or books in Onwas's camp. But there is entertainment. The women sing songs. And the men tell campfire stories, the Kabuki of the bush.

Onwas elongates his neck and moves around on all fours when he's playing the part of the giraffe. He jumps and ducks and pantomimes shooting a bow when he's illustrating his own role. Arrows whoosh. Beasts roar. Children run to the fire and stand around, listening intently. Onwas is demonstrating how he hunts; this is their schooling. The story ends with a dead giraffe—and as a finale, a call and response.

"Am I a man?" asks Onwas, holding out his hands.

"Yes!" shouts the group. "You are a man."

"Am I a man?" asks Onwas again, louder.

"Yes!" shouts the group, their voices also louder. "You are a man!"

Onwas then reaches into the fire and pulls out the skull. He hacks it open, like a coconut, exposing the brains, which have been boiling for a good hour inside the skull. They look like ramen noodles, yellowish white, lightly steaming. He holds the skull out, and the men, including myself, surge forward and stick our fingers inside the skull and scoop up a handful of brains and slurp them down. With this, the night, at last, comes to an end.

The baboon hunt, it seems, was something of an initiation for me. The next day, Nyudu hacks down a thick branch from a *mutateko* tree, then carefully carves a bow for me, long and gracefully

curved. Several other men make me arrows. Onwas presents me
with a pipe. Nkulu handles my shooting lessons. I begin to carry
my bow and arrows and pipe with me wherever I go (along with my
water-purification kit, my sunscreen, my bug spray, and my eyeglass-
cleaning cloth).

I am also invited to bathe with the men. We walk to a shallow,
muddy hole—more of a large puddle, with lumps of cow ma-
nure bobbing about—and remove our clothes. Handfuls of mud
are rubbed against the skin as an exfoliant, and we splash ourselves
clean. The men tell me that they prefer their women not to bathe
—the longer they go between baths, they say, the more attractive
they are. Nduku, my Hadza language teacher, said she sometimes
waits months between baths, though she can't understand why her
husband wants her that way. I also discover, by listening to Mille
and Onwas, that bickering with one's spouse is probably a universal human trait. "Isn't it your turn to fetch water?" "Why are you
napping instead of hunting?" "Can you explain why the last animal brought to camp was skinned so poorly?" It occurs to me that
these same arguments, in this same valley, have been taking place
for thousands of years.

There are things I envy about the Hadza—mostly, how free they
appear to be. Free from possessions. Free of most social duties.
Free from religious strictures. Free of many family responsibilities.
Free from schedules, jobs, bosses, bills, traffic, taxes, laws, news,
and money. Free from worry. Free to burp and fart without apology, to grab food and smoke and run shirtless through the thorns.

But I could never live like the Hadza. Their entire life, it appears
to me, is one insanely committed camping trip. It's incredibly risky.
Medical help is far away. One bad fall from a tree, one bite from
a black mamba snake, one lunge from a lion, and you're dead.
Women give birth in the bush, squatting. About a fifth of all babies
die within their first year, and nearly half of all children do not
make it to age fifteen. They have to cope with extreme heat and
frequent thirst and swarming tsetse flies and malaria-laced mosquitoes.

The days I spent with the Hadza altered my perception of the
world. They instilled in me something I call the "Hadza effect"
—they made me feel calmer, more attuned to the moment, more
self-sufficient, a little braver, and in less of a constant rush. I don't

care if this sounds maudlin: my time with the Hadza made me happier. It made me wish there was some way to prolong the reign of the hunter-gatherers, though I know it's almost certainly too late.

It was my body, more than anything, that let me know it was time to leave the bush. I was bitten and bruised and sunburned and stomachachy and exhausted. So, after two weeks, I told everyone in camp I had to go.

There was little reaction. The Hadza are not sentimental like that. They don't do extended goodbyes. Even when one of their own dies, there is not a lot of fuss. They dig a hole and place the body inside. A generation ago, they didn't even do that—they simply left a body out on the ground to be eaten by hyenas. There is still no Hadza grave marker. There is no funeral. There's no service at all, of any sort. This could be a person they had lived with their entire lives. Yet they just toss a few dry twigs on top of the grave. And they walk away.

IAN FRAZIER

Travels in Siberia

FROM *The New Yorker*

OFFICIALLY, THERE IS no such place as Siberia. No political or
territorial entity has Siberia as its name. In atlases, the word "Siberia" hovers across the northern third of Asia unconnected to any
place in particular, as if designating a zone or a condition; it seems
to show through like a watermark on the page. During Soviet times,
revised maps erased the name entirely, in order to discourage Siberian regionalism. Despite this invisibility, one can assume that Siberia's traditional status as a threat did not improve.

A tiny fraction of the world's population lives in Siberia. About
38 million Russians and native peoples inhabit that northern third
of Asia. By contrast, the state of New Jersey, where I live, has nearly
a quarter as many people on about .0015 as much land. For most
people, Siberia is not the place itself but a figure of speech. In fash-
ionable restaurants in New York and Los Angeles, Siberia is the section of less desirable tables given to customers whom the maître d'
does not especially like.

Newspaper gossip columns take the word even more metaphori-
cally. When an author writes a book about a Park Avenue apartment building, and the book offends some of the residents, and a
neighbor who happens to be a friend of the author offers to throw
him a book party in her apartment, and the people in the Park Avenue building hear about this plan, the party giver is risking "social
Siberia," one of them warns.

In this respect (as in many others), Siberia and America are
alike. Apart from their actual, physical selves, both exist as con-
structs, expressions of the mind. Once when I was in western Russia, a bottler of mineral water was showing my two Russian com-

panions and me around his new dacha outside the city of Vologda. The time was late evening; darkness had fallen. The mineral-water bottler led us from room to room, throwing on all the lights and pointing out the amenities. When we got to the kitchen, he flipped the switch but the light did not go on. This seemed to upset him. He fooled with the switch, then hurried off and came back with a stepladder. Mounting it, he removed the glass globe from the overhead light and unscrewed the bulb. He climbed down, put globe and bulb on the counter, took a fresh bulb, and ascended again. He reached up and screwed the new bulb into the socket. After a few twists, the light came on. He turned to us and spread his arms wide, indicating the beams brightly filling the room. "Ahhh," he said, triumphantly. "Amerika!"

Nobody has ever formally laid out the boundaries of the actual, physical Siberia. Rather, they were established by custom and accepted by general agreement. Siberia is, of course, huge. Three-fourths of Russia today is Siberia. Siberia takes up one-twelfth of all the land on earth. The United States from Maine to California stretches across four time zones; in Siberia there are eight. The continental United States plus most of Europe could fit inside it. Across the middle of Siberia, west to east for forty-six hundred miles, runs the Russian taiga, the largest forest in the world.

The Ural Mountains, which cross Russia north to south from the Arctic Ocean to Kazakhstan, are the western edge of Siberia. The Urals also separate Europe from Asia. As a mountain range with the big job of dividing two continents, the Urals aren't much. It is possible to drive over them, as I have done, and not know. In central Russia, the summits of the Urals average between one thousand and two thousand feet. But after you cross the Urals the land opens out, the villages are farther apart, the concrete bus shelters along the highway become fewer, and suddenly you realize you're in Siberia.

To the east, about three thousand miles beyond the Urals, Siberia ends at the Pacific Ocean, in the form of the Sea of Japan, the Sea of Okhotsk, and the Bering Sea. Since Soviet times, Russians have called this part of Siberia the Russian Far East.

The Arctic Ocean borders Siberia on the north. West to east, its seas are the Kara Sea, the Laptev Sea, and the East Siberian Sea. For most of the year (though less consistently than before), this line is obscured under ice. The land here for as much as 250 miles in from the sea is tundra—a treeless, mossy bog for the months of summer, a white near-wasteland otherwise.

In the south, Siberia technically ends at the border between Russia and Kazakhstan, Mongolia, and China, although Siberian watersheds and landforms continue on into them. This region is mostly steppe. The steppes of Siberia are part of the great Eurasian steppe, which extends from almost the Pacific westward as far as the Danube. For more than two thousand years, the Eurasian steppe produced nomadic barbarians who descended upon and destroyed cultivated places beyond the steppe's margins. The steppes were why China built the Great Wall. Out of the steppes in the thirteenth century came Genghis Khan and the Mongol hordes, civilization's then worst nightmare, the wicked stepfathers of the Russian state and of its tsars and commissars.

Sakhalin Island, which almost touches the Russian coast north of Japan, is considered part of Siberia. The island was a prison colony during tsarist times. Six hundred miles east of Sakhalin, the peninsula of Kamchatka descends from the Siberian mainland, dividing the Sea of Okhotsk from the Bering Sea. Kamchatka lies within the Pacific Rim's "Ring of Fire" and has active volcanoes. Kamchatka's Klyuchevskaya volcano, at 15,580 feet, is the highest point in Siberia. Among Russians, Kamchatka has served as a shorthand term for remoteness. Boris Pasternak's memoir, *Safe Conduct*, says that for Russian schoolchildren the far back of the class where the worst students sat was called Kamchatka. When the teacher had not yet heard the correct answer, he would cry to the back bench, as a last resort, "To the rescue, Kamchatka!"

Coincidentally, Kamchatka was the first geographic fact that many people my age in America knew about Siberia. I am of the baby-boom generation, who grew up during the Cold War. In our childhood, a new board game came out called Risk, which was played on a map representing the world. The object of Risk was to multiply your own armies, move them from one global region to the next while eliminating the armies of your opponents, and eventually take over the world. This required luck, ruthlessness, and intercontinental strategizing, Cold War–style. The armies were little plastic counters colored red, blue, yellow, brown, black, and green. Of the major global powers, you basically understood which color was supposed to stand for whom. The Kamchatka Peninsula controlled the only crossing of the game board's narrow sea between Asia and North America, so gaining Kamchatka was key.

On the Risk game board, the lines between regions and around continents were angular and schematic, after the manner of familiar Cold War maps having to do with nuclear war. On the walls at think-tank strategy sessions and as illustrations for sobering magazine articles, these maps showed the arcs of nuclear missiles spanning the globe—theirs heading for us, ours heading for them. Almost all the missile arcs went over Siberia. In the Cold War, Siberia provided the "cold"; Siberia was the blankness in between, the space through which apocalypse flew.

As a landmass, Siberia got some bad breaks geographically. The main rivers of Siberia are (west to east) the Ob, the Yenisei, the Lena, and the Amur. I have seen each of these, and though the Mississippi may be mighty, they can make it look small. The fact that the tributary systems of these rivers interlock allowed adventurers in the seventeenth century to go by river from the Ural Mountains to the Pacific Ocean with only five portages. Seeking furs, these men had crossed all of Siberia in a hundred years, and built fortresses and founded cities along the way. In western Siberia, there are cities more than four hundred years old. Siberia's rivers still serve as important north–south avenues for barge traffic and in the winter as ice highways for trucks.

The problem with Siberia's big rivers is the direction they flow. Most of Siberia's rivers go north or join others that do, and their waters end up in the Arctic Ocean. Even the Amur, whose general inclination is to the northeast and whose destination is the Pacific, empties into the stormy Sea of Okhotsk. In the spring, north-flowing rivers thaw upstream while they're still frozen at their mouths. This causes them to back up. This creates swamps. Western Siberia has the largest swamps in the world. In much of Siberia, the land doesn't do much of anything besides gradually sag northward to the Arctic. The rivers of western Siberia flow so slowly that they hardly seem to move at all. There the rivers run muddy; in eastern Siberia, with its real mountains and sharper drop to the Pacific, many of the rivers run clear.

In general, then, much of Siberia drains poorly and is quite swampy. Of the mosquitoes, flies, and invisible biting insects I will say more later. They are a whole other story.

Another bad geographical break is Siberia's continentality. The land simply stretches on and on; eventually you feel you're in the farthest, extra, out-of-sight section of the parking lot, where no one in the history of civilization has ever bothered to go. Only on the sea can you travel as far and still be in apparently the same place. The deeper into Siberia, and the farther from the mitigating effect of temperate oceans, the harsher the climate's extremes become. Summers in the interior of Siberia are hot, sometimes dry and dusty, sometimes hazy with smoke from taiga fires. In the winters, temperatures drop to the lowest on the planet outside Antarctica. In the city of Verkhoyansk, in northeast-central Siberia, the cold reaches minus 68 degrees centigrade (about minus 90 degrees Fahrenheit). When I mentioned this frequently noted Siberian fact to my friends and guides in St. Petersburg, they scoffed, as Russians tend to do. Then they said they knew of someplace in Siberia even colder.

Because of the cold, a lot of central Siberia and most of the east lies under permafrost—ground permanently frozen, sometimes to more than a thousand meters down. Permafrost also covers all the tundra region. Agriculture on any large scale is impossible in the permafrost zone, though in more forgiving parts of it people have kitchen gardens, and greenhouse farming occasionally succeeds. Much of Siberia's taiga rests on permafrost, implying a shaky future for the forest if the permafrost melts, and a shakier one, scientists say, for the earth's atmospheric chemistry. Huge amounts of climate-changing methane would be released into the air.

Cities and villages in the permafrost zone must have basic necessities brought in. Fuel comes in steel barrels that are about three feet high and hold fifty-three gallons. Around settled places these empty barrels are everywhere, sometimes littering the bare tundra surreally as far as you can see. In 1997, the *Los Angeles Times* estimated that in Chukotka, the part of farthest Siberia just across from Alaska, the Soviets had left behind about two million barrels, or about sixteen barrels for each person living there. Fewer people, and probably more barrels, are in Chukotka today.

What, then, is good about Siberia? Its natural resources, though hard to get at, are amazing. Its coal reserves, centered in the Kuznetsk Basin mining region, in south-central Siberia, are some of the largest in the world. The Kuznetsk Basin is also rich in iron ore, a combination that made this region Russia's armory. Siberia has minerals like cobalt, zinc, copper, lead, tin, and mercury in great abundance; in Norilsk, the second-largest city in the world above the Arctic Circle, the Soviets dug the world's largest nickel mine. The diamond mines at Mirny, near the Vilyui River, are second only to South Africa's. Siberia has supplied the Russian treasury with silver and gold since tsarist times; during the 1930s, the Kolyma region of eastern Siberia produced, by means of the cruelest mines in history, about half the gold then being mined in the world. Russia has some of the world's largest reserves of petroleum and natural gas. A lot of those reserves are in Siberia.

Along the route of the Trans-Siberian Railway, trains of oil-tank cars extend across the landscape for miles. Each tank car, black and tarry-looking, with faded white markings, resembles the one that follows it; slowly rolling past a grade crossing of the Trans-Siberian Railway, a trainload of these cars defines monotony. The Trans-Siberian Railway covers 9,288 kilometers between Moscow and the Pacific port of Vladivostok, or 5,771 miles. In other words, it's almost twice as long as Interstate 80 from New Jersey to California. Lying awake near the tracks in some remote spot, you hear trains going by all through the night with scarcely a pause. Sitting beside the tracks and observing the point in the distance where they and the cables above them merge — the Trans-Siberian Railway is all-electric, with overhead cables like a streetcar line — you find that the tracks are empty of traffic for only five or ten minutes at a time.

Besides oil, the railway carries coal, machinery parts, giant tires, scrap iron, and endless containers saying HANJIN or SEA-LAND or MAERSK on their sides, just like the containers stacked five stories high around the port of Newark, New Jersey, and probably every other port in the world. Now and then, a passenger train goes by, and, if the time is summer and the weather, as usual, hot, many shirtless passengers are hanging from the open windows with the curtains flapping beside them. Not even the most luxurious car on the Trans-Siberian Railway offers air-conditioning. Then more freight comes along, sometimes timber by the trainload. Siberian timber can be three or four feet in diameter, a size only rarely seen on logging trucks in America today. Some of these trees are called *korabel'nie sosni*—literally, "caravel pines," trees from which ships' masts were made.

Geologists have always liked Siberia, especially its eastern part, where a lot is going on with the earth. Well into eastern Siberia— to a north–south range of mountains roughly paralleling the Lena River valley—you are still in North America, tectonically speaking. The North American Plate, sliding westward, meets the Eurasian Plate there, while to the south the Amursky and the Okhotsky plates complicate the collision by inserting themselves from that direction. All this plate motion causes seismic activity and an influx of seismologists. Eastern Siberia is among the most important places for seismic studies in the world.

Paleontologists come to Siberia not for dinosaur fossils, which are not found nearly as often as in the Mongolian territory to the south, but for more recent fossils, of prehistoric bison, mammoths, rhinos, and other species that lived fifteen thousand to ten thousand years ago. The Siberian mammoth finds alone have been a bonanza, some of them not fossils but the actual creatures themselves, still frozen and almost intact, or mummified in frozen sediments. In the nineteenth century, discoveries of mammoth remains were so common that for a while mammoth ivory became a major export of Siberia.

To astronomers, Siberia provides the advantage of skies largely untroubled by light pollution and, in some places, cloud-free for more than two hundred days a year. Looking up at the clarity of the night in Siberia, you feel that you are in the sky yourself. Never in my life have I seen so many satellites and shooting stars.

Travelers who crossed Siberia in the eighteenth century noted the remarkable animals they saw—elk "of monstrous size," fierce aurochs, wild boars, wild horses and asses, flying squirrels in great numbers, foxes, hares, beavers, bears. Of the swans, cranes, pelicans, geese, ducks, bitterns, and other birds, one traveler wrote, "After sundown these manifold armies of winged creatures made such a terrific clamour that we could not even hear our own words." Philipp Johann von Strahlenberg, a Swede captured by Peter the Great's army at the Battle of Poltava, in 1709, and sent with other Swedish prisoners to Siberia, wrote that the region had six species of deer, including the great stag, the roe deer, the musk deer, the fallow deer, and the reindeer. He also mentioned a special kind of bird whose nests were so soft that they were used for socks. About 290 years later in Siberia, I saw few or none of these marvels, except in museums, where some of the specimens are facing a second extinction from moths and general disintegration.

The main four-legged animal I encountered in Siberia was the cow. Little herds appear all the time, especially in western Siberia, grazing along the road or moving at twilight from the woods or the swamp into a glade. Siberian cows are skinnier than the ones in America, and longer-legged, often with muddy shins, and ribs showing. Some wear bells. Herders, usually not on horseback, follow them unhurriedly. The boys have motorman's caps and sweaters with holes; the women, usually older, wear rubber boots, long trousers under their skirts, and scarves around their heads against the insects. Beef in Siberian stores is gristly, tough, and expensive. Siberian dairy products, however, are cheap and good. The butter and ice cream of Siberia are the best I've tasted anywhere.

At times, Siberia has supplied a lot of western Russia's butter, and some of England's and western Europe's, too. Just before the First World War, 16 percent of the world's exports of butter came from Siberia. N. S. Korzhanskii, a revolutionary who knew the father of the Russian Revolution, V. I. Lenin, when Lenin was living in England in 1903, recalled a meal in Lenin's London apartment: "I was amazed at the wonderful, beautiful-smelling creamy butter, and was just about to burst out with some remark about the wealth of the British, when Vladimir Ilyich said, 'Yes, that must be ours. From Siberia.'"

Lenin went to Siberia on two separate occasions. He was sent into exile there following his arrest for revolutionary activities in St. Petersburg in December of 1895. Lenin was twenty-five then, and still using his original name, Vladimir Ilyich Ulyanov. Sentenced to three years' exile, he was sent to Shushenskoye, a village on the Yenisei River, in south-central Siberia. Exile under the tsars could be a rather mild proposition, especially compared with what the Soviets later devised; during his exile Lenin received a government stipend of twelve rubles a month, which covered room and board along with extras like books. He was able to get a lot of reading done. All in all, Siberia seems to have agreed with Lenin splendidly, and seasoned him as a political thinker.

The second time Lenin was sent to Siberia he had been dead for seventeen years. After leading the revolution and maneuvering the Bolshevik state through the power struggles that followed, he suffered a series of strokes; a convalescence did not restore his health, and he died, of another stroke, in January of 1924. Because of Lenin's importance to the revolution and the saintlike status the Communists gave him, the Soviet government decided to have his body preserved. Embalmers and other technicians did such a skillful job that when they were done he looked better than he had in the months before he died. To house him, the government built a temporary and then a permanent tomb on Red Square, in Moscow, where his body went on display for the crowds who filed reverently by.

In 1941, with the Germans approaching, an icon as important as Lenin could not be left at risk of destruction or capture, so the body was packed into a railroad car and shipped to the western Siberian city of Tyumen for safekeeping. There, far from the front, it waited out the war. In 1945, after the Allied victory, Lenin again returned from Siberia, and went back to his Red Square tomb.

Like Lenin, many of the objects in museums and churches in western Russia have spent some time in Siberia. During the Second World War, state treasures and works of art and historic archives were put in crates and shipped east. A lot of western Russia's heavy industry also moved to temporary factories beyond the Urals. The instinct to withdraw, to disappear far into the interior, figures often in Russian history. During invasions from the west, Russia's strategic option of nearly unlimited retreat made it, in a sense, unkillable. After Napoleon began his invasion of Russia in 1812, an adviser told Tsar Alexander I, "I am not afraid of military reverses . . . Your empire has two powerful defenders in its vastness and its climate. The emperor of Russia will always be formidable in Moscow, terrible in Kazan, and invincible in Tobolsk." Tobolsk, at the junction of the Irtysh and Tobol rivers, was at the time the administrative capital and ecclesiastical seat of western Siberia.

On the question of whether Russia's vast size has benefited or hurt it overall, historians and others disagree. Those who take the negative side say that Russia has been too big and spread out ever to function properly, that it has been "crippled by its expanse," that much of its land is not worth the trouble, and that Siberia is a road leading nowhere. A few years ago, two public-policy experts at a Washington think tank wrote a book advising Russia to close down its remote and hard-to-supply Siberian cities and villages and concentrate the population in locations more practical for transportation and the global market. The far places should be left to a few skeleton-crew outposts, and the difficult environment allowed to revert to wilderness, the experts maintained.

Those on the positive side of the argument (a larger number, in total, than the nays) say, basically, that Russia was not really Russia until it began to move into Asia. Before, it was a loose collection of principalities centered on trading cities like Novgorod and Vladimir and Moscow. The pro-Siberians say that other nations became empires by crossing oceans, while Russia did the same by expanding across the land it was already on. At weak moments in Russia's history, it could have been partitioned between hostile countries that were then more powerful—Lithuania, Poland, Sweden, the Ottoman Empire, Germany—had not the resources and hard-to-subdue vastness of Siberia kept it alive. Possessed of Siberia, Russia became a continental country, not only an ethnic entity on the map of eastern Europe. Or, as Joseph Stalin once told a Japanese interviewer, "Russia is an Asiatic land, and I myself am an Asiatic." (Stalin, by the way, was exiled to Siberia an indeterminate number of times during his years as a young revolutionary, and claimed that he escaped from Siberia six times. He was, of course, alive during the Second World War, and so did not make a posthumous visit via cold storage.)

The first Russian ruler to style himself officially as tsar, Ivan IV (Ivan Grozny, Ivan the Fear-Inspiring, the Terrible), was also the first to add "Lord of All the Siberian Land" to his titles. He was able to do this because he had conquered the Tatar city of Kazan, a Muslim stronghold on the Volga River which had long blocked Russian moves eastward. With Kazan out of the way, Russian adventurers could go beyond the frontiers to previously unexplored lands across the Urals. In 1581 and 1582, a band of Cossacks led by a Volga River pirate named Yermak Timofeyevich followed rivers into the country of the Khan of Sibir, fought several battles with the Khan's forces, defeated him, captured his leading general, and occupied his fortress, Isker, on the Tobol River. Yermak sent envoys to Ivan with news of his victory and a rich tribute of sable furs, black-fox furs, and noble captives. This impressed Ivan favorably with Siberia's possibilities, and the state then secured Yermak's foothold with contingents of troops.

After Russia acquired Siberia, tsars of the seventeenth century sometimes were told by Westerners that their dominion exceeded the size of the surface of the full moon. This information pleased the tsars, who probably did not look too closely into the math of the statement. The surface area of the moon is about 14,646,000 square miles (although the tsars would have measured in desyatins, or square versts, or something else). When the moon is full, the part that's visible is, of course, half of the entire moon, or about 7,323,000 square miles. Whether Russia in the seventeenth century could honestly claim to be larger than that is not certain. It had not yet taken over the Baltic territories, the Crimea, Ukraine, or the Caucasus, and most of its Siberian territory was unknown in size. Mapmakers then had little information about Siberia's eastern regions, and were not even sure whether it joined North America. Those details weren't important, however. To say that Russia was larger than the full moon sounded impressive, and had an echo of poetry, and poetry creates empires.

The Van

Sergei Mikhailovich Lunev is a muscular and youthfully fit man in his mid-sixties. He looks like a gymnast, or a coach of gymnasts. He has a long, ectomorphic head whose most expressive feature is its brow, which furrows this way and that in thought, emphasizing his canny, mobile, and china-blue eyes. The neatly trimmed hair around his balding crown adds a professorial dignity, appropriately, because he is the head of the robotics lab at the St. Petersburg Polytechnical University. He used to work with the Soviet space program before it was reduced in size.

I met Sergei in the summer of 2001, in St. Petersburg; he was to be my guide for an automobile trip across Russia. Guiding was something he was doing for extra money. After knowing him for a while, I wondered if the discontent and suppressed anger that sometimes showed on his face were the result of having to do an extra job, one unequal to his talents. He speaks some English, I speak some Russian. We got along better as my Russian improved and I understood how prestigious his real job was.

One day in June, Sergei and I drove to a labyrinthine warren of single-vehicle garages in a far section of St. Petersburg. I had wanted to buy a Russian all-road vehicle like a four-wheel-drive Niva, but I was warned that that was a bad idea, because Russian vehicles constantly break down. (On our journey, after I'd seen the thousandth Niva by the side of the road with its hood up and the driver peering under it, I appreciated this truth.) Instead, with forty-five hundred dollars supplied by me, Sergei had bought a diesel-powered Renault step van. He promised me that this car was far more reliable.

In the narrow, low-ceilinged garage where Sergei was keeping it, the Renault struck me as not Siberia-ready. It looked more suited to delivering sour cream and eggs, the job it had done until recently. Sergei backed it out and we went for a quick test drive. Its shocks weren't much and its stick shift was stiff. Sergei said he would have it running smoothly in time for the journey. He said he planned to put an extra seat in the back, and a place to store our stuff, and a table where we could eat when it rained. I noticed that there were no seat belts, and said that each seat must have one. Sergei conceded that seat belts could be added if I wanted them. He treated this as an eccentric special request. Many Russians do not use seat belts and consider them an American absurdity.

Sergei described how he would arrange the back so we could sleep in there if necessary. I didn't see quite how this would work, especially when I learned there would be three of us—Vladimir Chumak, called Volodya or Vitya, who was a past associate of Sergei's, had been asked to come along as an assistant. Sergei and Volodya had been in Kamchatka together and had known each other since university. I was told that three men were better than two for safety. That sounded sensible to me. Sergei praised Volodya Chumak as a topnotch alpinist and a great guy. He lived in Sochi, a resort town on the Black Sea, where he employed his alpinist skills in his regular job as a building renovator, rappelling down the façades of buildings he was restoring. I would not meet him until just before the trip began.

There are very few motels in Siberia. Most of the time, Sergei and Volodya and I would be camping out, or else staying in people's houses. Sergei would supply tents, a propane stove, camp chairs, and other gear. I was to bring my own sleeping bag, eating utensils, personal items, etc. I asked if I should buy a travel directory of Siberian campgrounds, and he laughed. Sergei said that I would understand better what Siberia was like once I got there.

Early on the morning of the fifth of August, Sergei and Volodya brought the van to the back of Sergei's building. Volodya, who had arrived the day before, is a slim, broad-shouldered man who usually wears neat work shirts and pants in shades of gray. He was fifty at the time, with a full head of black, graying hair, blue eyes, and the thin nose and chiseled features of his Ukrainian ancestry. We did our final loading, Sergei said goodbye to his wife and grandson, and we climbed aboard. Setting out, I did not think about the enterprise before us or about our destination a third of the way around the globe. Instead I noticed that the rain, which had been sprinkling, had begun to pour, and that the windshield wiper on the passenger side worked only intermittently. The driver's-side wiper worked all right. The gray Neva River, beside us, reproduced the overcast drabness of the sky, and the speeding traffic threw up rooster tails of spray. By the time we reached the city limits, the oil-pressure warning light on the dashboard had come on. I pointed it out to Sergei and Volodya. They said it was nothing.

The van had been built with the cargo area in the back lower than the front seats, which rested on a raised platform. In the seat Sergei had installed in the back, one therefore had to sit straight up and lean forward in order to see over the dash. For comfort this was not ideal, but I had no choice, because there were no back windows on the van's sides. About the time the oil-pressure light came on, I also smelled a strange burning odor, mixed with diesel exhaust. When I mentioned this to Sergei, he rolled his window partway down.

Past the city, we turned onto the Murmansk highway eastbound. Its four lanes soon became two. Trucks were speeding toward us in the downpour. I thought Sergei was driving too fast but I couldn't tell for sure, because the speedometer needle, which had been fluttering spasmodically, suddenly lay down on the left side of the dial and never moved again for the rest of the journey. After a couple of hours, we came to the highway leading southeast to Vologda, and we pulled over at the intersection. The rain had let up by then. The intersection appeared to be a popular place to stop, with broad aprons of gravel beside the pavement and trash strewn around. We got out to use the facilities, which were bushes and weeds that had seen such employment before. Near the intersection stood a ruined brick church with grass and small trees growing from its upper towers and from the broken-off parts where the onion domes had been.

The Vologda road led through rural places with people selling potatoes along the narrow shoulder and irregularly shaped yellow meadows sometimes opening widely to the horizon. Then birch forest thronged close around, and Sergei said we were going into a huge swamp where many men had died in battles with the Nazis. People still go back in the swamp and find rusted grenades and skulls in helmets, he said. This conversation got Volodya talking about Ivan Susanin, the heroic Russian peasant who deliberately misled a Polish army deep into a swamp in order to save the life of the first Romanov tsar, in the Time of Troubles, during the seventeenth century. The Poles, discovering the trick too late, killed Ivan Susanin before perishing themselves. He is the main character of Glinka's opera *A Life for the Tsar,* Volodya told me. (Later, in my more uncertain moods, I wondered if my guides might be Ivan Susanin, and the Polish army might be me.)

The woods continued; now we came to a rotary completely enclosed by forest. On a pedestal in the middle of the rotary, pointing nose upward as if about to swoop into the sky, was a bright-silver MiG fighter jet. I had never seen a MiG up close. We had passed no air bases or factories that I recalled, so I couldn't figure out what it was doing here. Sergei seemed not to know, either. The shiny MiG was a strange object encountered inexplicably in a dark forest, spaceship-like.

The Vologda road had become a spill of pavement, untrimmed along its edges, with scalloping where the poured asphalt had flowed. Small villages followed, one after another, at regular intervals, roadside signs announcing their names. Often I looked up the names in my pocket Russian-English dictionary to see what they meant. According to my translations (verified by Sergei), that day we went through villages named Puddle, Jellies, Knee, New Knee, and Smokes.

All along the road, sometimes to heights of ten or twelve feet, grew a plant that Volodya identified as *morkovnik*. This plant resembles a roadside weed in America called Queen Anne's lace—except that *morkovnik* is like our modest, waist-high plant drastically and Asiatically enlarged. Queen Anne's lace and *morkovnik* are in fact related, both belonging to the carrot family (*morkov'* means "carrot"). Along the route we traveled, *morkovnik* grows abundantly from one end of Russia to the other.

In early afternoon, we stopped at an informal rest area like the one at the intersection of the Murmansk and Vologda roads. Here for the first time I encountered big-time Russian roadside trash. Very, very few trash receptacles exist along the roads of Russia. This rest area, and its ad hoc picnic spots, with their benches of downed tree trunks, featured a ground layer of trash basically everywhere, except in a few places, where there was more. In the all-trash encirclement, trash items had piled themselves together here and there in heaps three and four feet tall, as if making common cause. With a quick kicking and scuffing of nearby fragments, Sergei rendered a place beside a log bench relatively trash-free and then laid out our cold-chicken lunch on pieces of cellophane on the ground. I ate hungrily, though I did notice through the cellophane many little pieces of broken eggshell from some previous traveler's meal.

Back on the Vologda road, we continued in the direction of Cherepovets. After not many kilometers, the warning light for the engine generator lit up on the dashboard, making a companion for the oil-pressure light, which had never gone off. I expected that soon every warning light on the dashboard would be glowing. I pointed out the generator light to Sergei, and to humor me he said that we would stop and have the generator looked at in Cherepovets.

If that city consists of buildings, like a conventional city, you couldn't prove it by me, because all I saw of it was complicated highway ramps among a forest of power-line towers. The towers were everywhere, many stories high, sometimes clustering right up next to one another like groves of trees all striving for the daylight. Of daylight itself there was almost none; a tarpaulin of gray clouds overlay the entire scene. Somewhere Sergei spotted a garage in a roadside expanse of mud and gravel and pulled up in front of the garage-bay door. Just at that moment, the garageman came out, yanked a rope, and pulled the bay door down. He informed Sergei that the garage was now closed for the day. Then the garageman hurried to his car and sped away into the power-line forest. Sergei returned to the van, reseated himself behind the steering wheel, and turned the key. From the engine came no noise of any kind.

With this particular non-starting of the van we entered an odd zone — a sort of horse latitudes of confusion and delay caused by the mysterious problems of our vehicle. At low moments, I thought I might bounce around in this zone and stay in western Russia forever. The episode comes back to me in flashes:

Here are Sergei and Volodya and me pushing the van away from the garage-bay door, and then heaving and straining from behind to build up enough speed in order to start the engine by popping the clutch. Finally, at our breaking point, Volodya runs up to the open driver's-side door, leaps in, throws the gearshift into first, and the engine coughs alive.

Here we are in the city of Vologda, 135 kilometers down the road, where Vyacheslav, the brother of a friend of Sergei's wife, lives. Night has fallen. We are in a parking lot behind some buildings with our weakly idling van. Vyacheslav arrives. He is like a provincial nobleman from a nineteenth-century novel. He is tall and straight, with Tatar eyes, a round head, and Lenin-pattern baldness. He wears a well-tailored shirt of white, finely woven cotton, freshly pressed slacks, and polished brown loafers with silver buttons. His confident and peremptory manner shows not a particle of doubt. In the silvery aura of the headlights of his shiny new Volvo sedan, he says he knows an excellent mechanic who will repair the van tomorrow. For now, we will stay at his dacha, twenty-eight kilometers out of town. We will leave the van here in this parking lot overnight. Someone must stay with it to watch our things. This job falls to Volodya. He accepts it with a shrug.

Here we are in Vyacheslav's large dacha, in a densely packed village of dachas. Vyacheslav's is set off from the others by a concrete wall with a steel gate. On the other side of the driveway, but inside the wall, is a smaller dacha that Vyacheslav has told me is the dacha of his security staff.

Here we are rocketing back to Vologda in the early morning. The faithful Volodya, when we find him, is walking up and down unhappily in the parking lot. He looks a bit worn from his night in the van. Vyacheslav's mechanic has been summoned and is on his way. Now, Vyacheslav tells us, we will go to a tennis exhibition put on by his son, a rising tennis star. Then we will take a tour of Vyacheslav's factory. Meanwhile, Volodya will stay and deal with the mechanic and the van.

Here we are in Vyacheslav's factory. He owns a company called Start-Plus; it bottles a mineral water called Serebrenaya Rosa, which means "silver dew." The factory is a Soviet-era concrete-and-brick pile reconfigured into a bottling plant, with many hallways, storerooms, catwalks. As we go through it, Vyacheslav tells me that he was trained originally as an engineer in metallurgy, but after meeting the founder of the first Russian bottled-water company, he got the idea of starting such a business himself. With friends, he formed a company, hired a team of geologists to search for springs, found the water of one particular spring to be good-tasting and extremely healthful, and began to bottle it. The company's success has been enormous. He attributes this to the company's collective method of working, and to the water itself, which he says is better and purer than bottled water in America, where what is sold as spring water is actually fake—distilled, or piped from a public water supply. His bottled water is alive, he says, while bottled water in America is "dead water." In office after office, he introduces me to his employees, who stand at their desks and smile and say they are pleased to meet me.

Here I am taking a walking tour of the city of Vologda with Stanislaus, an executive of the Start-Plus company. The van, which we hoped would be done by now, has apparently presented some new difficulties. Stanislaus is in his seventies, with thinning blond hair combed back, faded blue eyes, and an easygoing style. He seems to have done this kind of duty before. He shows me a cathedral that Ivan the Terrible got built in record time by denying food to the workers when they progressed too slowly; soon after the cathedral was finished, it began to fall apart, and it wasn't consecrated for many years. Stanislaus also shows me the house of the first translator of Marx's *Das Kapital* into Russian, and the building where Lenin's sister lived while in exile, and a statue of Lenin that Stanislaus says is the only life-size statue of Lenin in the world. It looks painful—as if the powerful Bolshevik had simply stood on a pedestal and been bronzed alive.

Now here I am with Stanislaus and Vyacheslav in a restaurant in Vologda having a late lunch.

Here we are in Vyacheslav's office. Sergei and Volodya have just arrived. The van is out of the shop and supposedly ready to go. A conference of the executives of the Start-Plus company has been assembled to determine what we travelers should do now. My own plan is simple: Let's go. Oh, but that is an overly hasty idea, I am told. The afternoon is almost gone. We should not leave now, but instead stay another night at Vyacheslav's dacha. Sergei and Volodya both strongly favor this idea. What can I do but agree?

Here we are at Vyacheslav's dacha that evening. Dinner has ended long ago, but still we are sitting at the table, drinking our fifth or seventh cup of tea; and I am thinking that Russians can sit at a supper table while saying brilliant or ridiculous things longer than seems physically possible; further, this trait may explain Russia's famous susceptibility to unhealthy foreign ideas, with the post-mealtime tea drinking providing the opportunity for contagion; and, further yet, I am wondering whether tea perhaps has been a more dangerous beverage to the Russian peace of mind, overall, than vodka. At about midnight, Vyacheslav brings down his semi-automatic rifle and begins to tell us his adventures hunting bears.

Here we are saying goodbye to Vyacheslav and his wife on the steps of his dacha the next morning. Sergei walks over to the van. Against expectation, it starts. I am glad it has finally been repaired.

Of course, the van's ills were not cured—not then, nor were they ever, really. As we continued our journey, and new problems arose, I sometimes raged inwardly at Sergei for attempting to cross the continent in such a lemon. In time, though, I quit worrying. I noticed that, whatever glitch there might be, Sergei and Volodya did always manage to get the thing running again somehow. When the ignition balked, Sergei found a method of helping it along by opening the hood and leaning in with a big screwdriver from our gear. Soon his pokings would produce a large, sparking pop, the engine would start, and Sergei would extricate himself from the machinery, eyebrows a bit singed.

Once after Volodya had accomplished a similar maneuver, I asked if he could explain to me just what was the matter with this car. He thought for a while and then said that what was wrong with the car could not be said in words. I recalled the lines by Tyutchev:

Umom Rossiyu ne ponyat',
Arshinom obshchim ne izmerit':
U nei osobennaya stat'—
V Rossiyu mozhno tol'ko verit'.

(Russia cannot be understood with the mind, / She cannot be measured by ordinary measure: / She has her own particular stance— / All you can do is believe in her.)

Tsar's End

For days we motored eastward toward the Urals. Though the road went on and on, it never settled down and became what I would consider a standard long-distance highway. You never knew what it would do next. Sometimes it was no-frills two-lane blacktop for hours. Then without any announcement it would change to gravel, degenerating into mud and enormous potholes, and I learned the word *yama,* meaning "hole." Arriving in a village, the road might lead straight into an Olympic-size mud puddle or lose itself among streets apparently based on cattle paths. Many stops to ask directions would be required before we could pick up its thread again.

On long, desolate sections with no villages nearby, people sat along the road selling things, or not. You might see a very fat and not-young woman in a bright-yellow dress sitting on a folding chair and reading a newspaper, with nothing visible to sell; then, a kilometer later, a group of little boys with several buckets and a sign that said RAKI. I knew that *rak* means "cancer," but Sergei said it is also the word for crayfish, which the boys catch in nearby creeks and swamps. Day after day, men and women waited beside cardboard boxes filled with newspaper cones of mushrooms, gooseberries, strawberries, fiddlehead ferns, and cedar nuts. The term for these forest products is *podnozhnii korm,* Sergei told me; it means, literally, "feed found underfoot." Regularly, we passed women standing all alone and giving each passing vehicle a sideways, hangdog stare. When they realized the driver wasn't stopping, they would turn away with their eyes cast down. They reminded me of fallen women from an old novel; I had never seen prostitutes acting ashamed before.

Whenever we stopped to refuel, the stations were as minimal as could be. A couple of fuel pumps on a gravel apron and a sheet-metal kiosk with a glass or plastic pay window so thick and opaque you could hardly make out the attendant inside composed the total of their amenities. No advertising banners, vending machines, drinking fountains, or restrooms cluttered up this just-the-facts approach. Of course, no bucket or squeegee was available should your window need to be cleaned. We had entered a buggy part of the journey, and our windshield was usually covered with splattered insects. No problem: Volodya took some water from our supply, gave the windshield a few splashes, crushed an unfiltered cigarette in his fingers, and using the tobacco as a solvent washed the bugs from the glass with big sweeps of his hand. Sergei, meanwhile, removed the wiper mount from the windshield-wiper arm and with the blade of the wiper squeegeed the windshield dry and clean.

One day—a Saturday—we drove through five weddings in the course of the afternoon. I couldn't tell whether the bridal couples had actually been married on the highway or were just having their receptions there. In either case, a lot of participants and guests had shown up, their numbers perhaps swelled by curious passersby. The celebrants stood on the pavement and along the roadside, clutching champagne bottles by the neck, photographing one another, and shouting remarks. Late in the day, we came upon the biggest and most sociable wedding yet. The bride and groom themselves were square in the middle of the road with the wedding party milling around them and backing up traffic in both directions. A young woman in a fancy dress came to the passenger's-side window of our van and, talking fast, said we must give money to the newlyweds. Volodya handed her a few kopeks, and she said with indignation that that was not nearly enough. He asked how much and she said, "Ten rubles, at least." He found a ten-ruble bill and gave it to her. She then handed in a tray of little plastic cups of vodka, which Volodya declined, saying we were drivers on our way to the Far East.

Cities came and went—Kirov, some seven hundred miles from St. Petersburg, and then Perm. Both were big, gray, and industrial. For a while, the scenery had been getting hillier. Sometimes the road ran on ridge tops above pine forests, and beyond Perm the land reminded me of the Rocky Mountain foothills along Interstate 90 near Bozeman, Montana. Just when I was expecting the

sight of the mighty Urals themselves rising above their hilly pro-
logue, we were on flat ground again. The Ural Mountains had
been crossed. If there had been a moment when we crested the
continent-dividing range's summit, somehow it had slipped by me.
Then almost immediately we were coming up on Yekaterinburg,
considered the westernmost Siberian city; here the road did one of
its quick-change acts to become a crowded and roaring multilane
highway with furniture-store billboards alongside, and broken-
down vehicles, and extra-large heaps of trash, and stooped figures
poking through the heaps with old umbrella handles.

Having read a lot about the end of Tsar Nicholas II and his family and servants, I wanted to see the place in Yekaterinburg where
that event occurred. The gloomy quality of this quest depressed
Sergei's spirits, but he drove all over Yekaterinburg searching for
the site nonetheless. Whenever he stopped and asked a pedestrian
how to get to the house where Nicholas II was murdered, the reaction was a wince. Several people simply walked away. But eventually, after a lot of asking, Sergei found the location. It was on a low
ridge near the edge of town, above railroad tracks and the Iset
River. The house, known as the Ipatiev House, was no longer standing, and the basement where the actual killings happened had
been filled in. I found the blankness of the place sinister and dizzying. It reminded me of an erasure done so determinedly that it
had worn a hole through the page.

The street next to the site is called Karl Liebknecht Street. A
building near where the house used to be had a large green ad-
vertisement that said, in English, "LG—Digitally Yours." On an ad-
joining lot, a small chapel kept the memory of the tsar and his family; beneath a pedestal holding an Orthodox cross, peonies and
pansies grew. The inscription on the pedestal read, "We go down
on our knees, Russia, at the foot of the tsarist cross."

Beyond Yekaterinburg, the road lay straight through grain fields
like Nebraska's or Iowa's, and the sky unfolded itself majestically
outward and higher. Vistas kept appearing until the eye hardly
knew what to do with them—dark-green tree lines converging at a
distant yellow corner of the fields, and the lower trunks of a birch
grove black as a bar code against a sunny meadow behind them,
and the luminous yellows and greens of vegetables in baskets along
the road, and grimy trucks with only their license numbers wiped

clean, their black diesel smoke unraveling behind them across the sky.

And everywhere the absence of fences. I couldn't get over that. In America, almost all open country is fenced, and your eye automatically uses fence lines for reference the way a hand feels for a banister. Here the only fenced places were the gardens in the villages and the little paddocks for animals. Also, here the road signs were fewer and had almost no bullet holes. This oddity stood out even more because the stop signs, for some reason, were exactly the same as stop signs in America: octagonal, red, and with the word STOP on them in big white English letters. Any stop sign in such a rural place in America (let alone a stop sign written in a foreign language) would likely have a few bullet holes.

The Convicts' Road

In 1885, George Kennan, the journalist who became one of the most famous Siberian travelers of that century, went to Siberia to see prisons and interview political exiles. *Siberia and the Exile System,* the exposé he wrote afterward, appalled readers and contributed to the revolutionary spirit that brought down the tsar. I got interested in Kennan because he grew up in Norwalk, Ohio, where some of my family came from. Admiration for him was one of the reasons I had wanted to travel in Siberia in the first place.

Because I knew Kennan's route, I generally had it in the back of my mind. Though the human geography had changed in 116 years, I was confident that Kennan had traveled quite near where I was right now. Kennan and George Frost, his travel companion and sketch artist, arrived in Yekaterinburg on June 12, 1885, and left there soon afterward. During Frost and Kennan's first day on the Siberian road (also called the Sibirskii Trakt, or just the Trakt), they saw 1,445 freight wagons. The Trans-Siberian Railway had not yet been built, so the Trakt then served as Siberia's main artery. Traffic crowded it, especially tea caravans, which were among its chief nuisances—the great throngs of carts and wagons loaded with crates of tea from China, moving in herd formation all over the roadway at the will of their driverless horses, loosely controlled by a few caravan masters.

Of course, much of the Trakt's eastbound traffic consisted of exiles. Shackled or not, sometimes accompanied by their families, always under guard, parties of exiles journeyed to their various Siberian destinations on foot for most of the way. In tsarist times, many thousands of exiles walked the Trakt every year. It officially crossed into Siberia 150 miles east of Yekaterinburg, where the province of Perm, a western Russian province, met the Siberian province of Tobolsk. A square pillar of stuccoed or plastered brick marked the spot of this continental transition. One side of the pillar bore the coat of arms of Perm Province, and the other side that of Tobolsk.

At this pillar, Kennan said, exiles were allowed to stop and make a last goodbye, to press their faces to the ground and pick up a little of the earth of western Russia to bring with them. Beyond this spot they were, in a sense, jumping off into the void.

Naturally, I wanted to find this pillar and see what it looks like now. If I stood beside it, I would be in an exact place where the famous traveler had been. I explained about the pillar to Sergei and we kept our eyes open. Kennan had said that the pillar was about two days' travel from Yekaterinburg, between the villages of Markova and Tugulimskaya. I noted a large town named Tugulym on the map, but Markova was either too small to be included or didn't exist anymore. Then, about two hundred kilometers from Yekaterinburg, on the right-hand side of the road, there it was: Markova, barely a hamlet, just some houses and a sign. A short distance beyond it, tall markers announced the boundaries of two *raioni*, or regions. The marker facing westward said TUGULYMSKII RAION, and the eastward-facing marker said TAPITSKII RAION. We got out at the wide place in the road there. Pistachio shells and a Fanta Orange can littered the oil-stained ground, the trucks blew by, the trees leaned overhead. But nothing like Kennan's fateful pillar could be seen.

A woman in a roadside café nearby told Sergei that the road we were on was the new road, and the previous one, the original Trakt, used to run through the woods just to the north. She had never heard of any pillar such as Kennan had described. Following her directions, we went down a brushy lane until it ended at a collection of trash piles, and then Sergei and I continued on foot into deep forest with weeds and underbrush over our heads sometimes. Rain had fallen the night before and our clothes were soon soaked through, while grass seeds covered us all over. The woman had said that exiles who died along the road were buried beside the old Trakt, and you could still see the mounds. We did find mounds on either side of a declivity among the trees, and its barely visible path could once have been a roadway. But the mosquitoes were coming at us so madly that we had to wave our hands before us like windshield wipers on the fastest setting, and I soon decided that Kennan's pillar, if it did perhaps exist somewhere in these thickets, would not be found by me.

Back on the road, we drove slowly and asked people along it if they'd ever heard of the pillar—none had—and if they could show us sections of the old Trakt. Everybody we talked to pointed out pieces of the Trakt right away. Sometimes it was on one side of the new road, sometimes the other. Where it crossed grassy fields you could still see the deep depression the road had made in the ground. A man selling carrots on the new road told us that the Trakt had been the main street of a tiny village nearby called Maltsevo. Leaving the pavement and rambling along mud paths, we came upon Maltsevo in its backwater, where the new road as well as the railroad had passed it by. Every one of the dozen or so houses in the village was made of wood, and every piece of wood was the same shade of weathered gray. The houses' logs, thin pieces of overlying lath, decorative scrollwork, and plank window shutters all seemed to be in a slow-motion race to see which would be the first to fall completely down.

The single distraction that kept the village from epitomizing a dreary Russian peasant village for all time was the loud rock-and-roll anthem reverbing from speakers somewhere invisible but quite close by. I recognized the song as "It's My Life" (in English, the original), by Bon Jovi. As we stood on the town's one street, a small, unshaven, dark-haired man came walking along. He had on two sweaters, whose several large holes almost did not overlap. We asked him where the Trakt used to be, and he immediately said, "Right here!" gesturing backhand at the ruts at his feet. "Also, there," he said, and gestured far to the west. "And there!" This final gesture, to the east, was like an overhand throwing motion, and it pantomimed a hopelessness at even imagining how far the road went on.

I turned to where he gestured—first, back to the west, where the old road came on snakily but straight, a pair of muddy ruts in a wide and worn bed. The ruts entered the village, barely deigning to notice the weak attempt at domestication alongside, and then headed straight out of town. Across another empty field they dwindled eastward to the horizon and forever. I had seen some lonesome roads, but this one outdid them. I stood looking at it with Sergei and Volodya and the man wearing two sweaters. For a moment, I got an intimation of the sadness Kennan had talked about—the deep and ancient sorrow of exile.

In the ruts of the old Trakt, I tried to picture its former magnitude. This had been a continental highway, after all, a road of empire. I imagined parties of prisoners tramping along it, chains jingling; and sleighs slipping by in winter, and imperial couriers on horseback bound for Peking, and troops of soldiers, and runaway serfs, and English travelers, and families of Gypsies, and hordes of tea wagons in clouds of dust. If there were a museum of the great roads of the world, the Sibirskii Trakt would deserve its own exhibit, along with the Via Appia and the Silk Road and old U.S. Route 66.

In America, we love roads. To be "on the road" is to be happy and alive and free. Whatever lonesomeness the road implies is also a blankness that soon will be filled with possibility. A road leading to the horizon almost always signifies a hopeful vista for Americans. "Riding off into the sunset" has always been our happy ending. But I could find no happy-ending vista here, only the opposite. This had also been called the Convicts' Road or the Exiles' Road. Not only was it long and lonesome but it ran permanently in the wrong direction, from the exiles' point of view. Longing and melancholy seemed to have worked themselves into the very soil; the old road and the land around it seemed downcast, as if they'd had their feelings hurt by how much the people passing by did not want to be here.

Using a place as punishment may or may not be fair to the people who are punished there, but it always demeans and does a disservice to the place.

Insects

Eleven days from St. Petersburg, Sergei Lunev, Volodya Chumak, and I were well into the swampy flatlands of western Siberia. It was the summer of 2001, and we were driving across Siberia in a converted Renault step van that had formerly delivered eggs and sour cream and sometimes didn't start. Every night, we were camping out. In a country without fences or NO TRESPASSING signs, we had an abundance of places to camp, but each one required a certain amount of searching nonetheless. Sergei sometimes spent an hour or more in the evenings looking—stopping, getting out, walking around, then trying somewhere else. He wanted ground that was dry, not too low, not too many trash heaps, near water if possible, away from the road but not too difficult to get to. When he was satisfied with his find, he would pronounce it a *khoroshoe mesto*—a "good place."

The country's swampiness did not manifest itself in great expanses of water with reeds and trees in it, like the Florida Everglades. There were wide rivers and reedy places, but also birch groves and hills and yellow fields. The way you could tell you were in the swamp was, first, that the ground became impassably soggy if you walked at all far in any direction; and, second, by the mosquitoes.

I have been in mosquito swarms in beaver meadows in northern Michigan, in boreal wetlands in Canada, and near Alaska's Yukon River. Western Siberia has more. On calm and sultry evenings as we busied ourselves around the camp, mosquitoes came at us as if shot from a fire hose. Usually mosquitoes cluster in a cloud around their targets, but as Volodya made dinner I observed a thick and proximate cloud surrounding him head to toe, and then a whole other sort of candidate swarm around that inner swarm, and then more in all directions, minutely enlivening the sky.

With such astronomical numbers, Siberian mosquitoes have learned to diversify. There are the majority, of course, who just bite you anywhere. Those are your general-practitioner mosquitoes, or GPs. Then, you have your specialists—your eye, ear, nose, and throat mosquitoes. Eye mosquitoes fly directly at the eyeball and crash-land there. The reason for this tactic is a mystery. The ear mosquito goes into the ear canal and then slams itself deafeningly back and forth—part of a larger psyops strategy, maybe. Nose and throat mosquitoes wait for their moment, then surf into those passages as far as they can go on the indrawn breath of air. Even deep inside they keep flying as long as possible and emit a desperate buzzing, as if radioing for backup.

Nothing short of a good breeze keeps Siberian mosquitoes down.

They laugh at organic-based repellents. Strong repellent with deet is disagreeable to them, but they work around it. Thick smoke can be effective, but you have to stand right in it. In past times, native peoples and Russians wove fine netting of the long hairs in a horse's tail and wore the nets throughout the summer. Members of a tribe called the Tungus carried smoke pots with them wherever they went, while another native people, the Voguls, retreated into smoke-filled huts for the summer months and became dormant, doing most of their hunting and traveling in the wintertime. The sheer volume of mosquitoes might cause an observer not to mention the gnats, flies, and tiny biting insects (known as "no-see-ums" in America); there are plenty of all those as well. Sometimes in the evenings, I imagined I could hear the great insect totality tuning up all around, a continent-wide humming.

The mosquitoes kept tabs on us vigilantly everywhere we moved, indoors as well as out. Because our campsites were just places along the road, the bathroom arrangements had to be of the walk-off-into-the-bushes variety. Tending to necessities while under insect attack was a real experience. I recalled what a Siberian traveler named Hans Jakob Fries had written about this problem more than two centuries ago. Fries was a Swiss doctor, whose book, *Reise Durch Sibirien* (*Travel in Siberia*), described a journey he made in 1776 and, incidentally, became one of the earliest books to use that serviceable title. Fries wrote that during his passage through western Siberia he was bitten on a "delicate portion of my privy parts . . . so severely by a horse fly . . . that for three days I didn't know where to turn on account of pain, and I had the greatest trouble to prevent the setting in of gangrene." The recollection of Fries's misfortune filled me with caution, not to say fear.

Sergei had provided each of us with a special anti-mosquito hat, called a *nako-marnik,* that was draped with netting and resembled something a beekeeper might wear. When the mosquitoes were worst, we wore those hats, and gloves, and we tucked our pant legs into our boots. Dressed this way, we could move around and perform most essential activities. I found sketching and taking notes to be difficult with gloves on. Also, the no-see-ums got through the holes in the netting, and were hard to swat once inside. A few mosquitoes always sneaked in as well, and whined maddeningly. As Volodya cooked meals on the propane stove, mosquitoes attracted by the rising vapors flew over the pot, swooned from the heat, and fell in. When we ate our oatmeal in the morning, there were often a few mosquito bodies in it. Most of them we just ate, but sometimes there were ones that had bitten somebody and were full of blood . . .

Bugs are just part of the Siberian situation, as inescapable as distance and monotony. That long-suffering traveler Chekhov described a cockroach-infested room in the jailhouse where he spent the night in a tiny settlement on Sakhalin Island:

> It seemed as though the walls and ceiling were covered with black crepe, which stirred as if blown by a wind. From the rapid and disorderly movements of portions of the crepe you could guess the composition of this boiling, seething mass. You could hear rustling and a loud whispering, as if the insects were hurrying off somewhere and carrying on a conversation.

V. K. Arsenyev, the Russian army officer and explorer who in the early 1900s mapped some of the most inaccessible parts of the Primorskii Krai, north of Vladivostok, wrote about flies that fell so thickly they put out his campfire; Dostoyevsky waxed lyrical about the blessed moment in the cool of predawn in the prison barracks when the fleas stopped biting and the convicts could sleep; and John Bell, a Scottish doctor in the employ of Peter the Great, noted that his ambassadorial party, bound for Peking in 1719, changed their route across eastern Siberia partly because they were "much pestered with gnats and muskitoes." The swarms afflicted animals, too—descending on young foals in such numbers as to kill them, suffocating reindeer in Yakutia by clogging up their nostrils, tormenting cattle on the Barabinsk Steppe so that the herdsmen had to paint them all over with tar. Some of my Siberian notebooks still have squashed mosquitoes between their pages. The Lonely Planet guidebook to Russia that I consulted before I went on my journey states, in the section about Siberia, "By August, the air has cleared of mosquitoes." From my experience, this is no longer the case.

Camp Yermak

As we followed the banks of the Tura River going northeast, we came to the village of Pokrovskoye. I had wanted to check this village out because it was the hometown of Rasputin — not Valentin Rasputin, the Siberian writer, but the original, unhinged self-described holy man Rasputin, abettor of the downfall of the Romanov line. The village was all gray wood and stretched along the river for miles. Sergei did not care to look for Rasputin memorabilia — for an old church associated with Rasputin, perhaps, or a Rasputin museum. And Rasputin was not the kind of celebrity whose home place seemed eager to claim him; I saw no signs anywhere, including at either edge of town, that mentioned his name. Later, I heard that there is a small Rasputin museum in Pokrovskoye, but to visit it you have to make arrangements in advance. Sergei drove straight through the village without a pause while I fretted and said nothing. Rasputin, it was said, gave off a powerful odor of goat. What a museum you could make about a guy like that! Oh, well.

A few hours later, we came to a river I'd long wanted to see — the Tobol. This is the river that Yermak, the almost mythical conqueror of Siberia, traveled as he approached his decisive battle with the Khan of Sibir. The problem was, we could glimpse the river only off in the distance, because for most of its length it's really more like a deeper part of a continuous swamp. Trying to get close to it in the late afternoon, we drove up on a small hill. Birch groves and a meadow of long grasses covered the hill, which on its far side ended at a cliff descending steeply to the Tobol itself. Here the view swept far around a long continuation of the cliff that enclosed a wide swath of water made by a sharply turning river bend. This seemed an ideal camping place. Sergei parked the van back from the cliff, in a clearing in the birch woods, and set up the tents for the night.

Along the cliff a kilometer or two away, the roofs and smokestacks of a village mingled with the silhouetted trees. According to somebody we had talked to on the road, the village was called Berezovyi Yar — Birch Cliff. A breeze was blowing, rendering our supper pleasantly mosquito-free. After the meal, as the light was declining, Sergei and Volodya proposed that they walk over to the village, buy some bread, and find out about the area. While they were there, I would stay and keep watch over the camp and the van.

I did not like being left in camp, but I had brought that duty on myself. What with my awkwardness in the language, and the fact that I didn't drink, I sometimes preferred to stay in camp and read a book while Sergei and Volodya were hanging out and socializing with people they'd met along the way. But that does not quite describe the problem, either. By now we were in remote places where the arrival of a vehicle with St. Petersburg license plates was news. Even the highway police, when they waved us over at checkpoints, were a bit wide-eyed as they examined our documents— "Where do you live in America? What do you do?"—and so on. One young policeman, before he saw my passport, asked wistfully, "Is it expensive to live in St. Petersburg?" And this curiosity seemed to affect the local women even more strongly than it did the men.

I'm not saying that women paraded through our campsites wherever we happened to be; but they did show up occasionally, even when we were camped far from any village. A few nights before, in a glade well off the road, I had just got into my sleeping bag when Sergei rousted me out so that I could meet two women whom he described as schoolteachers eager to meet me. Dutifully, I got up and emerged and made conversation with the schoolteachers for a while. They had wanted to see the American, and I think Sergei had felt compelled to prove that he really did have one. Then he and Volodya and the schoolteachers went off—to a birthday party, Sergei said, at a picnic spot nearby. I demurred and returned to my tent. The idea of chasing women in Siberia would have made me nervous even had I not been married. Sergei and Volodya found my reluctance mystifying.

Tobolsk, our local destination—a must-see as far as I was concerned—was about an hour and a half away. In the morning, Sergei announced that we would drive to Tobolsk now, spend the day there, then come back here and camp for another night.

Rather tiredly, he and Volodya broke camp and packed the van. Then we drove off, with a first stop at the village, where three women were waiting for us. The youngest of them, a sturdy, round woman of about thirty with blond-streaked hair, came up to Sergei and took his hand. She seemed delighted with her luck in having met him. The other two women were in their late fifties or early sixties and did not appear to have been principals in last night's socializing. These two were sisters. One of them was the blond-streaked young woman's mother, the other her aunt.

Both the aunt and the mother had brown, deeply weathered faces. The mother wore a brown cloth Lenin-type cap, a dark-gray overcoat-smock with holes in it, brown bloused pants with red-brown patches, and knee-high rubber boots. The aunt was dressed similarly, but she had a head of wiry hair dyed yellow-orange. Both carried big galvanized pails. They were on their way to pick berries, and we were going to give them a ride to the berry patch, a few kilometers away. The mother started right in talking to me. Sergei must have told her that I was interested in Yermak, because she informed me that Yermak and his men had camped at the exact spot where we were last night. I asked how she knew this and she said, "It's a fact, everybody knows it," adding that the aunt had even written a paper about this subject. The aunt nodded her head in confirmation. The mother went on to tell us about the aunt's paper, and what it said, and where it was published. With more verifying nods, the aunt backed up each detail. I asked the aunt what her job was. "She's a philologist," the mother said. With matter-of-fact pride, the aunt nodded again.

At the berry patch, the mother showed me what they were picking—a small, round berry growing close to the ground on a plant with leaves like strawberry leaves. It looked like a holly berry and was very sour but sweet, with a big stone. There were thousands of them. The mother said its name was *kostyanika*. (The name means "stone berry.") She said they made a jam of it to put in tea.

As for her information about Yermak, later I read in a Russian chronicle from the late seventeenth century that the Cossack leader and his men, having fought one battle with the warriors of the Khan of Sibir, "sailed on the 8th day of June down the river To-bol, fighting and living on the alert. When they reached the landmark of Berezoviy Yar [!] a great battle was fought lasting many days. The infidels were like sheep rushing out of their folds but with God's help and the manifestation of heavenly hosts they too were defeated."

At Tobolsk, we saw the oldest stone fortress in Siberia, and the next days took us to and through the city of Omsk. I had been to Omsk twice before, but only at the airport. This city presented the usual row on row of crumbling high-rise apartment buildings, tall roadside weeds, smoky traffic, and blowing dust. For a moment, we passed an oasis scene—a crowded beach beside the Irtysh River, kids running into the water and splashing—before the urban grittiness resumed. Solzhenitsyn wrote in *The Gulag Archipelago* that he spent time in an ancient prison in Omsk that had once held Dostoyevsky, and that the prison's three-meter-thick stone walls and vaulted ceilings resembled a dungeon in a movie. I had wanted to explore Omsk looking for this prison, but forgot that idea entirely in our collective eagerness to get out of Omsk. We stopped just to buy groceries, then sped on.

A day beyond Omsk, the vastness of the Barabinsk Steppe stretched before us. For hours at a time, the land was so empty and unmarked that it was almost possible to imagine we weren't moving at all, and I often had trouble staying awake. Lenin himself had declared this a land "with a great future," but what I saw resembled more the blankness of eternity. And yet it was not like other flat places I've seen. The Great Plains of America tend to undulate more than this steppe does, and when the plains are flat-flat, as in southwest Texas, they're also near-desert hardpan with only stunted brush and trees. On the Barabinsk Steppe, by contrast, stretches of real forest often appeared here and there, intruding into the flatland like the paws of a giant dog asleep just the other side of the horizon.

The villages now were fewer, and their names seemed to reach new levels of strangeness. In far-apart succession, we went through Klubnika (Strawberry), Sekty (Sects), and Chertokulich (hard to translate, but something like Devil Bread, according to Sergei). In the village of Kargat (meaning unknown, probably a Tatar word), we stopped for a break in the late afternoon. I sat in the van with the window open and my feet up, watching. First, a man went by on a motorcycle with a sidecar. In a few minutes, he passed by going in the other direction, with the sidecar now full of hay. A flock of sparrows burst from a cluster of bushes by the corner of a house with a noise like heavy rain. A moment later, a small hawk hopped from the bushes onto a nearby pile of firewood, looked around, hunched down, and flew off after them.

A motorcycle again came by with its sidecar full of hay. I looked closely. It was definitely not the same as the previous motorcycle.

This motorcycle's driver was wearing an aviator's hat with goggles, and the sidecar was blue, not brown. As I considered that, a tall, shapely woman came walking from a long distance up the road. She wore a plain dress and had curly black hair. She passed the van and I smiled at her. She did not smile back. Then a beat-up car lurched into sight towing an even more beat-up car. As the cars came near I saw that they were connected back to front by a loop made of two seat belts buckled to each other. That was the only time I ever saw a Russian use a seat belt for any purpose at all.

Traveling Music

Now a short interlude of traveling music on the balalaika, and a few images from the road in no particular order, movie-style:

Trash. The more of it I saw, the better I understood how it differs from American roadside trash. Russian trash has less paper. Paper plates and paper cups, especially, are almost never seen. The basic and most common item of Russian roadside trash is the handmade plastic drinking cup, which is improvised on the spot by cutting off the bottom quarter or third of a plastic bottle that formerly contained water, soda, or beer. Some of these bottle-bottom cups are neatly trimmed at the lip, but most look ragged and slapdash. The sturdier ones are made from bottles with thicker sections of black plastic reinforcing their bases. After use, the cups are naturally left where they were created, along the road or at the picnic grounds. In more frequented parts of Siberia, from the Urals to the Pacific, you see these cups along the roads everywhere.

Ravens and Crows. For weeks as we drove, flocks of ravens and hooded crows remained a constant, ubiquitous in western Siberia no less than in St. Petersburg. The birds are easy to tell apart, because the ravens are all black, the hooded crows black and gray. On the Barabinsk Steppe, both kinds sometimes wheeled in great numbers that vivified the blank sky above the wide-open horizon. Past the city of Novosibirsk, however, it suddenly occurred to me that although I was still seeing ravens, I hadn't seen any hooded crows for a while. I began keeping a special watch for them, and did see a few stragglers. But after another few hundred kilometers no more hooded crows appeared.

Prisons. Sometimes I caught a glimpse of a prison, but invariably it went by too fast. Prisons cropped up in unexpected places on the outskirts of a city. Suddenly, I'd see a guard in boots carrying a machine gun and standing on a catwalk directly above an exercise yard. But always, it seemed, we were in traffic and couldn't stop. Outside Novosibirsk, I saw derelict guard towers, tumbledown buildings, and drooping barbed wire in a broad, open place beside the road. Whenever I pointed to such a site, Sergei and Volodya would say, "Military," without even turning their heads. My ongoing search for prisons did not sit well with either of them. After a while, I decided that pursuing it too much was impolite, and I let it drop for the time being.

Pigs. Although roaming herds of pigs were occasional in villages in western Siberia, east of Novosibirsk they became more common. Now every village we went through seemed to have big gangs of them. Because the weather was so hot, the pigs had generally been wallowing in a mudhole just before they got up to amble wherever we happened to see them ambling. Evidently, the wallowing technique of some pigs involved lying with just one side of themselves in the mud. This produced two-tone animals—pigs that were half wet, shiny brown mud, and half pink, relatively unsoiled original pig. The effect was striking—sort of harlequin. The other animals that roamed the villages in groups were geese. When a herd of pigs came face-to-face with a flock of geese, an unholy racket of grunting and gabbling would ensue. I wondered if the villagers ever got tired of the noise. Whether challenging pigs or not, the village geese seemed to gabble and yak and hiss nonstop. The pigs grunted and oinked almost as much, but always at some point the whole herd of pigs would suddenly fall silent, and their megaphone-shaped ears would go up, and for half a minute every pig would listen.

Birthplace of Volodya. About a half day past Novosibirsk, we passed close by a town called Yashkino. Seeing it on our road map, Volodya remarked that he had been born there. His mother's people were originally from this area, he said. His father, a tank officer who had been stationed in the Far East at the end of the war, had met his mother while crossing Siberia on his way back to western Russia. Volodya was still a baby when he and his parents left Yashkino, so he had no memory of it; no relatives he knew of still lived there. He felt no need to go there.

Cottage Cheese. Called *tvorog* in Russian, this was a favorite lunch of Volodya's and Sergei's. Usually it could be obtained in very fresh

supply from the grannies along the road. Sergei and Volodya especially liked their *tvorog* drenched in *smetana* (sour cream). I got to
like it that way, too. Once or twice, we had *tvorog so smetanoi* not
only for lunch but for a snack later in the day. The only drawback
to this diet was that it made us smell like babies. And as we were
able to bathe only infrequently our basic aroma became that of
grown-up, dusty, sweaty babies: the summertime smell of Mongols,
in other words.

Talk Radio. There is talk radio in Russia just as in America, and
call-in radio shows, and "shock jock" hosts who say outlandish
things. Sergei and Volodya enjoyed listening to these shows sometimes. Usually I understood nothing that was said on the radio,
except for one time when the host told a joke that Sergei and Volodya both laughed at. I picked out the word "Amerikantsi," so I
knew the joke was about Americans. I asked them to tell me the
joke, but they wouldn't. I kept bugging them, but Sergei said the
joke was not important. Finally, when he was off doing something
in the campsite, I asked Volodya about the joke again, and he told
it to me. The joke was: "Why do American men want to be present
when their wives are in childbirth?" Answer: "Because maybe they
weren't present during conception."

Smog

Until we left Novosibirsk, we had seen none of the large-scale environmental damage that Siberia is famous for. Then we hit the
small, smoky city of Kemerovo, in the Kuznetsk Basin coal-mining
region. Russians don't bother to hide strip mines with a screen of
trees along the road to spare the feelings of motorists, as we Americans do. Beyond Kemerovo, the whole view at times became the
gaping pits themselves, sprawling downward before us on either
side while the thread-thin road tiptoed where it could between.
Strip mines are strip mines, and I had seen similar scenery in North
Dakota and southern Ohio and West Virginia, though never quite
so close at hand. Often through this Siberian coal region the road
strayed and forgot its original intention, and more than one fork
we took dead-ended without warning at a city-size strip-mine hole.
We meandered in the Kuznetsk Basin for most of a day and drove
until past nightfall in order to camp on the other side.

After the Kuznetsk Basin came a long interval of meadows. We saw dark-clothed people working the hay fields in big groups as in an old bucolic painting, or riding to or from the work in horse-drawn flatbed wagons whose hard rubber wheels bouncing on the uneven pavement made the flesh of the passengers' faces jiggle fast. In this more peaceful region, we camped one night on the banks of the Chulym River at a popular spot with a gravel bank more convenient for bathing and washing than the usual swampy mud. While we ate supper, a group of Christians waded in not far from us, some of them in flowing white baptismal clothes. The worshippers sang songs accompanied by a guitar, held hands in a circle, swayed. A man in the middle of the circle took another man and a woman and two girls in his arms and then immersed them one by one.

Environmental blight resumed the next morning as we approached the city of Achinsk. Never, under any circumstances, go to Achinsk. I'm still coughing Achinsk out of my lungs to this day, probably. During Soviet times, 95 percent of everything—buildings, roads, bus shelters, playgrounds, fountains, telephone booths, lampposts—was made of cement. A particular kind of five-foot-by-eight-foot cement panel often used in fences and walls seems to be the basic visual element of urban Siberia.

Well, all that cement, or a hell of a lot of it, is made in Achinsk. Achinsk has mineral refineries, too. The thick, dusty air of Achinsk coats grass blades to death and desertifies everything in a wide radius around the city. Still forty minutes away from it, we rolled up the windows and sweltered in the van rather than breathe the emanations of Achinsk. Skirting the city at a far remove, we never actually saw it, but only its cement-dust cloud, which densified to a dark gray at what I took to be the city's middle. For a second or two, a haze-blurred smokestack could be seen.

Our passage through this almost-dead zone heightened the surprise a few hours later when we reached the river city of Krasnoyarsk. The name—from *krasnyi*, "red," and *yar*, "cliff"—refers to the red cliffs near the city, which give the landscape with its broad valley a slightly out-of-context look, as if this place might be in eastern Wyoming or South Africa. The city occupies a prominence above the Yenisei River just upstream from where a series of mountainous, tree-covered cliffs along both sides of the river suddenly descend to level ground. Chekhov judged Krasnoyarsk the most beautiful city in Siberia, and he was right, from what I'd seen. Many buildings in the city center were from the later nineteenth century, and in a style of brickwork done decoratively, almost whimsically. Recent renovations had emphasized a color scheme perhaps based on the earth-toned reds of the Yenisei cliffs, and with white or light-blue trim for intensity. The downtown boutiques, restaurants, clothing stores, and galleries called to mind shopping districts in any of a thousand gentrified antique-ish towns and small cities in America. And although a line of storefronts bearing the logos of Wrangler and Reebok and Benetton and Nike would not gladden me if I encountered it in New Jersey, seeing it in Siberia did, somehow.

Krasnoyarsk opens onto the Yenisei the way St. Petersburg opens onto the Neva. And the Yenisei here is huge, more like an estuary than a river. Many of Krasnoyarsk's streets end at the water and route its amplified daylight into the city; I recalled a similar effect on the streets of older Mississippi River towns. To get a better look at the whole picture, Sergei drove us to a scenic overlook he knew of on some heights west of town. This particular vantage dominated a graffiti-covered stone outcropping above a small parking lot. As we climbed up to it, a wedding party was coming down with surprising agility in their tuxedos and high heels. The viewing promenade, when we reached it, was strewn all around with shattered champagne flutes from their just-completed toasts. While we stood there, a storm came up the river, and you could see almost its entire extent—the dark clouds, the advancing netlike pattern of smooth and rippled water beneath the clouds, the wispy paleness of the rain. The city itself, off in the distance, was only a thumbnail-size patch of the scene's immensity.

The long view also revealed that Krasnoyarsk puts out an impressive smoky haze of its own. During Soviet times, a lot of heavy industry relocated here. The first thing you see in the main hall of Krasnoyarsk's regional museum is a banner with a slogan intended to inspire Soviet factory workers during the Cold War. In large white letters on a red background, it reads, DOGONIM I PEREGONIM AMERIKU! — "We Will Catch Up With and Surpass America!"

*

The road got worse after Krasnoyarsk, and soon deteriorated thoroughly. Long unpaved sections with many big rocks and *yamy* made for a bumpy and dusty ride. The van's low clearance underneath, which I'd worried about before, now caused problems as we began to scrape, and we almost high-centered from time to time. A boulder in the path knocked away a foot or so of tailpipe. A worse bump on an uphill grade crushed and scraped away the remaining two or three feet, leaving no pipe extending from the muffler's outlet to carry off the exhaust fumes. Immediately, the air in the van, which had never been good, became unbearable. Now I could detect an actual blue fog. I tried to remember what the signs of carbon monoxide poisoning were. Sergei, as expected, refused to go to a garage or muffler shop or do anything about the problem. That was not necessary, Sergei announced, sitting beside his open window and its plentiful incoming dust. Finally, Volodya, the swing vote among us, switched to my side and told Sergei that we had to fix the tailpipe right away or we'd all suffocate. Sergei said he would fix it, and with some annoyance he pulled over to the shoulder.

He got out. Volodya and I watched. Sergei was just wandering around a weedy patch of ground that paralleled the road, looking down and kicking occasionally at the dirt. After a minute or two, he bent over and stood up with something in his hand. It looked to be a piece of pipe. When we got out to see what he'd found, he showed us a somewhat rusty but still serviceable meter-long piece of tailpipe that must have fallen off another vehicle. It was exactly the same width as the one we'd lost. With Volodya's help, Sergei scooted under the van and wired the length of tailpipe in place at the muffler outlet and other points leading to the rear bumper. When we started driving again, the fumes were much better, though not by any means gone. Still, I had to praise Sergei for what an ingenious guy he was.

Beyond Krasnoyarsk, the road also began to run closer to the tracks of the Trans-Siberian Railway, crossing it over and back from time to time. Each crossing was watched over by a guard in a small shed. When the guard, usually a short, stout woman, saw a train coming, she would walk into the road, wave a flag to stop the cars, and lower the barricades. If the train was a long and slow one, as many were, the people in the waiting cars would unpack drinks and snacks, throw their doors open, stretch their legs out, and get comfortable. After the train had gone by, the guard would walk onto the tracks, look both ways to make sure all was safe, raise the barricades, and wave the cars through with her flag. At regularly spaced intervals on the road, piles of snack remains showed where each car had been.

Sometimes in the evening we camped not far from the tracks. During lulls in the train traffic, I climbed up the stones of the roadbed and looked down the rails to where they disappeared around a distant bend. As on the old Sibirskii Trakt, phantoms thronged along the railway. I pictured the flag-bedecked, celebratory trains that passed by here when the railway was first completed, in tsarist times, and the soldiers of the Czech Legion in their slow-moving armored trains in 1919, and the White Army soldiers dying of typhus by the thousands along the route, and the slave laborers who laid the second set of tracks in the 1930s, and the countless sealed Stolypin cars of prisoners dragged along these tracks to the deadly Gulag camps of the Soviet Far East. Osip Mandelstam, the great poet, on his way to death at the Second River transit prison in Vladivostok, had gone along this line. The ties and the steel rails and the overhead catenary wires all leading determinedly eastward still had a certain grimness, as if permanently blackened by history.

The Decembrists

On the afternoon of August 27, we reached Irkutsk, the onetime Paris of Siberia. Since leaving St. Petersburg, we had been on the road for twenty-two days.

Among the first places we went in Irkutsk was the house (now a museum) built in 1854 for Prince Sergei Trubetskoy. He was one of the leaders of the revolutionaries whose failed uprising of December 14, 1825, earned them the name Decembrists. Their plan, not thoroughly thought out, was to depose the tsar and establish a constitutional form of government; when the moment for action came, they collectively balked. Had the coup succeeded, Trubetskoy was supposed to become the country's interim dictator. Many of his comrades saw him as a George Washington figure. By logic, after the movement was crushed Trubetskoy should have been among the ones hanged. The loftiness of his family—in nobility, the Trubetskoys ranked just below the tsar—and the fact that his mother was a lady-in-waiting to the tsarina no doubt saved his life.

Like many other Decembrists, Trubetskoy was sent to Siberia. His wife, Ekaterina, followed him into exile. For twelve years, he served his sentence of hard labor in prison settlements east of Lake Baikal, and in 1839 he was allowed to relocate with his family nearer to Irkutsk, where he later moved and built this house. Though it may have been one of the grander houses of Irkutsk in its day, it is not overly fancy, but suggests instead the elegance of curtailed excess and of cultured taste making the best of materials at hand. The house has a brick foundation supporting smoothly joined logs that have been planed square and fitted together horizontally. Single-story wings on either side balance a central, peaked-roof section that rises to a tall second story. The overall effect is of an eccentric Greek Revival style married to the skill and intricacy of Russian-village woodworking. I thought I'd never seen a better-looking house. I wanted to find out what it was like inside, but unfortunately it was closed for renovation when we were there.

A block away is another Decembrist house-museum. It was the house of Sergei Volkonsky, whose nobility of birth equaled Trubetskoy's. The Volkonsky family descended from a prince, later a saint of the Orthodox Church, who fought the Mongols in the thirteenth century; Sergei Volkonsky's mother, Aleksandra Repnina, also happened to be the tsar's mother's highest-ranking lady-in-waiting and closest friend. Like Ekaterina Trubetskaya, Maria, the young wife of Sergei Volkonsky, voluntarily shared his exile. Nekrasov's poem "Russian Women," in praise of the Decembrist wives, compared Maria Volkonskaya to a saint. Pushkin rhapsodized that her hair was more lustrous than daylight and darker than night. Tolstoy, whose mother was a Volkonsky, and who came from the generation that followed the Decembrists, thought so highly of Sergei Volkonsky that he is said to have based Prince Andrei Bolkonsky in *War and Peace* on him and to have used the letters and journals that Volkonsky wrote during the Napoleonic Wars in creating the character.

The Volkonsky house-museum is large and imposing, in a Russian château style, though it's not a work of art like the Trubetskoys'. Its exhibits consist mainly of portraits and photographs of the Volkonsky family and the families of other Decembrists. The elderly lady guide who took us through gave us the biographical details of everybody. Zinaida Trubetskaya, born to Sergei and Ekaterina in Siberia in 1837, survived to 1924, long enough to receive a government pension granted by Lenin himself in honor of her revolutionary father. Among the ancillary characters, the museum also displayed the only picture I'd ever come across of Georges-Charles D'Anthès, the French army officer and ballroom roué who killed Pushkin in a duel. Had there been matinee idols in D'Anthès's day, he could have been one, with his wavy blond hair.

For a while, Tolstoy planned to write a book about the Decembrists, but he set the idea aside because all official papers relating to them were in secret archives and thus unavailable for his research. After the revolution of 1905, when documents withheld under the tsars became accessible, Tolstoy was seventy-seven years old and no longer able to take on such a big project. Why the Decembrists interested him is easy to grasp. Though their revolution fell apart and though their punishment was a humiliation and a waste, the Decembrists were inspiring nonetheless. Of the hundred and some Decembrists found most culpable by the Committee of Inquiry that followed the suppression of the uprising, only ten were over forty years old. Almost all the Decembrists were of the same youthful generation in 1825; and if I had to pick one generation as the greatest in Russian history theirs would be it. Alexander Herzen hailed the Decembrists as "a perfect galaxy of brilliant talent, independent character, and chivalrous valor — a combination new to Russia." Of those declared the most dangerous — in other words, the most prominent among them — the greater number lived out their lives imprisoned or exiled in Siberia.

Irkutsk does kind of look like Paris, it turns out — if you can imagine a Paris with the Seine gigantically expanded to the horizon-filling width of Irkutsk's Angara, and with diminished buildings and steeples poking up along the river's distant margins on either side. We drove down the Street of the Events of December, we parked, we bought supplies. But the afternoon had got late, and Sergei, as usual, was in a sweat to escape the city limits and find a good camping spot. He said he knew of an ideal place on the shores of Lake Baikal, fifty or sixty kilometers away. Before we set out for it, I stipulated that we return to Irkutsk the following morning; there was more here I wanted to see.

Sergei's camping spot was in a little regional park above the fishing town of Nikola. Centuries ago, eastbound travelers used to stop there and pray at the chapel dedicated to Saint Nicholas for safe passage across the lake. The park is on a hillside, and as Sergei navigated the van up its incline he made a sharp turn that came within a breath of tipping the vehicle onto its side. He then stopped, backed down, found a less steep route, drove to the campsite, and set up the tents without comment. This was the first "improved" campsite we had been in. Each site had a fire circle surrounded by stones, an iron grate for cooking, and two benches made of wood.

Sergei and Volodya spent the next morning climbing the cliffs above Baikal. Sergei said that these cliffs were so beautiful I must see them immediately. After lunch he led me there. We climbed past the camp and well beyond the village to a point where pale, columnar cliffs rose spirelike above. Single file, we started up. The rock had interstices and eroded places through which a handbreadth of trail snaked, mostly along the side closest to the water. I admired Sergei's quick footwork; mine was more uncertain, and at one or two places I got down on all fours. Lake Baikal, immensely blue, occupied the entire space on our right-hand side clear to the horizon. At the top of a spire, we stopped, and there, directly below us, maybe fifteen stories down, a naked couple was swimming in water of a clear, almost tropical greenish blue. We could hear the woman laugh; her figure was Rubensian. In another moment, they ducked into a grotto, maybe realizing we were there.

Seen close up, the city of Irkutsk (when we returned to it) resembled the Baikal cliffs' ancient and weather-beaten windings. During its early years, Irkutsk had grown unplanned, like coral, and when civic improvement tried to bring some order to the confusion the crews sent out for that purpose sometimes sawed houses in half to make crooked streets straight. In much of the city, they still aren't. A sense of almost microscopic embroidery fills the town's windingest lanes, where log homes sunk halfway to their eaves in the permafrost draw your attention with decorative woodcarving on shutters and doors and windows as ornate as the finest carved birch jewelry box. And yet almost every house also looked

gray and older than old, though never as decrepit as the defiantly
ugly high-rises that confront you whenever a big open space from
Soviet times scissors across the network of lanes.

Elsewhere on my Irkutsk ramblings, I came across the graves of
Ekaterina Trubetskaya and three of her children at Znamenskii
Monastery. In the first years of the Decembrists' imprisonment,
Katya Trubetskaya had been everybody's morale-builder, with her
good humor and levelheadedness, but after her children began to
die and her own health failed she became indifferent to life, and
she died about two years before the amnesty declared by Tsar Alexander II, on the occasion of his coronation, in 1856. Her death
stunned her husband; when he went back to western Russia, he
said goodbye forever to her grave.

In advertisements posted around the city, I also noticed that Admiral Kolchak, the White Army leader whose attempt to overthrow
the Bolsheviks ended in Irkutsk with his capture and execution, is
now a beer. Admiral Kolchak Beer is brewed locally. I picked up
an empty bottle of it that I found. The label has a portrait of the
admiral in his white naval uniform and even provides the history-
minded beer drinker with a brief bio, which plays up his heroism
in the Russo-Japanese War and the First World War, his polar ex-
plorations, and his improvement of the Russian navy, but makes
no mention of his violent exit. A beer garden on Irkutsk's Angara
riverfront sports a long striped awning with the Kolchak Beer logo
repeated prominently all along it; maybe the awning is within sight
of the place where the corpse of the unlucky admiral was shoved
through the ice back in 1920.

The Moon Road

That night, we again slept near the shores of Baikal. This time, owing to bad planning, we camped on the grounds of what was billed
as a resort. It had a gate, cabins, picnic shelters, and washroom
conveniences best left undiscussed. Its strewn heaps of trash were
extreme, even for Russia. Somebody who saw this campground
without context or explanation might come to the conclusion that
a group of confused people had mistakenly gone on vacation at
the town dump. We met a woman who "provided touristic services"
at the resort, and she had been driven to a near-frenzy by how aw-

ful it was. This became evident when Sergei invited her to have tea with us after supper, and she told us, with great drama and force-fulness and scorching irony, about the difficulties of her job. By one o'clock, her monologue had worn me out and I retired to my tent. Sergei had to evict her bodily at two-thirty. At an even later hour than that, when he and Volodya were again off somewhere, I came awake to a loud conversation between two passing drunks who were debating whether to do something or other—I did not recognize the verb—to our tents. Fortunately, the milder of the drunks prevailed after a while, and they went away. Cars then blasted up and down the resort's dirt lanes for an hour or so, blow-ing their horns. Just after dawn, the Big Brother–like speakers of the public-address system wired to nearby trees began playing bad music from many different cultures while exhorting everyone to get up and exercise.

Sergei assured me that he would find us a better place on Baikal, and the next day he did. We drove around the southern end of the lake and then followed the railroad tracks that ran between the road and the shore. At a place where a creek went under a railroad bridge, there was enough dry ground on one side for the van to squeak through, and we emerged onto a beach of small, smooth rocks with no sign of people anywhere for three or four kilometers. Sitting on the beach with nothing to do but look at the lake, I fi-nally got the point about Baikal.

I knew that it's the largest body of fresh water in the world, that it contains about 20 percent of the world's fresh water, that it's 1,637 meters (more than a mile) deep at its deepest, that it was created by continental landmasses moving apart, that it has species of animals found only here. But, beyond its facts, Baikal really does have a magic to it. Travelers who wrote ecstatically about it in the past were not exaggerating. Most of Russia's inland water is slug-gish, swampy, inert; Baikal's is quick. For sparklingness and clarity it's the opposite of swamp water. The surrounding hills and cliffs that funnel winds along it keep it jumping. It reflects like an opti-cal instrument and responds to changes in the weather so sensi-tively that it seems like a part of the sky rather than of the land.

When a wave rolls in on Baikal, and it curls to break, you can see stones on the bottom refracted in the vertical face of the wave. This glimpse, offered for just a moment in the wave's motion, is like seeing into the window of an apartment as you go by it on an elevated train. The moon happened to be full that night, and after it rose the stones on the bottom of the lake lay spookily illuminated in the moonlight. The glitter of the moon on the surface of the lake—the "moon road," Sergei called it—fluctuated constantly in its individual points of sparkling, with a much higher definition than any murky water could achieve. Light glitters differently on water this clear. I understood that I had never really seen the moon reflected on water before.

This camping spot was so great we decided to stay another day. True, trains did go by almost constantly just the other side of some shoreline trees; but the sound was not bad for sleeping at all. In the morning, a fisherman who put his boat in at the mouth of the creek brought us some *omul'* he had just caught. (The *omul'* is Baikal's tastiest fish.) To reciprocate, I opened a stash of presents I had brought along and got out a New York City snow globe, some Beanie Baby stuffed animals, and two folding pocket mirrors to give to him. He liked the snow globe and he accepted the Beanie Babies, but he gave me back the mirrors, saying he had no use for them. This made Sergei indignant and he scolded the guy for being a rude person who didn't know how to behave with foreigners. Chastened, the guy took the mirrors. I remembered I had a baseball cap with the logo of the Bass Anglers Sportsman Society on it—the logo shows a leaping bass, in bright green—and I gave him that cap, too. He put it on and examined it in the mirror, and above his broad face and brown bib overalls it looked exactly right. I liked the idea that I had successfully launched a BASS hat on the waters of Baikal.

Of the 437 rivers that are said to flow into Baikal (only one, the Angara, flows out), the Selenga is the principal stream coming from the south. Its origins are in the steppes of Mongolia. Genghis Khan made his capital, Karakorum, near a Selenga tributary called the Orkhon. The Selenga was the most authentic-looking Siberian river I'd encountered so far. Up to now I'd seen swampy rivers and ones bordered by mountains and trees; the bare hills along the banks of the Selenga and the wide-screen vistas of river and open country spoke of Asian steppes expanding to the southeast. Again, the fencelessness of the land amazed me. At a place where wheel tracks led through the sparse brown grasses beside the highway we drove down a hillside and stopped beside the Selenga to make that evening's camp.

The fact that the wheel tracks ended at the edge of the river should have tipped us off that this was a ferry crossing. We didn't notice that until the tents had been pitched; then, from the other side of the Selenga, arose the sharp rat-a-tat of an unmuffled engine whose sky-filling volume seemed out of proportion to the little craft that was its cause. In another few minutes, the sound came nearer, as a short, stubby power launch angled across the current with a small fenced raft in tow. On the raft sat a truck of the kind that carries troops, its box back enclosed by an awning. The launch approached the shore and then executed a neat, sharp turn that swung the towrope and the ferry raft at its end into an unfurling arc that ended with the front of the raft wedged against the shore. Someone undid the raft's gate and the truck drove off onto the bank, and a dozen or so passengers jumped from the raft into the back of the truck. It revved its engine smokily for a few minutes and then motored away.

Meanwhile, a few cars had arrived to go aboard for the return trip. I pointed out to Sergei that this traffic was likely to continue into the night, so maybe moving camp would be a good idea. A chronic fear I have of being run over while asleep in my tent had begun to flare up. Sergei replied that we had nothing at all to worry about, and, not wanting to be difficult, I went along. In fact the traffic did keep coming and going until late, and began again just at dawn, but its orderly rhythms didn't trouble me. I even found them comforting, somehow.

While Volodya was fixing supper, I went a distance down the bank and sat on a camp chair and admired the view. To the north, or downstream, the river spread so far from bank to bank that it seemed more like a landlocked sea. Facing that way, I did a sketch of the river and of the ferry launch arriving. In the other direction, upstream, a rock cliff came down to the water and cut off the vista that was beyond. I hiked a bit to get a look around the cliff and discovered only more cliffs and hills, and a narrowed river slipping out of sight among them.

In that direction—south—lay China. Our route here didn't lead toward it but veered away from the river and to the northeast. We spent the next day climbing out of the Selenga watershed through hilly country of mixed taiga and steppe. The many hilltop vantage points revealed one view after another, with endless uplands and ridges and low mountains; Sergei kept stopping and getting out to sweep the video camera slowly across the scene. Many trees in this part were dead and gray, I assumed from some infestation or disease. At first, I thought the cause might be the pine beetle, as in similar forest die-offs in North America, but I saw many dead birches, too.

Now we were passing fewer cars, people, or villages than at any previous stretch of the trip. I had rarely seen country this unused and empty anywhere. At midday, we stopped in a village called Desyatnikovo to buy potatoes. An old woman there told us that this was an Old Believer village, but it was dying. (Old Believers are dissenters from the Orthodox Church; many of them have sought refuge in Siberia since the seventeenth century.) She said that houses with the shutters closed meant that no one lived there now and the people who used to live there had died. The woman showed us her own house, a bright-painted cabin of trimmed logs on the central street with shuttered houses on either side. She seemed to be in permanent mourning and told us she was very sad. A somewhat younger guy we bought potatoes from said that only old people lived in the village nowadays. There is no work, so young people move away, he said.

We kept climbing, descending, climbing again. One hilltop overlooked a span of the Trans-Siberian Railway on which a train consisting entirely of black oil-tank cars stretched as far as one could see, west to east; it must have been four kilometers long. At about three o'clock in the afternoon, Sergei informed me that, according to the map, we had just crossed the divide between the watershed of central Siberia and the basin of the Amur River. The M55 highway goes over this divide near the village of Tanga. From that point, the road began to descend until it dropped into the broad valley of the Ingoda River—a familiar name. When the Decembrists were imprisoned in Chita, they bathed in the Ingoda.

In late afternoon, we found a good place to camp on its banks. The Ingoda is a pleasant, small river with a brisk flow and a bottom of sand and gravel in the parts I saw. Some boys near our campsite who came by to check us out told Sergei you could catch plenty of fish in it using crickets. I set up my fly rod and tied on an all-around attractor fly. Casting into slack water below some riffles, I got a lot of splashy strikes, but the fish were too small to fit their mouths around the fly. Finally, I hooked a flipping and flopping six-incher. It had delicate yellow markings on its side, like little reef fish I'd caught in Florida. I don't know what kind of fish it was.

I showed it to Volodya and he said he'd fry it up for an appetizer before supper. Then I waded back into the river and cast some more. Far downstream, I knew, the Ingoda joined the Onon to make the Shilka, which joined the Argun to make the Amur, which eventually emptied into the Pacific, which extended all the way to Dockweiler State Beach, in Los Angeles, where my sister-in-law brought her children to swim. In theory, from here I could take the all-water route home.

The Vagon

The following afternoon, we reached Chernyshevsk, an important point on our journey. I had been half dreading Chernyshevsk, because beyond it the road became undrivably bad for the next eight hundred or nine hundred kilometers. Owing to the swamps and the lack of local population and the difficulty of maintenance, from Chernyshevsk to the town of Magdagachi, a long way to the east, there was in effect no vehicle road. Therefore, all cross-country drivers had to stop in Chernyshevsk (or, if westbound, in Magdagachi) and load their vehicles onto Trans-Siberian car and truck carriers in order to traverse the roadless stretch by rail.

This situation had created a bottleneck at Chernyshevsk, where traffic backed up like leaves in a storm drain. The place was really just a village beside a large Trans-Siberian Railway train yard, and it offered travelers—who routinely had to wait forty-eight hours before an available transport appeared—almost no lodgings, no bathroom facilities you would want to enter without protective gear, and almost no restaurants. Meanwhile, the trucks and cars kept arriving.

Late in the afternoon, a train hauling vehicle transports arrived from the east. The transports carried used Japanese cars, most of them Toyotas, with their front ends covered in masking tape, like bandaged noses, to protect from flying gravel on the road. So far, I have not described this important aspect of Siberian trade: throughout the year, but especially in the summer, guys ride the Trans-Siberian to Vladivostok, buy used Japanese cars there, and drive the cars west across Siberia for resale. Cargo ships full of these vehicles arrive in Vladivostok all the time. A used car bought in Vladivostok for two thousand dollars can be resold farther west in Russia for three times that much. The guys who drive this long-distance shuttle tend to wear muscle shirts, shiny Adidas sweat-pants, and running shoes, and their short, pale haircuts stand up straight in a bristly Russian way. On the road, they are easy to rec-ognize by the tape on their vehicles and by the fact that they speed like madmen. The faster they finish each round trip, the more trips they can do and the more money they can make.

One of the drivers debarking in Chernyshevsk told Sergei that this load of cars and drivers had had to wait five days in Magda-gachi for transports, and then spent forty-eight hours on the train. In Chernyshevsk, the unloading was done one car at a time. Some of the drivers, when they finally did emerge with their vehicles onto the cracked pavement of the Chernyshevsk parking lot, shifted into neutral and raced their engines in automotive howls of liberation or rage. The emergence of each vehicle caused a crowd of begging children to swarm around it. Some drivers honked and yelled at the kids to go away; others rolled their windows partway down and held out little pieces of leftover food. I saw a girl with large hoop earrings trot to a window and snatch the back end of a kielbasa that a driver offered her.

At about ten-thirty that night, the stationmaster, a blocky woman with dyed red hair, a Dalmatian-spotted blouse, and an orange workman's vest, appeared among the vehicles and told us all that there would be no train tonight. Nor would there necessarily be one tomorrow, she added, with keen enjoyment disguised as non-chalance. The quiet way she savored giving out this disappointing news was a wonder to see. Maybe a train would come along tomor-row night, she speculated; but, then again, maybe it would not.

As we considered the prospect of spending the night in Cher-nyshevsk in the van, Sergei again showed his mastery of difficult situations. By distributing a small amount of cash to the drivers im-mediately in front of and behind us, he held our place for tomor-row. Then he backed out of the queue, sped away from Chernyshevsk, and found us a place to camp beside a quiet and clear and relatively untrashed stream a few kilometers outside town. We set up the tents, ate supper by lantern light, and turned in for a good sleep. In the morning, I took out my fly rod and caught a couple of little fish in the stream. Volodya made breakfast, then drove to Chernyshevsk to monitor what was going on. He returned in haste, saying the train was about to leave and we must get back there *begom*— "at a run."

The train was not about to leave, as it turned out. To my surprise, though, it did seem to have arrived. We spent another afternoon in the vehicle queue waiting to load. I had understood that we would be going on a vehicle transport, the usual open-air affair, where we would just sort of hang out like train-hopping hoboes until we reached Magdagachi. But Sergei had something better in mind. He had heard about a guy who had his own train car. The guy, a short, dark-haired, bushy-eyebrowed, villainous-looking party, appeared at the loading ramp surrounded by a small entourage. Yes, he did have his own *vagon*—a long, windowless boxcar with room inside for four ordinary-size vehicles. The guy's *vagon* represented the high end of Chernyshevsk vehicle transports. Sergei negotiated with the guy to ensure that our van would be one of the lucky four, and the guy agreed, for two hundred dollars.

Then our van was locked in the guy's *vagon* for a few hours while the train made up its mind about leaving, and we had to fend for ourselves in the Chernyshevsk train station with no vehicle to retreat to. I just kept moving, strolling and taking evasive action so as not to be swarmed on. Finally, we were let into the *vagon* and it somehow got hooked up to the train; and later, hours later, sprawled in the van, I felt the first few blessed inchings of forward motion. When a conveyance you are riding in fails to move and fails to move, and you hope and pray and apply all your mental powers in an attempt to get it rolling, and it finally does move, that's one of life's sweetest feelings. When the train at last left the yards after all that time in Chernyshevsk, I relaxed as if the sedative had finally reached my veins.

The *vagon*'s luxuries did not include interior lighting. Small planes of daylight came through narrow slots at the top of what might once have been windows; otherwise the space was completely sealed. Once darkness had fallen, everything in the *vagon* grew dim, except at the front end, where a glow came from an open door. Inside the door, the guy who owned the *vagon*—its *khozyain*, as he repeatedly instructed me to call him—occupied a sort of stateroom.

Past his room was a small between-cars passageway with doors on either side that opened at the top so you could look out. This place was great for fresh air, an antidote for the claustrophobia of the *vagon*. The *khozyain* kept his stateroom door open, and as I went by he would hail me, "Hey, comrade writer!" Sometimes we had short conversations. Generally, he was drinking vodka from a large bottle while lying on a bed that fit into the stateroom's corner. Beside him lay a blond woman so large and rumpled she seemed to be part bed herself. A TV sat on a shelf opposite them playing a Russian movie, and they were passing back and forth a sunflower blossom the size of a party pizza, pulling seeds from the blossom's center and chewing them and spitting the shells into cups.

On every trip there is a hump that must be got over, a central knot to be worked through. For us that knot pulled tight in the Chernyshevsk–Magdagachi part of our journey.

Being sealed in the *vagon* soon got to me. I mean, here were four vehicles parked inches apart in a closed space, maybe twenty gallons of gas in each vehicle; and there were no windows, no fire extinguishers on the walls, no EXIT signs, the *vagon*'s back doors secured tightly from the outside . . . Safety is never the Russians' primary concern. Meanwhile, the guy in charge of the *vagon* is drunk and watching TV. Of course, I understood that there was no point in mentioning any of this to anybody.

Besides our van, the *vagon* carried two Japanese-made SUVs driven by families on their way back to their home cities in the Sakha Republic, in northeastern Siberia, after their summer vacations. One family consisted of a hard-drinking dentist and his fourteen-year-old daughter, Kira. The other family was a mother and father, a young son, and a fourteen-year-old daughter named Olya. The two girls lived far apart and had never met. They hung out together in the passageway and talked, and when they found out I was from America they had a lot of questions for me, mostly about Jewel (the singer), Sylvester Stallone, and the Hard Rock Cafe. Both girls said that Yakutsk, the capital of the Sakha Republic, was a really boring place. Olya gave me a piece of paper with her address and wrote "Write to me!" all over it; naturally, I lost it soon afterward. At one point, I was sitting in the van and I took a nervous look behind us—making sure no wisps of smoke were rising, signs of coming inferno—and Olya happened to sit up in the front seat of her car where she'd been napping, and she smiled at me so beautifully that all my malaise lifted for a while.

The guy in the fourth car, a Russian vehicle right in front of the van, was a scuba diver. He said that he worked on oil platforms and also gathered shellfish off the coast of Sakhalin Island, to which he was returning. He was wiry-haired and ruddy and he wore a vest of black leather. With other people and by himself, he drank vodka night and day. Our first morning in the *vagon*, after I'd slept pretty well on the front seat of the van complicatedly propped between the door and the steering wheel, I woke, sat up, and rubbed my eyes. The scuba diver woke at the exact same moment and got out of his vehicle rubbing his eyes. He saw me, broke into a huge grin, and made the "Do you want a shot of vodka?" gesture, tapping his throat below the jaw with a flip of his fingers. From his car he pulled a half-full bottle of vodka to show me. I shook my head no politely, it was about eight in the morning.

Quietly, I slid from the van and went to the passageway for a look outside. The sun had risen on a cool, clear day in early fall. Our train was making a steady thirty kilometers (about twenty miles per hour) through taiga mixed with hay fields. During the night, a heavy frost had covered the countryside. It rimed the leaves of the birch trees, some of which had already turned yellow, and made the needles and knobby branches of a tree I took to be a larch a soft white. At this speed, I could see the trackside weeds, curved like shepherds' crooks by the spiderwebs attached to them, the frost on the web strands glistening in the sun. When the tracks went around a bend, the rest of the train was revealed extending far ahead. Our *vagon* was the second-to-last car. A broad hay field we passed had just been cut. The short stubble, all frost-white, lay like a carpet among the haystacks spaced regularly across it. In the cool morning air, the top of every haystack was steaming, and each wisp of steam leaned eastward, the direction we were going.

All day the train moseyed on. During stretches where the track was really bad, it slowed to walking speed. It stopped, it started,

it waited on sidings, started again, stopped. In the *vagon*, a temporary lobotomy seemed to have leveled everybody. Sometimes as
the train sat awhile at a station I got out and walked around, never
wandering too far, from fear of being left. Every station I observed
was dark, cracked, in the process of being colonized by weeds, and
with the lights of its platform broken.

People thronged the stations nonetheless—old ladies selling
pirozhki (small pies of cabbage or meat or mushrooms), skinny
guys with big bottles of foamy, off-color beer, girls displaying boxes
made of birch and carved wooden shoes on pieces of carpet, vodka
sellers with their bottles lined up in rows on folding card tables.
Here and there, black electrical wires drooped above the assembly.
The *khozyain* and the scuba diver, hopping down for quick vodka
runs, were the only ones in our car who got off besides me.

The day went by, and again the twilight in the *vagon* dimmed to
almost-darkness. I ate an energy bar I'd brought along and experi-
mented with new sleeping positions in the front seat. If I hit upon a
workable one, I could get an hour or so of napping time, provided
the train kept up its regular motion. When it stopped, I grew rest-
less and thrashed around.

During a long stop in the middle of the night, I emerged into
consciousness with a sense of something being different now. I got
up, opened the van door, walked to the passageway. As I stepped
out onto it, my awareness of space expanded enormously: our
vagon was sitting by itself in a vast, irregularly lighted train yard.
This must be Magdagachi. In a minute the *khozyain* joined me,
looking a bit rusty from the entertainments of his journey, and
confirmed that we had arrived. Suddenly a beam of light swung
down on us, backed up by a resounding diesel noise. Behind the
light, I could just make out, by shading my eyes, a train engine's
massive form. Out of the brightness, stepping onto the coupling at
the engine's front, the engineer appeared.

Without preamble the engineer began to yell an abusive stream
of complaint or instruction at the *khozyain*, who yelled even more
heatedly at him. Amounts of rubles were shouted back and forth.
Then the *khozyain* went into his stateroom and reemerged, cursing,
with a wad of bills. He handed it to the engineer, who counted it in
the engine's headlight, then put it in his bib. I was told to get out
of the way. The engine was then maneuvered around and the *vagon*

coupled to it. In another minute we had been pulled up to the unloading ramp. All the drivers in the *vagon* woke up, the sealed-shut back doors opened, and the vehicles rolled down the ramp into the Magdagachi night.

It was one-thirty in the morning when we emerged from the *vagon*. We knew nothing about Magdagachi except its name. The hard-drinking dentist, father of fourteen-year-old Kira, told Sergei that he could lead us to a fuel station that he thought would be open, so we followed him there. He also said that he knew how to find the road out of Magdagachi; but after he had fueled up he drove off without waiting for us, and when we tried to make our way by the directions the fuel-station man gave us we soon were meandering on roads and non-roads in Magdagachi. Finally, we got so turned around that we were driving on gravelly nothing zones between unlit buildings, and Sergei pulled over in a weed lot where we spent another few uncomfortable hours attempting to sleep in the van.

A little after dawn, we awoke and set out again, and with more people available at that hour to ask for directions we did find the road. Driving in our dusty, exhaust-fume, no-shock-absorbers van seemed like carefree travel after the gloomy limbo of the *vagon*. A leisurely three hundred kilometers or so farther on, we stopped in the early afternoon and camped on the banks of the Zeya River outside the city of Svobodnyi (Free).

From the Zeya we took a detour off the main road in order to see the Amur River and the city of Blagoveshchensk. *Blagoveshchenie* means "annunciation," and the name is not too lofty for the city, which I thought the handsomest we'd been through since St. Petersburg. Blagoveshchensk is fortunate for two reasons—its light, and China. Something about the Pacific Ocean, maybe, gives a reddish gold tint to light that spreads up the river and this far inland. The benign and hopeful sunniness of Blagoveshchensk reminded me somehow of Palo Alto, California. Blagoveshchensk and other Amur River cities could be the Golden East, as California was the Golden West. Or maybe this notion was just my homesick imagination. Still, the sun and blue sky and reddish gold light as we drove around Blagoveshchensk struck me as imported, not quite Russian.

Second, China: The Chinese industrial city of Heihe is just across the Amur. Our radio had begun picking up Chinese radio stations. On the other side of the pale-brown, slow-moving, dauntingly wide Amur the tops of the tallest buildings of Heihe could be seen. Like other Amur River cities, Heihe and Blagoveshchensk participate in an agreement that locally suspends certain visa and customs regulations for the purposes of encouraging trade. I saw several big buildings under construction in Blagoveshchensk, a rarity in these remote areas, and Chinese laborers working on them. The hard hats the workmen wore were made of wicker. A lot of the smaller structures in the city were new. Some had pagoda-style roofs. No thickets of *morkovnik* or other weeds grew along the streets, and the usually omnipresent trash, in heaps or promiscuously strewn, seemed to be gone.

We headed out of Blagoveshchensk in its California evening light and settled back for a few hours of driving in what remained of the day, but the road we were on—a major road, and in fact the only one here that continued cross-country, a road marked in red on the map—suddenly came to an end. It reached the Bureya River and just quit. Reexamining the map, I noticed that the red of the highway did become a dotted line for a very short span at this spot. There was no bridge, no nothing. I had never known a major road to do that before. After a bit of searching, however, we found a ferry landing, albeit sans ferry. The ferryman had apparently taken the ferry to the other side of the Bureya, and no one among the two dozen waiting cars knew when he might return. Sergei backtracked up the road to look for a camping spot, figuring we'd just wait till morning. All we could find were small openings in the thick woods where the weeds grew six feet high. Finally, we plunged the van into an out-of-the-way opening, tramped down some weeds beside it, and pitched our tents.

At the ferry landing the next morning, there were only a few cars, but still no ferry. Soon more cars and several trucks showed up.

Finally the ferry came, loaded a few cars and our van with great slowness, and slowly took us to the other side. A lot of other vehicles were waiting there for the return trip. I could not understand why this one river should be without a bridge; clearly, some of the people in the queue would be there all day. But we seemed to have entered a forgotten zone. As we continued on this alleged cross-country highway, it quit trying altogether and became little more than a swamp lane. On its rare paved stretches you couldn't get too comfortable, because in another moment you'd have to slow down and negotiate mudholes in lowest gear.

Half a day of this brought us to the border of Birobidzhan, the Jewish Autonomous Oblast. Under Stalin in the 1920s and '30s, the idea of setting aside this region in the drainage of the Bira and Bidzhan rivers for a Jewish homeland attracted support among Jews in the Soviet Union, America, and elsewhere. Here sparsely occupied land extending for two hundred miles along the Trans-Siberian Railway offered the advantages of plenty of room and no unwelcoming nationalities who needed to be removed. On the other hand, Birobidzhan is a swamp in the middle of nowhere. Although many thousands of Jews, including groups from America, did move here, almost all of them left within a few years. Birobidzhan's Jewish population was 4 percent in 1990, and it has gone down since.

By the Sea

Dersu Uzala, the memoir and narrative of exploration by Vladimir K. Arsenyev, begins in 1902, when Arsenyev is a young army officer assigned the job of exploring and mapping the almost unknown regions east and northeast of Vladivostok, including Lake Khanka and the upper watershed of the Ussuri River. The name for the whole area is the Primorskii Krai—the By-the-Sea Region. It and much of the Khabarovskii Krai, just to the north of it, consist of a unique kind of Pacific forest in which tall hardwoods hung with vines grow beside conifers almost equally high, and the lushness of the foliage, especially along the watercourses, often becomes quite jungly. In Arsenyev's time, this jungle-taiga was full of wildlife, with species ranging from the flying squirrel and the wild boar to the Siberian tiger. Back then (and even recently) tigers could also be seen on the outskirts of Vladivostok, where they sometimes made forays to kill and carry off dogs. Arsenyev describes how tigers in the forest sometimes bellowed like red deer to attract the deer during mating season; the tiger's imitation betrayed itself only at the end of the bellow, when it trailed off into a purr.

The humans one was likely to meet in this nearly trackless forest were Chinese medicine hunters, bandits, inhabitants of little Korean settlements, and hunter-trappers of wild game. Dersu Uzala, a trapper whom Arsenyev and his men come upon early in their 1902 journey, is a Siberian native of the Nanai tribe whose wife and children have died of smallpox and who now is alone. After their meeting, Dersu becomes the party's guide. The book is about Arsenyev's adventures with Dersu on this journey and others, their friendship, and Dersu's decline and end.

In the 1970s, a Soviet film studio produced a movie of *Dersu Uzala*, directed by Akira Kurosawa. It won the Academy Award for Best Foreign Film of 1975. The movie is long and slow-paced, like a passage through the forest, and wonderfully evokes the Primorskii country. I own a cassette of the movie and in my many viewings of it even picked up some useful fractured Russian from the distinctive way Dersu talks.

Khabarovsk, the city, figures importantly in the movie—when Dersu, whose sight is failing, moves to Arsenyev's house in the middle of town. Finding the house where Arsenyev lived in Khabarovsk was another of my Siberian goals. Sergei and Volodya completely approved, for a change; they were even bigger fans of Dersu and Arsenyev than I was.

From far off, Khabarovsk looks nothing like the trim little community of the movie. The city occupies one of the great river junctions in this part of the world: at Khabarovsk, the Amur River, having been the border between Russia and China for about sixteen hundred kilometers, turns left, or northeastward, and crosses Russian territory for the rest of its course until reaching the ocean. Meanwhile, the Ussuri River, joining the Amur from the south, takes over as the Russian-Chinese border. Travelers coming to Khabarovsk from the west cross the Amur on a bridge that goes on and on. Sergei said it was the longest bridge in the country. Up ahead, spread out in a succession of ridges above the confluence, Khabarovsk seemed endlessly large. With its tall sky and sprawling landscape, it could have been a city designed for animals considerably larger than humans—mammoths, maybe, or midsize dinosaurs.

We soon learned that Arsenyev's house no longer stands. An exhibit about Arsenyev in the regional museum said that an Intourist hotel had been built on the spot where the house used to be.

The next day, we continued southward, passing villages called Roskosh (Luxury), Zvenevay (Small-Group Town), and Tigorovo (Tigerville), and rivers called Pervaya Sedmaya Reka (First Seventh River) and Vtoraya Sedmaya Reka (Second Seventh River). At noontime, we stopped to buy bread in the small city of Bikin. Like most cities of military importance, Bikin had been closed to foreigners until after the end of Soviet times. With the Chinese border only twenty kilometers away, Bikin formerly was fortified with active military installations all around it, and now their barbed wire dangled and their concrete works had turned ramshackle in predictable post-Soviet style. And yet Bikin still had the cloistered feel of a garrison town.

Soon after Bikin, we suddenly entered a weird all-watermelon area. Watermelon sellers crowded both sides of the road under big umbrellas in beach-ball colors among wildly painted wooden signs. Sergei pulled over and bought a watermelon for a ruble, but as we went along the heaps of them kept growing until melons were spilling into the road and the sellers were giving them away. A man with teeth like a crazy fence hailed us and in high hilarity thrust two watermelons through the passenger's-side window. By the time we emerged at the other end of the watermelon gauntlet, we had a dozen or more in the van. The watermelons were almost spherical, antifreeze green, and slightly smaller than soccer balls. We cut one open and tried it — delicious. This was not a part of the world I had previously thought of as a great place for watermelons.

Rather than continue south, directly to Vladivostok, our ultimate destination, we had decided to turn east again, cross the Sikhote-Alin Mountains, and arrive at the Pacific (technically the Sea of Japan) in a less inhabited place on the mountains' other side. The Sikhote-Alins, once we were among them, seemed more like hills, and not very forbidding, but the depth and silence of their forest made up for that. Arsenyev had described the taiga here as "virginal, primeval timberland." From the altitude of the trees and the venerable length of the vines depending from them, I would guess that the taiga we saw was still original growth. That night, we camped above the small gorge of a river named for Arsenyev — the

Arsenyevka. The sound of it was pleasant to sit beside; this was our first genuinely rushing stream. I stayed up for a while after Sergei and Volodya had gone to bed, listening to it and looking up at the stars and at the satellites tracking past.

The next day, we continued winding generally eastward through the mountains. I noted villages called Uborka (Harvest), Shumnyi (Noisy), and Rudnyi (Oreville). Now we were in Arsenyev's very footsteps. A little beyond Rudnyi, we crossed a mountain pass that hardly looked like one. This was the divide between the waters that flow roundabout to the Pacific via the Ussuri and the Amur, and those which drain down the front of the Sikhote-Alins and into the Pacific directly. At the crest of the divide, back among the roadside weeds, stood a cement obelisk on which was inscribed: CROSSED OVER THIS PASS: M. I. VENÝUKOV 1858; N. M. PREZHEVAL-SKII 1887; V. K. ARSENYEV 1906.

Arsenyev's passage across this divide happened during a mapping expedition guided by Dersu and described in detail in the book. The party continued from here until they came to the Pacific and the port village of Olga, where they were resupplied. Sergei said that we would also aim for Olga and camp near there.

Often the taiga stood so close to the road that the vines almost touched the side of the car, and on the upgrades we were looking into the canopy. At one point in the movie *Dersu Uzala*, a tiger stalks Arsenyev's party, and the Siberian tiger used for the scene was a splendid animal, all liquid motion and snarling growls. Though near extinction, the Siberian tiger has not yet been wiped out, and the thought that this Pacific forest—reminiscent in some ways of the American and Canadian Northwest—had tigers in it gave the shadows far back among the trees a new level of authority. I had been in a few forests that held grizzly bears, but a forest with tigers in it seemed even more mysterious and honorable.

Rather than go straight to Olga, we turned off at a little road where a sign pointed to Vesyolyi Yar—Merry Cliff. This road as it led eastward and Pacificward was not particularly merry. The closer we approached to the coast, the more falling-down military structures cluttered the scene. Overhead, the sky got bluer and lighter simultaneously in an ever-brightening expansiveness that could only be a reflection of the Pacific just beyond. At the top of each rise, I thought I'd see it. Then we came over a crest above an unusually steep descent, and there ahead, in the notch between two hills: the Pacific Ocean. Against the green of the trees it was a deep pelagic blue, with many white waves.

Past a few more hills and an abandoned gate checkpoint, and then we were on a level, sandy road that served as the main street of another military ghost town. On either side of the road, block after block of three- or four-story cement residential buildings with most of their window glass out showed only occasional signs of human presence. An onshore breeze rattling through the ruins smelled like the sea and made the vacant place spookier.

I saw the water just in glimpses between the buildings, but then the road bore left and we were driving alongside the shore. We stopped and got out. Here we had arrived not at a regular beach, with big rollers coming in, but at the semi-fortified edge of Vladimirskaya Bay. The Pacific rollers I had hoped for could be seen in the distance, at the bay's entrance between its northern and southern headlands. At this spot there were just rocks and broken concrete and pieces of rusted iron, and a small black cow looking for something to eat among them. Between the road and the water a four-meter-high observation tower leaned to one side, and the hulks of two wrecked ships, one still with its stacks and superstructure, sat grounded and tilted over not too far out in the bay.

On the ocean-facing side of a big rock, someone had spray-painted the NY logo of the New York Yankees and the LA logo of the Los Angeles Dodgers. Also in big white letters on the rock was the word RAP.

We drove along the shore a little farther, until there were fewer ghost buildings around. In this part, the beach was more beach-like and offered a better setting for our momentous arrival. Wave-smoothed stones and actual sand inclined down to clear and cold waves that were breaking hard on this windy day. Strands of kelp lay here and there like pieces of reel-to-reel tape. I went to the water and put my hand in and cupped some of it and tasted salt. Sergei immediately stripped down to his briefs and dove in and swam. Volodya recorded the event with the video camera while I made a sketch of the bay and the ocean and the sky. During his dip, Sergei stepped on a sea-urchin spine, a painful development, but he mentioned it only in passing among the shouting, hilarity, and mutual congratulations. Finally, we were here. Today was Tuesday, September 11, 2001. We had crossed Russia by land from the Baltic Sea to the Pacific Ocean in five weeks and two days.

Batman Returns

FROM *Outside*

NEAR DUSK ON OUR FIRST NIGHT in the Surinamese capital of Paramaribo, my dad stood outside our hotel watching the sky fill with bats. I took this as a sign that they were generally thriving, even amid the throng and crush of the city. Dad shook his head.

"Look around," he said. "What do you see?"

This is our familiar dynamic — the dim but diligent seeker and the beleaguered but bemused scientist.

I studied the scene hard. I saw the whitewashed cinder-block buildings of our hotel lined up like boxcars. I saw a rum distillery, a bike-rental stand, half-collapsed homes held together by plywood and scavenged fencing.

"What am I looking for?"

He pointed across the street to a tall palm spreading over a trash-strewn lot, holding his finger steadily, waiting. Then I saw: like drips from a leaky faucet, bats trickling from a hole in the trunk.

"*Molossus molossus*," Dad said. Pallas's mastiff bat. A junk species. "They're lousy fliers," he explained. "Very fast but not very agile. They need wide-open spaces to hunt in, because they're not nimble enough to navigate tight spots. So for them to be this abundant means that an area has been extremely disturbed."

We were after something more elusive: *Lophostoma schulzi*, Schulz's round-eared bat, a species discovered by my father deep in the Amazon in 1979. Like many bats of the old forest, *schulzi* is a nimble flier that has the ability to thread dense undergrowth. Whenever timber is cleared, faster competitors take over, so our only hope of catching one was to go out among the tall trees, far from human development. We would confine ourselves to the areas where Dad had collected *schulzi* before—jungle outposts inside Brownsberg Nature Park and at the base of the uncharted Tafelberg Plateau, in the Central Suriname Nature Reserve (CSNR). In Dad's heyday, he led teams of well-trained, well-equipped researchers, but this time it would be just the two of us, using a few ten-foot-tall nets. Dad didn't equivocate: he didn't like our chances.

"It's like casting out a net in the middle of the ocean and hoping to catch a specific fish," he said.

The night had deepened and cooled, and the streetlights and neon signs of Paramaribo blazed in the twilight. A bass-heavy club beat struck up in the distance. Dad scratched his grizzled beard with mock seriousness, as if contemplating the half-moon climbing over the rooftops.

"But we came all this way," he said. "So, what the fuck, let's go get one."

Even as a kid, I knew my dad wasn't like other dads. Most boys' fathers in the North Hills of Pittsburgh were mechanics, welders, steelworkers—many of them Vietnam vets, laid off from the mills and scraping by. But my dad was Dr. Hugh H. Genoways, curator of mammals at the Carnegie Museum of Natural History. He started the job in 1976 and soon after undertook a multiyear project, sponsored by Alcoa, the Pittsburgh aluminum giant, to study mammals in the isolated central highlands of Suriname. Those expeditions became the foundation of his career, but they also made him—to my young eyes—larger than life. He had been held at gunpoint in Mexico, housed his crew in a whorehouse in Jamaica, smuggled weapons into Guatemala. But Suriname represented a higher order of adventure: he was surmounting a remote plateau, hacking through dark jungle, returning with unknown species. The newspapers compared him to Indiana Jones. They called him Batman.

And the bat he discovered was as exotic as the place in which it originated. It had a hairless face and a band of wartlike bumps that came to a point on its brow. Every visible inch of it was covered with these bumps—its ears, its nose leaf, its arms, even the long digits that formed its wings. It was a ghastly little creature, but Dad's jesting affection for all bats became my genuine love for *schulzi*. It was

Dad's bat—and so somehow felt like *my* bat, my inheritance. Since its discovery nearly thirty years ago, however, only ten specimens of *schulzi* have been caught. The International Union for Conservation of Nature (IUCN) placed it on the Red List of Threatened and Endangered Species more than a decade ago, due to "ongoing human-induced habitat loss"—a fact that, I long ago assumed, doomed it to imminent extinction.

Then, in 2007, a Conservation International expedition co-funded by Alcoa announced the discovery of twenty-four new species—fish, snakes, toads, insects—in two weeks of collecting on the Lely and Nassau plateaus of eastern Suriname. What caught my eye was the rediscovery of an armored catfish introduced to science fifty years ago but since given up on as extinct when run-off from illegal gold mines poisoned the only creek where it was known to exist. Its reappearance raised hopeful questions: Are species like *schulzi* really critically endangered or simply understudied? Was it possible they hadn't been seen in years only because no one had gone out to look?

But what drew me to South America wasn't just the adventure of netting bats. I also wanted a chance to take fuller measure of my father. Every summer, for most of my childhood, we rode around the country in our Chevy camper, my dad and his team setting traps and stringing the delicate lacework webs known as mist nets. But when night fell and they started for the woods, I stayed at my mom's side, drawing pictures and writing stories while she cooked over the hiss of the propane stove. My dad never expressed anything like disappointment that I didn't take an early interest, but how could he not have felt a twinge?

A friend of his once confided, "I think it would be hard to be Hugh Genoways's son." I knew what he meant. My dad is a gruff, barrel-chested giant—a former college football player who approaches science and life with gridiron resolve. Experience tells him he's not only the smartest person in the room but the most tenacious. The refrain of my boyhood was this: "Nobody ever said it'd be fair." But that didn't mean you gave up; it meant the only way to succeed was to outwork everybody else. To this day, our every phone conversation begins with him asking, "What are you working on?" and ends with him saying, "Get back to work." But his grit is more than just runaway midwestern rearing. My father sees himself in an unwinnable race against the rest of humanity.

Twenty-five years ago, Dad told an international gathering of scientists that it was his goal to "preserve as much of the native habitat of South America as possible in an unaltered state for future generations." But his pursuit of this legacy was interrupted. In 1982, at the height of his research, Suriname's military dictator, Desi Bouterse, ordered the so-called December murders, in which opposition leaders—journalists, university professors, lawyers—were rounded up and shot. The ensuing chaos cut short Dad's work. He spent the rest of his career studying neotropical bats, but he never returned to Suriname.

When he retired last year, in his late sixties and slowed by diabetes, he vowed to go into the field only a few more times, just enough to wrap up unfinished business. So when I called him to say I'd booked tickets to Suriname, he seemed more resigned than enthusiastic. After so many years, I don't think he ever expected to go back. Nor, fearing what he might find, did he really want to.

Nestled on the north coast of South America, just above Brazil, Suriname (formerly Dutch Guiana) was colonized by successive waves of English and Dutch traders more than three centuries ago, but three-quarters of it remains unexplored. Some 80 percent of the nation's half-million people are strung along the Atlantic coast or crowded on the muddy banks of the Suriname River in Paramaribo, cut off from the interior by the verdant wall of the Amazon.

Our first morning out, we headed toward Brownsberg Nature Park—the country's first national nature reserve, three hours south of Paramaribo. As our Toyota pickup sped past the clapboard houses rotting in the blanketing humidity and blistering sun, it was hard not to feel that centuries of human effort have amounted to little more than a temporary stay against the encroaching jungle. On the outskirts of town, clouds broke into rain, forcing us to roll up our windows partway, until they whistled. The howl was so shrill that Dad had to tap me on the shoulder to get my attention.

"There it is," he shouted.

In the distance rose the great, rusting bulk of a refinery, its even rows of smokestacks belching into the air. In 1941, Alcoa opened the Paranam processing plant to support cavernous bauxite mines along the Para and Suriname rivers. The mines were productive, but the cost to power them and process ore skyrocketed during World War II. When Holland granted Suriname limited self-rule in 1954, Alcoa saw an opening. The company negotiated an agreement with the new government for permission to dam the Suriname River and harness hydroelectric energy for a new smelter, aluminum oxide plant, and power station. The dam would bring electricity to a nation lit by kerosene. Alcoa called the dam Afobaka —"back to African ways," a return to ancestral glory for the Maroons, former slaves who inhabit the region.

But progress carried its own price. The lake created by the dam flooded at least seven Maroon villages and decimated the Suriname River they depended on. According to one long-term study, there were 172 species of fish just before the damming in 1964; within four years, that number was down to 62. The Maroons dubbed the lake Brokopondo—literally, "the canoe is broken," a way of life scuttled.

In 1969, to counterbalance this disaster, the government created the Foundation for Nature Conservation in Suriname (STINASU), and Alcoa started underwriting expeditions from the Carnegie Museum, headed by my father. Their charge was to survey Brownsberg and other subsequently created provincial nature reserves while training a generation of Surinamese scientists under STINASU's first director, Johan Schulz, for whom my dad eventually named his bat.

As we neared the town of Brownsweg, the blacktop gave way to the greasy red clay typical of bauxite-rich soil. We fishtailed through puddles and throbbed over washboard. Dad snored contentedly in the backseat, but I was edgy, eager to get to work and away from the despoiled highway corridor. As we began our slow ascent up the plateau, out of the midday heat, I began to breathe easier. At a fork in the road, a park sign—painted with a smiling, brown-faced monkey—pointed the way through the trees.

By mid-afternoon, we'd set up in an abandoned World Wildlife Fund education center at the far end of the park headquarters. We threw open the windows and started unpacking gear—nets, machetes for chopping poles, and an assortment of muslin bags to hold live bats. A clearing nearby served as the trailhead to several paths into the forest and provided a good spot to string our nets.

"Bats are as lazy as people," Dad explained. "If they find a trail, they use it."

After setting nets and returning for dinner at a makeshift restaurant known as Rocky's, we met up with our guide, a young man from Brownsweg named Ramond Finisie. Known to everyone as Melkie (Dutch for "Milky"), he was only days from twenty but looked baby-faced, with wide, searching eyes. Wearing a traditional wrap around his neck and brandishing his machete, he had a mock swashbuckling air.

The night was cooling. The pale trunks of distant trees turned ghostly in the setting sun, then faded as fog rolled in. Before long, the socked-in plateau was cast in a hazy half-moon glow until, unexpectedly, the park lights buzzed to life. Their klieg-light brilliance—the product of Alcoa's hydroelectric dam—flattened everything into depthless overexposure. As we rounded a corner, we could see a bulb high overhead, its blinding fluorescent glare clearly illuminating our first net. Dad cursed under his breath.

We walked deeper into the foggy darkness but found the other nets empty, so Dad sat down under a palm-topped picnic shelter and waited. There's something maddeningly stubborn yet Buddha-like about him at moments like this—not insistent, just unyielding, as if prepared to wait until the world comes to him. Melkie, too, seemed contented by the calm, circling the shelter, swinging his machete idly, crooning some unrecognizable snippet of song. I checked the nets obsessively, until I found one twitching with life, an irate bat that twisted in the nylon threads as it tried to bite its way out.

To remove a captured bat, you clasp it with a leather-gloved hand to keep it still. As it bites the glove's thumb, you work its rubbery wings free from the netting with your other hand. I'm no good at it and harbor the dual fear of being bitten and of dislocating their shoulders. Not Dad. He handled the bats with ease, talking to them all the while. "You're having a really bad night, aren't you?" Or: "Easy, now, don't be like that."

Bit by bit, he educated me on what we were seeing. "OK, this little guy is a *Saccopteryx bilineata*," he said, adjusting his headlamp to give me a better look. "See these sacs on his wings? He spends all day filling those with saliva and fluid from his glands, then he grooms that into his fur all over his body to attract females. Like Old Spice for bats. And see the two white racing stripes down the

middle of his back? Also very distinctive. Sac-winged, double-lined
— *Saccopteryx bilineata*." After each lecture, he took a muslin bag
and dropped the bat in, then slipped the knotted drawstring under his belt like a scalp. That night we caught several bats, but no
schulzi.

I could have slept the next day away, but Dad was up with the
sun, skinning bats for scientific use. It's a process I learned as a
small child. "You find the V in the rib cage," he said back then,
tapping my sternum, "then lift and push until the heart stops, the
lungs collapse." In seconds, the bats go from fierce animals to limp
specimens. He slits them open and turns them inside out, working
the pelts free, then stuffs the empty skin with cotton and wire, pin-
ning it to a foam-core board until the hide dries.

While Dad skinned, I decided to hike down from the rim of the
plateau to Witi Creek — to scout the spot where the last two specimens of *schulzi* were collected, in 2002. Harry Hunfeld, STINASU's
bluff, white-haired grounds manager, had warned that we might
not be able to net in the area, because it had become a target for
illegal gold miners known as "pork knockers" — a term coined in
the fifties when the miners lived in the bush on a diet of salt pork
and worked with pickaxes and shovels. Today the operations are
huge, using bulldozers to level trees, backhoes and hydro cannons
to trench the soil, and a mercury-separation-and-sluicing process
that poisons the water.

Melkie and I descended the steep, rocky incline, weaving around
fallen trees and hacking through undergrowth. We zigzagged from
one bank to the other until the path leveled a bit and Melkie
hopped into a bright patch of sunlight. Stepping out behind him, I
saw that we were on the edge of a mud superhighway punched
through the forest. Sun-hardened ruts left by heavy machinery
stood two feet deep, pooled with standing rainwater and teeming
with mosquito larvae.

We followed the road up a short embankment into a stadium-
size hole that pork knockers had slashed in the forest. The temperature must have climbed fifteen degrees when we stepped into
the sun. The area was devastated and, now, abandoned. There was
no chance that forest-dwelling *schulzi* could thrive in an environment like this.

"Had the miners been down here for years?" I asked Melkie.

"Eight months."

"Months?"

"Before that," he said with a sweep of his machete, "all trees."

Back in Paramaribo, we took off from the Zorg en Hoop airstrip and flew deep into the interior—nothing but forest canopy below us, the coffee-brown Saramacca River snaking through. Our co-pilot was Henk Gummels, the owner of Gum Air, the same airline that flew Dad's crews to the foot of Tafelberg decades ago. Over the roar of the twin engines, I asked whether the Saramacca's muddy current was caused by tidal surge.

"Nee," Henk said. "Pork knockers."

As we flew deeper into the mountains, we saw their camps—piles of slash, bulldozed gravel, and bright-yellow gashes of dirt carved from the lush green. Henk's wife, Jennifer, chatted in Dutch with her brother, Anton Brandon, the second in command at Suralco, the Surinamese subsidiary of Alcoa.

Before long, the distinctive flattop silhouette of Tafelberg appeared on the horizon, shrouded in clouds, its dark profile jutting some three thousand feet above the forest floor. No one knows exactly when Tafelberg, or "Table Mountain," was discovered—it may have been during a Dutch voyage up the Coppename River in 1901 or an expedition on the Saramacca a year later. Either way, it remained imposing but remote, seemingly unreachable, marooned and embowered by the limitless forest, until in 1944 the New York Botanical Garden undertook a thorough probe of the forested mountaintop. Bassett Maguire, the garden's longtime curator, spent fifty-four days exploring the mountaintop and naming the Edenic places he encountered. But in nearly two months of collecting botanical specimens, his team didn't record a single word about the animal populations.

My dad set out to correct that in the fall of 1981, when two of Henk's planes carried his thirteen-person crew to the Rudi Kappel airstrip, where a pilot named Foster Ford ferried their gear on five round-trips to a sandy clearing on the edge of the plateau.

This mountain occupied such a large place in my childhood imagination that it seemed nearly unreal as we banked by the caprock. But there would be no trip to the top this time; Henk assured me that there was only one helicopter charter company in all of

Suriname and that climbing was out of the question. I would have to settle for this flyby view, the plateau's square black shoulders already disappearing into the afternoon clouds. The engines revved, then smoothed to a hum as we swooped down toward the airstrip.

On the ground, we were greeted by the guide Henk had hired, Atinjoe Panekke. A Tiriyó Indian, Atinjoe had a pro wrestler's physique, a shaved head, a goatee, and facial tattoos, but he wore Air Jordan shorts and flashed a quick smile whenever we managed to get something across in our mishmash of English, Spanish, and Dutch. He cut twelve perfect poles for our mist nets, wielding his machete with unnerving force and accuracy, then heaved them casually over one shoulder.

The first night we set up near a handmade wooden bridge spanning a creek. Over the next six hours we caught only four bats—all rare and diverse, from *Trachops cirrhosus*, which uses echolocation to pluck piping tree frogs from the lower canopy, to *Artibeus obscurus*, which thrives on guava and soursop. But Dad couldn't understand why we weren't catching more. He had expected ten, fifteen; if we got lucky, twenty. Four seemed like a bad sign. Bats are bellwethers, he reminded me. Without bats, the whole forest is in trouble.

But Dad wasn't about to give up that easy, so the next night we got ambitious, spending hours setting up six nets, including some that were nearly sixty feet long, at spots that effectively cut off three major trails. We caught just two bats—again, uncommon species, but only two, and no *schulzi*. The night passed with so little action that Atinjoe dozed in the tall grass, snoring until he woke himself.

Well after midnight, we sat on the porch of the airstrip lodge, drinking warm Parbo beers while Dad reviewed the field notes from his old expeditions, tallying the incredible numbers of bats —forty and fifty each night—caught at these very sites. To boost our spirits, I checked to see whether the rain barrel had caught enough water to allow for a much-needed shower. But when I twisted the spigot, only a miserable trickle bubbled out. Dad laughed at my stricken expression. "Come on, rookie," he said, and, by the dim light of our perched flashlights, he hopped breathlessly under the icy dribble, before handing the soap off to me.

"Sorry," he said with a toothy grin. "I think I used up all the hot water." I laughed in spite of myself, a gallows laugh. Whether or

not we caught that goddamned bat the next day, our last at Tafelberg, I knew the moment would stand alongside tales of past mis-
adventures that my dad and his friends told over howls of laughter.
This was my initiation.

So I commended myself to the frigid water—the sound of my
hollering rattling the rafters and echoing out into the starless
night.

For our final night in the CSNR, Dad decided to move deeper
into the forest. All through the cloudy afternoon, he scouted the
canopy on the other side of the airstrip for bulging termite nests,
explaining that two of *schulzi*'s closest relatives—*Lophostoma silvicolum* and *Lophostoma carrikeri*—are known to day-roost in cracks
in arboreal mounds. Spotting several along a trail, Dad selected
net placements on either side of a grove of tall palms. Of the few
schulzi ever taken, several have been netted in palm-dominated forest, leading some to speculate that the bats may use them for hunting roosts at night. As Dad explained all this, I felt an irrational
surge of optimism. The conditions were perfect; of course we'd
catch one there.

Maybe Dad was feeling optimistic too, because he decided to
string only one more net, the largest we had. We'd set it up across a
stream at the top of a spectacular waterfall. The water there was
thick froth so suffused with leaf tannin that it had turned the color
of port wine. Both banks were blanketed with razor grass, but Atinjoe mowed the way clear with a few swift machete strokes. Dad decided to make the most of the dwindling daylight, so we unfurled
the net, the low sun dappling the orange water. No sooner had we
tied off the poles and switched on our headlamps than a light rain
started to fall. Then it got heavy. Then heavier. By the time we returned to the first net, it sagged with rain, glistening in the beams
of our lamps. The trees were piping with frogs.

"Will bats fly in the rain?" I asked.

"Not rain like this," Dad said. "Not many, anyway."

We tramped to the shelter of a deck overhanging the newer,
larger lodge where Henk's family was staying. They stretched
out in their hammocks drinking cabernet and enjoying the downpour. After a few drinks of our own, I asked Anton about Suralco's
plans for the Nassau and Lely plateaus, east of Brownsberg. Now

that so many endangered species had been found, would Alcoa still mine?

"You must understand," he said. "The Paranam mines, when they were opened, were estimated to contain sixty years of bauxite. It has now been sixty-five. The ore cannot last."

He acknowledged that the research team had found many rare species, but they'd also found evidence of illegal hunting by Maroons and illegal gold mining, most of it by French Guianese and Brazilians. "Saying these lands are off-limits to development," he said, "would change nothing." Averting the sort of wholesale devastation that has occurred at Brownsberg requires research and enforcement. Both require money. And the only money in Suriname comes from bauxite.

The rain continued to fall as Dad and I zipped our jackets and headed back out. "He's right, you know," Dad said. "We can't expect the Surinamese to sit on their natural resources. You look around here, you see the rainforest, but people like Henk or Anton see their country. This is where they live."

"But he's as much as admitted they're going to mine there," I said. "That doesn't shock you?"

Dad was quiet as we walked. "Alcoa is going to do what's in its best interest," he said finally. "That doesn't shock me. Suriname will do what's in its best interest. That doesn't shock me. And everybody in Suriname sees Alcoa mines in their best interest, so, no, I'm not shocked. Besides, what's the alternative? Mine iron instead? What does that solve?"

This is my father—no pundit, no poet, no profiteer. He makes no value judgments, argues for no outcome. He is a thoroughgoing scientist and professor, intent only on the twin purposes of mapping the rich complexities of the world and teaching others to do the same. He had no stake, no investment, in whether we found his *schulzi* or not. So when the final bat of the night, twisted and rain-sopped in the net, turned out to be *Lophostoma silvicolum*, it didn't bother him in the least. "So close," I groaned. Dad shook his head. It's not about one species, he reminded me—no matter how rare, no matter what sentimental attachment you may feel to it. It's about observing and learning, rather than consuming and destroying.

Surrounded by perfect darkness, rain soaking through my coat,

I finally understood. *Lophostoma schulzi* isn't Dad's bat at all; it's Schulz's bat. My father didn't name his discovery for himself but for those who stayed in Suriname. And those who continue to fight for the forest are its true inheritors. In that expanse, more than anywhere, his simple lessons applied: "Nobody ever said it'd be fair. Now get back to work."

I pulled on my glove. "It's OK, Dad," I said. "I got this one."

On our last morning, as we scanned the skies wondering if the rain would clear enough to fly, we heard chopping rotor blades. Suddenly a helicopter hove into view and landed at the airstrip. I sprinted down and started talking—begging, bargaining, bribing our way to the top of Tafelberg. The pilot, Jerome, worked for Hi-Jet, the company that runs the Surinamese medical-emergency service, but he'd flown out that morning to pick up some tourists from an illegal lodge under construction atop the plateau. We were shocked to hear such a place existed, but there was no time to consider. We agreed to Jerome's offer: for six hundred dollars, he would take us up on his way back to Zorg en Hoop.

We'd be allowed only a few minutes on top, but that didn't matter. If we hadn't been able to net even one of Dad's bats, to assure ourselves of its survival, at least there was this unexpected gift. And in the months after our return, we would learn that a team of Canadian scientists, working in far-western Suriname, had netted several specimens of *schulzi*, dramatically increasing its range and likely population. Their expedition was so encouraging that in October the IUCN took *schulzi* off its list of endangered species.

But, at that moment, all we knew was that we'd chanced upon this small, personal redemption before we were gone from Tafelberg. So we squeezed into the helicopter and zoomed up the escarpment and over the lip of the plateau, a dizzy-making sensation of falling even as you felt your body rise. Jerome laughed over the intercom. "It feels like a roller coaster, huh?" He took us over the Arrowhead Basin, then around the southwestern edge to a tiny clearing barely big enough for the chopper's whirling blades. We touched down and hopped out, stumbling as we went. "Five minutes," Jerome yelled. "I'm not even going to power down. *Five minutes.*"

We wouldn't need more. I couldn't believe that I was standing

atop Tafelberg—but especially with my dad. And as he looked
over the edge of a cascading waterfall, then turned back into the
chopper's rotor wash, I had a flash of a photograph I've carried
in my mind all these years. When Foster Ford's helicopter lifted
off in 1981, leaving my dad and his crew isolated for eleven days,
someone thought to lean out of the passenger's seat and snap a
single black-and-white frame. It's my dad, a camera slung around
his neck, wearing a T-shirt with the distinctive seventies logo of the
Carnegie Museum. All around him, the vegetation swirls, but he
stands with feet planted, hands on his hips.

But it was Dad's expression that brought the image back to me.
His face had drawn and slackened, his stance grown less certain;
still, his gaze was set now, as it was then, in a tight squint—probably nothing more than a wince and a square-jawed grimace against
the blast of the departing chopper, but it looked for all the world
like defiance.

J. C. HALLMAN

A House Is a Machine to Live In

FROM *The Believer*

> It is clear that if there is to be any revival of the utopian imagination in the
> near future, it cannot return to the old-style spatial utopias. New utopias
> would have to derive their form from the shifting and dissolving movement
> of society that is gradually replacing the fixed locations of life.
> —Northrop Frye, "Varieties of Literary Utopias"

> Nowadays we do not resist and overcome the great stream of things, but
> rather float upon it. We build now not citadels, but ships of state.
> —H. G. Wells, *A Modern Utopia*

AT THE START OF William Alexander Taylor's 1901 utopian
novel, *Intermere,* a small steamship runs into a fog bank three days
north of the equator and drifts into a whirlpool. "I felt myself being
dragged down to the immeasurable watery depths," the hero recounts. He loses consciousness, and promptly wakes in a hammock
on the curved deck of an entirely different kind of vessel—one
with a "succession of suites and apartments, richly but artistically
furnished." The hero imagines for a moment that he is already
in paradise, but the ship, a "merocar" propelled by "supernatural
agencies," turns out to be one of many technological advances en-
gineered by a perfect society hidden inside the earth.

The jump from steam-powered transport to luxury yacht places
Intermere midway along an evolution in utopian thought: a range
of authors, architects, and engineers first identified paradise as a
floating island, then as an island accessible by ship, and finally as
the ship itself. Transport became destination.

In 2002, when the 43,000-gross-ton vessel the *World* shoved off from an Oslo wharf—christened by a triumvirate of Norwegian priests with a cocktail of holy water and champagne—it marked the first time it was possible to own real estate on board a ship.

The launch was greeted with telling fanfares.

"A global village at sea," said the *Boston Globe*.

"Utopia afloat," said *Maclean's*.

I flew to Norway to meet the man who had coaxed utopian ships off the drawing board. Knut Kloster Jr. met me at the airport wearing a sea captain's cap low on his brow so I could recognize him. It was odd to be met by Kloster himself. He was the father of the modern cruise industry, and the visionary scion of one of Norway's oldest shipping families.

"I'm glad I don't have to wear this hat anymore," Kloster said.

On the drive into Oslo, he felt obliged to point out the city's new high-speed train, and for the next couple of days he would sustain that act of reluctant tour guide. Kloster was almost eighty, but he was a large, buoyant, alert man, and he sluiced smartly through the streets, mumbling recriminations to drivers who didn't quite grasp the system of signal-less intersections. We sat in the lobby of my hotel to begin our discussions. Almost all of my discussions with Kloster would be about what we would discuss in the event that we decided, collectively, that his was a story worth telling. I liked him immensely.

Kloster didn't have a high regard for consistency, and even in our first chat he turned on a dime.

"Of course it's an interesting story," he said, of the grand megaship scheme he had first proposed in the 1970s. This wasn't the *World*. It was a plan originally code-named the "Phoenix Project," and over the years Kloster had spent tens of millions of dollars on it.

Then, in the very next moment, he said, "I'm a failure. I failed. You won't get whatever you're looking for from me. I'm not interested in cruise ships anymore."

He took me to the only park in Oslo where he could walk his German shepherd off-leash, a sculpture garden filled with pieces by Gustav Vigeland. We climbed together to the centerpiece, *Monolith Plateau*, which featured a huge granite column of piled and twined bodies, people helping one another, straining against one another.

"It's about life," Kloster said. "Do you want to take a picture?"

I told him I didn't have a camera.

"Good." He was terribly relieved. "I thought you would want me to take pictures."

Families and youths gathered around the statue, adding to the collage of forms.

"It's about life," Kloster said again.

Utopian literature is so full of ships and shipwrecks that no history of floating utopias would be complete without the story of a voyage.

My voyage began when a deliveryman ignored the threshold of my screen door and left a box in my foyer. I discovered the trespass with a little jolt of fear. Inside the box was another box, wrapped like a present with gold twine. Inside that was a leather document wallet stamped with a curious symbol. And inside that was my invitation to the *World*.

I met the boat in Luleå, Sweden, on the Gulf of Bothnia. The town was not exactly a tourist destination, and the only word my taxi driver needed by way of address was "ship." At any given moment, the *World* might have a population of 200 guests and 250 crew members, giving it a unique passenger-to-staff ratio. Except there were no passengers, really. Apartments on the *World* ranged in price from $1 million to $8 million, and many of the residents used the ship as a second home—or third, or fourth. The *World* circled the globe endlessly, following world events and stopping at ports most cruise ships ignored. Like Luleå. Thus, it sometimes accepted humble moorings, and was now docked just up the coast from town, past some broken-down railroads and in line with a barnacled icebreaker named *Twin Screws*.

The taxi passed through the ship's cyclone-fence checkpoint—manned by members of its Gurkha-recruited security force. I hurried up the gangway because it was raining.

A crowd of residents huddled inside, pressed together in the ship's onboard security lock, waiting to disembark. I'd been told that privacy was the ship's highest priority, but the residents looked friendly enough, bright and cheery, though not like tourists, and with a glow to them. The glow of knowing your time belonged to you.

Plato's Atlantis, home to a "wonderful empire" that no man can visit for "ships and voyages were not as yet," implies having floated on the surface of the ocean by sinking beneath it.

Callimachus the librarian describes Delos, birthplace of Apollo, as "a tiny island wandering over the seas."

Lucian's *True History* (circa 150 C.E.) satirizes a Greek tendency toward exaggeration, poking fun at Jason and the Argonauts. Its mock-epic sea voyage preludes with nymphomaniacal sirens and men using their erect penises for masts. The narrative takes off when a gust of wind lifts the ship to the moon. Back on earth, the crew witnesses a battle among giants who sail about "on vast islands the way we do on our war galleys."

The archetypal island paradise became fixed in Sir Thomas More's *Utopia,* which in 1516 gave birth to the entire utopian genre. You needed More's narrator, Raphael Hythloday, a fool of a sea captain, to get to Utopia, but at least it stayed in one place. And so did maritime utopias, at least for a while. A couple centuries after More, utopian novels began to explore advances in naval technology, and the mobile, floating paradise was born anew.

While Francis Bacon's *New Atlantis* (1626) looks to the distant past when the science of navigation "was greater than at this day" (think Noah), Tommaso Campanella's *The City of the Sun* (1623) looks to the future, when vessels would move not with oars or wind but "by a marvelous contrivance." After James Watt, inventor of the steam engine, proved Campanella right, it was utopian authors who anticipated ships that would become as much home as vehicle. Étienne Cabet's *Travels in Icaria* (1839) describes a ferry that offers drawing rooms with fireplaces, and cabins outfitted with "all the . . . furnishings one might need," and Theodor Herzl's Jewish utopia, *Old-New Land* (1902), depicts the repopulation of the Promised Land via a vessel called *Futuro* that features an onboard orchestra and a daily newspaper. One delighted passenger never leaves, declaring, "This ship is Zion!"

In 1833, J. A. Etzler, a German inventor, proposed a fleet of huge propeller-powered landmasses closer to *True History*'s "war galleys" than Cabet's or Herzl's proto–luxury liners. Etzler un-got the joke of Lucian. *The Paradise Within the Reach of All Men, Without Labor, by Powers of Nature and Machinery* describes floating islands large enough for gardens and palaces, with room for "thousands of families," and promises inhabitants the ability to "roam over the whole world . . . in all security, refinements of social life, comforts and luxury." The islands could be built in a decade, he said, if only he found enough investors. He never did.

Six decades later, Jules Verne returned the idea to fiction with *The Floating Island,* a novel as cautionary as it is utopian. The book begins with the carriage of a French chamber quartet breaking down twenty miles north of San Diego. The hapless musicians wander onto a massive, docked "Floating Island" filled with millionaires, nouveau-riche robber barons who have shoved off to a different kind of life. The vessel is a perfect oval of five thousand acres, driven by hundreds of propellers and two dynamos that produce ten million horsepower. Floating Island's main town is Milliard City. The population is ten thousand, its army five hundred strong. The chamber group is contracted to offer performances for the mobile civilization, and for a time they are delighted. Yvernès, the first violin, anticipates that "the twentieth century would not end before the seas were ploughed by floating towns."

Floating Island encounters various dangers—pirates, volcanoes, wild animals. Halfway through the book, the Floating Island Company Ltd. appoints a liquidator. "The Company had gone under" —pun intended. The millionaires produce the obvious solution: they buy the vessel themselves. Four hundred million dollars later, they're back to island-hopping. But Verne will not permit utopia to last. In a clumsy deus ex machina, the unsinkable Floating Island begins to break apart, embodying tensions brewing between characters for hundreds of pages. The island snaps and sinks.

A century later, in 2002, French architect Jean-Philippe Zoppini un-got the joke of Verne. He proposed several designs based on *The Floating Island.* The shipyard that built the *Queen Mary II* agreed to construct the ship if anyone came along with the funds and infrastructure to operate it. None did.

On my second day in Norway, in the living room of his Oslo home, Kloster and I embarked again on discussions of the discussions of his story that we might eventually have.

The home reminded me of a Russian dacha: wide-open spaces, furniture from a range of centuries and cultures, original art on the walls that intimidated the viewer by looking a little familiar. Kloster was doubting himself again, and I found myself offering a pep talk to an earnest, broken utopian.

The Kloster shipping empire started with ice. Kloster's grandfather hauled blocks by the shipload from northern Norway before refrigeration, and his father moved the business into oil when deposits were discovered in the North Sea. For a time the Kloster tanker fleet was as large as any in the world. Kloster studied naval architecture at MIT, and took over the family business at age thirty. He set the company on a new tack almost at once, constructing an almost-nine-thousand-ton ship called the *Sunward* to ferry British retirees to Gibraltar. Kloster's visionary streak poked through even then: the *Sunward* offered amenities unusual for a ferry—overnight cabins, onboard restaurants.

The Gibraltar plan snagged when Franco claimed the peninsula in a final power grab. As Britain and Spain waged a miniature Cold War, Kloster was left with a ship but nowhere to sail it.

In Florida, future Carnival Cruise Line founder Ted Arison had precisely the opposite problem. He had built an infrastructure to fill a hole in the Caribbean cruise industry, but the Israeli vessel he had leased was recalled as a troop transport for the Six-Day War of 1967. He had a destination but no ship.

Arison rang up Kloster, and three weeks later the *Sunward* arrived in Miami.

The partnership was wildly successful—they added the *Starward,* the *Skyward,* and the *Southward*—but Norwegian Cruise Line (NCL) wound up in court. Kloster and Arison were different kinds of capitalists. Arison was ruthless, driven solely by profit and competition. Kloster wound up in tears on the deck of the *Sunward,* reading Charles Reich's *The Greening of America.* Kloster held to capitalism like a faith, but tempered it with conscience and a belief that the cruise industry was uniquely positioned to battle back against cultural alienation and malaise, to become a medium for global communication.

The lawsuit ended with Arison retreating for the time being and Kloster moving to Florida to take over the business. In 1972, he envisioned a wholly new kind of ship. In an address titled "The

Shape of Things to Come," delivered to British travel agents in Vienna, Kloster quoted Emerson and laid out plans for a split-hull catamaran-style "ultramodern design" that would offer both an on-board observatory for astronomy and an underwater observation room for the study of marine life. The ship was no longer just a ship. Vessels of the future, Kloster told the agents, must serve as a "nexus" for three groups of people: those who visit them, those who live and work on them, and those who are visited by them.

In 1979, NCL was ready to move beyond words. The company bought the world's last great ocean liner, the *France*, overhauling and rechristening it the *Norway*. This ship marked a paradigm shift. To that point, it was believed that twenty thousand tons was about as large as a cruise ship could get and still count on a profit. The *Norway* tripled that figure overnight—and it profited just fine. The ship featured a variety of shops and boutiques along "streets" called Champs-Élysées and Fifth Avenue.

Kloster hailed the "megaship" as "a destination in and of itself."

Thirty years later, Kloster was the nice guy who had finished last. Arison had rebounded, using money that was rightfully Kloster's to start what would eventually become the largest cruise company in the world. In the eighties, Kloster bet everything he had on the Phoenix Project, his vision of a utopian city afloat—and lost.

In his living room, as I tried to convince him his story was worth telling, Kloster stared me down with a look that combined disbelief and corporate savvy.

He had an idea. He produced a small model of the underside of a boat, a tandem rudder system, and placed it on the coffee table between us.

"Say you are in a large ship. It is moving toward an island, some rocks. You need to turn—turn quickly."

He explained that when ships reached a certain tonnage, single-rudder systems snapped from the pressure exerted on them. The solution was a second, much smaller rudder, positioned behind the first. This rudder was called a "trim tab." The trim tab turned the *wrong way*, shifting the current and creating a vacuum so that the larger rudder could turn the right way without breaking. Kloster demonstrated this with the model between his knees, moving the rudders back and forth and steering his hypothetical ship away from the rocks. The trim-tab rudder lent itself to metaphor — engineer Buckminster Fuller had been the first to suggest that it demonstrated "what one little man could do" — but sitting across from Kloster, I was baffled.

He stared at me. I asked for the toilet.

When I came out Kloster acted defeated and offhandedly showed me his home office. It was modest, a square meter beside the washroom — the office not of a mariner but of a submariner. The walls were jammed with bound collections of the correspondence that Kloster had conducted while attempting to bring the Phoenix Project to pass. The room was a dead child's shrine. Kloster didn't want to talk about it, but he wouldn't throw it all away either. Now I understood. Kloster was the trim tab. He had turned himself the wrong way to steer us all clear of the rocks. It was the dilemma of all earnest utopians.

Kloster's dilemma evolved in this way: After the cruise business had been born anew with the unholy matrimony of Kloster and Arison, Kloster charted the industry's course with a kind of moral sextant for the next decade and a half. NCL bought an island and a few of its rivals. In 1984, the *Norway* was the largest cruise ship in the world, and the company dominated the business.

Then Kloster suggested an even wilder revolution.

Others had followed NCL's lead in converting old ocean liners, but now there were none left. The only option for a revolutionary ship was to build one from scratch. Describing the initial planning of the Phoenix Project, Kloster said, "The design objective was to give passengers a sense of community . . . We talked about a 'downtown' featuring broad streets and village squares, lined with shops, boutiques, and restaurants, nightclubs, cinemas . . . In short, a city afloat."

The *Phoenix* would exceed 250,000 gross tons, quadrupling the size of the *Norway*. Its aft split-hull would serve as a marina for four-day cruisers, each with the passenger capacity of the *Sunward*. Kloster announced "the dawn of a new age at sea," and the plan came to include a number of smaller ships that, acting as remora to the *Phoenix,* would amount to a "global Chautauqua circuit."

I gestured to the shrine.

"If there's nothing here, then why are you keeping all these?"

"That's a good question." He shrugged. "There *is* a story here. Someday someone may want to know about it."

Kloster had two sons, both of whom offered up innovative ideas for cruise ships. The older son, also named Knut, envisioned the *World*. The younger proposed a kind of floating beach resort. Like the father of prodigal twins, Kloster denied that either ship had anything to do with the Phoenix Project. To my mind, the *World* completed the story the elder Knut was reluctant to tell.

During the *World*'s first sail, the ship struck the same reef as Verne's Floating Island. Its management company lost $100 million struggling through the climate of the post-9/11 travel industry. Its lender foreclosed, tried to run the ship on its own, and lost another $150 million. The future looked bleak until the residents stumbled onto the same solution as Verne's millionaires: they bought it.

"The vessel is now a co-op," said the *San Francisco Chronicle*.

I stepped on board the *World* just in time to attend a crew recognition ceremony in the Colosseo, the ship's theater. Almost the entire staff had gathered so that Captain Ola Harsheim, a man who looked exactly like a self-portrait of Van Gogh, could offer congratulations to various crew members on their years of service. The crew's lodgings on the lower decks of the ship—the decks without verandas—made it easy to liken the *World* to a floating version of the phalansteries of utopian Charles Fourier, whose bourgeois vision retained class distinctions. E. M. Cioran had once described Fourier's hotel-like phalansteries as "the most effective vomitive I know," but nevertheless, a benign expression of "community" was on the lips of both residents and staff of the *World* for my entire stay. We're all in the same boat, they said.

After the ceremony I was shown to my apartment. Mine was one of several spaces on board that had been compiled out of two studio apartments during a period of reorganization, and as my rooms were mirror images of each other the apartment had an odd doubling quality to it. I had two bathrooms, and two verandas with two sliding-glass doors. I had two flat-screen televisions, but only one kitchen, only one bottle of champagne waiting for me, and only one bathtub (double-size). A number of strategically placed mirrors expanded the space and provided another source of doubling—or quadrupling—the result being that at one moment I could look through the pocket doors into one room and not be entirely certain that I was not already standing there, and at another moment glance into a chamber and experience a kind of vampire thrill at not seeing a reflection where I expected one. The apartment was a homey fun house, which was another way of saying that I sometimes got lost in it. It was one of the smallest spaces on board.

I stepped out onto one of my verandas just as a Swede, down by the dock, took a picture of the ship with me in it. In some ports, the *World* is a spectacle.

Lewis Mumford: "The autonomous machine, in its dual capacity as visible universal instrument and invisible object of collective worship, itself has become utopia."

It took another French architect and the U.S. military to make the Phoenix Project even conceivable.

"If we forget for a moment that a steamship is a machine for transport and look at it with a fresh eye," wrote Le Corbusier in 1931, "we shall feel that we are facing an important manifestation of temerity, of discipline, of harmony, of a beauty that is calm, vital, and strong." The son of a watchmaker, Le Corbusier was fond of saying a house was a machine to live in. In *Towards a New Architecture*, he used a profile of the *Lusitania* superimposed over the Arc de Triomphe to argue that ocean liners already rivaled the world's most impressive structures. Le Corbusier went on to design buildings that looked like ships, and proposed apartment living with maid service, a kitchen staff, and a communal dining room like a luxury vessel. He insisted that "the steamship is the first stage in the realization of a world organized according to the new spirit."

At about the same time, the U.S. military was getting serious about bringing back the old floating-island idea. Edward R. Armstrong—once a circus strongman, later an engineer and inventor—proposed a battery of "seadromes," floating airports that would enable fighter planes to hopscotch the Atlantic. The plan caught FDR's eye, but advances in aircraft flight ranges made them obsolete. Another war-era plan was the top-secret Project Habakkuk, named for a biblical prophet ("Thou didst tread the sea with thy horses"—Habakkuk 3:15) and reportedly a favorite of Churchill's. It was an artificial iceberg: a huge vessel made of "pykrete," an ice-and-sawdust blend that rendered it impervious to torpedo strikes.

Habakkuk never came to pass either. But the floating-island concept would never fade from the military imagination. After the seadrome, the basic concept underwent periodic revision: the "megafloat" and the "Mobile Offshore Base." In 1996, plans were drawn for the "Joint Mobile Offshore Base," a multimodule platform like a floating Guantánamo, featuring an artificial beach for hovercraft, space for a POW camp, and room for 3,500 vehicles, 150 aircraft, and 3,000 troops. It was Lucian's "war galley" with airports and Quonset huts.

I was given a tour of the public areas of the *World*, what in ship parlance was called "the Village." The main hallway through the Village was "the Street," and along it were the theater, a small sanctuary space, a (very) high-end jewelry store, an equally impressive boutique, a deli for gourmet foods or simple groceries, a cigar lounge, a small casino, an Internet café, a four-thousand-volume library, a handful of restaurants, a couple of bars, and a spa that sported quasi-spiritual massage facilities and a state-of-the-art gym. The *World* had been criticized as something of a ghost ship, and it was true that a lot of the time it didn't seem like there were many folks around: the shops and the casino never opened while I was on board. But the residents argued that if others wanted a lot of cruise zaniness, late-night parties, and lines for dinner, they were welcome to it. It was not for them. Their apartments were not staterooms where they slept while on vacation. They were homes.

I was shown what a couple of the larger homes looked like. The first was a larger, grander version of my own apartment, a space that was for rent while the owner was not on board. It went for thousands per night. The second would have suited Captain Nemo. Each of the three bedrooms had its own bathroom. The whole place was paneled. The master bedroom had its own veranda and what my guide called "a religious experience of a closet." The residents spent a good deal of time customizing their spaces, and the upper-tier staff said they'd been surprised at how unique the apartments could be made to look, transformed and modified, sometimes with furnishings, sometimes with art worth more than the apartment itself.

I met no one who had seen every space on board.

I had dinner that night with James St. John, former president and CEO of ResidenSea, the resident-owned company that managed the *World*. We ate at East, the ship's generic Asian restaurant. The ship actually had too many restaurants — they opened on a rotating schedule — but East was a favorite. Most of the restaurants offered outdoor eating when weather permitted; the annual food budget was in the millions. Later, I stopped by the Colosseo to see a local combo (sax, bongos, harp, accordion, xylophone) rush through a variety of show tunes so they could disembark before the ship left Sweden. I met an older couple walking through the Village after the show. They liked the performance, they said, but they were fonder of the ship's lecture series. Wherever the *World* went, it was accompanied by a team of scholar–tour guides who gave talks that put the region into historical context. The ship was now in the middle of its "Bothnian Expedition."

"You kind of schedule your day around it," the woman said.

It was their second time on board; they were thinking of buying an apartment. They were renters, but came for stays of around six to eight weeks. I converted weeks to dollars.

"That's a good chunk of — time."

"It is," the man said. "And now it's time to go to sleep."

I wandered the Village. The cigar lounge was empty; the chess tables in the game room had no pieces. The *World* was less like a ghost ship, I thought, than an amusement park you'd leased. Or bought. At an empty bar on Deck Eleven, I chatted with a Filipino barman. He somehow knew my name. He'd been on the ship since the beginning, and had traveled around the world several times as a result. An hour after the engines grumbled to life, he looked out the window and became excited.

"Mr. Hallman — we're moving!"

We stepped out to the rail to watch the land slink by, passing steel foundries on the edge of Luleå, their towers topped by a blue and spectral fire, the negative signature of heat. Below us, the Gulf of Bothnia was a dark winter's sea, choppy and pleated in moonlight, like skin viewed through a microscope.

"This may be the last time I see Sweden," I said.

"Really." There was a touch of pity in the barman's voice.

It was Fuller—of trim-tab fame—who was the first to marry Le Corbusier's maritime idealism to something that actually had a chance to hit the water. Early in the 1960s, a Japanese patron commissioned Fuller to create a "tetrahedronal floating city" for Tokyo Bay. Fuller designed three floating cities, one for harbors, one for semiprotected waters, and one for deep sea. In *Utopia or Oblivion,* Fuller cited a claim that visions for perfect worlds failed because they were unrealistic from the get-go. Ship design, however, offered hope, as it required a different sort of design discipline. All of a ship's functions had to be comprehensively understood in advance. If you were unrealistic, you sank.

Fuller's patron died in 1966, which cleared the way for the U.S. Department of Housing and Urban Development to get interested. HUD passed the tetrahedronal city on to the navy, which deemed it both water worthy and economically feasible. Baltimore, Maryland, remained interested in a city for the Chesapeake Bay until LBJ, also a fan of the plan, left office. Johnson took two of Fuller's models to his presidential library in Texas. They're still there.

The strange symbol on my document wallet—the symbol of the *World*—was not a picture of a ship. It was a picture of an island.

The original frontispiece of More's *Utopia* featured not just one island but two. It's generally held that the shape of Utopia—a crescent whose points almost touch, making for a large inner harbor —comes from Plato's description of Atlantis. Plato, it's been suggested, may have been thinking of the Greek island of Santorini, which is crescent-shaped and has smaller islands situated between its points. This suggested to Plato a tactically perfect location to erect a fortress that would make one's inner harbor impenetrable.

Utopia, however, did not start out as an island. It was a peninsula when the land was first conquered by King Utopus. Utopus dredged the narrow band of earth connecting it to the mainland, snipping its figurative umbilicus and delivering the infant of a better world. That Utopia was now suspiciously womb-shaped nodded both to Hesiod's Elysium (circa 700 B.C.E.), whose "islands of the blessed" were swaddled in the ocean's amniotic fluid, and to first-century gnostic mystic Simon Magus, whose Eden was comfortably in utero. More hyperextended the metaphor. An inner harbor

guarded by a jutting phallic tower made the book jacket of *Utopia* a
rather clinical depiction of coitus.

I would sail with the *World* from Luleå to Vaasa, Finland, and
then down the Finnish coast to Mariehamn in the Åland Islands,
a curious archipelago in the mouth of the gulf. The islands technically belonged to Finland, but the population spoke Swedish
and they were recognized by the United Nations as autonomous.
The tactically advantageous location of the Ålands had long been
known, though it wasn't until centuries after More that anyone
tried to build a fortress there—first the Swedes, then the Russians.
Nevertheless, it seemed perfectly reasonable to wonder whether
More, in designing Utopia in Antwerp (far closer to Finland than
Greece), might not have been thinking of Bothnia rather than
Plato.

I woke at 5 A.M. to a peach-colored world, the chill blue water strip-
ping by at seventeen knots, a warm wind puffing my curtains, and a
sound like light surf rising from the waterline. From the bathtub's
window I watched the first spark of sun ignite the horizon, and
room service brought a light breakfast. The ship had encountered
gale-force winds and four-meter waves overnight, but the captain
had deployed the stabilizers, the ship's ten-meter wings, and we
barely felt the heavy seas. From that point on in my voyage, as
though the secret sharer of my subconscious recognized the feel of
warm, moist containment and the possibility of months-long rest, I
would be torn between trying to see the ship and just coming back
to my apartment, my home, to survey the gulf. It was a womb with a
view.

After breakfast I went back to sleep on the spot where sunlight
had warmed the bed.

The ship had arranged a Thai lemongrass-oil massage for late
morning, and my masseuse apologized for the lack of candles and
incense (ship regulations) before she went to work. ("Mr. Hallman,
put your face in the hole, please, sir.") I met St. John for lunch and
then had a tour of the back of the house. He was jolly, something
like the Skipper from *Gilligan's Island*. St. John had once considered the seminary, but life had tacked, and time in the military, in
the hotel business, in the shipping business, and finally as the manager of a private community on Jupiter Island, Florida, left him
with the perfect résumé for the *World*.

As we climbed downstairs, St. John insisted the *World* was the cleanest ship in the industry. As above, the main hallway in the back of the house was a "street." It was utilitarian but tidy. There were two below-deck saloons, an officers' club, and a crew bar, but in keeping with the lean-toward-egalitarian theme of the ship, staff, officers, and crew mixed freely. We visited the mooring decks as a team of men were tying us off to the dock in Vaasa with cleats the size of anvils and capstans the size of barrels. We visited the recycling facility. Ecological progressiveness was one of the few traits common among the residents, St. John said, and the ship, in addition to being the first vessel of its class to run on industrial diesel instead of heavy bunker fuel, took pains to recover as much of its waste as it could. Everything not crushed and stored for recycling was incinerated — including sewage.

"We even capture our ash," St. John said.

The residents' routine was morning exercise in the pools, or a walk on the track or on treadmills in the gym, and a leisurely breakfast as the ship pulled into port. Some vacated their apartments early so that the crew could get their work out of the way and go ashore for the day. The residents did the same, either renting cars for private excursions or signing up for prearranged tours that were announced in several onboard publications and on the ship's morning TV news show. I didn't disembark for a day or two. I played Pebble Beach on the ship's high-tech golf simulator, I lunched with the captain, and I got a peek at the cargo-van-size engines and the onboard water treatment facility that could produce three times the two hundred tons of fresh water the ship used daily.

I went to a lecture about the Åland Islands. The archipelago sat right on an ancient line between hunter-gatherer and agrarian civilization, and the lecturer offered us his theory on how the Ålands' aborigines, who butchered people and seals alike and buried them all in the same mound graveyards, eventually became cultural Swedes but Finnish nationals. The Gulf of Bothnia was curious not just for the Ålands, he said, but for the fact that it was all becoming slowly shallower.

The islands were moving — up.

The *Phoenix* pitted Kloster against his family. The strain began when NCL took off; the *Phoenix* was simply too risky. Kloster stepped down from the chairmanship in 1986, divesting himself entirely, taking only the plan with him. He turned his full attention to bringing the *Phoenix* to pass. A team formed around the effort, and came to include administrators of maritime organizations, two former admirals, and a former commandant of the Coast Guard. Various retrofits of the blueprint saw the ship renamed *Phoenix World City* and *America World City*. When it turned out that the vision future-shocked everyone it touched, the *America World City* team tried the imagery of Le Corbusier: the ship's profile superimposed on the Citicorp Building and the Waldorf Astoria.

It didn't work. *America World City* came closest to being built in 1989, but Citicorp pulled out at the meeting that would close the deal. Kloster suspected Arison was involved. In 1996, Westin Hotels and Resorts backed the project, but the ship's in-house champion was ousted in a squabble over personalities. The project stalled there.

At about the same time, Kloster's son's vision was just hitting the drawing board. The *World* suffered through five years of downsizing before construction began.

"This is the new lifestyle," the younger Knut said when the *World* finally got wet. "To travel the world without leaving home."

On my last day on board, I was invited along with forty or so residents to visit a few sites of interest in the Ålands. We assembled in the Village, filed down the gangway, piled onto a chartered bus. The residents were millionaires to a man, but as we pulled away they chattered and laughed like kids riding home from school.

"They're affluent people, but warm," I'd been told, the caveat added as though it ran contrary to expectation.

. Which made me wonder whether the *World,* beyond allowing you to stay at home while you traveled, offered the possibility of community, of kinship, to those whose success tended to alienate them. It may be wasted compassion to empathize with the wealthy, but it seemed to me that the wealthy remained apart not because they liked being apart, but because an economic system that encouraged class division—a system in which not everyone was in the same boat—chopped people into insoluble bits: wealthy and poor, cold and warm. Dichotomies. Did utopia have to eliminate class? Could a class system figure out how to retain dignity for all involved—without inducing vomiting? Was Fourier right to imagine perfection without aspiring to economic equality? Was that the best possible world? The *World* was born of capitalism, but it seemed to me that it took at least one step toward transcending it. It wasn't just the community on board, the resident poker games that sprouted up spontaneously, or the karaoke nights that revealed the wealthy had the same plebeian tastes as everyone else. It was, too, a conspicuous lack of currency—of transactions—on board; it was the green values they embraced, not because it was profitable, but because they thought it right; it was the government they had formed themselves, intentionally, when they bought the ship.

"By the way," St. John told me, "I don't think it's utopia." I wasn't so sure.

Among the sights we were on our way to see in Mariehamn were the fortresses that had tried to take the tactical advantage of the Ålands that More and Plato prescribed. The Swedish castle stood boxy and tall, but it had failed to fend off the Russians, who had moved in and begun their own construction. The Russian fort was only half complete when ten thousand Frenchmen and forty British ships under Admiral Nelson attacked and brought it to the ground. It was another of the *World*'s lecturers—Noel Broadbent, an archaeologist with the Smithsonian—who told us this story as we stood before the ruins of one of the fortress's walls. The residents wandered, petting the cold, thick cannon still in place and admiring the impact marks of the British ball.

We went home to the ship.

I left the following morning, taking the same plane out of Mariehamn as Broadbent. We chatted in the tiny airport. I likened the *World* to a votive ship we had seen in a church on our tour the day before. Common in Scandinavia, the model ships hanging from church ceilings symbolized the spiritual journey of the early Christian community. Broadbent nodded, but thought the *World* was closer to something from the work of Swedish poet Harry Martinson, who had mulled real-life merchant-marine experiences in books of poems called *Ghost Ship* and *Trade Wind*. Then Martinson shared the 1974 Nobel Prize in Literature for an epic poem called *Aniara: A Review of Man in Time and Space,* which imagined huge space vessels called Goldondas ferrying émigrés from a polluted earth to a better Mars.

"It's an interesting concept," Broadbent said, when we'd taken our seats in the island-hopper to Stockholm. "If you're self-contained—if you can do it on your own—then you're almost like those sci-fi stories of ships carrying civilization off after cataclysm. It's not far from that. And islands are not so different. They're moving, too—in geologic time. Either way, it's all about boundaries and travel."

As the plane banked up, we had a view of the *World* at its mooring, as large as the city beside it but as small as a toy from our vantage.

"I was depressed all yesterday," Kloster told me on my last day in Norway.

I wasn't supposed to see him at all—his German shepherd had fallen ill and needed to go to the vet—but then the plan changed. When we met in the lobby, Kloster was sad not because of the dog, but again because he thought his story was uninteresting.

We drove down to Oslo's fjord. Several cruise ships were docked monolithically alongside the city. Kloster's walrus-like benevolence gave him the naive serenity of a mystic. He pretended not to notice a prostitute streetwalking the pier.

We visited a series of maritime museums together. The first was dedicated to Thor Hyerdahl's *Kon-Tiki* expedition. If Hyerdahl's ocean crossing on a balsawood raft dabbled usefully with the past, I thought, then Kloster's imaginary megaship had tinkered with the future. The second was devoted to unearthed Viking ships. I climbed a parapet to look down into the ancient wooden hulls, then glanced back at Kloster in the middle of a hallway, tourists streaming around him as though he were an atoll. The last museum was a tribute to Norway's shipping business, a gallery of models and to-scale mock-ups of tiny crew quarters. We walked directly to the back of the museum and found the original miniature of the *Sunward*, set without fanfare among notable old tankers.

After Kloster left NCL, the company abandoned his guiding principles, his "process of vision." It sailed into a whirlpool of bad luck and bad publicity. It reflagged its vessels in the Bahamas, dumped agreements that protected third-world staff, and tried to go public in 1987 only to have its IPO fall on the day after Black Monday. In the nineties, it tried to reverse course with a more aggressive approach, but was already taking on water. Eventually even Arison joined in the bidding when the company was put on the auction block.

After the final deal to realize *America World City* petered out, Kloster became a different kind of utopian, proposing smaller projects that were even bigger long shots. In 2001, he suggested a seventy-story glass globe for the World Trade Center memorial, called Planet Earth at Ground Zero. A year later he wrote to Secretary General of the United Nations Kofi Annan proposing *Gaiaship,* a goodwill vessel that could be paid for, he suggested, if all the countries of the world contributed one-tenth of one percent of their military budgets.

Arthur C. Clarke wrote a letter of support—he called ocean liners "a microcosm of the Earth"—but an aide to Annan rejected the proposal.

In the meantime, Kloster's original vision kept creeping toward reality.

After the *Norway,* cruise ships started getting bigger. A number of ships in the eighties came in at around 40,000 tons, and in 1988 the *Sovereign of the Seas* upped the ante to 73,000 tons. Carnival broke 100,000 tons in 1996, only to be eclipsed two years later by the *Grand Princess* at 109,000 tons. More followed—142,000; 151,000; 160,000. Recently, Royal Caribbean proposed the *Genesis Project,* a 220,000-ton vessel scheduled to sail in 2010. Similarly, the *World* can spot competitors in dry dock: Residential Cruise Line plans a luxury ship called *Magellan;* Ocean International Holdings Ltd. has promised a similar vessel, the *Four Seasons;* and Condo Cruise Lines International claims 90 percent sales on a plan to convert old cruise ships to condominiums.

"The luxury of new views every day," the *St. Louis Post-Dispatch* said of the last of these.

At the shipping museum, Kloster and I came around to the model of the *Norway.* Kloster showed me how the *Norway* differed from newer monstrosities: it was small enough that its hull was curved all the way around. More recent ships were boxier, their cross sections interchangeable. Each section of the *Norway* was unique.

"It was a good ship," Kloster said, as though speaking over the remains of a man in state, one who had lived long and perhaps made a difference. Kloster went a bit woozy looking through the model's glass case. The *Norway* had had a tough run. In 2001, it sprouted dozens of leaks in its sprinkler system, incurring fines, and two years later an explosion in its boiler room killed eight. It was decommissioned not long after.

I asked Kloster where it was now. He said he'd heard it was lying on a beach in India, but he wasn't sure.

"It's OK." His lips formed a smile for the first time all day. "A ship can't last forever."

PETER HESSLER

Strange Stones

FROM *The New Yorker*

ALL ALONG HIGHWAY 110 we saw signs for Strange Stones.
They first appeared in Hebei Province, where the landscape was
desolate and the only color came from the advertising banners
posted beside the road. They were red and had big characters
promising QI SHI — literally, "Strange Stones" — and had been tattered and torn by the wind. We were driving northwest, right into
a spring storm. There was only rain at the moment, but we could
see what lay ahead — the forecast was frozen on top of the oncoming traffic. Most vehicles were big Liberation-brand trucks carrying
freight south from Inner Mongolia, and their stacks of boxes and
crates were covered with Ice. The trucks had fought a crosswind on
the steppes, and now their frozen loads listed to their right, like
ships on a rough sea.

It was 2002, I was driving a rented Jeep Cherokee, and Mike Goettig was along for the ride. If things went well, we might eventually
make it to the Tibetan Plateau. We had met in the Peace Corps
years earlier, and after finishing our time as volunteers we had each
found a different way of staying in China: I worked as a freelance
writer; Goettig opened a bar in the southwest. But every once in a
while we met up on the road, for old times' sake. We passed a half-
dozen signs for Strange Stones before either of us spoke.

"What's up with this?" Goettig said at last.

"I have no idea. I haven't driven this road before."

The banners stood in front of small shops made of concrete and
white tile, and they seemed to grow more insistent with every mile.
"Strange Stones" is the Chinese term for any rock whose shape

looks like something else. It's an obsession at scenic destinations across the country; in the Yellow Mountains you can seek out natural rock formations with names like Immortal Playing Chess and Rhinoceros Watching Moon. Collectors buy smaller rocks; sometimes they've been carved into a certain shape, or they may contain a mineral pattern with an uncannily familiar form. I didn't have the slightest interest in Strange Stones, but their proliferation in this forgotten corner of Hebei mystified me. Who was buying this stuff? Finally, after about twenty banners, I pulled over.

Inside the shop, the arrangement seemed odd. Display tables completely encircled the room, leaving only a narrow gap for entry. A shopkeeper stood beside the gap, smiling. With Goettig behind me, I squeezed past the tables, and then I heard a tremendous crash.

I spun around. Goettig stood frozen; shards of green lay strewn across the concrete floor. "What happened?" I asked.

"He knocked it off!" the shopkeeper said. He grabbed the hem of Goettig's coat. "Your jacket brushed it."

Goettig and I stared at the scattered shards. Finally, I asked, "What is it?"

"It's jade," the man said. "It's a jade ship."

Now I recognized pieces: a corner of a smashed sail, a strand of broken rigging. It was the kind of model ship that Chinese businessmen display in their offices for good luck. The material looked like the cheap artificial jade that comes out of factories, and the ship had exploded — there were more than fifty pieces.

"Don't worry about it," the shopkeeper said brightly. "Go ahead and look around. Maybe there's something else you'll want to buy."

We stood in the center of the room, surrounded by the ring of tables, like animals in a pen. Goettig's hands were shaking; I could feel the blood pulsing in my temples. "Did you really knock it over?" I said, in English.

"I don't know," he said. "I didn't feel anything, but I'm not sure. It fell down behind me."

I had never seen a Chinese entrepreneur react so calmly when goods were broken. A second man emerged from a side room, carrying a broom. He swept the shipwreck into a neat pile, but he left it there on the floor. Silently, other men appeared, until three more of them stood near the door. I was almost certain it was a setup; I had heard about antique shops where owners broke a vase and blamed a customer. But we were hours from Beijing, and I didn't even know the name of this county. Goettig had become extremely quiet—he was always like that when things went wrong. Neither of us could think of a better plan, so we started shopping for Strange Stones.

Goettig and I had both joined the Peace Corps in 1996, when it seemed slightly anachronistic to become a volunteer. President John F. Kennedy had founded the organization in 1961, at the height of the Cold War, and back then it was immensely popular, attracting idealistic young people who were concerned about America's role in the developing world. Later, after the Vietnam War, the Peace Corps suffered as the nation experienced a wave of cynicism about foreign policy. Since the attacks of September 11, the significance of the Peace Corps has changed again—nowadays anybody who joins is likely to have thought hard about personal responsibility in time of war.

During the mid-nineties, though, there were no major national events that weighed on volunteers. It was hard to say what motivated a person to spend two years abroad, and we went for countless reasons. Most of the volunteers I knew possessed some strain of idealism, but usually it was understated, and often people felt slightly uncomfortable speaking in such terms. Goettig told me that during his interview with the Peace Corps the recruiter had asked him to rate his "commitment to community" on a scale of one to five. Goettig gave himself a three. After a long pause, the recruiter started asking questions. You've worked in a drug-treatment center, right? You're teaching now, aren't you? Finally, the recruiter said, "OK, I'll put you down as a four." Goettig told me later that one reason he signed up was that he had a girlfriend in Minnesota who wanted to get serious. I heard the same thing from a few other volunteers—the toughest job you'll ever love was also the easiest way to end a relationship.

Back then, I wouldn't have told a recruiter my own true motivations. I wanted time to write, but I didn't want to go to school anymore and I couldn't imagine working a regular job. I liked the idea of learning a foreign language; I was interested in teaching for a couple of years. I sensed that life in the Peace Corps would be unstructured, which appealed to me; but they called it volunteerism, which would make my parents happy. My mother and father, in Missouri, were Catholics who remembered Kennedy fondly—later I learned that the Peace Corps has always drawn a high number of Catholics. For some reason, it's particularly popular in the Midwest. Of the thirteen volunteers in my Peace Corps group, six came from midwestern states. It had to do with solid middle-country liberalism, but there was also an element of escape. Some of my peers had never left the country before, and one volunteer from Mississippi had never traveled in an airplane.

None of us were remotely prepared for China. Nobody had lived there or studied the language beyond a few basics; we knew virtually nothing about Chinese history. One of the first things we learned was that the Communist Party was suspicious of our presence. We were told that during the Cultural Revolution, the government had accused the Peace Corps of links with the CIA. These things were no longer said publicly, but some factions in the Chinese government were still wary of accepting American volunteers. It wasn't until 1993 that the first Peace Corps teachers finally showed up, and I was part of the third group.

We must have been monitored closely. I've often wondered what the Chinese security officials thought—if our cluelessness confused them or simply made them more suspicious. They must have struggled to figure out what these individuals had in common, and why the United States government had chosen to send them to China. There were a few wild cards guaranteed to throw off any assessment. A year ahead of me, an older man had joined up after retiring from the U.S. Coast Guard. Everybody called him the Captain, and he was a devoted fan of Rush Limbaugh; at training sessions he wore a Ronald Reagan T-shirt, which stood out on the Chinese college campus where he lived. At one point, I was told, a Peace Corps official said, "Maybe you should change your shirt." The Captain replied, "Maybe you should reread your Constitution." (This was in the city of Chengdu.) One day, while teaching a class of young Chinese, the Captain drew a line on the blackboard and wrote "Adam Smith" on one side and "Karl Marx" on the other. "OK, class, short lesson today," he announced. "This works; this doesn't." In the end, the Peace Corps expelled him for breaking a cabby's side-view mirror during an argument on a Chengdu street.

(This altercation happened to occur on Martin Luther King Day, a detail that probably escaped the Chinese security file.)

After a while, though, it was almost possible to forget who had sent you and why you had come. Most of us taught at small colleges in remote cities, and there wasn't much direct contact with the Peace Corps. Only occasionally did a curriculum request filter down from the top, like the campaign for Green English. This was a worldwide project: the Peace Corps wanted educational volunteers to incorporate environmental themes into their teaching. One of my peers in China started modestly, with a debate about whether littering was bad or good. This split the class right down the middle. A number of students argued passionately that lots of Chinese people were employed in picking up garbage, and if there wasn't any litter they would lose their jobs. How would people eat when all the trash was gone? The debate had no clear resolution, other than effectively ending Green English.

The experience changed you, but not necessarily in the way you'd expect. It was a bad job for hard-core idealists, most of whom ended up frustrated and unhappy. Pragmatists survived, and the smart ones set small daily goals: learning a new Chinese phrase or teaching a poem to a class of eager students. Long-term plans tended to be abandoned. Flexibility was important, and so was a sense of humor. There had been nothing funny about the Peace Corps brochures, and the typical American view of the developing world was deadly serious—there were countries to be saved and countries to be feared. That was true of the Communists, too; their propaganda didn't have an ounce of humor. But the Chinese people themselves could be surprisingly lighthearted. They laughed at everything about me: my nose, the way I dressed, my use of their language. It was a terrible place for somebody stiffly proud to be American. Sometimes I thought of the Peace Corps as a reverse refugee organization, displacing all those lost midwesterners, and it was probably the only government entity that taught Americans to abandon key national characteristics. Pride, ambition, impatience, the instinct to control, the desire to accumulate, the missionary impulse—all of it slipped away.

At the shop, a few Strange Stones looked like food. This has always been a popular Chinese artistic motif, and I recognized old favorites: a rock-hard head of cabbage, a stony strip of bacon. But in my nervousness most of the shapes looked the same to me. I selected one at random and asked the price.

"Two thousand yuan," the shopkeeper said. He saw me recoil—that was nearly $250. "But we can go cheaper," he added quickly.

"You know," Goettig said to me, "nothing else in here would break if it fell."

He was right—it was all Strange in a strictly solid sense. Why had a jade ship been there in the first place? As a last resort, I hoped that Goettig's size might discourage violence. He was six feet one and well built, with close-cropped hair and a sharp Germanic nose that the Chinese found striking. But I had never known anybody gentler, and we shuffled meekly toward the door. The men were still standing there. "I'm sorry," I said. "I don't think we want to buy anything."

The shopkeeper pointed at the pile of green shards. "*Zenmeban?*" he said softly. What are you going to do about this?

Goettig and I conferred, and we decided to start at fifty yuan. He took the bill out of his wallet—the equivalent of six dollars. The shopkeeper accepted it without a word. All the way across the parking lot, I expected to feel a hand on my shoulder. I started the Cherokee, spun the tires, and veered back onto Highway 110. I was still shaking when we reached the city of Zhangjiakou. We pulled over at a truck stop for lunch; I guzzled tea to calm my nerves. The waitress became excited when she learned we were Americans.

"Our boss has been to America!" she said. "I'll go get her!"

The boss was middle-aged, with dyed hair the color of shoe black. She came to our table and presented a business card, with a flourish. One side of the card was in Chinese, the other in English:

United Sources of America, Inc.
Jin Fang Liu
Deputy Director of Operations
China

Embossed in gold was a knockoff of the Presidential Seal of the United States. It looked a lot like the original, except for the eagle: the Zhangjiakou breed had pudgy wings, a thick neck, and legs like drumsticks. Even if it dropped the shield and arrows, I doubted that this bird would be capable of flight. The corner of the card said, in small print:

President Gerald R. Ford
Honorary Chairman

"What kind of company is this?" I asked.

"We're in the restaurant business here in Zhangjiakou," the woman said. She told me that her daughter lived in Roanoke, Virginia, where she ran another restaurant.

I pointed at the corner of the card. "Do you know who that is?"

"Fu Te," Ms. Jin said proudly, using the Chinese version of Ford's name. "He used to be president of the United States."

"What does he have to do with this restaurant?"

"It's just an honorary position," Ms. Jin said. She waved her hand in a way that suggested, *No need to tell Mr. Fu Te about our little truck stop in Zhangjiakou!* Ms. Jin gave us a discount and told us to come back anytime.

We stopped in the city of Jining for the night. The temperature had plummeted into the teens; the rain had turned to snow; I pulled into the first hotel I could find. It had a Mongol name — the Ulanqab — and the lobby was so big that it contained a bowling alley. We registered at the front desk, surrounded by the crash of balls and pins, and by now I had a pretty good idea where this trip was headed.

Traveling with Goettig was always a calculated risk. Interesting things happened when he was around, and he was unflappable, but his standards of comfort and safety were so low that he essentially had no judgment. Of all the midwestern refugees I had known in the Peace Corps, he had come the farthest, and he seemed the least likely ever to return home. When our group first met for departure from San Francisco, Goettig had shown up with the smallest pile of luggage. He carried less than a hundred dollars, his entire life savings.

He was from southwestern Minnesota, where he had been raised by a single mother. She had two children by the age of nineteen, and after that she found jobs wherever she could — bartending, office work, waitressing at the Holiday Inn. Eventually, she took a position on the production line of a factory that manufactured bread-bag ties, in Worthington, Minnesota, a town of ten thousand people. The family stayed in a succession of trailer courts and rental apartments, and much of their home life revolved around motorcycles. Goettig's mother was a devoted biker, and in the summer they attended Harley-Davidson rallies and rodeos around the Midwest. He watched his mother's friends compete in events like Monkey in the Tree, in which a woman leaps from the back of a motorcycle to a low-hanging rope, where she dangles while the man continues around an obstacle course, returning so that the woman can drop down perfectly onto the seat. Another contest involves seeing which woman on the back of a moving bike can take the biggest bite out of a hot dog hanging from a string. When Goettig first told me about these events, I realized that I hadn't seen anything stranger in China. Goettig said that he had always disliked motorcycles.

He was the only one in his family who enjoyed reading. After high school, he had majored in English at the University of Minnesota at Morris, and then he went to graduate school at the Mankato campus of the state university. While studying for his master's, he applied to the Peace Corps. He'd seen commercials as a child, and he figured it was the best way to go overseas for free.

In China, he was assigned to a job teaching English in Leshan, a small city in southern Sichuan Province. With two other volunteers, he organized a play: a student version of *Snow White*. Soon, college administrators recognized an opportunity for publicity, and they developed a traveling variety show. The other Peace Corps volunteers quickly washed their hands of the project, but Goettig was game for anything. He went on the road with *Snow White*, traveling by bus to small towns around the province, performing at middle schools three times a day. Originally, the Woodsman was a villain, but college officials insisted that the play end with a more favorable view of the proletariat, so the Woodsman reformed and gave self-criticism. As part of the variety show, a student sang Richard Marx's "Right Here Waiting," a brass band played the "Internationale," and Goettig went onstage with a blue guitar and sang "Take Me Home, Country Roads." He was mobbed for autographs everywhere. During the bumpy rides between towns, the *Snow White* players sang songs at the top of their lungs and gorged on raw sugarcane, spitting the pulp onto the floor of the bus. Goettig told me that those were the longest ten days of his Peace Corps service.

He learned Chinese quickly. The Peace Corps gave us two and a half months of intensive training upon arrival, and after that we could hire tutors if we wished. But the best strategy was simply to wander around, talking to people in the street. Goettig had the ideal personality for this: he was patient and curious and tireless. He was also, as the Chinese like to say, a very good drinker.

One autumn, he journeyed to Xinjiang, a wild region in China's far west. He camped alone in the Tian Shan Mountains, and one day, while hiking off trail, he clambered over some rocks and was bitten on the finger by a snake. First the finger swelled, then the hand. It took four hours to make it back to Ürümqi, the provincial capital. By then, the swelling had spread to his arm; the pain was excruciating. He found a public phone and called the Peace Corps medical officer in Chengdu. She recognized the symptoms: it sounded like a tissue-killing venomous snake, and he needed to get to a hospital, fast.

He asked bystanders for directions, and a young Chinese woman offered to help. She spoke perfect English, which was unusual, and she was dressed in a bright-orange sleeveless sweater that hung loose from her upper body like a bell. At the time, Goettig thought that the woman seemed slightly strange, but he wasn't in a position to worry about it. She accompanied him to the hospital, where doctors sliced open the bitten finger. They had some traditional Chinese medicine; Goettig figured it was a good sign that the box showed a picture of a snake. The doctors used a mortar and pestle to grind up the pills, and then they shoved the powder directly into the incision.

The swelling continued to spread. Goettig's arm turned purple at the joints, where the venom was rupturing capillaries. By evening, he realized that the woman in the orange sweater was completely insane. She had brought her luggage to the hospital; she refused to leave his side; she told everybody that she was his official translator. She wouldn't answer any personal questions—Goettig still had no idea how she had learned English. Whenever he asked her name, she responded, "My name is . . . Friend." Every time she said this, it sounded creepier, until he finally gave up on the questions. She spent the night in a chair at the foot of his bed. The next day, the doctors cut open the hand three times to shove more powder inside. The pain was intense, but at least Goettig was able to persuade some nurses to kick the crazy woman out. After the third day, the swelling began to subside; he stayed in the hospital for a week. He was so broke that the Peace Corps medical officer had to wire money to cover the bill, which was less than $150. His hand recovered fully. He never saw the woman in the orange sweater again.

A solitary bowler was hammering the pins when we checked out of the Ulanqab Hotel. At the entrance to Highway 110, the local government had erected a sign with changeable numbers, like the scoreboard at Fenway Park:

AS OF THIS MONTH
THIS STRETCH OF ROAD
HAS HAD 65 ACCIDENTS AND 31 FATALITIES

Yesterday's storm had passed, but the temperature was still in the teens. From Jining to Hohhot the highway crossed empty steppe—low, snow-covered hills. We passed Liberation trucks that were stopped dead on the road; their fuel lines had frozen, probably because of water in their tanks. After fifteen miles, we crested a hill and saw a line of hundreds of vehicles stretching all the way to the horizon: trucks, sedans, jeeps. Nobody was moving, and everybody was honking; an orchestra of horns howled into the wind. Never had I imagined that a traffic jam could occur in such a desolate place.

We parked the Cherokee and continued on foot to the gridlock, where drivers explained what had happened. It had all started with a few trucks whose fuel lines had frozen. Other motorists began to pass them on the two-lane road, and occasionally they encountered a stubborn oncoming car. Drivers faced off, honking, while the line of vehicles grew behind them; eventually it became impossible to move in either direction. Some had tried to go off road, and usually they made it fifty yards before getting stuck. Men in loafers slipped in the snow, trying to dig out cars with their bare hands. There was no sign of police or traffic control. Meanwhile, truckers had crawled beneath their vehicles, where they lit road flares and held them up to the frozen fuel lines. The tableau had a certain beauty: the stark, snow-covered steppes, the endless line of vehicles, the orange flames dancing beneath blue Liberation trucks.

"You should go up there and get a picture of those truckers," Goettig said.

"*You* should get a picture," I said. "I'm not getting anywhere near those guys."

At last, here on the unmarked Mongolian plains, we had crossed the shadowy line that divides Strange from Stupid. We watched the flares for a while and then took the back roads to Hohhot. The moment we arrived, the Cherokee's starter failed; we push-started the thing and made it to a garage. The mechanic chain-smoked State Guest cigarettes the whole time he worked on the engine, but after Highway 110 it seemed as harmless as a sparkler on the Fourth of July.

The hardest thing about the Peace Corps, they said, was going home. Near the end of our two years, the organization held a pre-departure conference. They handed out job-search materials, and they talked about how we might feel when we got back to America and people said things like "I didn't know they still had the Peace Corps." A few volunteers sat for the foreign-service exam. One of them got halfway through and couldn't take it seriously; for the essay section he wrote about how his worldview had been influenced by the film *Air Force One*. The others passed the exam but failed the interview. Over the years, I came to know more volunteers who also took that exam, and all of them were befuddled by the process—virtually nothing they had learned in the field seemed relevant.

From the beginning, the Peace Corps had represented a type of foreign aid, but another goal had been to produce Americans with knowledge about the outside world which could benefit their own country. The organization had been inspired in part by the 1958 book *The Ugly American*, which criticized a top-down approach to foreign affairs. At some level, I came away with a deep faith in the transformative power of the Peace Corps: everybody I knew had been changed forever by the experience. But these changes were of the sort that generally made people less likely to work for the government. Volunteers tended to be individualists to begin with, and few were ambitious in the traditional sense. Once abroad, they learned to live with a degree of chaos, which made it hard to have faith in the possibility of sweeping change.

Many of my peers in China eventually became teachers. It was partly because we had been educational volunteers, but it also had to do with the skills we developed—the flexibility, the sense of humor, the willingness to handle anything an eighth grader could throw at us. A few became writers and journalists; some went to graduate school. Others continued to wander, and Goettig stayed in China for years. During the summer, he worked for the Peace Corps, training new volunteers, and the rest of the time he picked up odd jobs: writing freelance newspaper stories, working part-time as a translator and researcher. Periodically, he came through Beijing and slept on my couch for a week. The term of Peace Corps service is lifetime when it comes to guests. Sometimes I had three or four ex-volunteers staying in my apartment, all of them big midwesterners drinking Yanjing beer and laughing about old times.

In the southwestern city of Kunming, Goettig opened a bar with a Chinese partner. They found space in an old bomb shelter; the lease explicitly stated that they had to abandon the premises if China went to war. They had two pool tables and a stage for bands. Not long after they opened, there was a bad knife fight—one of the bartenders got stabbed multiple times, and part of a lung had to be removed. The bar didn't have much business, and Goettig and his partner barely scraped together enough money to cover the medical bills. Goettig had named the place the Speakeasy.

The year after we drove across northern China, Goettig finally returned to the United States. He was thirty years old and nearly broke. He went back to southwestern Minnesota, but he couldn't imagine living there again; after a month, he caught a Greyhound bus heading south. Some other former volunteers were living in Starkville, Mississippi; they let Goettig crash in their home and found him a job teaching English to foreign students at Mississippi State. It paid $24,000 for the school year. When Goettig looked into teacher-certification programs, he realized that they took almost as long as law school. He bought some books about the LSAT, studied on his own, and scored off the charts. The next time I saw him, he was living on Riverside Drive, studying at Columbia Law School. In his spare time, he did Chinese-language research for Human Rights Watch. Eventually, he became the editor in chief of Columbia's *Journal of Asian Law.* He wore a certain expression I recognized from China—slightly stunned, a little overwhelmed, completely out of his element. He had no idea where this was going, but he was happy to hang on for the ride.

At the end of the drive, we followed Highway 215 to the Tibetan Plateau. The two-lane road was flanked by high-desert landscapes of rock and dirt, punctuated by highway-safety propaganda. Along one stretch, the government had perched a wrecked car on spindly ten-foot poles beside the road. The vehicle had been smashed beyond recognition: the front end was crumpled flat and the remains of a door dangled in strips of steel. Across the back were painted the words FOUR PEOPLE DIED. It was like some gruesome version of a children's treat—a Carsicle. Another sign presented the speed limit like options on a menu:

40 KM/HR IS THE SAFEST
80 KM/HR IS DANGEROUS
100 KM/HR IS BOUND FOR THE HOSPITAL

The road climbed steeply to the border of Qinghai Province. We passed slow-moving Liberation trucks, their engines whining in the thin air; my altimeter read nearly twelve thousand feet. For 150 miles we saw almost no sign of human habitation. There were no gas stations or restaurants or shops; the first town we passed had been recently razed. Roofless walls stood stark on the plateau, lonely as the traces of some lost empire.

In Qinghai, Goettig's left eye began to act up. First it watered and then it hurt; he sat in the passenger's seat, rubbing his face with his fist. We crossed another twelve-thousand-foot pass and descended to Qinghai Lake. It's the largest body of water in China, a salt lake more than two hundred miles in circumference and blue as a sapphire. We camped on the banks, pitching my tent on a finger of land. It was one of the most beautiful places I had ever visited in China, but by now Goettig could hardly see a thing.

The next morning, he lay in the tent, moaning. "It hurts like hell," he said. "It just keeps burning." He had taken out his contacts, but his eyes still hurt; he asked how many hours it would be to Xining, the provincial capital. "Maybe we'll have to find an eye doctor in Xining," he said. It occurred to me that this was the most ominous sentence I'd heard in about six thousand miles. The eye would eventually recover, and he later learned that the problem had been caused by his contact lenses. In Kunming, a friend had told him that a local shop was selling Johnson & Johnson lenses for half the usual price—a great deal, and Goettig stocked up. It turned out that the contacts were counterfeit. That became a new rule: when in Kunming, don't buy contact lenses on sale. China was full of lessons; we were still learning every day. Don't hike off trail in Xinjiang. Don't shop for Strange Stones in a bad part of Hebei. Don't hang out with people who light flares under stalled trucks. Driving alongside the lake, we passed another Carsicle, although Goettig's eyes were watering so badly he couldn't see it. He wept all the way across Qinghai—he wept along the salt lake's barren banks, and he wept past the stranded Carsicle, and he wept through the long descent from the roof of the world.

CHRISTOPHER HITCHENS

The Lovely Stones

FROM *Vanity Fair*

THE GREAT CLASSICIST A. W. Lawrence (illegitimate younger
brother of the even more famously illegitimate T. E. "of Arabia")
once remarked of the Parthenon that it is "the one building in the
world which may be assessed as absolutely *right.*" I was considering
this thought the other day as I stood on top of the temple with Maria Ioannidou, the dedicated director of the Acropolis Restoration
Service, and watched the workshop that lay below and around me.
Everywhere there were craftsmen and -women, toiling to get the
Parthenon and its sister temples ready for viewing by the public
this summer. There was the occasional whine of a drill and groan
of a crane, but otherwise this was the quietest construction site I
have ever seen—or, rather, heard. Putting the rightest, or most
right, building to rights means that the workers must use marble
from a quarry in the same mountain as the original one, that they
must employ old-fashioned chisels to carve, along with traditional
brushes and twigs, and that they must study and replicate the ancient Lego-like marble joints with which the master builders of antiquity made it all fit miraculously together.

Don't let me blast on too long about how absolutely heart-
stopping the brilliance of these people was. But did you know, for
example, that the Parthenon forms, if viewed from the sky, a perfect equilateral triangle with the Temple of Aphaea, on the island
of Aegina, and the Temple of Poseidon, at Cape Sounion? Did you
appreciate that each column of the Parthenon makes a very slight
inward incline, so that if projected upward into space they would
eventually steeple themselves together at a symmetrical point in

the empyrean? The "rightness" is located somewhere between the beauty of science and the science of beauty.

With me on my tour was Nick Papandreou, son and grandson of prime ministers and younger brother of the Socialist opposition leader, who reminded me that the famously fluted columns are made not of single marble shafts but of individually carved and shaped "drums," many of them still lying around looking to be re-assembled. On his last visit, he found a graffito on the open face of one such. A certain Xanthias, probably from Thrace, had put his name there, not thinking it would ever be seen again once the next drum was joined on. Then it surfaced after nearly twenty-five hundred years, to be briefly glimpsed (by men and women who still speak and write a version of Xanthias's tongue) before being lost to view once more, this time for good. On the site, a nod of respect went down the years, from one proud Greek worker to another.

The original construction of the Parthenon involved what I call Periclean Keynesianism: the city needed to recover from a long and ill-fought war against Persia and needed also to give full employment (and a morale boost) to its citizens. Over tremendous conservative opposition, Pericles in or about the year 450 B.C.E. pushed through the Athenian Assembly a sort of stimulus package which proposed a labor-intensive reconstruction of what had been lost or damaged in the Second Persian War. As Plutarch phrases it in his *Pericles:*

> The house-and-home contingent, no whit less than the sailors and senti-nels and soldiers, might have a pretext for getting a beneficial share of the public wealth. The materials to be used were stone, bronze, ivory, gold, ebony and cypress-wood; the arts which should elaborate and work up these materials were those of carpenter, molder, bronze-smith, stone-cutter, dyer, veneerer in gold and ivory, painter, embroiderer, embosser, to say nothing of the forwarders and furnishers of the material . . . It came to pass that for every age almost, and every capacity, the city's great abundance was distributed and shared by such demands.

When we think of Athens in the fifth century B.C.E., we think chiefly of the theater of Euripides and Sophocles and of philoso-phy and politics—specifically democratic politics, of the sort that saw Pericles repeatedly reelected in spite of complaints that he was overspending. And it's true that *Antigone* was first performed as the

Parthenon was rising, and *Medea* not all that long after the temple was finished. From drama to philosophy: Socrates himself was also a stonemason and sculptor, and it seems quite possible that he too took part in raising the edifice. So Greece might have something to teach us about the arts of recovery as well. As the author of *The Stones of Athens,* R. E. Wycherley, puts it:

> In some sense, the Parthenon must have been the work of a committee . . . It was the work of the whole Athenian people, not merely because hundreds of them had a hand in building it, but because the assembly was ultimately responsible, confirmed appointments, and sanctioned and scrutinized the expenditure of every drachma.

I have visited many of the other great monuments of antiquity, from Luxor and Karnak and the pyramids to Babylon and Great Zimbabwe, and their magnificence is always compromised by the realization that slaves did the heavy lifting and they were erected to show who was boss. The Parthenon is unique because, though ancient Greece did have slavery to some extent, its masterpiece also represents the willing collective work of free people. And it is open to the light and to the air: "accessible," if you like, rather than dominating. So that to its rightness you could tentatively add the concept of "rights," as Periclean Greeks began dimly to formulate them for the first time.

Not that the beauty and symmetry of the Parthenon have not been abused and perverted and mutilated. Five centuries after the birth of Christianity the Parthenon was closed and desolated. It was then "converted" into a Christian church, before being transformed a thousand years later into a mosque—complete with minaret at the southwest corner—after the Turkish conquest of the Byzantine Empire. Turkish forces also used it for centuries as a garrison and an arsenal, with the tragic result that in 1687, when Christian Venice attacked the Ottoman Turks, a powder magazine was detonated and huge damage inflicted on the structure. Most horrible of all, perhaps, the Acropolis was made to fly a Nazi flag during the German occupation of Athens. I once had the privilege of shaking the hand of Manolis Glezos, the man who climbed up and tore the swastika down, thus giving the signal for a Greek revolt against Hitler.

The damage done by the ages to the building, and by past empires and occupations, cannot all be put right. But there is one desecration and dilapidation that can at least be partially undone. Early in the nineteenth century, Britain's ambassador to the Ottoman Empire, Lord Elgin, sent a wrecking crew to the Turkish-occupied territory of Greece, where it sawed off approximately half of the adornment of the Parthenon and carried it away. As with all things Greek, there were three elements to this, the most lavish and beautiful sculptural treasury in human history. Under the direction of the artistic genius Phidias, the temple had two massive pediments decorated with the figures of Pallas Athena, Poseidon, and the gods of the sun and the moon. It then had a series of ninety-two high-relief panels, or metopes, depicting a succession of mythical and historical battles. The most intricate element was the frieze, carved in bas-relief, which showed the gods, humans, and animals that made up the annual Pan-Athens procession: there were 192 equestrian warriors and auxiliaries featured, which happens to be the exact number of the city's heroes who fell at the Battle of Marathon. Experts differ on precisely what story is being told here, but the frieze was quite clearly carved as a continuous narrative. Except that half the cast of the tale is still in Bloomsbury, in London, having been sold well below cost by Elgin to the British government in 1816 for $2.2 million in today's currency to pay off his many debts. (His original scheme had been to use the sculptures to decorate Broomhall, his rain-sodden ancestral home in Scotland, in which case they might never have been seen again.)

Ever since Lord Byron wrote his excoriating attacks on Elgin's colonial looting, first in *Childe Harold's Pilgrimage* (1812) and then in *The Curse of Minerva* (1815), there has been a bitter argument about the legitimacy of the British Museum's deal. I've written a whole book about this controversy and won't oppress you with all the details, but would just make this one point. If the *Mona Lisa* had been sawed in two during the Napoleonic Wars and the separated halves had been acquired by different museums in, say, St. Petersburg and Lisbon, would there not be a general wish to see what they might look like if reunited? If you think my analogy is overdrawn, consider this: the body of the goddess Iris is at present in London, while her head is in Athens. The front part of the torso of Poseidon is in London, and the rear part is in Athens. And so on. This is grotesque.

To that essentially aesthetic objection the British establishment has made three replies. The first is, or was, that return of the marbles might set a "precedent" that would empty the world's museum collections. The second is that more people can see the marbles in London. The third is that the Greeks have nowhere to put or display them. The first is easily disposed of: The Greeks don't want anything else returned to them and indeed hope to have more, rather than less, Greek sculpture displayed in other countries. And there is in existence no court or authority to which appeals on precedent can be made. (Anyway, who exactly would be making such an appeal? The Aztecs? The Babylonians? The Hittites? Greece's case is a one-off—quite individual and unique.) As to the second: Melina Mercouri's husband, the late movie director and screenwriter Jules Dassin, told a British parliamentary committee in 2000 that by the standard of mass viewership the sculptures should all be removed from Athens and London and exhibited in Beijing. After these frivolous and boring objections have been dealt with, we are left with the third and serious one, which is what has brought me back to Athens. Where should the treasures be safeguarded and shown?

It is unfortunately true that the city allowed itself to become very dirty and polluted in the twentieth century, and as a result the remaining sculptures and statues on the Parthenon were nastily eroded by "acid rain." And it's also true that the museum built on the Acropolis in the nineteenth century, a trifling place of a mere 1,450 square meters, was pathetically unsuited to the task of housing or displaying the work of Phidias. But gradually and now impressively, the Greeks have been living up to their responsibilities. Beginning in 1992, the endangered marbles were removed from the temple, given careful cleaning with ultraviolet and infrared lasers, and placed in a climate-controlled interior. Alas, they can never all be repositioned on the Parthenon itself, because, though the atmospheric pollution is now better controlled, Lord Elgin's goons succeeded in smashing many of the entablatures that held the sculptures in place. That leaves us with the next-best thing, which turns out to be rather better than one had hoped.

About a thousand feet southeast of the temple, the astonishing new Acropolis Museum will open on June 20, 2009. With ten times

the space of the old repository, it will be able to display all the marvels that go with the temples on top of the hill. Most important, it
will be able to show, for the first time in centuries, how the Parthenon sculptures looked to the citizens of old.

Arriving excitedly for my preview of the galleries, I was at once able
to see what had taken the Greeks so long. As with everywhere else
in Athens, if you turn over a spade or unleash a drill you uncover at
least one layer of a previous civilization. (Building a metro for the
Olympics in 2004 was a protracted if fascinating nightmare for this
very reason.) The new museum, built to the design of the French-
Swiss architect Bernard Tschumi, has had to be mounted above-
ground on one hundred huge reinforced-concrete pillars, which
allow you to survey the remnants of villas, drains, bathhouses, and
mosaics of the recently unearthed neighborhood below. Much of
the ground floor is made of glass so that natural light filters down
to these excavations and gives the effect of transparency throughout. But don't look down for too long. Raise your eyes and you will
be given an arresting view of the Parthenon, from a building that
has been carefully aligned to share its scale and perspective with
the mother ship.

I was impatient to be the first author to see the remounted figures and panels and friezes. Professor Dimitrios Pandermalis, the
head of the museum, took me to the top-floor gallery and showed
me the concentric arrangement whereby the sculpture of the pedi-
ment is nearest the windows, the high-relief metopes are arranged
above head height (they are supposed to be seen from below), and
finally the frieze is running at eye level along the innermost wall.
At any time, you can turn your head to look up and across at the
architectural context for which the originals were so passionately
carved. At last it will be possible to see the building and its main
artifacts in one place and on one day.

The British may continue in their constipated fashion to cling to
what they have so crudely amputated, but the other museums and
galleries of Europe have seen the artistic point of reunification and
restored to Athens what was looted in the years when Greece was
defenseless. Professor Pandermalis proudly showed me an exqui-
site marble head, of a youth shouldering a tray, that fits beautifully
into panel No. 5 of the north frieze. It comes courtesy of the collec-

tion of the Vatican. Then there is the sculpted foot of the goddess Artemis, from the frieze that depicts the assembly of Olympian gods, by courtesy of the Salinas Museum, in Palermo. From Heidelberg comes another foot, this time of a young man playing a lyre, and it fits in nicely with the missing part on panel No. 8. Perhaps these acts of cultural generosity, and tributes to artistic wholeness, could "set a precedent," too?

The Acropolis Museum has hit on the happy idea of exhibiting, for as long as following that precedent is too much to hope for, its own original sculptures with the London-held pieces represented by beautifully copied casts. This has two effects: It allows the visitor to follow the frieze round the four walls of a core "cella" and see the sculpted tale unfold (there, you suddenly notice, is the "lowing heifer" from Keats's *Ode on a Grecian Urn*). And it creates a natural thirst to see the actual reassembly completed. So, far from emptying or weakening a museum, this controversy has instead created another one, which is destined to be among Europe's finest galleries. And one day, surely, there will be an agreement to do the right thing by the world's most "right" structure.

GARRISON KEILLOR

Take In the State Fair

FROM *National Geographic*

THE STATE FAIR is a ritual carnival marking the end of summer and gardens and apple orchards and the start of school and higher algebra and the imposition of strict rules and what we in the North call the Long Dark Time. Like gardening, the fair doesn't change all that much. The big wheel whirls and the girls squeal and the bratwursts cook on the little steel rollers and the boys slouch around and keep checking their hair. It isn't the World's Columbian Exposition, the Aquarian Exposition, the Great Exhibition of the Works of Industry of All Nations, the Exposition Universelle, the Gathering of the Tribes, or the Aspen Institute. It's just us, taking a break from digging potatoes.

The Ten Chief Joys of the State Fair are:

1. To eat food with your two hands.
2. To feel extreme centrifugal force reshaping your face and jowls as you are flung or whirled turbulently and you experience that intense joyfulness that is indistinguishable from anguish, or (as you get older) to observe other persons in extreme centrifugal situations.
3. To mingle, merge, mill, jostle gently, and flock together with throngs, swarms, mobs, and multitudes of persons slight or hefty, punky or preppy, young or ancient, wandering through the hubbub and amplified razzmatazz and raw neon and clouds of wiener steam in search of some elusive thing, nobody is sure exactly what.
4. To witness the stupidity of others, their gluttony and low-grade obsessions, their poor manners and slack-jawed, mouth-breathing, pop-eyed yahootude, and feel rather sophisticated by comparison.

5. To see the art of salesmanship, of barking, hustling, touting, and see how effectively it works on others and not on cool you.
6. To see designer chickens, the largest swine, teams of mighty draft horses, llamas, rare breeds of geese, geckos, poisonous snakes, a two-headed calf, a 650-pound man, and whatever else appeals to the keen, inquiring mind.
7. To watch the judging of livestock.
8. To observe entertainers attempt to engage a crowd that is moving laterally.
9. To sit down and rest amid the turmoil and reconsider the meaning of life.
10. To turn away from food and amusement and crass pleasure and to resolve to live on a higher plane from now on.

The Midwest is State Fair Central, and it thrives here because we are the breadbasket of America, Hog Butcher, Machinemaker, Stacker of Particleboard, Player with Chain Saws, Land of the Big Haunches. And also because midwesterners are insular, industrious, abstemious, introspective people skittish about body contact, and a state fair is liberation from all of that, a plunge into the pool of self-indulgence, starting with a thick pork chop hot off the grill and served on a stick with a band of crisp brown fat along one side. The fat is not good for you. You eat the pork chop, fat and all, and your child eats her pork chop, and then you score a giant vanilla shake from the Dairy Bar to cushion the fall of a bagful of tiny doughnuts. Now you're warmed up and ready to move on to the corn dog course.

But first here is a flume ride your child is agitating for, so you climb onto a steel raft and plunge into a concrete gorge and over a waterfall, and a two-foot wave washes over the gunwales, and now your pants are soaked. You disembark. You look like a man who could not contain his excitement. For cover, you hide in the crowd. You walk close behind people. You join the throng at the hot-corn stand and comfort yourself with a salty ear of buttered corn. Your pants chafe. You wander among booths of merchandise looking for men's pants and find encyclopedias, storm windows, lawn mowers, vegetable peelers and choppers, humidifiers, log splitters, and home saunas. Your search for dry pants leads you through buildings where champion jams and jellies are displayed on tables draped with purple, blue, red, yellow ribbons, and also champion cakes (angel food, Bundt light, Bundt dark, chiffon, chocolate, chocolate chiffon, German chocolate, jelly roll, pound, spice, sponge, vegetable, or fruit) and pickles (beet, bean, bread-and-butter, cucumber sweet, dill without garlic, dill with garlic, peppers sweet, peppers hot, watermelon). And through an education pavilion where headhunters lie in wait for you to pause and make eye contact, and they leap on you and make you hear about the benefits of beautician training, the opportunities in the field of broadcasting.

The way to dry out your pants is to get on a motorized contraption that whirls you through the air. Your child suggests you ride the giant Slingshot that is across the street. A long line of dead-end kids wait to be strapped into a cage and flung straight up in the air. The mob of onlookers waiting for the big whoosh looks like the crowds that once gathered to watch public executions.

You pass up the Slingshot for the double Ferris wheel. An excellent clothes dryer, lifting you up above the honky-tonk, a nice breeze in your pants, in a series of parabolas, and at the apex you look out across the gaudy uproar and the blinking lights, and then you zoom down for a close-up of a passing gang of farm boys in green letter jackets and then back up in the air. You tell your child that this Ferris wheel is the ride that, going back to childhood, you always saved for last, and so riding it fills you with nostalgia. She pats your hand. "You'll be all right, Dad," she says. After ten minutes you come down nice and dry, and also the food has settled in your stomach, and you're ready for seconds.

Of the Ten Joys, the one that we midwesterners are loath to cop to is number three, the mingling and jostling, a pleasure that Google and Facebook can't provide. American life tends more and more to put you in front of a computer screen in a cubicle, then into a car and head you toward home in the suburbs, where you drive directly into the garage and step into your kitchen without brushing elbows with anybody. People seem to want this, as opposed to urban tumult and squalor. But we have needs we can't admit, and one is to be in a scrum of thinly clad corpulence milling in brilliant sun in front of the deep-fried-ice-cream stand and feel the brush of wings, hip bumps, hands touching your arm ("Oh, excuse me!"), the heat of humanity with its many smells (citrus deodorant, sweat and musk, bouquet of beer, hair oil, stale cigar, methane), the solid, big-rump bodies of Brueghel peasants all around you like dogs in a pack, and you—yes, elegant you of the refined taste and the commitment to the arts—are one of these dogs. All your life you dreamed of attaining swanhood or equinity, but your fellow dogs know better. They sniff you and turn away, satisfied.

Some state fairs are roomier, some gaudier, but there is a great sameness to them, just as there is a similarity among Catholic churches. No state fair can be called trendy, luxurious, dreamy— none of that. Nothing that is farm-oriented or pig-centric is even remotely upscale.

Wealth and social status aren't so evident at the fair. The tattooed carnies who run the rides have a certain hauteur, and of course if you're on horseback, you're aristocracy, but otherwise not. There is no first-class line, no concierge section roped off in the barns. The wine selection is white, red, pink, and fizzy. Nobody flaunts his money.

The state fair, at heart, is an agricultural expo, and farming isn't about getting rich, and farmers discuss annual income less than they practice nude meditation on beaches. Farming is about work and about there being a Right Way and a Wrong Way to do it. You sit in the bleachers by the show ring and see this by the way the young women and men lead their immaculate cows clockwise around the grumpy, baggy-pants judge in the center. They walk at the cow's left shoulder, hand on the halter, and keep the animal's head up, always presenting a clear profile to the judge's gaze, and when he motions them to get in line, the exhibitors stand facing their cows and keep them squared away.

You and I may have no relatives left in farming, and our memory of the farm, if we have any, may be faint, but the livestock judging is meaningful to us—husbandry is what we do, even if we call it education or health care or management. Sport is a seductive metaphor (life as a game in which we gain victory through hard work, discipline, and visualizing success), but the older metaphor of farming (life as hard labor that is subject to weather and quirks of blind fate and may return no reward whatsoever and don't be surprised) is still in our blood, especially those of us raised on holy scripture. The young men and women leading cows around the show ring are relatives of Abraham and Job and the faithful father of the prodigal son. They subscribe to the Love Thy Neighbor doctrine. They know about late-summer hailstorms. You could learn something from these people.

Twilight falls on the fairgrounds, and a person just suddenly gets sick of it all. You've spent hours gratifying yourself on deep-fried cheese curds, deep-fried ice cream, testing one sausage against another, washing them down with authentic American sarsaparilla, sampling your child's onion rings, postponing the honey sundae for later, and now it is later, and the horticulture building and the honey-sundae booth are four blocks and a river of humanity away. You and the child stand at the entrance to the midway, barkers barking at you to try the ringtoss, shoot a basketball, squirt the water in the clown's mouth and see the ponies run, win the teddy bear, but you don't want to win a big blue plush teddy bear. You have no use for one whatsoever. There is enough inertia in your life as it is. And now you feel the great joy of revulsion at the fair and its shallow pleasures, its cheap tinsel, its greasy food. You are slightly ashamed of your own intake of animal fats. Bleaugh, you think. Arghhhh. OMG. You have gone twice to ATMs to finance this binge, and you regret that. No more of this! You take the child's hand. There will be no honey sundae tonight, honey. We got all that out of our system. We are going home and sober up and get busy.

You hike toward where you recollect you parked your car this morning, and by a stroke of God's grace you actually find it, and your child does not have to watch a father roaming around pitifully, moaning to himself. You get in, and you drive back to the world that means something, the world of work. The Long Dark Time is coming, and you must gather your herds to shelter and lay in carrots and potatoes in the cellar.

The fair is gone the next day, the rides disassembled, the concessions boarded up, the streets swept clean. Dry leaves blow across the racing oval, brown squirrels den up in the ticket booths, the midway marquee sways in the wind. You drive past the fairgrounds a few days later on your way to work. It looks like the encampment of an invading army that got what booty it wanted and went home. And now you are yourself again, ambitious, disciplined, frugal, walking briskly, head held high, and nobody would ever associate you with that shameless person stuffing his face with bratwurst and kraut, mustard on his upper lip, and a half-eaten deep-fried Snickers in his other hand. That was not the real you. This is. This soldier of the simple declarative sentence. You have no need for cheap glitter and pig fat and pointless twirling. You have work to do. Onward.

PETER LaSALLE

Walking: An Essay on Writing

FROM *Agni*

1. Roller Luggage

Both times it had to do with walking, and both in what you might call "other places." Not so oddly, I guess. In Paris I had been walking for about a half hour already that Sunday afternoon.

I had no real agenda, other than getting out of my apartment in the Marais for a while in the good weather, heading up toward the Place de l'Opéra and the streets behind it with the big department stores. I wanted to see if I could maybe determine where the old Café Certa had been, the spot that figures prominently in what has to be one of the neglected masterpieces of French Surrealism, Louis Aragon's *Paris Peasant*. I was in Paris for a semester, teaching at a university there, and at the moment I was immersing myself in a personal project of reading as much as I could Surrealist prose, which overall tends to get sold short at the expense of the movement's poetry.

I had logged enough long walks around the city already that I knew it was wise to always have a mini umbrella poked into the pocket of my zip-up jacket—in Paris in autumn the weather can often change, dramatically and fast. But this day the sky was so big and blue over the stately buff stone buildings lining the empty thoroughfare of Boulevard de Magenta, the plane trees showing leaves as fiery as anything in New England, that I soon realized I definitely wouldn't need it. I probably also realized, or assured myself, that wearing the springy, and basic, black-and-white nylon Reeboks had been a good idea, the essential bounce of them, even if they did look a little goofy. Actually, continuing along, I tugged off the jacket and carried it under my arm, eventually deciding the day wasn't *quite* warm enough for that, and when I did put it back on, I spotted the Gare du Nord. Which is when I think it started.

I hadn't been in the Gare du Nord for a while, so I thought it might be worth taking a swing through it now on this walk. I headed that way.

There was the cluster of cafés and hotels surrounding the station and then the façade of the impressive edifice itself. A central fan window rose almost the height of it, with sculpted toga-clad personages atop the entrance's long row of heavy swinging doors. (While walking, I suppose that I was thinking of the woman I had been seeing before I came to France. I suppose I was thinking some about my classes, too, there in the university's stark classroom building over by the Panthéon, where I went to teach only once a week, on Fridays. One class was in creative writing, delivered in English to sweet, hopeful first-year Anglo-American Studies students whose English really wasn't very good and who probably weren't ready for creative writing even in their own language; the other was in the theater department, a class on Tennessee Williams, where the equally sweet and hopeful students, budding actors and actresses, had next to no English for the most part and I often had to resort to conversing in French, despite the departmental powers that be repeatedly telling me that the whole idea was to stay tough and give them only English.) The concourse of the Gare du Nord within stretched enormous, a wide polished floor and the bright afternoon light coming through the lofty glass-and-cast-iron roof providing a pleasant glare to it all, like sunshine on a frozen pond, maybe; automated signs clickingly shuffled arrival and departure information. At the dead ends of the platform tracks were the sleek, streamlined snouts of the high-speed TGV locomotives repeated one after another, massive silver machines, about a half dozen of them in a line facing that main lobby with its newsstands and coffee counters. And gathered before one locomotive, in the glare and amidst a spread-out clutter of all sorts of bags and bulky suitcases, was a pack of young women, chicly dressed and very blond; they were chatting and laughing, occasionally looking up to the schedule announcements above. I told myself they must have been Dutch or Scandinavian—all strikingly blond like that, nearly uniformly so—and, of course, the Gare du Nord does serve northern European destinations.

As I said, it *started* then, but I wasn't sure of it yet.

Farther on, it was admittedly strange to be walking through the pocket with the famous Parisian department stores, true Belle Époque landmarks, and seeing the streets thoroughly deserted. I passed the window displays and their many mirrors that tossed back moving images of me, and I even poked around the alleys behind the stores and the scruffy loading docks; it was cooler there in the shadows, but once out in the sun again, walking in the comfortable Reeboks, it became warm again, though not quite as much so now as an hour before when I'd first set out.

Louis Aragon's 1926 *Paris Peasant* is a long personal essay, more or less a journal, about the author's life and metaphysical imaginings at twenty-five. In the book, the Café Certa serves as the central meeting place for the group of then relatively unknown young writers and painters who are his close friends, an iconoclastic coterie that began with Dada interests and would eventually be celebrated worldwide as a bona fide movement, the Surrealists. The café also becomes for Aragon, when alone, a good nook for writing. There he works on his poems and essays. He rubs elbows with the habitués from the neighborhood, soon backing their struggle to try to keep the vintage shopping arcade that houses the Certa from being demolished in the name of progress, before it belatedly falls prey to Baron Haussmann's controversial master plan to rehab Paris that lingered well into the twentieth century. Why, at one point in *Paris Peasant*, Aragon goes as far as reproducing on the page, as part of the text, an exact facsimile of the café's cocktail menu, a "Tarif des Consommations," ranging from (untranslated) the "Kiss me Quick" and the "Pick me Hup" and the "Sherry Cobler" (one *b*), to what seems to be the very special, and undoubtedly extremely dangerous, "Pêle-Mêle Mixture" (*prix 2 F.50*).

But walking now, it was tough for me to get a bead on exactly where the Café Certa had been, there in the vicinity of the big, open plaza in front of yet another of those full six train stations in Paris, this time the Gare St.-Lazare. On the city's western side, it serves the lines going to and coming from the UK, via the old pre-tunnel ferry connection, and I told myself that the Certa's menu with its endearing English might have been practical rather than affected when considered in that light, seeing that some of its customers would have been British. However, looking around, going up and down streets between the station and the Boulevard des Italiens, I realized much had certainly changed, and I conceded that many of the buildings were completely different now and sometimes also renumbered, so that for me it wouldn't be, after all, a matter of at least seeing where the café had *once* been.

I had looked up the address for the current Café Certa in the *Bottin*, the hefty Paris phone book, before I left my apartment, and it matched the information that Aragon himself had given back in 1926. In a footnote he explains that at the time of his publishing *Paris Peasant* the Café Certa was already gone, moved to a "new location" on Rue d'Isly and "near the old London Bar," though he makes no mention of going there anymore. And a couple of blocks from the station, deep in a nest of more Sunday-empty side streets, I did find the Rue d'Isly and I did see the current Certa. I would have gone in for a coffee, but for me the place looked too neat today, even after so many years of operation in this location, too upscale. There was a pricey dinner menu in the front window, and on the other side of the glass waiters in proper black trousers and crisp white shirts were preparing tables for what might have been the evening's well-heeled dinner clientele—I understood why Aragon himself had perhaps kept his distance.

And still walking, starting to head back, I knew I was appreciative of the fact that attempting to locate the Café Certa had, if nothing else, given me a destination, a vague reason to get out of my apartment on such a fine October afternoon, to just walk and walk like this. (I possibly thought some more about my classes, thought, too, much more about the woman I had been seeing back home and who had become, well, dear to me.) I checked my watch, saw that the time it gave was exactly the same as that on the clock atop the Gare St.-Lazare. I figured I would work my way back to the Marais along the Grands Boulevards, and there would be plenty of cafés en route to choose from if I wanted to take a bit of a rest—which was when it started again.

Or, more so, when it *happened*.

I waited for the light to turn at sort of a traffic semicircle—devoid of any traffic, it faced the plaza in front of the station, with Gare St.-Lazare as impressive as Gare du Nord even without the latter's ornate carved statuary—and I saw what I maybe hadn't noticed when I had been looking around there only a half hour before. I saw how from all sides of the traffic semicircle people on foot seemed to be converging on the station, not a crowd, but people approaching the station—singly or sometimes in couples—from all directions. It was the end of a weekend, a Sunday with the sunshine beginning to soften and taking on a thick, honeyish hue that made the recently sandblasted Gare St.-Lazare more golden than it was, also made the colors of the clothing of the people converging on the station from the empty streets—moving in a diminishing fan toward it and then across the paved plaza—yes, those colors more true than they were, too, a red jacket here, a very royal blue one there. Many of them were pulling roller luggage, walking along with the suitcases on little wheels with quiet reservation, expressionless, as if it was just so much work they had to do. Everybody returning.

I stared at it all.

I don't know what it was. It would be easy to say it was a combination of understandably intriguing imagery—travelers at the end of a weekend heading home, not only the lovely contingent of blond young women in the Gare du Nord standing around in front of the long-snouted futuristic locomotives, a scene that was pretty wondrous in itself, but travelers from everywhere seeming to have materialized from all the deserted streets of Paris now. And there was that clock high on the station's topmost gable at the head of the sloping plaza, its sizable Roman numerals and tapering hands, black on white, telling them they had trains to catch, weary as they were, they had eventual destinations somewhere in what would surely be the dark night of a station platform in some distant town or other faraway city—it would be very easy indeed to give the whole thing a somewhat logical explanation like that.

But the truth of the matter, and what I honestly still remember to this day, is that I didn't want to explain it, there was nothing to be interpreted. And what I know is that it simply left me with an undeniable feeling, not about the scene in particular then or wanting to later depict or write about it, but just a feeling, strong and sure and almost dizzying in my longing, an overwhelming and tangible need.

I really felt like I wanted to be writing my own fiction, like nothing else in the world, to pick up where I had left off earlier that morning on the short story I had been working on. I really felt that I just wanted to be there again at the desk, writing that short story, or anything else, for that matter.

The traffic light changed. I crossed the street and headed toward the Place de l'Opéra and the Grands Boulevards. I didn't stop for a coffee in the course of the long walk back, and I just desired, very much so, to be in the apartment in the Marais, *writing again.*

2. *The Statue of Chopin by the Sea*

This time I was in Brazil, Rio specifically.

You see, lately I have been doing something. I go to a place where literature I love is set, and the travel doesn't entail any other express purpose, like that of the teaching appointment I had been lucky enough to land in Paris—this kind of travel is always altogether different. What I do is pack a small bag with a few changes of clothes and a few texts, and I head off for a couple of weeks, solo, to reread a writer there, immersing myself in the work "on the premises," so to speak. I've read Borges's stories in Buenos Aires, and I've read Flaubert's meditation on ancient Carthage, the novel *Salammbô,* in Tunisia. I've read Faulkner in Oxford, Mississippi, holed up in a great little twenty-five-buck-a-night motel called the Ole Miss right off the main square with its antebellum white courthouse there, and I've read what could be ensconced among the handful of my absolutely favorite modern novels, Malcolm Lowry's *Under the Volcano,* in Cuernavaca.

And in Brazil it was Machado de Assis's 1881 *Epitaph of a Small Winner.* The novel recounts the odd life of an elegant Rio gentleman, Brás Cubas, and is presented in the form of an autobiography written from the other side of the grave; actually, the spooky narrative strategy gets announced right up front by an alternate, but not as good, English translation from the Portuguese that sticks to the original title, *The Posthumous Memoirs of Brás Cubas.* Machado's book is essentially an experimental one that was far ahead of its time, a text that became important to a lot of the generation of daring American writers who made their mark in the 1960s and '70s—everybody from John Barth to Donald Barthelme to Susan Sontag, it seems—and I guess it took hold in my writer's psyche about that time, too. The power lies in the sheer virtuosity of the performance, a tour de force both in its nervous, darkly humorous take on life, with a postmodern (Beckettian?) mind-set well before even modernism, and an unflagging commitment to startling invention in style and structure throughout.

And after over a week in the city, rereading Machado, exploring some of the Rio associated with him (where he had lived; his burial crypt built into a hillside in São João Batista cemetery; the forgotten little museum room of manuscripts and artifacts from his life tucked upstairs in the Brazilian Academy of Letters building downtown, etc.), I found myself leaving my hotel in Catete one sunny, very hot weekday afternoon, and, again, just walking.

Or maybe not just walking, because I was certainly thinking about a lot of things. (Things like what I had, in fact, learned here concerning Machado de Assis and his work, as well as, and more importantly, a new friendship I had formed with a Brazilian ex-diplomat/poet, whom I'd been told by a Brazilian acquaintance in Austin to contact in Rio. The acquaintance had assured me that the ex-diplomat/poet would be somebody I could talk to about Brazilian literature and who also represented a long tradition of the country's writers often having careers in the foreign service. I had spent a wonderful afternoon with him—an older man and a bachelor himself—out at his sprawling and pretty cluttered apartment in an aging tropical high-rise in Copacabana, a thunderstorm pounding darkly outside as we talked for several hours about literature ranging well beyond that of only his native Brazil. Since that session, he had been phoning me at the hotel just about every morning, for long, intense conversations on many more matters literary. The talk could involve an assortment of topics, including his extended, and damn interesting, ruminating in his whispery voice about the comparative poetic potentials of various languages, of which he spoke several—French versus English versus Portuguese, let's say—and also what he had noticed just the night before in reading one of my own short stories in a collection I had given him; that call came at nine in the morning on the day I took the walk, and, whispery-voiced as ever, he gently offered the observation that I had used the word "incessant" twice within three pages in the short story and said that I should be careful of such slips, or I should always be as *very* careful as a poet even when writing fiction—and I knew he was right.) The small hotel I'd set myself up in was a fine and cheap enough family-run place in the Catete neighborhood, a few streets up from the sea and not far from the city center; the turn-of-the-century yellow building, formerly a townhouse, backed up to the public park that had once been the formal gardens of the very faded pink old presidential palace, when Catete—run-down and comfortably funky now—had actually been chic. There was no literary landmark of any variety I was looking for this day, though I did pass the inlet of Botafogo with its extensive sailboat harbor, a locale that turns up several times in Machado's work. I think I simply wanted to do what I hadn't yet done—go clear to the other side of Pão de Açúcar, the umber, rocket-shaped seaside mountain that is, of course, *the* Rio de Janeiro icon, and see the neighborhood of Urca; I had heard that it remained one of the most handsome older pockets of the city.

I could have gone out there by rattling city bus, but I decided that while it was a couple of miles, the route along the sea and beside the old winding expressway would be nice, perfect for walking. Not that walking in Rio was always entirely casual, I'd learned. One of the sad truths of this particular moment in Brazilian history was that street crime was rampant, a product of the larger truth that Rio is a place where the third world of utter poverty seems to be thrust flat against a first world of economic success and even outright glitz; the whole city is laced with steep, conical hills bearing mazes of makeshift tin-and-terra-cotta squatters' shacks, the *favela* slums that repeatedly rise up like maybe just so many remembered and very haunting dreams, everywhere. And I will admit I was a bit uneasy when I had to make my way through the urine-pungent pedestrian tunnel below the empty freeway and to the other side of it by the inlet at Botafogo, where there was a concrete concourse surrounding the tunnel's exit and a bus stop stranded there, no buildup of anything nearby. Men in rags—and some not men, only teenage boys—slept in nooks along the concrete walls splattered

with graffiti; my being alone and obviously not Brazilian—somebody wandering uninvited through their sleep world, you might
say—I undoubtedly stood out as a tourist, and one now in a territory where I really shouldn't be at that. I usually kept a good supply of coins for the shoeshine boys in Catete, to pay them *not* to
shine my shoes and at least smilingly give them something, telling
myself that I'd tried to help; here, however, it might not be that
simple, I knew, and muggings, often at gunpoint, were more than
rampant in Rio, almost to the stage of being mere commonplace
occurrences and apparently part of the accepted give and take of
daily city life. Nevertheless, once beyond the bleak concrete concourse at the tunnel, then taking a turn to the other side of Pão de
Açúcar and walking down a wide, straight palm-lined boulevard in
the heat—it must have been an even ninety degrees in December,
Brazil's summer, with humidity to match—I felt a little stupid, or
possibly guilty, for having been so apprehensive. While everybody I
met in Rio kept warning me to always be careful and keenly on
guard, I personally wanted to believe the situation *wasn't* as bad as
often described.

I continued on, toward the village of Urca and the little beach I
knew was there, called Praia Vermelha.

The boulevard stretched before me, with those tall, spindly
palms and the roadway lanes divided by a grassy central island
landscaped with overgrown oleander, the stars of the fleshy blos-
soms bursting white or pink. Steep and seemingly jungled emerald
embankments rose up on both sides, and it was still empty on the
sidewalk, though soon there were many more people for a while.
Especially young people. They were obviously students, getting on
and off the sooty yellow city buses with book packs, because in the
stretch I now passed through was an older campus of the University of Rio de Janeiro; it continued to be used for some classes,
though lately was mostly a venue for conferences and the work of
various research institutes. The fine nineteenth-century university
buildings faced the street and were sort of a wedding-cake architecture—neoclassical and bright white—with lumpy red-tile roofs
and no shortage of balustraded balconies and definitely "grand"
front staircases, all surrounded by well-kept gardens and lawns. I
could already see the sea up ahead, shimmering in the distance
and at the end of the wide boulevard, where there seemed to be a
rather formal, and somewhat out-of-place, open square.

And I could already smell the sea, along with the wafting perfumy fragrance that no matter where you are in Rio, a city of everblossoming flowers, does define the place. And here's where it gets tricky again, because continuing on toward the end of the boulevard, past some functional 1950s-style buildings now, squat highrises painted pale green and part of the national military school, I started to anticipate something.

I mean, it was as if suddenly the whole outing wasn't merely a walk, and it was as if I was being drawn along, was moving toward something very definite even if I didn't know what it was, the soles of yet another pair of springy black-and-white nylon Reeboks again rhythmically slapping, yes, I was moving with nearly somnambulistic conviction to whatever it was I would find at the end of this boulevard and the Praia Vermelha there at the sea waiting before me.

I passed what looked like a parade concourse for the military school, studded with a commemorative pillar, and there was a parking area, formed by a traffic-circle bulge in the boulevard, for the cable-car station that offered airy rides up to Pão de Açúcar; reportedly, the peak afforded spectacular views perhaps surpassed only by those from even higher up above Rio, at the enormous white statue of Christ the Redeemer with arms perpetually outstretched, perched on its own lofty mountain behind the city. And I then came to the end of the boulevard and the open square, empty. It was paved with large rectangular slabs of dark stone laid like tiles, and there were old-fashioned lampposts and benches, everything set at right angles and geometrically precise somehow, for a design that you couldn't quite peg as to period, or—this is it—pretty much timeless, I'd say, easily the stuff of a de Chirico canvas. This square opened onto the perfect crescent of the little beach tucked in by the mountains, and the brown sands actually had a reddish tinge, living up to the name, Praia Vermelha. The low, glassy waves lapped lazily and whisperingly in the stillness of the day, and at the far edge of the square, on the side facing the water and at the exact midpoint of the plaza, was a single bronze statue—green going to black—set on a pedestal.

In that afternoon heat, I walked toward the figure.

Youthfully slim and hair swept back, dressed in breeches and high-collared jacket with a puffy cravat, Chopin was captured in a stance that had him romantically listing to one side, very contemplative and facing forever Guanabara Bay and the sea. I stared at

the statue. I'm not even sure whether what was provided on the
plaque affixed to the granite pedestal sank in for me; there was
some rubric explaining how the statue itself had been a gift of the
Polish citizens of Brazil to their country, though in what year or to
commemorate what particular occasion I would never really know
or later investigate. But that didn't matter, and all that did matter
while I stood there was that again, as on the walk in Paris, I had
ended up where I hadn't expected to have ended up. In other
words, a rather random walk had taken me to a place—and a
scene—I surely never expected to have come to, but it was, I fully
realized now, a place where I very much wanted, and even needed,
to be.

I looked out at the beach. It was no more than a few hundred
feet wide and with but a dozen or so people in swimwear sitting
here and there on low canvas chairs on this a weekday mid-
afternoon. There were some fine waterfront villas, the hand-
someness of the Urca architecture that I had read about in guidebooks, at the foot of the sheer stone cliffs on either side; farther
out, where the water striped alternately aqua and a very dark blue,
almost purple, was a long red-hulled freighter heading out to sea,
moving toward the horizon, I guess, but in a way not moving whatsoever.

I sat down for a while on one of the benches in the open square.
I slipped off my shoulder the little day pack I had been carrying
and took out a bottle of mineral water, to slowly sip from it and
think some more about things. (At this point in my life, unlike
in Paris a few years earlier, there wasn't the woman in question
to think about, and that hadn't worked out, though I wished it
had. But there was more to think about concerning what the ex-
diplomat/poet had told me, many things to think about on that
front, also his latest poems that he had shown me as we sat together
at the big mahogany dining room table in his apartment in Copa,
his handing me the carefully typed sheets to read, some in English
and some in French. They were good poems that I went through
one by one as that thunderstorm outside intensified and as the
younger man who lived with him—a pleasant, handsomely muscular Brazilian of African descent in T-shirt and shorts named José—
did ironing in the kitchen then brought us a large pitcher of fresh-
squeezed orange juice, smiling as he set it on the table, gentle and

polite. I suppose that out at Praia Vermelha I even thought about the writer I had journeyed to Brazil to *think* about, Machado de Assis, the triumph of the novel *Epitaph of a Small Winner,* which had become, for a time, a veritable cause taken up by many contemporary American writers and that probably could rank as the single greatest contribution of all South American literature written in the nineteenth century, for me, anyway.) But to be honest, I have no recollection today exactly what I thought about while sitting on the bench.

There was just something about being there, something about the whole idea of a lost little beach, more or less deserted, and a statue of Chopin contemplating forever the sea. And at this place, and as when I saw the travelers with the roller luggage all slowly moving toward the Gare St.-Lazare, I realized it wasn't that this was a setting I was ever going to write about and use in a short story of my own.

It was just that overwhelming feeling, again and more than anything else in the world, that I wanted to be writing my fiction, getting back to it as soon as I could, in this case to somehow immediately dispose of the several thousand miles and many hours of an overnight jet hissing on and on through the darkness, then a change of planes in Atlanta and finally a taxi ride on the freeway back to my place in Austin. I wanted to write as much as I had ever wanted to in my entire life, including when I was a kid taking undergraduate creative writing classes to the point that I held some kind of record at my college then for the number of them taken, dreaming of someday publishing, or even when I did get some attention and good reviews on at least one of the books I eventually went on to publish, granting the book never did sell very well—yet all of that had encouraged me, made me want to continue on with writing.

Or maybe this was so much more than anything I had known before. And right then and there I intensely wanted, now that I was indeed older and admittedly didn't have the luxury of any full arc of a career ahead of me, to once again be sitting down at my desk in the back room in my apartment there at 1407 West 39th 1/2 Street in Austin, Texas, to simply be writing, even if so much else in my life—the failed relationships I didn't try hard enough to make work, a longtime job in a stifling English department in Austin where the so-called scholarly colleagues around me too often seemed like only busy careerists far removed from the genuinely important in literature, the students deserving better—true, just to be writing again

*seemed to be all that mattered, even if most everything else in my life, to be
entirely honest about it, could at times feel as if it had never added up to
very much.*

I was still sitting on the bench.

"A statue of Chopin by the sea."

I think I whispered it aloud, liking the very sound of it, as I then
sipped from the bottle again. The water was cool, and for insula-
tion I had wrapped the clear plastic bottle in a thick towel from the
hotel before leaving, an old trick I had learned years ago in traveling.

I screwed the blue cap back onto the bottle, put the bottle back
in the day pack, and zipped the thing up. I got up, slipped the
pack's strap over one shoulder; I walked around the open square
some more.

Two uniformed soldiers—young and smiling, from the nearby
military school, most likely—were chatting with the guy who had a
handcart marked PIPOCA at the far corner of the esplanade, under the limbs of a shading grove of eucalyptus trees; the cart on its
bicycle wheels was a red contraption with shiny chrome trim, and
the freshly popped corn itself, *pipoca*, lay heaped up high behind
its glassed sides.

I listened a while longer to the low waves softly lapping on the
sand before starting back toward the palm-lined boulevard, to finally wander through the sweet little neighborhood there directly
below Pão de Açúcar, the whitewashed village of Urca proper and
its maze of hilly side streets, everything impeccably groomed.

Until eventually, sure enough—and this is where it all gets
stranger and even amazing, or that's the way I see it now, anyway
—three days later I somehow *was* back at my desk in Austin again,
putting together the words that as always (somehow magically?
somehow inevitably a minor miracle?) became the sentences that
became the paragraphs, as I worked on a new short story that was
going well, one I was feeling very good about.

Which is to say—at the desk once more and at long last, I was
writing.

PETER JON LINDBERG

In Defense of Tourism

FROM *Travel + Leisure*

ONCE I GOT INTO AN ARGUMENT with a friend over the hot-button issue of cannoli. We were standing in Mike's Pastry, a popular stop for bus tourists and presidential candidates in Boston's North End. My friend's problem was not so much with the cannoli (which he called "flaky" and "cheesy") as with a prominently displayed photograph of Bill Clinton gobbling one up. "How can you like this place?" Alex ranted. "It's like a funnel siphoning the souls out of hapless tourists."

"Really? And I thought the filling was ricotta."

My side of the argument was also less about Mike's cannoli (which I call "Proustian" and "delicious") than Alex's counterintuitive conviction to boycott Mike's Pastry because Bill Clinton and bus tours went there. When his own grandparents had come to town asking about "that bakery the president likes," Alex shanghaied them across Hanover Street to Modern Pastry—a shop serving an adequate cannoli and not one headshot. God forbid they be suckered into the sublime, "touristy" rendition at Mike's.

I admit, though, that I'm prone to thinking like Alex when I travel. Maybe you are too. We'll come upon this fabulous Japanese *izakaya* or Czech jazz club or Parisian zinc bar—some corner of the universe that seems to have been created to our own specifications—and then, suddenly, all these other people show up. And then more of them. And then still more. Ohhhhhh, this is all wrong, we think; our beloved discovery is a *tourist trap*.

Yet recently I got to wondering: maybe it was my worrying that was all wrong. What did I really care about the presence or absence of fellow travelers, or the character thereof? Was this precious zinc bar so fragile it couldn't withstand the affection of a hundred other like-minded visitors? Perhaps it wasn't the place that needed saving, but my outlook. Doesn't every traveler start out as a tourist?

You know how politicians are always saying this is no time to engage in politics? Well, what *politics* is to politics, *tourist* is to tourism. and *touristy* has devolved from "of or relating to tourists" to "ignoble, tacky, cloying, ersatz." For travel writers, *touristy* is the ultimate slander. Even *flea-ridden flophouse* seems less damning. We're forever distinguishing between hip travelers and sheeplike tourists. We parse the world's offerings into things tourists do versus things "locals" do, as if the mere act of residing somewhere confers a sense of style. For all the times I've indulged that facile distinction, I offer my apologies. Because frankly, this ridiculous fixation on what is and what isn't "touristy"—and who is or isn't a "tourist"—can ruin a vacation.

In the age of mass tourism, high-end travel becomes increasingly about exclusivity—seeking out isolated places and rarefied encounters that only a lucky few can enjoy. (It was easier back in the day: when Delacroix visited Tangier, there were no bus tours to flee from.) By this equation, the merit of an experience corresponds inversely to the number of people we're obliged to share it with. In the urge to legitimize, singularize, and privatize our travel experiences, we trade the proverbial hell of other people for the hell of trying in vain to avoid other people. That's a terribly cool way to travel, and when I say *cool* I mean chilly, and when I say *chilly* I mean obnoxious.

Sure, certain places are so extraordinary we forgive them their teeming hordes. No traveler could honestly dismiss as tourist traps the terra-cotta warriors at Xi'an, Machu Picchu, the Taj Mahal, or the British Museum. But when it comes to choosing what other sites to visit, where to have dinner, or which show to see that evening, we go out of our way to leave the hoi polloi behind. Exclusivity threatens to become an end in itself, wherein we base our itineraries not on what's actually worth seeing but on where other Americans aren't.

For most of my life, I believed independent travel was the only route to the real unfiltered stuff. I eschewed group experiences like the plague, running from cruises, luaus, dinner shows, and, most of all, anything incorporating the word "tour": carriage tours, walking tours, eight-seat tandem-bike tours, gondola tours, duck-boat tours, harbor tours, sunset harbor tours, ghost tours, foliage tours . . . To me they all sounded silly and artificial. Why would I actually plan to put other people between me and what I'd come to see?

My mistake. Since being cajoled into what turned out to be a brilliant London Walks ramble through Hampstead Heath, I've gained some of my best travel memories from being herded around with a bunch of strangers—on a Big Onion Walking Tour of Irish New York; on a twenty-person nature trek in the Malaysian jungle; on a National Park Service stroll through new Orleans's French Quarter under the tutelage of an erudite ranger in a funny hat. It struck me that independent travelers, so adamant about seeing the world on their own terms, tend not to line up to listen to People Who Know Things, and therefore tend not to learn about, say, the Great Boston Molasses Flood of 1919. Seriously, Google that. I lived in Boston for years, yet the first time I heard of this sticky and surreal episode was on a Boston Duck Tours boat with my nephew.

Being a tourist can give you access to experiences you wouldn't have otherwise—experiences that aren't so much exclusive as *inclusive*, drawing their appeal from the company of other people. Independent travel may offer the tantalizing possibility of disappearing into a place, nametagless, and acting the part of the vaunted native, but that rarely pans out. Traveling solo through India, I always expected some local shopkeeper or templegoer to invite me home for chai and divulge all the secrets of the culture. Never happened. Last year a couple I know took a Road Scholar tour of Rajasthan with a dozen other Americans; every day they shared tea or a home-cooked meal with Rajasthanis, several of whom they still correspond with. If that's "touristy," somebody strap a Nikon around my neck.

Snooty travelers would instinctively dismiss a place like Bukhara as a feedlot for tourist cattle. Every New Delhi guidebook recommends this boisterous kebab restaurant, which is why it's always packed to its exposed rafters. Whole planeloads of tour groups come through Bukhara each evening, and guess what: they're having a way better meal than you are tonight. The chicken and lamb kebabs are easily the best I've tasted (and not a word to my Iranian mother-in-law). After one visit, Bukhara shot to the top of my Really Is list—as in, "No, no, it *really is* that good." I laughed and thought of my old friend Alex as I scanned the house specialties: the "Presidential" platter and the "Chelsea" platter, the former named after Alex's North End cannoli nemesis, who dined here during a state visit to India in 2000. Judging from the proportions of their namesake dishes, Bill and Chelsea Clinton not only took a village, they devoured most of its livestock. Yet the crowd at Bukhara is so consumed with enjoying themselves that one can imagine the Clintons hardly making a stir. British honeymooners, Elderhostel groups from Sarasota, Kuwaiti businessmen, Indian clans with toddlers in tow—all are having a blast. And in the ultimate mark of a proud tourist haunt, every last patron is wearing a gingham bib.

The problem with the term "touristy" is that it broadly applies to—and condemns—a whole lot of things that are merely guilty of being popular with out-of-towners. The leather-bound guest directory at New Orleans's Ritz-Carlton recommends a night at Vaughan's Lounge with Kermit Ruffins & the Barbecue Swingers. If I were a hotel guest directory, I would too: Ruffins's Thursday sets at Vaughan's are incendiary, and a favorite even among (ahem) locals. Should it matter that a bunch of people from Minneapolis and Osaka are there too? When something inherently cool is adopted by tourists, does that render it uncool? In Reykjavík, Iceland, the Islandia shop is exactly what you'd expect of a state-sponsored tourist emporium, packed with souvenir puffin dolls, die-cast Viking figurines, and overpriced wool sweaters for your dad. They also sell the complete discographies of Björk, Sigur Rós, and the Sugarcubes. So: Is Björk "touristy"? Is Kermit Ruffins? No. The answer is no.

Considering that only 28 percent of Americans have passports, you sort of have to hand it to anyone who leaves home in the first place, no matter how often they show up in your photos of the Pont Neuf. Rather than resenting your compatriots for the audacity of choosing the same vacation spot as you, why not tip your hat to them for having found their way there at all? Would that more of us had the time and money to travel. As for cynical travelers, they can arguably learn, or relearn, something from the wide-eyed "tourist"—from the sense of wonder and unmitigated joy he brings to those top-of-the-Eiffel-Tower, crest-of-the-Cyclone, edge-of-the-Grand-Canyon moments that all travelers, no matter how jaded, long for. This involves surrendering to the inherent awkwardness of being a stranger in a foreign land, yet somehow losing yourself—and your self-consciousness—at the same time. It means letting go of the suspicion, letting down the defenses, and allowing for a genuine response, even if that response is simply "*Wow.*" It means enjoying a Central Park carriage ride or a London walking tour or a sunset cruise on San Francisco Bay without second-guessing whether you should be doing so. It means finally quieting—or ignoring—that nagging inner voice that asks, Do I dare to eat a peach? Or are peaches just a little too . . . touristy?

SUSAN ORLEAN

Where Donkeys Deliver

FROM *Smithsonian*

THE DONKEY I COULDN'T FORGET was coming around a corner in the walled city of Fez, Morocco, with six color televisions
strapped to his back. If I could tell you the exact intersection
where I saw him, I would do so, but pinpointing a location in Fez
is a formidable challenge, a little like noting GPS coordinates in a
spiderweb. I might be able to be more precise about where I saw
the donkey if I knew how to extrapolate location using the position of the sun, but I don't. Moreover, there wasn't any sun to be
seen and barely a sliver of sky, because leaning in all around me
were the sheer walls of the medina—the old walled portion of Fez
—where the buildings are so packed and stacked together that
they seem to have been carved out of a single huge stone rather
than constructed individually, clustered so tightly that they blot out
the shrieking blue and silver of the Moroccan sky.

The best I can do is to say that the donkey and I met at the intersection of one path that was about as wide as a bathmat and
another that was slightly larger—call it a bath sheet. The Koran
actually specifies the ideal width of a road—seven cubits, or the
width of three mules—but I would wager that some of Fez's paths
fall below Koranic standards. They were laid out in the late eighth
century by Idriss I, founder of the dynasty that spread Islam in Morocco, and they are so narrow that bumping into another person
or a pushcart is no accident; it is simply the way you move forward,
your progress more like a pinball than a pedestrian, bouncing from
one fixed object to the next, brushing by a man chiseling names
into grave markers only to slam into a drum maker stretching goat

skin on a drying rack, then to carom off a southbound porter hauling luggage in a wire cart.

In the case of my meeting the donkey, the collision was low-
impact. The donkey was small. His shoulders were about waist-high,
no higher; his chest was narrow; his legs straight; his hooves quite
delicate, about the size of a teacup. He—or she, perhaps—was
donkey-colored, that is, a soft mouse gray, with a light-colored muz-
zle and dark-brown fur bristling out of his ears. The televisions,
however, were big—boxy tabletop sets, not portables. Four were
loaded on the donkey's back, secured in a crazy jumble by a tangle of plastic twine and bungee cords. The remaining two were attached to the donkey's flanks, one on each side, like panniers on a
bicycle. The donkey stood squarely under this staggering load. He
walked along steadily, making the turn crisply and then continuing
up the smaller path, which was so steep that it had little stone stairs
every yard or two where the gain was especially abrupt. I caught
only a glimpse of his face as he passed, but it was utterly endearing, all at once serene and weary and determined. There may have
been a man walking beside him, but I was too transfixed by the
sight of the donkey to remember.

This encounter was a decade ago, on my first trip to Fez, and
even amid the dazzle of images and sounds you are struck with in
Morocco—the green hills splattered with red poppies, the gorgeous tiled patterning on every surface, the keening call from the
mosques, the swirl of Arabic lettering everywhere—the donkey
was what stayed with me. It was that stoic expression, of course. But
even more, it was seeing, in that moment, the astonishing commin-
gling of past and present—the timeless little animal, the medieval
city, and the pile of electronics—that made me believe that it was
possible for time to simultaneously move forward and stand still.
In Fez, at least, that seems to be true.

Just a mile outside Casablanca's Mohammed V Airport, on the side
of a four-lane high-speed roadway, underneath a billboard for a
cellular service provider, a dark-brown donkey ambled along, four
huge sacks filled to bursting strapped to a makeshift harness on his
back. I had been back in Morocco for less than an hour. My recollection already felt concrete—that there were donkeys everywhere
in the country, that they operated like little pistons, moving people

and things to and fro, defying the wave of modernity that was washing gently over the country—and that the television donkey of Fez
had not been just an odd and singular anecdote.

On my first trip to Morocco, I had seen the television donkey
and then countless more, trudging through Fez with loads of groceries, propane tanks, sacks of spices, bolts of fabrics, construction
material. When my trip was over and I returned home, I realized
I had fallen in love with donkeys in general, with the plain ten-
derness of their faces and their attitude of patient resignation and
even their occasionally baffling, intractable moods. In the United
States, most donkeys are kept as pets and their pessimism seems
almost comical. In Morocco, I knew that the look of resignation
was often coupled with a bleaker look of fatigue and sometimes de-
spair, because they are work animals, worked hard and sometimes
thanklessly. But seeing them as something so purposeful—not a
novelty in a tourist setting but an integral part of Moroccan daily
life—made me love them even more, as flea-bitten and saddle-sore
and scrawny as some of them were.

The medina in Fez may well be the largest urbanized area in the
world impassable to cars and trucks, where anything that a human
being can't carry or push in a handcart is conveyed by a donkey,
a horse, or a mule. If you need lumber and rebar to add a new
room to your house in the medina, a donkey will carry it in for you.
If you have a heart attack while building the new room on your
house, a donkey might well serve as your ambulance and carry you
out. If you realize your new room didn't solve the overcrowding in
your house and you decide to move to a bigger house, donkeys will
carry your belongings and furniture from your old house to your
new one. Your garbage is picked up by donkeys; your food supplies
are delivered to the medina's stores and restaurants by mule; when
you decide to decamp from the tangle of the medina, donkeys
might carry your luggage out or carry it back in when you decide
to return. In Fez, it has always been thus, and so it will always be.
No car is small enough or nimble enough to squeeze through the
medina's byways; most motorbikes cannot make it up the steep,
slippery alleys. The medina is now a World Heritage site. Its roads
can never be widened, and they will never be changed; the donkeys
might carry in computers and flat-screen televisions and satellite
dishes and video equipment, but they will never be replaced.

I am not the first American woman to be fascinated by the working animals of the medina. In 1927, Amy Bend Bishop, wife of eccentric, wealthy gallery owner Cortlandt Field Bishop, passed through Fez on a grand tour of Europe and the Mediterranean, and was intrigued by the forty thousand donkeys and mules working at the time. She was also disturbed by their poor condition, and she donated $8,000—the equivalent of at least $100,000 today—to establish a free veterinary service in Fez. The service was named the American Fondouk—*fondouk* is Arabic for "inn"—and after a stint in temporary quarters the clinic opened up in a white-washed compound built around a shaded courtyard on the Route de Taza, a busy highway just outside the medina, where it has operated ever since. The Fondouk has become well known in Fez, even among the animals. Dozens of times creatures have shown up at the Fondouk's massive front gate, unaccompanied, needing help; just days before I arrived, for instance, a donkey having some sort of neurological crisis stumbled in on its own. It is possible that these wanderers were left at the door by their owners before the Fondouk opened in the early morning, but Fez and Morocco and the American Fondouk all seem to be magical places, and after spending even a few hours in Fez, the idea that animals find their own way to the Fondouk's shady courtyard doesn't seem unlikely at all.

The highway from Casablanca to Fez rushes past fields and farms, along the edge of the busy cities of Rabat, the capital, and Meknes, rolling up and down golden hills and grassy valleys, lush with swaths of yellow broom and chamomile in bloom, and, dotted among them, hot-red poppies. The highway looks new; it could be a freshly built road anywhere in the world, but several mules trotted across the overpasses as we zoomed underneath, claiming the image as Morocco.

King Mohammed VI makes frequent visits from Rabat to Fez; some speculate that he might relocate the capital there. The king's presence is palpable. The Fez that I encountered ten years ago was dusty, crumbling, clamorous, jammed. Since then there's been restoration at the massive royal palace; at least a dozen fountains and plazas now line a long, elegant boulevard where there used to be a buckling road. New development followed the royal family's interest in the city; as we headed to the Fondouk, we drove past a gaping excavation soon to be the Atlas Fez Hotel and Spa and a score of billboards touting shiny condominiums such as "Happy New World" and "Fez New Home."

But the medina looked exactly as I remembered it, the dun-colored buildings tight together, hive-like; the twisting paths disappearing into shadow; the crowds of people, slim and columnar in their hooded *jalabas,* hurrying along, dodging and sidestepping to make their way. It is rackety, bustling. I chased after my porter, who was wheeling a handcart with my luggage from the car. We had parked it outside the medina, near the gorgeous swoop of Bab Bou Jeloud, the Blue Gate, one of the handful of entryways into the walled city. In a moment, I heard someone shout, *"Balak, balak!"*—Make way, make way!—and a donkey carrying boxes marked AGRICO came up behind us, his owner continuing to holler and gesture to part the crowd. And in a few moments came another donkey, carrying rusty orange propane tanks. And in a few moments, another one, wearing a harness but carrying nothing at all, picking his way down one of the steepest little roads. As far as I could tell, the donkey was alone; there was no one in front of him or beside him, no one behind. I wondered if he was lost, or had broken away from his handler, so I asked the porter, who looked at me with surprise. The donkey wasn't lost, the man said. He was probably done with work and on his way home.

Where do the donkeys of the medina live? Some live on farms outside the walls and are brought in for work each day, but many live inside. Before we got to my hotel, the porter stopped and knocked on a door. From the outside, it looked like any of the thousands of doorways of any of the thousands of medina houses, but the young man who answered the door led us through a foyer, where it appeared he had been practicing electric guitar, to a low-ceilinged room, a bit damp but not unpleasant, the floor strewn with fava beans and salad greens and a handful of hay. A brown goat with a puppy-size newborn kid sat in a corner, observing us with a look of cross-eyed intensity. The young man said that ten donkeys lived in the house; they were stabled in the room each night, but they were all out working during the day.

So a good donkey is respected and valued—it is estimated that 100,000 people in the Fez area depend in one way or another on a donkey for their livelihood—but the animals are not sentimental-ized. Out of habit, every time I spoke to someone with a donkey, I asked the donkey's name. The first man I asked hesitated and then answered, "H'mar." The second man I asked also hesitated and then answered, "H'mar," and I assumed that I had just stum-bled upon the most popular name in Morocco for donkeys, the way you might by chance meet several dogs in the United States named Riley or Tucker or Max. When the third told me his don-key's name was H'mar, I realized it couldn't be a coincidence, and then I learned that *H'mar* is not a name—it's just the Arabic word for "donkey." In Morocco, donkeys serve, and they are cared for, but they are not pets. One afternoon, I was talking to a man with a donkey in the medina and asked him why he didn't give his don-key a name. He laughed and said, "He doesn't need a name. He's a taxi."

I woke up early to try to beat the crowd to the Fondouk. The doors open at seven-thirty each morning, and usually there is a crowd of animals already outside the gate by then, waiting to be examined. I have seen old photographs of the Fondouk from the 1930s, and it is uncannily unchanged; the Route de Taza is prob-ably busier and louder now, but the handsome white wall of the Fondouk with its enormous arched wooden door is unmistakable, as is the throng of donkeys and mules at the front door, their own-ers, dressed in the same somber long robes that they still wear to-day, close by their side. In those old pictures, as is still the case, an American flag is flying from the Fondouk's walls; it is the only place in Morocco I know of besides the U.S. Embassy to display an American flag.

These days, the Fondouk's chief veterinarian is Denys Frappier, a silver-haired Canadian who had come to the Fondouk planning to stay just two years, but fifteen years have now gone by and he has yet to manage to leave. He lives in a pleasant house within the Fon-douk property—the old stables, converted to the staff residence sixty years ago—along with ten cats, nine dogs, four turtles, and a donkey, all of them animals who were either left here for care by their owners, who never came to get them, or were walk-ins who never walked out. In the case of the donkey, a tiny knock-kneed creature whose Arabic name means "Trouble," he was born here but his mother died during birth, and the owner wasn't interested

in taking care of a baby donkey, so he left it behind. Trouble is the
Fondouk pet; he likes to visit the exam room and sometimes snuf-
fle through the papers in the Fondouk office. An awkward, ill-built
animal with a huge head and a tiny body, he was adopted by the
veterinary students who were doing internships at the Fondouk;
one of them used to let the newborn donkey sleep in her bed in
the small student dormitory. When I arrived that morning, Trouble was following Dr. Frappier around the courtyard, watching him
on his rounds. "He is nothing but trouble," Dr. Frappier said, looking at the donkey with affectionate exasperation, "but what can
I do?"

Previously, Dr. Frappier had been the chief veterinarian of the
Canadian Olympic Equestrian Team, tending to pampered performance horses worth $100,000 or more. His patients at the Fon-
douk are quite different. That morning's lineup included a bony
white mule who was lame; a donkey with deep harness sores and
one blind eye; another donkey with knobby hips and intestinal
problems; a hamster with a corneal injury; a flock of three sheep;
several dogs with various aches and pains; and a newborn kitten
with a crushed leg. A wrinkled old man came in just behind me,
carrying a mewling lamb in a shopping bag. By 8 A.M., another six
mules and donkeys had gathered in the Fondouk's courtyard, their
owners clutching little wooden numbers and waiting to be called.

The Fondouk's original mission was to serve the working animals of Morocco, but long ago it began to dispense free care to all
manner of living things, with the exception of cattle—a luxury in
Morocco, and therefore free care seemed unnecessary—and pit
bulls. "I was tired of patching them up so the owners could take
them out and fight with them again," Dr. Frappier said, as he was
checking the hooves of the lame mule. The mule was poorly shod,
as are many of the donkeys and mules in the medina, with rubber pads cut out of old automobile tires; the corners of his mouth
were rubbed raw by a harsh bit; he would have looked better if he
weighed another thirty or forty pounds. It took Dr. Frappier several years to adjust to the condition of the animals here; at first
he was utterly discouraged and put in a request to resign his post
and return to Montreal, but he settled in, and he has learned to
sort out "dire" from "acceptable." The Fondouk has quietly pushed
an agenda of better care, and in large part it has been successful:

it managed to spread the word to the mule and donkey owners that sticking cactus thorns in harness sores didn't encourage the animals to work harder, and that rubbing salt in their eyes, a folk remedy to get them to walk faster, was not only ineffective but left the animals blind. There are animals everywhere you look in Fez, and in Morocco. Cats tiptoe around every corner; dogs lounge in the North African sun; even on the roaring roads of Casablanca, horse-and-buggies clatter alongside SUVs and sedans. Twelve full-time veterinarians work in Fez, but even so, on two separate occasions the royal family of Morocco, which could certainly afford any veterinarian in the world, has brought its animals to the Fondouk.

On my first trip to Morocco, I had heard of Souk el Khemis-des Zemamra, one of the country's largest donkey markets, held every Thursday, about two hours southwest of Casablanca, and ever since hearing of it I had wanted to go. I wanted to see the epicenter of the donkey universe in Morocco, where thousands of creatures are bought and sold and traded. A few years ago, the government began visiting Khemis-des Zemamra and the other large souks to take stock of the transactions and levy sales tax on them, and since then more of the trade has migrated away from the souks toward word-of-mouth impromptu markets, out of reach of the tax man. The number of donkeys sold in Khemis-des Zemamra these days is perhaps a third less than what it was five years ago. Still, the souks thrive—besides donkeys, of course, they sell every single food product and toiletry and household item and farm implement you could ever imagine, serving as a combination Agway, Wal-Mart, Mall of America, and Stop & Shop for the entire population for miles around. If you want chickpeas or hair dye or a fishing net or a saddle or a soup pot, you can find it at the souk. If you want a donkey, you will certainly find the one you want any Thursday morning in Khemis-des Zemamra.

I set out on the five-hour drive from Fez to Khemis-des Zemamra on a Wednesday night. The market starts at the crack of dawn; by noon, when the sun is searing, the fairground where it takes place would be empty, the grass trampled down, the mud marked with wagon wheel tracks and hoof prints. I was traveling there with a young Moroccan man named Omar Ansor, whose father had worked at the American Fondouk for twenty-five years until his recent retirement; Omar's brother, Mohammed, has been working there with Dr. Frappier since 1994. Omar told me he loves animals, but he found my fascination with donkeys puzzling. Like many Moroccans, he considered them tools—good, useful tools, but nothing more. Maybe to him, my enthusiasm about donkeys was like being enthusiastic about wheelbarrows. "A donkey is just a donkey," he said. "I like horses."

The drive took us back past Casablanca, with its smoking chimneys and thicket of apartment buildings, and then to El Jadida, a whitewashed resort town on a flat spread of pinkish beach, where we stayed the night. Thursday morning was warm and clear, the light pouring over wide fields of corn and wheat. In several fields, donkeys and mules were already at work, pulling irrigation machines and plows, leaning into their harnesses. Carts hurtled alongside us on the shoulder of the road, loaded with entire families and nearly toppling loads of bulging burlap bags, boxes, and miscellany, heading in the direction of the souk, the donkey or mule or horse moving snappily, as if the sound of the car traffic was egging them on. By the time we arrived, just after 7 A.M., the fairground was already mobbed. We had no trouble parking, because there were only a handful of cars and another handful of trucks, but the rest of the parking area was cluttered with wagons and carts and scores of donkeys and mules—a few hundred of them at least, dozing, nibbling on the scraps of grass, swaying in place, hobbled by a bit of plastic twine tied around their ankles. These weren't for sale—they were transportation, and they were parked while their owners were shopping.

A roar floated over the fairground; it was the combined chatter of hundreds of buyers and sellers haggling, and the smack and thump of boxes being opened and sacks being slapped down to be filled, and vendors hollering for attention and a blast of Moroccan music playing out of an unattended laptop computer that was hooked to man-size speakers, beneath a tent of fabric cut from a Nokia cell-phone billboard. We walked in through a section of the souk where vendors sat behind mountains of dried beans in baskets four feet wide, and past stalls selling fried fish and kebabs, the greasy smoky air trapped in the tents, and then we arrived at the donkey area. At the entrance were rows and rows of vendors selling donkey and mule supplies. A young man, deep furrows in his face, was selling bits made of rusty iron—his inventory, hundreds of bits, was in a stack three feet high. Beside him, a family sat on a blanket surrounded by harnesses made of tan and orange and white nylon webbing, and every member of the family, including the children, was stitching new harnesses while they waited to sell the ones they had already made. The next row had a dozen stalls, all offering donkey saddles—V-shaped wooden forms that sit on the animal's back and support the cart shafts. The saddles were made out of old chair legs and scrap lumber, the corners nailed together with squares cut from old tin cans; they were rough-looking but sturdy, and they had thick padding where they would rest on the animal's skin.

Just past the saddle sellers was a small field jammed with donkeys for sale, their owners scanning the crowd for buyers, the buyers strolling among them, stopping to glance at one, size up another. There was much milling around, the crowd moving in and out of the clusters of donkeys; the donkeys, though, stood quietly, nodding off in the warming sun, idly chewing a bit of grass, flicking off flies. They were a rainbow of browns, from dusty tan to almost chocolate, some sleek, others with the last patches of their thick winter coats. For someone who loves donkeys, it was an amazing sight. I stopped near one dealer who was in the center of the field. A small woman with piercing blue eyes, covered head to toe in black fabric, was completing her transaction—she had traded her older donkey and some cash to the dealer for a younger animal. The donkey dealer was tying a hobble on his new acquisition, and when he finished, he told me he was having a busy day and had sold eight donkeys already that morning. His name was Mohammed, and his farm was ten miles from the souk; he brought his load of donkeys here on the back of a flatbed truck. It was a good line of work. His family had always been donkey dealers—his mother and his father, his grandparents, their grandparents—and business was steady, fifty donkeys or so sold each week. He had brought eleven donkeys to the souk that morning, so he had three small, sturdy animals left.

"How old is this one?" I asked, patting the smallest of them.

"He's three years old," Mohammed said. As he said this, a young man behind him grabbed his elbow and moved him aside and said, "No, no, he's only one."

"Well, is he three years old or one year old?"

"Uh, yes," Mohammed said. "And very strong." He leaned down and began untying the donkey's hobble. "You will not find a better donkey here at the souk. Just give me fifteen thousand dirhams."

I explained that I lived in New York and that it didn't seem practical for me to buy a donkey in Khemis-des Zemamra. Moreover, the price—the equivalent of about eighteen hundred dollars—sounded exorbitant. Donkeys here usually go for under seven hundred dirhams.

"Tell me, what is the price you want to pay?" Mohammed asked. He was a dark-skinned man with sharp features and a loud chesty laugh. He led the donkey a few feet away, and then turned him in a circle, displaying his fine points. By now a crowd of other donkey sellers was gathering. I explained again that I was not being coy, that as much as I would love to buy the donkey, it was more impractical than even I, an often impetuous shopper, could possibly be.

"Then we'll make it twelve thousand dirhams," he said, firmly. "Very good."

By this time, the crowd had become emotionally invested in the idea that I might buy the donkey; a gaggle of little boys had joined in, and they were giggling and jumping up and down with excitement, dodging under the donkey's head to glance at me, and then dashing away. The donkey was unperturbed by the commotion; he seemed wise, as they all seem to be, to the fleeting nature of the moment, and the inconsequential nature of the outcome, that life would just roll on as it has, and will, for thousands of years, and that certain things like the hard work of animals and the mysterious air of the medina and the curious and contradictory nature of all of Morocco will probably never change.

I left without that small, sturdy donkey, who was undoubtedly named H'mar, but I know that if I return to that field in Khemis-des Zemamra years from now, I will find another brown donkey for sale with the exact same air of permanence and the exact same name.

DAVID OWEN

The Ghost Course

FROM *The New Yorker*

IN 2005, A SCOTTISH GOLF COURSE consultant named Gordon Irvine took a fishing trip to South Uist, a sparsely populated island in the Outer Hebrides, fifty miles off Scotland's west coast. South Uist (pronounced YEW-ist) is about the size of Martha's Vineyard and Nantucket combined. It is virtually treeless, and much of its eastern third is mountainous and uninhabited. Gales from the Atlantic strike it with such force that schoolchildren hope for "wind days." Irvine had approached the island's golf club, called Askernish, and offered to barter greenkeeping advice for the right to fish for trout and salmon in the lochs nearby, and the club had welcomed the free consultation. It had just nine holes and a few dozen members, and the golfers themselves mowed the greens, with a rusting gang mower pulled by a tractor. Irvine walked the course, in driving rain, with the club's chairman, Ralph Thompson, and several regulars, and then the group went to lunch at the Borrodale Hotel, a mile and a half down the road.

At lunch, one of the members surprised Irvine by saying that Askernish was more than a century old and had been designed by Old Tom Morris, a towering figure in the history and folklore of the game. Morris, who was born in 1821 and looked a little like Charles Darwin in an ivy cap, was the founding father of modern golf. In the 1860s, he won four of the first eight British Opens and became the head professional of the Royal and Ancient Golf Club of St. Andrews, serving there for four decades as the chief greenkeeper of the Old Course, golf's holiest ground. He also designed or redesigned several of the world's greatest courses, among them

Muirfield, Prestwick, and Carnoustie, in Scotland, and Royal County Down, in Northern Ireland.

Irvine was polite but dismissive: the course he'd walked that morning was a cow pasture with flagsticks stuck in the ground, and he doubted that Morris, whose courses he knew well, had ever come near it. But another club member said that this was not the original Askernish, and that Old Tom's layout had had eighteen holes and was situated closer to the sea. Most of the original holes, apparently, had been abandoned, probably beginning around the time of the Second World War. Ralph Thompson said that the club possessed a news clipping from 1891 which described Morris's creation of the course that year, and which quoted Morris calling the layout "second to none." Irvine was curious enough to take another look, and after lunch Thompson drove him back.

This time, Thompson led him to a grassy dune at the western end of the seventh hole, and when Irvine climbed to the top and looked toward the Atlantic he saw a stretch of undulating linksland running along the ocean, between the beach and the existing holes. For Irvine, the experience was like lifting the corner of a yard-sale velvet painting and discovering a Rembrandt. There were no surviving signs of golf holes in the waving marram grass, but the terrain, which had been shaped by the wind into valleys, hollows, and meandering ridges, looked so spectacularly suited to the game that he no longer doubted the Morris connection. Despite the rain, Irvine could easily imagine greens and fairways among the dunes, and he told Thompson that, if the club's members would agree to work with him, he would donate his time and expertise, and help them restore their lost masterpiece. A resurrected Askernish, he said, would provide a unique window on the birth of the modern game.

Not everyone on South Uist was pleased with this idea. The land in question had long been used as a common grazing area by local tenant farmers, called crofters, and a group of them protested that the construction of golf holes would violate their legal rights. One of the crofters described the golf project as a "land grab," and said that old property documents relating to the area made no mention of Old Tom Morris. For the aggrieved crofters, the plans brought to mind one of the most notorious periods of Scottish history, the Highland Clearances. Beginning in the eighteenth century, wealthy landlords gained possession of large sections of northern Scotland, which until then had been controlled by Gaelic-speaking clans. The new landlords attempted to impose what they viewed as economic rationality on their holdings, most of which were still farmed and grazed as they had been during the Dark Ages, by subsistence farmers working tiny plots. This transformation, which has been described as the wholesale substitution of sheep for people, involved waves of eviction, consolidation, and forced expatriation. By the late nineteenth century, the chieftains of the northern clans had either sold out to others or become landlords themselves, and the old Gaelic culture had been weakened or obliterated in many places, and sentimentalized elsewhere. A fad for kilts, tartans, and bagpipes took hold in the rest of the country, even as genuine Highlanders were being shipped off to Canada or put to work in the factories of Birmingham.

The Askernish project seemed, to the protesting crofters, like the clearances all over again. Ralph Thompson soon began to speak of making the restored Askernish—which the sportswriter John Garrity has described as a "ghost course"—the anchor of a much larger development, including additional golf courses and a hotel. He created a Web site and solicited nonresident life memberships, at £2,500 apiece, in the hope that fees from abroad would help to finance the construction. The crofters complained that the club's members were courting golf-playing "dandies" from the mainland and the United States, and were doing so at their expense. "What a cheek," one crofter said this past December. "They have gone on top of our *grazing* land and done with it what they want." The crofters began legal action to stop them.

Getting to South Uist today isn't as hard as it was in 1891, when the sole option was a slow, unreliable steamer, but it still requires determination. When I visited the first time, in 2007, I flew from Inverness to Benbecula, one island to the north; South Uist doesn't have its own airport but is connected to Benbecula by a half-mile-long causeway. In the air, I looked down, through breaks in the clouds, on the fjord-like creases that rumple Scotland's west coast and on the waters of the Minch, the stormy channel that separates the Outer Hebrides from mainland Scotland. This past December, I visited again, taking a ferry from Oban, which is a two-and-a-half-hour drive from Glasgow, by way of Loch Lomond. The ferry sails three or four times a week and sometimes makes a brief stop at Barra, which has a tiny airport whose schedule depends on the tides, since the runway is a beach. The South Uist ferry passes Mull, Coll, Muck, Eigg, Rum, Sanday, Sandray, Vatersay, Hellisay, Gigha, and other small islands, and in good weather the trip takes about six and a half hours. Until 1974, cars had to be loaded and unloaded with a crane, like freight; nowadays, you drive on and drive off.

The first time I visited South Uist, Ralph Thompson, the Askernish chairman, came to meet me. He manages the island's main agricultural-supply store, which stocks sheep feed, onion sets, shotguns, and other local necessities. He was born on the mainland in 1955, but as a child, he spent summers on South Uist, where his grandparents lived. One reason he liked those visits, he told me, was that he was allowed to go for weeks without bathing, because his grandparents' house, like almost all houses on the island at that time, had no running water.

Even today, South Uist is short on modern conveniences. The lights went out one afternoon as Thompson and I were having a beer in the bar at the Borrodale, and he began counting. When he got to "five," the lights came back on, and he said, "If you count to five and the power comes back, it means a swan hit the line." Later, we drove south on the island's main road—a single lane for most of its length, with frequent bump-outs for yielding to oncoming traffic and for overtaking sheep—and crossed a causeway to Eriskay, a smaller island. Thompson spotted, in the distance, a ferryboat approaching from Barra, and he pulled over to watch it. He wasn't expecting anyone, but there are so few activities on South Uist that residents have evolved an unusually low threshold of amusement. We watched the ferry for fifteen or twenty minutes, and didn't pull away until the last of a handful of departing passengers had boarded.

Sometimes, entertainment arrives on the island unexpectedly. Early in 1941, a freighter, the SS *Politician*, ran aground in the sandy shallows between South Uist and Eriskay. Its cargo included more than twenty thousand cases of whiskey, and over several weeks, groups of islanders rowed to the wreck and made off with thousands of bottles. They hid the whiskey in cowsheds, rabbit holes, and lobster traps—and significant portions of the adult population of several Hebridean islands stayed drunk for weeks. In 1947, the Scottish novelist Compton Mackenzie wrote a fictional-ized account of the wreck and its aftermath, called *Whisky Galore.* Two years later, the book was made into a movie, filmed mostly on Barra. For its release in the United States, it was retitled *Tight Little Island;* too late, James Thurber suggested *Scotch on the Rocks.*

Most people think of the word "links" as a synonym for "golf course," but it's actually a geological term. Linksland is a specific type of sandy, wind-sculpted coastal terrain—the word comes from the Old English *hlinc,* "rising ground"—and in its authentic form it exists in only a few places on earth, the most famous of which are in Great Britain and Ireland. Linksland arose at the end of the most recent ice age, when the retreat of the northern glacial sheet, accompanied by changes in sea level, exposed sandy deposits and what had once been coastal shelves. Wind pushed the sand into dunes and rippling plains, ocean storms added more sand, and coarse grasses covered everything. Early Britons used linksland mainly for livestock grazing, since the ground closest to the sea was usually too starved and too exposed for growing crops. When significant numbers of Scotsmen became interested in smacking small balls with curved wooden sticks, as they first did in 1400 or so, the links was where they went (or were sent), perhaps because there they were in no one's way. On South Uist, linksland is called *machair,* a Gaelic word. It's pronounced "mocker," more or less, but with the two central consonants represented by what sounds like a clearing of the throat.

The major design elements of a modern golf course are the syn-thetic analogues of various existing features of those early Scottish playing fields, and the fact that golf arose so directly from a par-ticular landscape helps explain why, more than any other main-stream sport, it remains a game with a Jerusalem: it was perma-nently shaped by the ground on which it was invented. Groomed fairways are the descendants of the well-grazed valleys between the old linksland dunes; bunkers began as sandy depressions worn through thin turf by livestock huddling against coastal gales; the first greens and teeing grounds were flattish, elevated areas whose relatively short grass—closely grazed by rabbits and other animals and stunted by the brutal weather—made them the logical places to begin and end holes. ("A rabbit's jawbone allows it to graze grass lower than a sheep," Gordon Irvine told me recently, "and both those animals can graze grass lower than a cow.")

On the great old courses in the British Isles, the most celebrated holes often owe more to serendipity and to the vicissitudes of animal husbandry than they do to picks and shovels, since in the early years course design was more nearly an act of imagination and discovery than of physical construction. One of Old Tom Morris's best-known holes, the fifth at Lahinch, in southwestern Ireland, is a short par 3 whose green is concealed behind a tall dune, so that the golfer's target is invisible from the tee—a feature that almost any contemporary architect would have eliminated with a bulldozer. The greatest hole on the Old Course at St. Andrews is often said to be the seventeenth, a long par 4 called the Road Hole, which violates a list of modern design rules: the tee shot not only is blind but must be hit over the top of a tall wooden structure that reproduces the silhouette of a cluster of old railway sheds; the green repels approach shots from every direction and is fronted by a vortex-like circular bunker, from which the most prudent escape is often backward, away from the green; a paved public road runs directly alongside the green and is treated as a part of the course, meaning that golfers who play their way onto it must also play their way off. Over the centuries, every idiosyncratic inch of the Old Course has acquired, for the faithful, an almost numinous aura.

For Gordon Irvine, Askernish was in some ways an even more compelling historical artifact than the Old Course—so much so that shortly after his first visit to the course he called it "the holy grail." Unlike most other early links courses, Askernish had never been stretched to accommodate high-tech clubs and balls, and its original quirks had not been worn smooth, over the years, by motorized maintenance equipment. "Askernish was as Old Tom left it," Irvine told me. "Because the old holes were abandoned so early, there had been no real proactive maintenance done with machinery or chemicals, and it had never been revisited by other architects. The last time the old holes were played, the greens were probably cut with scythes."

In 2006, he enlisted the help of Martin Ebert, a golf architect whose specialty is links courses. No plan of Morris's Askernish lay-

out was known to exist, so the men's first task was to identify eighteen likely green locations among the dunes. A round of golf consists of eighteen holes primarily because the Old Course ended up
with that many in 1764, when four very short holes were combined
to make two longer ones—although the number took a while to
catch on. Prestwick, where the first dozen Opens were played, had
twelve holes until 1883. Leith, where golf's first rule book was written, in 1744, had five. Montrose had twenty-five.

Finding a lost golf course isn't as simple as you might think: the
creators of early layouts did so little in the way of earthmoving that
unambiguous evidence of their work can be difficult to detect,
even for someone who knows where to look. My hometown, in
northwestern Connecticut, had a small golf course in the 1890s,
contemporary with Askernish. I know exactly where it was and have
seen old photographs of it, but during a long afternoon spent
tramping over the area I was unable to find a single undeniable
surviving feature. In the earliest days of the game, golfers created
courses the way children do when they knock balls around a vacant
lot, by devising interesting ways to go from Point A to Point B.

Ebert developed his restoration design by hiking over the *machair*
and visualizing golf shots (Old Tom's method) and by studying satellite photographs, which helped him weigh various schemes for
connecting the greens in a logical sequence. He also extrapolated
from his knowledge of Morris's designs elsewhere, and from his
own work in restoring old links courses. When I visited Askernish
in 2007, he and Irvine had placed eighteen flags in the ground,
denoting provisional green locations, and were taking readings
with a laser range finder and a handheld GPS device, so that Ebert
could enter accurate coordinates into his laptop—enabling him,
among other things, to leave a clearer record of his thinking than
Old Tom Morris did. Ebert told me that he and Irvine were fairly
certain they had identified a number of the original greens, in
some cases because the ground appeared to have been slightly flattened, most likely by hand, at some point in the past, and in other
cases because particular formations simply looked like golf greens
to them and so presumably would have looked like golf greens to
Old Tom Morris, too. One such site—the fourteenth green in
Ebert's layout—occupied a plateau surrounded by dunes, which
resembled ocean billows. "That green plays well from many differ-

ent directions, but I think it plays best the way we've laid it out, as a par 3," Ebert told me. "It just seems like a par 3 green, set high on the dune with everything dropping away."

While Ebert and Irvine worked, Ralph Thompson, a couple of his friends, and I followed along, hitting golf balls into the marram grass, and losing many. At one point, we all hit shots toward the top of a distant dune directly above the beach, so that Ebert could get a sense of whether it was reasonable to expect golfers to hit such a long shot to such a small target and into the prevailing wind. Putting wasn't really possible yet, although a few of the proposed greens had been encircled by single strands of barbed wire, to keep sheep and cattle from wandering onto them.

The most vocal opponents of the Askernish project have been Gilbert Walker and William Macdonald, both crofters. I went to see them this past December at Walker's house, down the street from the Borrodale Hotel. Walker, who is seventy, went upstairs to find his hearing aid, and Macdonald rolled a cigarette and took a seat near the hearth, so that he could blow his smoke toward the flue. Macdonald is fifty-four but looks and sounds at least ten years older. He apologized for his hair, which was pointing in several directions, and explained that he'd fallen asleep in his chair, at home, while waiting for Walker to pick him up. When Walker returned, I asked the men if they could explain crofting to me, and Macdonald smiled and said, "It is complicated."

Most of northern Scotland used to be occupied by clans, whose leaders had a conception of real estate which Macdonald likened to that of American Indians before the arrival of Europeans. "The clan chieftain did not regard himself as the owner," he said, relighting his cigarette, which had gone out. "He regarded himself as the chief of his people, and he considered his wealth in terms not of the number of acres he occupied but of the number of fighting men he had, or the number of cattle, or these things combined." Beginning around the time of Macbeth, the Scottish government (and, later, the British) increasingly viewed the northern clans as military, political, cultural, and religious threats, and took various steps against them. In the mid-eighteenth century, the rule of the clans began to be replaced by a modern system of land tenancy—the beginning of the clearances.

South Uist was bought in 1838 by Colonel John Gordon of Cluny, who lived in a castle on the other side of Scotland. Most of the island's residents spoke only Gaelic and subsisted by growing potatoes, raising cattle and sheep, fishing, and collecting seaweed for fertilizer. Their cottages, which they often shared with their animals, usually lacked chimneys; smoke from smoldering peat fires inside seeped out through thatched roofs. Colonel Gordon— whose name in historical accounts is often preceded by "heartless," "brutal," or some similarly grim epithet—eventually transported more than two thousand of these people, perhaps half of South Uist's population at the time, to Quebec, and consolidated their plots into large livestock farms, which were more profitable. His treatment of his tenants was among the reasons that the government acted, in the late nineteenth century, to bring the clearances to an end, by giving small tenant farmers protection from arbitrary removal. Crofters continued to pay rent to their landlords, but eventually gained many of the powers of ownership, including the ability to bequeath their crofting rights. The system, with various modifications, remains in place today.

After Colonel Gordon died, South Uist passed to his son and then to the son's widow, Lady Emily Gordon Cathcart. It was she who commissioned the first Askernish golf course, in 1891. A major golf boom was under way, and her decision to hire the most famous golfer of the day probably reflected a hope of attracting sportsmen from the mainland. When Old Tom Morris traveled to South Uist at her behest, he was accompanied by Horace Hutchinson, who was both a champion golfer and one of the first golf correspondents. An account of their trip, probably written by Hutchinson, appeared in the *Scotsman* and reported, "On a stretch of beautiful links ten miles in length it was difficult to select the best site for a course, as half-a-dozen courses, each having special points of interest, could have been marked off on the available ground. After a survey, a part of the farm of Askernish was selected, principally on account of its proximity to the excellent hotel at Lochboisdale, which at this season is usually crowded with anglers."

In 1922, most of Askernish Farm was divided among eleven tenants, one of whom was William Macdonald's grandfather. Each of the Askernish crofters received the permanent right to occupy a portion of the old farm and to graze animals on common land near the sea, while Lady Gordon Cathcart, who still owned the farm and the rest of the island, retained the manor house, a portion of the arable land, and the right to play golf on the *machair.*

The meaning of that last stipulation was central to the golf course dispute. Macdonald told me that the golf provision, in his opinion, expired with Lady Gordon Cathcart's death, and that the crofters on her former property tolerated continued golf playing only as a favor. He and Walker said that they had no issue with the old nine-hole course, which didn't extend into the dunes, but that the new course was an outrage. Walker, rising from his seat, said, "What they have now is four times the size of what was there. The whole *machair* is 437 acres. What they've taken over is 340!"

In 2003, new legislation enabled communities in Scotland's crofting regions to collectively purchase the land they occupied. Three years later, the people of South Uist, Eriskay, and Benbecula paid £4.5 million for their islands, which are now owned and managed by a community-run nonprofit company called Stòras Uibhist —Gaelic for "the treasure of Uist." In 2006, Stòras Uibhist confirmed the decision of the previous owner to allow the golf club to restore the course—a decision that the Askernish crofters contested. The vice chairman of Stòras Uibhist is Father Michael Macdonald, who is the priest of the Catholic parish at South Uist's northern end. When I asked him about the complaints, he shook his head. "I can't figure out what's behind it all," he said. "It's hugely expensive to go down this road. And for what benefit?"

Walker's and Macdonald's objections to the golf course are less straightforward than they may seem: although each man has a croft at Askernish, Macdonald doesn't graze animals there, and Walker owns only a few. In addition, the people who run the golf club, far from asking anyone to remove livestock, have said repeatedly that they wish the crofters would graze more animals on the course. Hungry sheep and cattle are good for a links course, Irvine and Ebert told me, because they fertilize the soil and help keep the rough under control.

Part of the difficulty may lie with crofting itself. Father MacDonald, when I asked, defined a croft as "a small piece of land surrounded by legislation." This is an old joke in Scotland, but it's apt. Crofting was devised to protect small tenant farmers from abusive landlords, but the system was already becoming an anachronism by the time it was put in place. The land on South Uist is so marginal and the plots are so small—an average of forty or fifty acres—that no one on the island today makes a living from crofting alone, despite substantial government grants and subsidies, and legally protected rents of less than a pound an acre. The system successfully preserves a sanitized form of medieval land tenancy, but it makes cost-effective agriculture impossible, since it divides the land among far too many tenants.

Perhaps for that reason, modern debates about crofting tend to focus more on symbols than on practicalities. The Askernish controversy has been portrayed as a class conflict, between struggling crofters and wealthy golfers, but the distinction makes no sense on South Uist, since virtually everyone on the island has at least one croft, including Ralph Thompson, the other local members of the golf club, and Father MacDonald. South Uist's economy—and therefore crofting itself—depends heavily on visitors from elsewhere, and has since at least the era of Lady Gordon Cathcart. Ralph Thompson has said that Askernish could eventually contribute as much as a million pounds a year to the local economy, a big deal on an island with a population of eighteen hundred and falling.

In early 2008, the protesting Askernish crofters asked the Lochmaddy Sheriff Court to halt the golf project. The court declined to intervene, and the crofters took their case to the Scottish Land Court, in Edinburgh. Meanwhile, construction of the golf course began. Actually, "construction" is the wrong word. At Askernish, Ebert and Irvine were determined to create golf holes the way Old Tom Morris and his contemporaries did, by doing virtually nothing beyond cutting the grass and filling in old rabbit burrows. (The 1891 article in the *Scotsman* about Askernish suggests that the first round of golf there was played within a few days of Morris's visit.) Modern golf course designers usually work closely with contractors called shapers, who use heavy earthmoving equipment (and, often, explosives) to transform existing terrain to suit a designer's vision of what golf holes ought to be. For Askernish, Ebert didn't need a shaper, because he and Irvine intended to be no more aggressive than a nineteenth-century course builder would have been. Only a few small areas were subjected to more than trivial amounts of

soil disturbance. One of those was the seventh green. Irvine and
Ebert were both fairly certain that the seventh had been one of the
original holes, because the valley in which it was situated looked so
much like a fairway. But in what seemed to be the logical location
for the green Irvine found virtually no organic matter beneath the
grass. This led him to deduce that the old putting surface, if there
was one, must be buried beneath six or seven decades' worth of
windblown sand. He and a crew of local volunteers removed the
beach grass from that spot and then raked away sand, looking for
the original contours. A few feet down, they reached topsoil (or
what passes for it on South Uist), confirming his hunch. Another
green that required significant work was the eleventh—the target
overlooking the sea which Ebert, in 2007, had asked several of us
to hit shots to. Irvine and Ebert suspected that the original green
(and most of the fairway leading up to it) had been lost to ero-
sion, but they still wanted to use what remained of the dune, both
because it formed an invitingly level plateau, and because the required shot, though challenging, had been so deeply appealing to
all of us who had tried it. (Part of golf's addictiveness, for those
who are hooked, arises from the thrill of effecting action at a distance—a form of satisfaction also known to antiaircraft gunners.)

   Ebert and Irvine used no pesticides or artificial fertilizers, and
they didn't install an irrigation system. The entire cost of the golf
course construction was less than £100,000, a fraction of the usual
bill for even a modest golf course nowadays. (Ebert helped to keep
the price low by agreeing to work for Old Tom's fee, which was
£9.) Ebert told me, "Askernish goes back to the roots of the game,
where you're just sort of playing across the landscape." Modern
golf course architects have individually recognizable styles, but
most of them adhere to certain hole-design conventions: that golfers should be able to see their targets, that hazards and other obstacles should not be arbitrarily punitive, that fairways and greens
should be shaped to reward good shots. In Old Tom Morris's era, a
designer's main function was not to recontour the ground in order
to conform to golfers' expectations, but to direct play over existing
terrain in thought-provoking ways, and to capitalize on lucky topographical accidents. Because Ebert and Irvine did their work at
Askernish in that spirit, some of the holes pose challenges of a type
that most modern players are unaccustomed to meeting. "Golfers
who have only experienced modern courses will find some of the

Askernish greens very, very difficult to understand," Irvine told me. "Some of them look as if they were sloping the wrong way, but that's only because we've got so used to pandering to the golfer." The sixteenth hole, called Old Tom's Pulpit, has an elevated green whose rear half falls off severely, into a sort of bowl, where many players' approach shots are likely to come to rest. The green breaks any number of design rules, but the hole is both memorable and fun to play, as well as challenging—just like Old Tom's blind par 3 at Lahinch.

The restored Askernish course opened officially on August 22, 2008. The retired Scottish soccer legend Kenny Dalglish played in the first group and was named the club's honorary president. Five months later, the Land Court heard two days' worth of testimony from the attorneys representing the protesting crofters and Stòras Uibhist, and in late February it issued a ruling. It affirmed Stòras Uibhist's right to create golf holes anywhere on the *machair*, as well as to build a clubhouse and make other improvements, while stipulating that the golf club must not deprive the crofters of the right to graze their animals adequately. (If the crofters and Stòras Uibhist can't settle the grazing details on their own, the Land Court will hold a hearing in May.) Ralph Thompson had told me beforehand that Stòras Uibhist's attorneys were confident they would prevail, but, even so, the scope of the ruling surprised him. "It's miles above what we expected," he said.

Crofting remains an important part of life on South Uist, and many residents, Father MacDonald among them, believe that it serves a critical social function, by enabling the island to sustain a larger full-time population than would otherwise be possible. But crofting, because it spreads residents so thinly across the settled parts of the island, also undermines any deep sense of community: most of the houses on South Uist are widely scattered rather than clustered in true villages. The golf club, which is open to all and costs very little to join, has the potential to become a community anchor, and its junior golf program, which the club and Stòras Uibhist have both treated as a priority, may keep at least a few of the island's young people interested in hanging around instead of pursuing careers on the mainland. At any rate, it will give them something interesting to do on weekends while they wait for their chance to escape.

I got to play a couple of rounds at Askernish in December. Even though the course is farther north than Sitka, Alaska, the Gulf Stream keeps temperatures on South Uist mild through most of the winter and creates the possibility of a twelve-month golf season, at least for die-hards. I played one day with Ralph Thompson and Donald MacInnes, who is the club's captain, as well as a builder and a crofter. There was a film of frost on some of the beach grass when we began, but the sky was virtually cloudless, and I never needed the stocking cap that I had tucked in my golf bag. On the fifth hole, we passed a spot where an Askernish crofter had plowed a small potato plot up to the very edge of the fairway, most likely as a provocation. I expected Thompson to be angry, but he laughed. "We never would have got the course finished so fast if it hadn't been for the crofters," he said. "They turned Askernish into international news."

MacInnes had brought along his dog, which ran ahead of us over the dunes, pausing occasionally to enlarge a rabbit hole. The fairways and the greens were ungroomed, in comparison with a typical course at home, and we sometimes had to play around a rut or a bare spot or a half-buried skeleton of a sheep. But roughness is part of the course's charm. The bunkers looked like real hazards, rather than like oversize hotel ashtrays, and the slanting winter light made the beach grass glow. We were a little worried, when we began, that we wouldn't have time for eighteen holes, because the winter solstice was approaching and the sun had seemed to begin setting almost as soon it came up. But we finished with visibility to spare, and had time for a beer in the tiny clubhouse, which MacInnes had built. We were able to play quickly because we had the golf course to ourselves, except for a few cows.

GEORGE PACKER

The Ponzi State

FROM *The New Yorker*

ALL ALONG STATE ROAD 54 in Pasco County, Florida—forty-five minutes northeast of Tampa—the pine trees and palmettos and orange groves have been cleared to make way for new developments. Over the past few years, these inland subdivisions, which are sometimes called "boomburgs," appeared as if overnight. Developers dreamed up instant communities and christened them with names evoking the ease of English manor life: Ashton Oaks, Saddle Ridge Estates, the Hammocks at Kingsway. Across flat and empty fields of wire grass, the developers paved suburban streets and called them Old Waverly Court and Rolling Greene Drive. They parceled out lots smaller than a quarter acre and built, with concrete blocks and stucco, look-alike two-story beige and yellow houses; columned archways over the front doors lent an illusion of elegance. The houses sold for $200,000 or $300,000 to some of the thousand or so people who moved to Florida every day, or to middle-class people who already lived there but wanted to get farther away from Tampa, where most of them had jobs. Nearby, shopping malls and megachurches sprang up. By last year, Pasco County, where twenty thousand people lived in 1950, had nearly half a million residents. A few days after the Presidential election of 2004, the *New York Times* devoted an article to Pasco County, saying that it was the kind of place that had given Florida, and the White House, to George W. Bush. The county's growth fueled a real-estate boom that, by the middle of this decade, was bigger and gaudier than anything the state had ever seen.

Recently, I drove around some of the subdivisions on State Road

54, as well as in other parts of Tampa Bay and in southwest Florida. A friend from Tampa, who accompanied me on one outing, called them "ghost subdivisions." I didn't understand what he meant until we drove into a development called Twin Lakes, where there was nobody on the gently curving streets except for a solitary middle-aged woman, who was watering her lawn in hip-hugging capri jeans, a sleeveless top, and silvery-green eye shadow. Her name was Bunny—"just Bunny"—and she was a native New Yorker who had grown up on Utopia Parkway, in Queens. She had pursued the sun and the good life to Hawaii, Arizona, and West Palm Beach, before ending up in Twin Lakes. Some of the houses around Bunny's were occupied, she said, but a good number were for sale. In the past two years, property values in Twin Lakes had dropped by more than $100,000. One house had been for sale for almost two years.

Farther east on State Road 54, in a subdivision called Country Walk, there were streets whose pavement stopped a few feet from where it began, as if the developer had changed his mind. I saw streets with signs and streetlamps but no houses, and streets with houses but no occupants. Overhead, the sky was brilliant aquamarine, and the structures looked like cardboard cutouts. Dozens of houses had FOR SALE signs in the front yard, some of them standing next to collapsed inflatable Santa Clauses. On Pumpkin Ridge Road, house after house appeared to be waiting for inhabitants—carpeted white rooms with no furniture—or deserted. Five minutes after I rang the doorbell at one house, an old woman missing two front teeth opened her door a few inches and peered out. I asked where her neighbors had gone. "I don't know anything," she said. "I've only been here since October." In front of the house at the corner, three copies of the *Tampa Tribune*—one of them dated September 27—lay on the pavers. I looked through the kitchen window: the refrigerator doors hung open and on the floor were piles of trash, including a sign that said FOR SALE BY OWNER. The grass outside was overgrown, and yellow from a recent drought.

To the south, on a rural road off U.S. 301 in Hillsborough County, I turned into a subdivision called Tanglewood Preserve. The sales center was shuttered and construction had been arrested: 32 lonely houses were scattered around 366 lots, with patchy fields for back yards. At the corner of Tangle Brook Boulevard and Tangle Bend Drive, there was a two-story beige stucco house with a black Ford Explorer and a Chevy Venture parked in the driveway. A woman named Angie Harris lived there with her five children. She was thirty-six years old, a navy veteran, black, with short hair and a stout, powerful body. She was the wife of a sailor stationed in Bahrain who was not due to return home until 2010. He had found the place in Tanglewood Preserve online, marked down from $326,000 to $226,000. "Go look," he told her. "There's something wrong, for that price." But there was nothing wrong, other than the head-high grass out back, and so Harris bought it and moved in this past July. She placed four leopard-skin-patterned chairs around a table in the dining nook and put a brown leatherette sofa set in the carpeted living room. When I visited, Harris's two younger daughters were watching cartoons on a large plasma television, with the volume low. On the kitchen counter were audio CDs of Dave Ramsey, a personal-finance adviser. Other than a few military plaques above the TV, the walls were bare. The blinds were drawn against the sunlight.

A group of original homeowners in the subdivision, who paid full price in 2006, had held a Thanksgiving get-together to which newcomers like Angie Harris, who had bought in for much less, were not invited. She knew the name of only one other family in Tanglewood Preserve—she'd heard it from the real-estate agent. "It used to be people would wave," she said, standing in her darkened living room in a Verizon Wireless sweatshirt and jeans. "Now they don't, maybe because of the economy. It used to be southern hospitality. Now it's, like, grab your purse."

After the development went into foreclosure and was sold, Harris received a letter from the new developer. It said that the building of new houses remained on indefinite hold, but also promised better maintenance of the vacant lots, and included a gift certificate to Publix, the supermarket chain.

I asked Harris if she wanted a few more neighbors. "Not really," she said. "I want them to upkeep the property. And the playground they promised." She had annual passes to all the theme parks around Tampa for her five kids; when she moved in, her back yard was a breeding ground for snakes, the subdivision's common areas were not tended, and the open fields had become dumping grounds, so Harris seldom let her children play outside. She had grown up in Baltimore, where neighbors could spank one another's children, and had lived in Brooklyn, and she had fond memories of street life in those old cities. But at Tanglewood Preserve, Harris was filled with suspicion, as if transience and isolation made her vulnerable. (Valrico, the town a few miles to the northeast where she had lived before, was overcrowded and beset by gangs.) "When we moved to Florida, the auto insurance went up a hundred dollars. 'Florida is a fraudulent state' — that's how they explained it. I don't know if it's like that across the board. It's so much stuff that's going on — in this day and age, you can't trust people. The neighbors are leery of me, and maybe I'm leery of them."

On State Road 54, there was a gated community called Hamilton Park. Toward evening, a woman was sitting in her open garage, smoking and talking on the phone. A covered Corvette was parked in the driveway. Exposed to the darkening street, the woman resembled a figure on a lighted stage, an impression deepened by the theatrical amount of clutter surrounding her: pots and pans, Masonic emblems, Art Deco fireplace tools, a metal desk, an Army Air Corps scrapbook from the Second World War, a fiftieth-wedding-anniversary album, piles of photographs and letters, brown porcelain canisters, a Kodak Brownie Reflex camera with external flashbulb, *The Good Housekeeping Cook Book*.

"I'm liquidating everything at an auction," the woman said, after hanging up. Her name was Lee Gaither. She had been on the phone with Verizon, trying to keep her Internet service from being cut off. The water bill was past due, and Gaither, who was renting the house, was facing eviction. (To avoid it, she had sold off her mother's silverware, and some vintage furniture and jewelry, for $1,300.) Gaither, forty-seven years old, was slender and blond, with an educated voice; but her face was lined with exhaustion, and a scar ran under her left eye. She suffered from fibromyalgia, she said, and "something called lupus." Disability payments were her only income. She was from Ohio by way of Virginia, and around her lay the precious debris that her family had passed down to her, including a document dated March 11, 1830, transferring from Kentucky to Ohio the remaining balance of a Revolutionary War veteran's pension. In November 2007, after financial ruin forced her to sell the family house in Vienna, Virginia, she had moved to Florida. She apologized for the disorder in the garage. "These are family heirlooms," Gaither explained. "I might get a little for it."

Gaither traced her disaster to her third husband, whom she'd met in Virginia. "He asked me to marry him in three weeks, and that was a big thrill," she said, with a hint of apology. She had invested her savings in the man's construction business, which turned out to be fraudulent. He is currently in jail in Virginia. He had put two race trucks and the Corvette in her name, leaving her with payments of $3,300 a month. One truck had already been repossessed, and the second had been totaled by a man who borrowed it from her. She was still hoping to sell the Corvette, which carried a balance due of $26,000. "I don't have it," Gaither said, in a tone of quiet defeat.

Gaither's only consolation was her son from her second marriage. He was an A student at the local high school and hoped to attend law school. "I'm really proud of him, obviously," Gaither said. "It's too quiet here. I thought it'd be a great neighborhood for him, but he really has no friends to do things with." Next door, a couple had moved in and then suddenly moved out again, and another couple was now renting.

Other than her son, there was no one, she said. "It would be nice to have living relatives," she said. "My family home — everything is gone. And here I sit, wondering if I can get the phone company not to cut me off." Pinned to the back wall of the garage was a small card with the words "PEACE: it does not mean to be in a place where there is no noise, trouble or hard work. It means to be in the midst of these things and still be calm in your heart."

I had begun to think that Gaither was alone in Hamilton Park when a bright-red Hummer lumbered into her driveway, and a massive man with a long gray ponytail and a Harley T-shirt got out. He said that his name was Dan, and described himself as a friend who was helping Gaither out. Dan had a bass twang and a bone-crunching handshake. He was a retired state trooper and had been earning money serving subpoenas on foreclosures, until the high cost of gas made the business unprofitable. "It's not their first rodeo, most of the people who are bailing," Dan said, waving at the houses up and down the street, which were disappearing in the dusk. "The reason you don't see FOR SALE signs is they just pack up over the weekend and get out. They know the tricks to keep from getting traced." He shrugged. "I'm going on credit cards myself. I took some of my retirement money and bought things I liked." Dan nodded toward the Hummer. On his wrist was a Rolex watch.

Gaither was looking at a family picture, from 1942, of her father putting his Army Air Corps cap on her grandfather's head. "There's so much history here, and it's heartbreaking," she said. "But I just don't have the time to sell it on eBay." The auction would be held in two days. Gaither was trying to sell possessions of no value to anyone but her.

This is one of the places where the financial crisis began. Florida has epitomized the boom-and-bust cycle of American business ever since a land rush in the 1920s ended with the devastating hurricane of 1926. The state's economy depends almost entirely on growth—that is, on new arrivals and the wealth they generate in construction and real estate. "Until two years ago, this was a growth machine that was the envy of the world," said Gary Mormino, a professor of history at the University of South Florida, in St. Petersburg, which is across the bay from Tampa. "Florida, in some ways, resembles a modern Ponzi scheme. Everything is fine for me if a thousand newcomers come tomorrow. The problem is, except for a few road bumps—'73, '90, and they were really minor—no one knew what would happen if they stopped coming."

Only Nevada has a lower proportion of native residents than Florida. The state's growth machine did not depend on higher education or high-paying professional jobs; it depended on real estate and sunshine. Tourism and migration allowed Florida to become a low-tax, low-wage state, where living was relatively cheap. "The Florida economy has been based on selling Florida," David Reed, who runs the Florida operation of an investment fund called CapitalSouth Partners, said. "Our growth is all about population growth. When you take that away, what have you got?"

Florida is one of only nine states without an income tax—the state constitution bans it—and its taxes on corporations and financial transactions have been gutted with exemptions. The state depends for revenue on real-estate deals and sales taxes. In 2005, the LeRoy Collins Institute, at Florida State University, released a report warning that the state budget was overdependent on the housing boom and would soon experience deep shortfalls. Politicians in Tallahassee generally dismissed it. "Florida has a political culture, and one of its little phrases is 'If it ain't broke, don't fix it,'" Lance deHaven-Smith, a public-policy professor at Florida State, said. In exurban counties like Pasco, property taxes were kept low to attract homebuyers, and the schools and fire stations that new arrivals expected were often paid for with bond issues floated on the projection of future growth—a system that Ben Eason, who owns *Creative Loafing,* an alternative weekly in Tampa, also likened to a Ponzi scheme. DeHaven-Smith called Florida's policies "the most disingenuous system of government."

By 2005, the housing market in Florida was hotter than it had ever been, and the frenzy spread across all levels of society. Migrant farmworkers took jobs as roofers and drywall hangers in the construction industry. Nearly everyone you met around Tampa had a Realtor's license or a broker's license or was a title agent. Alex Sink, the state's chief financial officer and a Democrat, said, "When the yardman comes and says he's not going to mow your yard anymore because he's going to become a mortgage broker, that is a sure sign that something is wrong." Flipping houses and condominiums turned into an amateur middle-class pursuit. People who drew modest salaries at their jobs not only owned a house but bought other houses as speculators, the way average Americans elsewhere dabble in day trading. Ross Bauer, a manager at a Toyota dealership in Tampa, told me that between 2000 and 2007 he bought and sold half a dozen properties, in a couple of instances doubling his money within two years. "Looking back, it was right in our face," he said. "That's a heart attack. It's not normal."

Jim Thorner, a real-estate reporter in the Tampa office of the *St. Petersburg Times,* said, "There were secretaries with five to ten investment homes—a $35,000 salary and a million dollars in investments. There's no industry here, only houses." When Thorner went to buy a new house, in 2005, the customer ahead of him in line at the sales center said that he intended to turn his property around in six months and make $50,000. It was not an outlandish plan. Home values around Tampa rose 28 percent that year. "I'm telling you, it was the Wild West," Alex Sink said. "And Florida has always been susceptible to the Wild West mentality. If it's too good to be true, we're going to be involved in it."

In Fort Myers and the neighboring city of Cape Coral, two hours

south of Tampa, things got wilder than anywhere else. A Fort Myers real-estate agent named Marc Joseph, who entered the business
right out of college, in 1990, and had the jaundiced eye of a veteran, told me, "Money was flowing, easy money. Anybody could
qualify—I mean anybody." He knew a bank teller with an annual
salary of $23,000 who had received a $216,000 mortgage, with no
money down and no income verification—not even a phone call
from the lender. "I wish I could say the market here was driven by
end users and retirees, but it wasn't. Two-thirds were speculators.
You could flip 'em before you had to close on 'em." Karen Johnson-
Crowther, another real-estate agent in Fort Myers, showed me the
sales history of a property in an upscale gated community which
she had recently bought at a foreclosure auction. Building had begun in 2005. On December 29, 2005, the house sold for $399,600.
On December 30, 2005, it sold for $589,900. On June 25, 2008, it
was foreclosed on. Johnson-Crowther bought it in December for
$325,000. I said that the one-day increase in value must have been
some kind of record, and she looked at me pityingly: "No."

When I told Alex Sink about the house that had appreciated by
almost 50 percent overnight, she said, "That's a fraudulent transaction." According to an investigative series in the *Miami Herald,*
oversight by the state's Office of Financial Regulation and its commissioner, Don Saxon, was so negligent that more than ten thousand convicted criminals got jobs in the mortgage business, including four thousand as licensed brokers, some of whom engaged in
fraudulent deals. Until the rules were recently changed, felons in
Florida lost the right to vote but could still sell mortgages. (Under
pressure from Sink, Saxon resigned this past August.) Kathy Castor, Tampa's representative in Congress, told me, "Florida was particularly lax when it comes to mortgage regulation." She connected
the mortgage crisis and the lack of oversight with state politics and
the political power of developers. "We were hit by two Bushes,
George and Jeb"—Florida's governor from 1998 to 2006—"and
there was very loose growth management. Because Jeb was aligned
with the development industry, it was a speculator's paradise." Before running for Congress, in 2006, Castor was a commissioner in
Hillsborough County. She said that developers held sway there,
benefiting from "a very costly urban-sprawl model." The county
sold off agricultural land "in places that are miles from the jobs."

The Web site for Country Walk, in Pasco County, promised buyers "a comfortable distance from the higher prices, taxes, and congestion of big city living. Come enjoy the home Tampa residents can only dream about."

Last fall, Michael Van Sickler, of the *St. Petersburg Times,* tracked the real-estate deals of a local tattoo-parlor owner named Sang-Min Kim, also known as Sonny. Starting in 2004, Sonny Kim made ninety sales around Tampa, mostly in poor neighborhoods, on which he cleared $4 million. Van Sickler found that many of Kim's buyers, who put little or no money down, were untraceable; some had been convicted of drug dealing and other crimes. Kim, who has not been charged with any crimes and could not be reached for this article, closed a third of his deals with a title agent named Howard Gaines, who now faces up to forty-five years in prison on a fraud conviction elsewhere in Florida. According to law-enforcement experts, drug dealers often become flippers, in order to launder money.

One night in December, Van Sickler took me on a tour of some of the abandoned and foreclosed properties that had once belonged to Sonny Kim's real-estate empire. We stopped at an ill-lit corner in a mostly black slum of single-family houses called Belmont Heights, which is cut off from downtown Tampa by Interstate 4. Van Sickler—incongruous-looking in a dress shirt and dark slacks—pointed out a decaying two-story stucco house. Its windows were boarded up, and mattresses lay in the overgrown yard, near a FOR SALE sign. Van Sickler learned that Kim acquired the house in 2006 with a deed that was witnessed by a convicted drug dealer, then flipped it for the sum of $300,000, with the help of a no-money-down mortgage from a subsidiary of Washington Mutual Bank, which later foreclosed on the house. (Last year, WaMu went into receivership, after becoming the largest bank failure in American history.) According to mortgage-fraud experts, the straw buyer is typically paid a small slice of the flipper's take and then disappears without moving in. When Van Sickler recently asked a real-estate agent about the house, he was told, "That's selling for $52,000, but it can be yours for $35,000 in cash."

"Sonny Kim may not be the biggest, he may not be the worst, but he really epitomizes the laxness of the banks during the boom years," Van Sickler said as we stood outside the house. "It raises the question, Did anyone from the bank do a drive-by to eyeball this place?" Kim's deals had been financed by Wachovia, Wells Fargo, Bank of America, Lehman Brothers, Fannie Mae, and Freddie Mac. While Van Sickler, who was having trouble selling his own house in Tampa, was investigating the trail of Sonny Kim in September, the country plunged into the worst economic crisis since the Great Depression, and the banks that had greased Kim's deals were at the center of it. "We're not *all* to blame for this," Van Sickler said. "Decisions were made, and people looked the other way. This did go all the way up the ladder."

Van Sickler was right: the diagram of moral responsibility looked like an inverted pyramid, with the lion's share belonging to the banks, mortgage lenders, regulators, and politicians at the top. And yet anyone buying and selling property in Florida in the middle of the decade must have known that the system was essentially a confidence game, that everyone involved was both being taken and taking someone else. Easy credit and mistrust are two sides of the same economy. This explained, at least in part, why Angie Harris avoided her neighbors in Tanglewood Preserve, and why they shunned her: she made them feel that they'd been duped. A Ponzi scheme succeeds only when enough people are willing to put aside common sense, and on some level they know they are doing it. The result is universal credulousness and universal fear.

A Tampa police car pulled up outside the derelict house, and a cop got out. "Someone around here doesn't like you," he said. A neighbor had complained about two men snooping around the abandoned property.

Flipping and fraud burst the boil. But in places like Pasco County and Cape Coral it was the ordinary desire of ordinary people to buy their own homes that turned things septic. Southwest Florida isn't Las Vegas or Palm Beach: this is conservative, churchgoing country, with antiabortion signs scattered among the highway billboards advertising model homes and liposuction. Unlike the upscale Atlantic Coast of Florida, it was settled by middle- and working-class people who followed the I-75 trail down from Michigan, Ohio, and other places that nurtured midwestern frugality and caution. The memory of these values haunts conversations about what happened here. Karen Johnson-Crowther, the real-estate agent in Fort

Myers, who bought five houses at one Sunday auction in December, said, "You open the paper and read the foreclosures in the back
of the classified section—you can't help but feel for all of those
people who wanted the American dream." Johnson-Crowther,
the mother of grown children, comes from Illinois. "My parents
were always savers," she said. "My father was an asphalt contractor
up there. He retired here because he saved. Today, we're so different from that generation. After seeing this, is it going to swing back
the other way?"

Anita Lux also came from Michigan. She and her husband, Richard, live in a one-story house along a canal in Ponderosa Shores,
a quiet older subdivision of St. Petersburg. Her father worked at
Ford's Rouge River plant in Dearborn, Michigan, for forty-seven
years, long enough to have known Henry Ford and Walter Reuther.
Anita had a job with the city of Dearborn until 1985, when Richard, an architect, accepted an offer to start a new office in Florida.
They wanted to get away from the winters.

The Luxes invited me for coffee out on their screened-in porch
overlooking the canal. Richard, in his early sixties, was bearded
with thinning hair; Anita, who was in her late fifties, had large,
heavily mascaraed eyes behind glasses.

"Her father was very frugal," Richard said. "All of this rubbed off
on Anita. Anita has been known as the Coupon Queen."

"You know how they tell you at the end of the receipt how much
you've saved?" Anita said. "I love that!" She added, "We've always
tried to live not beyond our means. We have credit cards, but not
maxed out. One or two cards." They saved for two years in order to
take a vacation to Yellowstone. "We don't have big-screen TVs. We
don't have fancy cars." They owned a Ford and a Mercury. "Bought
used," she added.

When the recession of the late eighties caused Richard's office
to close, Anita took a job as an administrative assistant at Wachovia.
Earlier this decade, she watched the bank get into the subprime-
loan business. In 2006, Wachovia bought World Savings, a California mortgage lender operating under the umbrella of Golden West
Financial, which that year was named by *Fortune* as one of the most
admired mortgage-services companies in America.

"Who would have thought that all those loans would cause . . ."
Anita didn't finish her sentence. At World Savings, the loans were

called "Pick a Pay." Customers were invited to design their own mortgages, choosing an interest rate and a payment plan. "They were going to have all the lenders for Wachovia follow the same scheme" as World Savings, she recalled. "A lot of our mortgage lenders thought this was pretty nutty. But World Savings was pretty successful, for a while."

"For its owners," Richard added.

"He saw all this coming," Anita said.

"What triggered it for me was all these high-rise condos for a million dollars," Richard said. "In Tampa, in St. Pete. Who in the world can afford those? This is Podunk. This isn't Chicago, this isn't Paris. Who is dumping all this money?" Anita smiled—they knew each other's conversational turns—as Richard went on: "We changed as a society. Prior to the concept of the government getting into the lottery business, we were a nation built on the value of a dollar. We became a nation based on the *volume* of the dollar."

"Part of the problem is they allowed people to have too much credit," Anita said. "Every day, you get something in the mail that says you've been preapproved for a credit card, and people don't know how to say no. You've got people with thirty credit cards."

"Then people compound it—they get a line of credit to pay their taxes," Richard said. "The American people don't have an education in money. They didn't learn it from their parents."

Alex Sink, the state treasurer, was president of Bank of America in Florida until she retired in 2000, just before her colleagues started to lose their bearings. "What were the banks thinking?" she asked. "My alma-mater bank, one of their early write-offs—they came up with this idea that they were going to make lines of credit up to $100,000 available to small businesses without any history. You know, the Kevin Cate Tattoo Parlor." (Kevin Cate is Sink's press secretary, and though he has a real-estate license, like everyone else in Florida, he doesn't own a tattoo parlor.) On a recent visit to Bank of America headquarters, in Charlotte, North Carolina, Sink confronted one of the bank's most senior executives. "I said, 'What were you thinking?' He just looked at me. He thought they'd outsmarted themselves."

In 2003, Jennifer Formosa and her husband, Ron, bought a house in Cape Coral, across the Caloosahatchee River from Fort Myers.

Until the late fifties, Cape Coral didn't exist, except as an uninhabited spit of land called Redfish Point. In 1957, two salesmen from Baltimore, Leonard and Julius Rosen, bought it for $678,000, gave it a more alluring name, and began pitching their new development on television. In *Land of Sunshine, State of Dreams: A Social History of Modern Florida,* Gary Mormino, the historian, writes, "The first national ads for Cape Coral offered shivering Northerners the opportunity to buy into the Florida dream on the installment plan." Today, 167,000 people live there.

Jennifer Formosa, who is twenty-five, with brown hair and a practical manner, came from Michigan, like Anita Lux, but she was raised by a single mother and moved to Florida when she was nine. A month after graduating from high school, she went to work as a teller with BankAtlantic. (In the state's employment hierarchy, the lower-middle-class job for those without a college education was bank teller. For men who didn't finish high school, it was construction. The middle class worked as real-estate agents and brokers. The upper class were developers.) At nineteen, Jennifer had her first child with Ron, whom she met in high school. They've since married and had a second child. Ron, who has the short haircut and earnest look of a fifties jock, was abandoned by his parents and raised by a grandmother. He didn't finish high school, and went to work pouring cement in the construction industry around Cape Coral and Fort Myers. At the height of the building boom, he was making thirty dollars an hour. ("I was thinking, I don't need no diploma.") Using Jennifer's income of about $20,000 a year and Ron's sweat equity as a down payment, they took out a $110,000 mortgage and began construction on a three-bedroom house in Cape Coral. To pay their bills, they refinanced with Washington Mutual, then took out an equity line.

"Our $100,000 house got up to $280,000," Ron said.

"With the final equity line, we put the patio in, paid off the cars, and bought the boat," Jennifer said.

"Blew some of it," Ron admitted.

"Vacations, cruises," Jennifer said matter-of-factly. "Going to Orlando, taking the kids to Disney."

By 2006, even though the Formosas had almost no savings, and kept borrowing against the value of their house—with its apparently endless path upward—their position seemed pretty solid. At least they didn't have an adjustable-rate mortgage, with no money down and a low teaser rate that would soar in two years.

I met the Formosas through Marc Joseph, the Fort Myers real-estate agent. He was a cheerful booster of his hometown and his trade, but he also wanted me to know the local roots of the financial crisis and the human faces behind it. "A lot of it originated right here, with greed and easy money, greed and easy money. That was the germ. It wasn't location, location, location—it was greed and easy money."

And then it all came to an end.

Some people in Florida can identify the precise moment when the economy turned. "It was almost like somebody had turned the light switch off," Karen Johnson-Crowther said. Marc Joseph remembered a week in December 2005 when the median price per unit in Fort Myers and Cape Coral was at its high of $322,000, and suddenly the phone wasn't ringing as much. "It was as if the car came to a stop and all the air went out of the tires," he recalled. For real-estate agents like Johnson-Crowther and Joseph, who stood on the precipice of Florida's economy, the plunge to today's depth started earliest and was steepest. For other Floridians, the past few years have been a slow agony of contraction.

When, at the Florida market's dizzying mid-decade height, speculators lost confidence, the faith that kept the state aloft gave way and the economy plummeted like a Looney Tunes character who, suspended in midair, suddenly looks down. Property values did what the lenders and borrowers somehow never imagined was possible: they started to decline. Today, the average unit in Fort Myers and Cape Coral is selling for just $158,000, less than half of what it sold for at its height. When housing prices dropped, owners like the Formosas could no longer use their homes as cash machines. Even luxury properties, usually insulated from downturns, took big hits: in St. Petersburg, a real-estate agent named Alona Dishy showed me a waterfront house that had originally been advertised for $4.4 million but sold for $2.4 million. With fewer interested buyers, the volume of new building decreased, and the construction industry began to dry up.

In Naples, the wealthy retirement community south of Fort Myers, Ron Labbe owned a lumberyard that sold materials to the town's high-end builders. Labbe, who came from a working-class family in Akron, Ohio, had started out driving a forklift in the yard thirty years ago, and in 2005 he bought out the company's owners with the help of CapitalSouth Partners, David Reed's investment fund. In the summer of 2006, Labbe noticed a sudden drop in building permits around Naples—a warning sign in the construction trade. He cut his workforce, then closed his truss-fabrication plant, sold off the plant's equipment and land, and waited for the downward spiral to stop. But it kept going. Labbe's water coolers were replaced with drinking fountains. The company shrank from two hundred employees to forty, and revenue dropped from $50 million in 2006 to $16 million in 2008. This past summer, Labbe—a self-deprecating, meticulous sixty-year-old—stopped paying himself and put his own cash back into the business. When I visited the lumberyard, on January 7, he told me that it was the worst single day of sales he had ever had. And there was no end in sight. I asked whom he blamed for the wasting away of his company. Labbe shook his head and smiled. "There are big forces out there that are much larger than we are," he said. "It would just eat away at you if you think about what's happening now." He added, "There's not one thing you have to blame. You'd have to blame everyday people. What's the saying? I met the enemy, and it's us."

By early 2008, the cement company where Ron Formosa worked in Cape Coral started laying guys off. Ron first saw his hours cut in half, and then he lost his job. At the same time, interest rates crept upward, which meant that borrowers who were already watching their income and property values melt away had an even harder time making monthly payments.

Thus the foreclosure epidemic began. By last year, the highest rate in the country could be found in Fort Myers and Cape Coral, where 12 percent of the area's residences were in foreclosure, including the Formosas'. In Tampa, a third of the properties sold by Sonny Kim passed into the hands of some of the country's leading banks, which had lent millions of dollars to his straw buyers without asking questions. In Pasco County, the foreclosure rate jumped fivefold between 2005 and 2008. And in New York and Washington the term "mortgage-backed securities" came to inspire dread, like the name of a new virus. Having incubated along the Gulf Coast of Florida, it was spreading around the world.

But this was only the beginning of Florida's calamity. In early 2007, Alex Sink attended a meeting of the Chamber of Commerce in Tallahassee, where an official from Allied Van Lines reported that the company was moving more people out of Florida than in. "That really got people's attention," she said. "It's even worse now." In the 2003–2004 fiscal year, Florida's population grew by nearly 400,000. The projection for 2009 is 5,000, making it the first year since the early seventies, when statistics began to be recorded, in which the net flow of migration is negligible. Residential electrical hookups show the same trend: preliminary numbers suggest a decline in 2008, the first decrease in the four decades since the Bureau of Economic and Business Research at the University of Florida has been keeping the data. The engine of Florida's growth has quit. In Gary Mormino's metaphor, the Ponzi scheme has collapsed.

Because real estate stands at the center of the state's economy, very little in Florida survived the bust intact. A harbor pilot named Jorge Viso told me that at the port of Tampa, where the bulk of the traffic is in construction materials, the volume of shipping had imploded over the past two years—steel was down by 67 percent, cement by 73 percent, wood products by 89 percent. It was the worst decrease in his two decades there. Ross Bauer, the Toyota manager who sold properties on the side, said that the car dealership had enjoyed double-digit increases throughout the decade. "Business was insane," he said. In 2007, sales leveled off. In 2008, they dropped precipitately. Twenty percent of auto sales were paid off through home equity, Bauer said, and now a fifth of the vehicles financed by Toyota's southeastern distributorship were in repossession. In the final months of 2008, half a dozen auto dealerships in Tampa closed or declared bankruptcy.

The construction workers who had scaled the economic ladder from the strawberry fields and orange groves began sliding back down. Latino farmworkers without houses or families in Florida boarded buses bound for Mexico. The Hillsborough County sheriff reported tent villages full of the homeless sprouting behind strip malls, along with an outbreak of strange new crimes. Carl Grooms, a strawberry grower in Plant City, explained, "The economic situation is so bad that you've got a low-rent element coming in that will steal anything. They steal our copper from our churches, they strip the wiring out of the trailers." Jim Joyce, a supervisor with Hillsborough County's health and social-services department, said that his caseworkers were seeing "a new face" coming in for help: "People who were in their homes, were living the American dream, and then lost it. And they don't have the knowledge to navigate social services, how to get food stamps. People who were employed in the real-estate market—we see people who were making quite a nice living, and they end up in our office." Unemployment in Hillsborough County was close to 8 percent, and retailers in the strip malls were closing down. Tampa was awash in out-of-work brokers and busted developers. On the streets outside his condo, Ross Bauer began to see something new: homeless people who looked like him.

In Room 416 of the George E. Edgecomb Courthouse, in downtown Tampa, Laura Donaldson, twice divorced, was having another face-off with her first husband, Dennis Johnson. They were both in their forties, both blond, both good-looking, though a little drawn around the eyes and mouth—she in a navy-blue blazer, he in a yellow button-down shirt. It was easy to imagine the couple, in better times, out on the emerald bay together, in the boat whose valuation became a subject of argument at their divorce hearing, in 2001. Johnson was a property developer—his niche was subdividing and flipping empty lots in the wealthy areas of South Tampa —and in 2005 he earned $830,000, by far his career high, after which his ex-wife demanded a second increase in support payments for their son.

By the time the case came before Judge Bernard C. Silver, of the Hillsborough County Circuit Court, Johnson's fortunes had taken a disastrous turn—two straight years of deficits, totaling more than $300,000. He had fired his secretary, sold his million-dollar house at a loss, moved his new family into a rental, and was paying bills and debts with credit cards, stock sales, a loan from his in-laws, and proceeds from his business properties, which were losing value every month and which he was liquidating as quickly as possible. He had plotted a graph to show the judge, labeled "Declining Net Worth." The line began in May 2006 at $3,759,000 and descended, first gradually, then steeply, to last August: $220,500.

And yet, on the witness stand, Johnson parried his ex-wife's

lawyer with the almost jaunty equanimity of a ruined man in a
screwball comedy. Once or twice, without knowing who I was, he
caught my eye and shook his head with a grin. "It appears right
now there's a multitude of people with my expertise out there,"
Johnson said when questioned whether he was looking for work.
"Everybody's been laid off. I'm a cheap commodity right now." His
ex-wife's lawyer, Adrian Castro, kept suggesting that Johnson had
money hidden away, and Johnson kept answering with the verbal
equivalent of turning out his pockets and shrugging. It seemed
as if he'd finally found a way to keep his ex-wife's hands off his
money.

"Your net worth drops $3 million in one year, and that's not your
big problem," Johnson said later, over lunch at Pipo's Cuban Café.
"I'd take three more years of real-estate hell if my lawyer could get
me out of court."

I thought of Lee Gaither, sitting amid the detritus of her life in a
garage up in Pasco County. Gaither had said that her ex-husband
was "an incredible actor," and now the only thing of value she
owned was a red Corvette. Johnson had a white Lexus. He also
owned an interest in a piece of property in Pasco County—twenty
acres of orange groves and a pretty lake, north of the developments
along State Road 54. When the economy recovered, the orange
groves could be subdivided and developed. He was going to hold
on to them—he was still in the game.

At a table outside a Tampa Starbucks, Ross Bauer, the Toyota
dealer, was sipping a latte and smoking in the December afternoon
sun, wearing an Abercrombie & Fitch T-shirt, sunglasses, and a few
days' stubble. "I personally laid off thirty guys in the last ninety
days," he said. "It was brutal. I had to let a guy go who worked there
for many years. His wife was sick. 'Did I do something wrong?' 'No.'
'Does someone not like me?' 'No.' The bottom line was he was a
highly compensated person we could do without."

Then it was Bauer's turn. "I was a victim of my own cost-cutting,"
he said.

When we met, Bauer had been unemployed for three weeks.
He admitted that he enjoyed sleeping in and was delaying the moment when he would go looking for a new job. He had stopped
shopping at Nordstrom's, and no longer dined out at Ruth's Chris

Steak House. In his condo, there was an expensive Viking gas stove that he'd turned on only two or three times, because he hardly ever cooked. "I never thought about it—it was just how I lived," he said. "And it just stopped. Now you go to Hooters for a burger and a beer."

Bauer's condo, which he'd bought for half a million dollars at the peak, was currently worth maybe $300,000, and he was negotiating a short sale with the bank to avoid foreclosure. Nearby, the streets were deserted around the Towers at Channelside—twin twenty-nine-story luxury high-rises, built in the past two years in a warehouse district near the port. At the end of last year, the project nearly went bankrupt. At night, the Towers themselves looked nearly empty, almost all the windows dark, except for a string of Christmas lights halfway up one tower and the blue light of a television flickering in the other.

When Anita Lux worked in the complaints office of Dearborn's public-utilities department, a framed quotation hung on the wall, next to the time clock. She could still recite it word for word a quarter century later, as we drank coffee on her screened-in porch by the canal:

> If you work for a man, for heaven's sake work for him: speak well of him and stand by the institution he represents. Remember, an ounce of loyalty is worth a pound of cleverness. If you must growl, condemn, and eternally find fault, why not resign your position? And when you are on the outside damn to your heart's content, but as long as you are part of the institution, do not condemn it. If you do, the first high wind that comes along will blow you away and you will never know why.

It came from an essay by Elbert Hubbard, a popularizer of the Arts and Crafts movement and a philosopher of homespun wisdom, who celebrated the American virtues of know-how and can-do a hundred years ago.

Last July, Wachovia told Anita Lux that her eighteen years at the bank were over. They were very nice about it: the vice president who spoke to her was also being fired, and the two women cried together and talked about severance packages and health insurance. Anita had seen it coming, but she couldn't get over the feeling of rejection.

"I had always been active in the bank," she said. "I volunteered for Big Brothers Big Sisters, the American Cancer Society. I liked doing it, but I also felt it was doing good for the bank." Now Elbert Hubbard's exhortation kept coming back to her. "You see my point?" Anita asked, her eyes welling up. "I thought as long as I worked for a company and stood by a company and spoke well of a company, the company would stand by me. And it didn't. The sign was wrong, in my case."

Anita was fifty-eight when she got fired. A lot of the downsizing at Wachovia hit women her age, and she was afraid that no one would want to hire her. She'd had no luck yet, despite attending job fairs and having had two or three phone interviews. It was a shock to be on unemployment, and there were so many out-of-work professionals like her that the unemployment office had begun holding special classes for them. Richard's work as a self-employed architect had dried up in early 2008, and Anita's health insurance will run out in July. The one saving grace was that the Luxes had always been more frugal than Wachovia, which was bought by Wells Fargo on the last day of 2008 and will soon cease to exist.

Across the bay from the Luxes, in Tampa, Dan and Ronale Hartzell live in a cramped, featureless two-bedroom apartment in a strip of apartment complexes and motels near MacDill Air Force Base. Until last March, Dan had a ten-dollar-an-hour job laminating plastic snack-food bags, at a small plant in Tampa. He was laid off without explanation. Dan said that his supervisor, who had gone to high school with him, made someone else give him the news. He was still angry about that.

Dan had been looking for work ever since — Home Depot, Sam's Club, Publix, at least sixty applications — with no luck. "It's just been so hard out there, it's so saturated," he said. "When you apply, they tell you you're the twenty-fifth person to apply." He was a short, potbellied man in his thirties, with a wispy goatee and a shaved head under his Steelers cap. (He came from Pittsburgh.) He was missing some teeth and spoke in a loud voice, owing to deafness in one ear, and it was easy to imagine the wariness of prospective employers in the low-wage service sector, the only area where jobs seemed to be available. "I would classify myself as a blue-collar-type guy," he said. "I'm not the behind-the-counter-take-your-money-can-I-help-you-find-your-dress-size type. That's not my kind of thing." But no one was advertising blue-collar jobs.

"He was an excellent worker," Ronale said. Like her husband, she had extensive tooth decay, and was beset with numerous other medical problems, for which there was no money. "He's always been that way. And he's a fast learner."

"All I've got is my work habits—what can I do?" Dan said. "I've got two children."

"He doesn't drink. He doesn't do drugs."

We were sitting in their living room around a cheap flat-screen TV showing the local news—they had bought it with last year's Earned Income Tax Credit. Brent, in fifth grade (and unusually small for his age), sat on the dingy carpet, holding the hand of Danielle, in second (with hearing loss). Their father was a high school dropout, which he regretted intensely and blamed for his inability to find a job. But Dan also felt that the world was holding something against him: "You almost get to the point where, what's the point? You apply and apply, and nothing happens. I start to wonder, What's wrong with me? Why do all these people out there view me as such a bad person? They don't know me, they don't know my work history, they won't give me a chance. I'm blue-collar. You work for what you have, that's all anyone can do, and then all of a sudden the economy gets so bad and instead of thirty people looking for work there's three thousand," he said. "To be honest, I'm just actually starting to lose heart now."

Dan and Ronale were estranged from their families, and since most of the people they knew were heavy drinkers, they had few friends. Dan said, "As far as the support system, you're looking at it."

The Hartzells didn't take out a subprime mortgage. They hadn't lived beyond their means. After Dan lost his job, they stopped renting DVDs and buying toys. They hadn't even turned against each other. "I thank God every day that I have her," Dan said, and Ronale said, "One thing we don't argue about is money, because we don't have none." They felt lucky to have avoided eviction, but now they were facing the real possibility of homelessness. It would be hard to find more unambiguous victims of the housing bust and its thousand cascading effects.

Dan knew that his plight was the result of rising unemployment in a bad economy that was shedding the few remaining manufacturing jobs. In Hillsborough County, forty-eight thousand people had no work. And yet, in pondering the causes of his trouble, Dan couldn't avoid the feeling that the world had singled him out for some terrible payback, that it must have been his fault, that the failure was his alone and he had no right to anyone else's help. It occurred to me that this was an attitude that no senior figure on Wall Street had adopted.

After going a full year without making a mortgage payment, Jennifer and Ron Formosa realized that they were about to lose their house in Cape Coral. "When they were going to put that ugly yellow auction sticker on it, I didn't want to live there," Jennifer said. They found a place to rent nearby that was larger and less expensive, and in January they vacated their house and moved. Even in the new place, Jennifer dreaded the ringing telephone, with various creditors threatening to have her wages garnished. The Formosas wanted to file for bankruptcy, but they couldn't quite afford the $1,400 fee, even though Ron had found a job working for a locksmith, at nine dollars an hour, plus commission. Most of the work involved changing the locks on foreclosures.

One evening in January, the Formosas sat at the kitchen table in their new house while the children did their homework. On a large-screen TV, Barack Obama was explaining the terms of the bailout. "I'm not saying what we did was perfect," Jennifer said. "We spent our money and didn't save it. But we had it, and we didn't see that this was going to happen." She thought for a moment. "This whole situation—I won't do things the way I did before."

"Lessons learned," Ron said.

"I'll save my money instead of spend it," Jennifer said. "I don't think I'll ever want to buy a house again."

Richard and Anita Lux were using their new free time to read more and take long morning walks together. As they walked, they discussed books they were both reading—Herman Wouk's *War and Remembrance* was a recent one—which helped fortify the mind, Richard said, against all the depressing news. He said, "The good thing about this is people are talking to people, families are talking to families, and eventually people are going to get it that there's more to life than the greed-is-good arrogance of recent years, and back to the pleasures of life."

"Back to the value of the dollar, not the volume," Anita added. She had not yet found a new job.

In the office of Pam Iorio, who, at forty-nine, is Tampa's mayor, a map was spread across the table. It was titled "2035 M.P.O. Long Range Transportation Plan DRAFT"—a blueprint for Tampa's first light-rail system. Greater Tampa, with nearly three million people, is, after Detroit, the largest metropolitan area in the country without one. For nearly two decades, while planners carried out $14 million worth of studies, local politicians refused to push the project, which would require voters in Hillsborough County to pass a referendum raising the sales tax by one cent.

Iorio is determined to have mass transit approved before her term ends, in 2011. "We are twenty years behind the rest of the country, in terms of light rail," she said. "It will put us at a huge economic disadvantage without it." In Iorio's view, the industries of the future won't come to an area without mass transit. The project interested me, because it cut directly against the way people around Tampa Bay lived. It would get them out of their cars, lure them back to the city, and develop the metropolitan area with taxes and services, rather than depend on endless growth.

"The reason we don't have it now is people have thought for years we don't need it," Iorio said. "Florida's already growing fine—why should we make those long-term investments? We need them precisely because of the crisis we're in. We'd have our own long-term economic-stimulus package right here, right now, if we had this in place." Instead, with the federal government poised to spend hundreds of billions of dollars on infrastructure, Tampa has no big "shovel-ready" transportation projects lined up, except for a widening of the connector between Interstates 4 and 275.

Iorio had been described to me as a competent, unimaginative public servant, but in our conversation she sounded almost visionary. "If there can be any good from this economic calamity that is occurring, it is causing us to reassess ourselves as a country, as a state, as a city," she said. "We have to reassess the institutions that we trusted and can't trust anymore. We have to reassess the role of government in the private sector. And, locally and as a state, we have to reassess the basis of our economy. A state that is so dependent on the ebb and flow of construction does not have a strong foundation for its economic future." Putting a light-rail system to the voters would be part of the reassessment. "It goes beyond the SUV. It goes to how we're going to live in this community. We can't continue to build four-thousand-square-foot houses miles outside cities."

A number of people in Florida told me that the state needs a fundamental change in its political culture. Ben Eason, the owner of *Creative Loafing,* said, "In the next ten years, growth will return to the cities from the suburbs," but he added that Tampa's leadership lacks a "forward-thinking core to propel the dynamic of the city." The Florida state government estimates that it will have an $8.5 billion shortfall in revenues by 2012, which Governor Charlie Crist and the legislature are trying to remedy by dipping into short-term reserve funds and by deeply cutting spending. (The governor's office did not respond to requests for comment.) Libraries are closing, university budgets are being slashed, and social services are cutting back, even as demand soars. In Hillsborough County, civil circuit court judges are carrying some three thousand cases at a time. "You can't say this too loud, because you get shot around here," David Reed, the investment-fund manager in Tampa, said. "But we need an income tax."

During the era of George and Jeb Bush, places like Pasco County and Cape Coral voted heavily Republican, and became the political center of gravity in Florida. But in 2008 a right-wing former professional wrestler lost his seat on the Hillsborough County Commission to a gay ex-cop who supports mass transit. And, to many people's surprise, Barack Obama won the county, helping him carry Florida. With his election, political power has begun shifting away from the sprawling suburbs and back to the cities. When, in his inaugural address, Obama called for "a new era of responsibility," he was speaking about Wall Street and Washington, but he was surely also speaking about Florida, which holds up to the rest of the country a fun-house mirror of distorting accuracy.

Driving around Florida's ghost subdivisions, you feel not just that their influence is waning but that they are physically hollowing out. In a place like Lehigh Acres, near Fort Myers, where half the driveways are sprouting weeds, and where garbage piles up in the bushes along the outer streets, it's already possible to see the slums of the future. More and more of the residents in Hamilton Park will be renters like Lee Gaither. The vacant houses in Country Walk will be boarded up. The St. Augustine grass in the front yards of Tanglewood Preserve will grow three feet high. The open fields with streetlights but no houses will become dumps.

"It's Florida," Doug Bennett, the chief of the Riverview bureau of the *St. Petersburg Times,* in eastern Hillsborough County, said. "Most of the governors never saw a developer they didn't like." He was looking through the window of his second-floor office: outside, a vast open field was littered with construction equipment and trailers. Another development had stalled—the shopping mall and offices were built, but the "faux village" never materialized. "Stucco ghettos," Bennett said. "I live in one, so I can say that. Too many houses, not enough water, the economy's terrible, no tourists. This is the capital of the low-wage jobs, and when things go bad people just have no safety net. It's very unfortunate." He turned back to his desk. "This is the epicenter of everything that's bad in America."

The sense of urgency among a few people was less striking than the strange calm among everyone else. It was either grace under pressure or blind folly, but I encountered it everywhere: the serene conviction that visitors would start coming again, and everything would be the way it was before. "The sun's still shining—go down to the beach and it's packed," Marc Joseph, the real-estate agent in Fort Myers, said. "This is just a hiccup, and we'll get through it. It just happens to be a little longer than most hiccups, because it's not just here—it's globalized."

Joseph was already adapting his business to the new reality. He had started Fort Myers's first foreclosure bus tour—an efficient way for speculators to mop up cheap properties. And he was about to launch a foreclosure boat tour, on the canals of Cape Coral. It was, he told me more than once, a great time to buy.

MATTHEW POWER

Lost in the Amazon

FROM *Men's Journal*

IQUITOS, PERU, POPULATION 360,000, bills itself as the largest
city in the world that cannot be reached by road. The capital of the
Peruvian Amazon, it is an island in a vast ocean of jungle, a seaport
two thousand miles from the sea, linked to the outside world only
by air or by the roiling waters of the Amazon River. At the height of
the rubber trade in the late nineteenth century, Iquitos was one of
the richest cities in South America, a boomtown that could afford
to ship in a prefab mansion designed by Gustave Eiffel or ship out
dirty linens to be laundered in Paris. Today it is a filthy, crumbling
frontier town, choked with motokars, three-wheeled taxis that turn
the dusty streets into a buzzing and honking chaos. Iquitos is also
a launching point for exploration of the two-million-square-mile
rainforest that spreads across the Amazon basin, home to a tenth of
the world's known species, several of which I can see as I walk along
the waterfront, where hawkers sell stuffed piranhas, mounted butterflies the size of paperbacks, and twelve-foot anaconda skins un-
rolled with a theatrical flourish. But I have no time to barter for
souvenirs. It's the rainy season, and black-bellied thunderheads are
piling up on the horizon as the pressure drops in the soupy tropical air. I am hurrying to the port to catch a boat heading downriver, through the vast unsettled territory that lies between Iquitos
and Peru's frontier with Brazil and Colombia.

If all goes according to plan, somewhere on the banks of the
mile-wide river I will rendezvous with a thirty-three-year-old former
British army captain named Ed Stafford. But Stafford has warned
me that in the Amazon things rarely go according to plan. He

should know: since April 2008 he has been on an expedition to be the first person in history to travel the entire four-thousand-mile length of the Amazon River on foot, through the heart of the largest jungle on earth. He's attempting to walk every step of the river's route from source to sea, wherever it is possible to walk. There are also several hundred tributaries he will need to cross using an inflatable raft he carries with him, and he must traverse three countries and the territories of dozens of indigenous tribes. In his expedition blog, Stafford writes: "Walking from the source to the sea is one of the last great feats of exploration."

We live in an age of diminishing firsts, so those wishing to find fame or notoriety through adventure are forced into increasingly baroque categories: summiting Everest on prosthetic legs, or climbing Kilimanjaro on Rollerblades. The Amazon has been run several times by kayaking expeditions, and a Slovenian named Martin Strel has even swum most of its length, but nobody has ever crossed it on foot. When I first read about Stafford's mission, I immediately wondered what made Stafford believe he could actually make it.

Perhaps more than any other landscape, the Amazon jungle is steeped in myth and mystery, looming over the human imagination as a symbol of both untamed wilderness and environmental vulnerability. The mind shudders at its enormity. The river that begins as a trickle of glacial meltwater at 20,000 feet in the Andes discharges 32 million gallons a second. Twenty percent of all fresh water flowing into the world's oceans passes through its mouth, which gapes 150 miles wide. For five centuries the river has been the obsession (and undoing) of countless outsiders, from the lunatic conquistador Lope de Aguirre to the vanished 1920s explorer Percy Fawcett. The lore of Amazon exploration is filled with starvation, madness, disease, and murder.

I understood the region's undeniable allure, but I was still curious why anyone would subject himself to two years crossing a landscape largely populated by anacondas, jaguars, vampire bats, pit vipers, scorpions, wasps, army ants, electric eels, piranhas, drug smugglers, hostile tribes, dengue *and* yellow fever, malaria, fifteen-foot black caimans, and eighteen-inch leeches. Not to mention the candiru, a pin-size catfish that has the ability to swim up a stream of urine and lodge itself irretrievably in the urethra. There are almost no roads along Stafford's route, and since the most common way of traveling is by boat, even trails are scarce. So to try to understand whatever impulse inspires Stafford onward, I arranged to join him for a few weeks of his journey. But first I had to find him.

At the Iquitos docks I board a rusting double-decker ferry, whose every inch of deck space is strung with hammocks. I am the only gringo aboard, and everything I do meets with stares. The sky is flame orange; cumulonimbus clouds boil over the forest as the boat noses out into the current. The water is the color of cappuccino, and putting green–size mats of floating vegetation drift along in it. Dugouts with outboards hug the banks and beat their way upstream against the flow. The ferry steams along swiftly with the current, the river lashing in broad meanders between the unbroken walls of jungle.

As darkness falls and most of the passengers climb into their hammocks, I stand by the wheelhouse, watching as the pilot navigates around huge floating logs. After several hours of staring into the blackness, we see a tiny cluster of lights on the far bank. As we get closer, I see two men, and the taller one, wearing a baseball cap, waves to me. The big boat grounds itself against the muddy bank, and I jump down, the only passenger disembarking at this stop. The two men approach. I can't resist: "Mr. Stafford, I presume?"

"Have a beer," he replies, laughing.

Ed Stafford stands about six feet tall, wearing flip-flops, tattered cargo pants, and a filthy T-shirt, and walks with the bouncy gait of someone who has just set down a heavy load. He has two weeks' growth of beard, an easy laugh, and dark glimmering eyes. He introduces me to his expedition partner, Gadiel Sanchez Rivera, a twenty-eight-year-old Peruvian nicknamed Cho. It is 3 A.M., and percussive cumbia music blasts from the town's only bar, where we drink beer as Stafford fills me in on his story so far. In more than ten months of walking he has faced poisonous snakes, navigated perilous footpaths above Class V rapids, and had his life threatened by angry tribesmen. He has traveled about two thousand miles so far and is almost halfway to the Atlantic. "Unfortunately, this has been the easy half," he says.

Inauspiciously expelled from his posh British private school at age seventeen for chopping down a tree planted by the queen,

Stafford spent four years in the British army, making the rank of captain. He was once a competitive rugby player and has a false incisor in place of the one he lost on the cricket field. He organized security logistics for the UN during Afghanistan's 2004 elections and led an expedition for a BBC nature documentary in Guyana. He wanted a life of adventure, like that of his hero Sir Ranulph Fiennes, so he and a colleague named Luke Collyer brainstormed possible expeditions they could undertake. Stafford's jungle experience in Belize and Borneo—expeditions he led to raise money for charity—gave him the idea of walking the length of the Amazon. To their surprise, it had never been done.

The expedition began on Peru's Pacific coast in April 2008, with Collyer. The pair hiked up the Colca Canyon and into the Andes, traversing several of the possible sources of the Amazon to cover all their bases. They crossed the mountains with pack burros, and from eighteen thousand feet began their long descent into the Amazon basin.

As Stafford sees it, there was an imbalance from the beginning. During the months of planning, securing sponsors, permits, and equipment, Collyer was busy with work, so Stafford handled most of the logistics himself. When Collyer arrived in Peru he was out of shape, didn't speak a word of Spanish, and had gotten engaged a few weeks before. "He was totally unprepared for what we were about to do," Stafford tells me. "And that became more and more apparent as we went on. His heart just wasn't in it."

Three months in, Collyer placed a supply order that contained just one MP3 player. Stafford got angry and asked why Collyer hadn't also gotten one for him. Collyer announced that the player was for Stafford and that he was quitting the expedition. The breakdown had been a long time coming. "The MP3 player was just the final straw," says Stafford. "He claimed he was leaving because our friendship was more important to him than the expedition. For me the expedition is more important than anything." The two men haven't spoken in five months.

When I later contacted Collyer for his side of the story, he e-mailed a polite "no comment": "A lot of time has passed and I've removed myself from anything to do with the expedition," he wrote. "And I'm happy to keep it that way."

Stafford continued on alone, walking with a succession of local guides. Then, in August 2008, he met Cho in the town of Satipo, Peru. Cho had worked for some time as a forester, hiking deep into the jungle to find large specimens of the most desirable timber hardwoods: mahogany, cedar, tornillo. He had initially agreed to walk with Stafford for five days. The two didn't get along at first, but Cho grew enthusiastic about the mission and proved a tireless and loyal companion, and so Stafford brought him on as a paid partner for the remainder of the expedition.

"He's got balls of steel, and he's as keen as I am to complete this expedition," says Stafford. "He's taken the whole thing on as a sort of personal challenge as much as I have. And to find someone like that has been a real key. You just can't do something like this alone." Stafford now has someone to share the weight of food and gear and help bridge the language gap, but Cho's greatest value is psychological: the sheer relief of having someone to watch your back. They have been walking together for seven months now, and Cho has committed to sticking with Stafford until they reach the Atlantic, however long that takes.

Which may be a very long time. Stafford originally planned to travel about ten miles a day, which he soon realized was "vastly overoptimistic." At that rate he would have reached the Colombia-Brazil border by Christmas. But it was already February, and Colombia is more than one hundred miles east of us. The rainy season is in full swing, and the forests alongside the main channel have begun to flood. Stafford and Cho have gotten a taste of that in the last two weeks, crossing the wide delta where the Rio Napo joins the Amazon. "The forests were completely flooded, waist-high, sometimes head-high," Stafford tells me. "We were scrambling over tree trunks under the water. There's a species of palm here where the entire trunk is covered with three-inch spikes. They were like needles driving straight into our knees."

In the morning the children of the village sit in a hut to watch a badly dubbed version of Jean-Claude Van Damme's *Kickboxer*, and then spill out into the intense sunlight to practice their new moves. They watch raptly as Stafford, Cho, and I organize our gear. My frame pack is stuffed with a waterproof canoe bag; within that are smaller dry bags and ziplocks, a system that keeps things dry while making them impossible to find. Stafford's bag, a battered one-hundred-liter monster that weighs in at seventy-five pounds, contains everything he needs to be a self-documenting, one-man, twenty-first-century expedition. "My kit would be a lot lighter if I wasn't trying to blog this whole thing," he says, as he double- and triple-bags the sensitive electronics that are his only link to the outside world.

Part of Stafford's mission statement is to document the customs and perceptions of the tribes he encounters and the environmental issues facing the region, as well as raise $200,000 for a host of charities. Yet he is the first to admit that he is doing this mainly because it has never been done, and because he wants to have an extraordinary life and support himself with adventures. There's something anachronistic about the project, a "because it's there" attitude that could be criticized as a risky ego trip. I ask Stafford if he feels as if he belongs in an earlier era, perhaps that of Captain Cook or Admiral Byrd. "I feel like I was born at exactly the right time," he says. "I don't think a middle-class individual would have been able to do this sort of thing before." And he admits to an "element of pride about the whole thing," adding, "If anyone has got a problem with it, they should come try it themselves."

Stafford has acquired a full set of forty-year-old National Geographic Institute of Peru 1:100,000 topographical maps, still the most accurate available. In conjunction with his handheld GPS, they actually provide fairly decent route finding. He shows me his new route, tracing a band of altitude that should—he hopes—help us avoid walking through a swamp and make for faster travel. "One of the odd things about *walking* the length of the Amazon," he says, "is that you don't actually see the river very much."

For each leg of his walk, Stafford tries to hire a local guide, someone with knowledge of the forest who can help pick the most efficient route. In Oran he has engaged the services of Mario, a sixty-two-year-old farmer and father of twelve, who has been hunting these forests for five decades. Mario doesn't stand an inch above five feet, and his gear is the minimalist opposite of Stafford's: everything he needs is stuffed into a small flour sack that he carries by a cloth strap across his forehead. The only other items he has are rubber boots, a machete, and an ancient rusting shotgun, in case he stumbles across dinner.

Shouldering our packs, we turn away from the river and cross a cow field behind the village, the tropical sun crushing down on us. A few one-hundred-foot shade trees have been left standing alone, a sobering indication of the original height of the rainforest's triple canopy. This part of the Amazon, too remote and flood-prone to be easily exploited, still offers glimpses of the devastation wrought elsewhere.

We make our way up a slope, and within minutes we plunge into the tangled green wall that closes off the edge of the forest, leaving the bright world behind. Even at noon on the equator, the jungle is dim, the filtered green sunlight offering little sense of direction or time. The air is cooler, sounds are muffled, and the line of sight is reduced to a dozen yards through the dense understory tangle of creeping vines, lianas, and sprawling root systems. Huge trunks shoot up through the canopy, clung to by vines and strangler figs, giant bromeliads hanging like chandeliers. An astonishing amount of biomass claws upward, trying to bridge the gap between the limitless water of the ground and the limitless sunshine of the forest roof. You can almost hear it growing. The leaf litter on the ground is a foot-deep cushion, and there is no sound but the drone of insects and the distant calls of birds.

Mario leads the way along a barely perceptible path. His machete seems to be an extension of his body, and he parts the jungle with deft ease, using only the tip of the blade to slice thick vines and huge leaves. Stafford has also become adept with the indispensable machete but still relies on brute force to hack his way through obstacles. The diminutive Mario doesn't even sweat and seems to expend almost no effort as the trail parts before him with a flick of his wrist.

Taking up the rear, I'm already soaked through with sweat as we balance our way across mossy logs spanning tea-colored streams and scramble over waist-high buttress roots. Mosquitoes swarm around us, and hordes of stinging ants brush off from overhanging leaves or the trunks of trees. Even the vegetation has evolved with its own aggressive microspecializations. There are spike-covered roots that seem to grow exactly where a handhold is required, vines like rubber bands that wrap around my ankles, and thorny tendrils that snatch the hat right off my head. The worst by far is serrated razor grass, which slices through clothing and skin with the lightest touch. Stafford has been told there are endless stretches of razor

grass downriver in Brazil, another obstacle to add to the preposter-
ously overfull roster that stands between him and the mouth of the
Amazon.

A few times Mario stops dead and points off into the underbrush. I see nothing moving at all. "Pit viper," Stafford tells me. I've
researched enough about the variety of horrible deaths on offer
in the Amazon to know that a pit viper's hemotoxin causes massive hemorrhaging, bleeding from the eyes and ears, necrosis, then
death. "Oh, don't worry," Stafford says cheerfully. "We've got six
doses of dry antivenin, enough to last eighteen hours, and there's
a military rescue helicopter in Iquitos. The worst-case scenario is if
you were bit at sunset, because the helicopters can't fly at night.
But we'd be able to keep you alive until dawn." Well, then. No worries. The expedition has already come across ten pit vipers, all but
one of which have been quickly dispatched by their guide's machetes. In stark contrast to our own conservation dogma, no local
guide would let a poisonous snake escape if he could help it.

The only anaconda they had come across while walking was a
beautiful twelve-footer that Stafford stopped to film. When he'd
finished, his native guide hacked the creature into pieces. "He said
it was to feed to his dog," Stafford tells me. "But one of the things I
learned early on was that there was no point in trying to impose my
Western sensibility on the people who live here. They do what they
do to survive. They don't think of animals as having any value except food."

In late afternoon we find a small stream and stop for the night.
After months of sleeping out, Stafford and Cho have reduced setting up camp to a science. I have not reached that point and very
nearly dismember myself with the machete while trying to clear an
area of underbrush. Eventually I get a tent fly strung between two
trees as a shelter. This way camp can be made even in a driving
rain. The key piece of equipment is the expedition hammock, enclosed by mosquito netting and entered via a Velcro-sealed slit in
its bottom.

Cho and Stafford assemble a structure of damp green wood on
which to build a fire and support the cook pot, gathering standing deadwood from the forest for fuel. It's a miracle the fire will
catch with wood that is drenched daily, but Cho soon has a crack-
ling blaze and puts on a pot of stream water. Dinner is boiled rice

with canned tuna bought from a supply store in the last village we'd passed through. "When I first began, I thought there would be much more of a survivalist element, fishing and living off the land," says Stafford. "But as it's happened, we come across villages often enough that we can resupply or pay villagers to cook for us. That's been the most surprising aspect: how much we've had to deal with people. I had imagined it would be emptier, more man versus nature." He realized that the cultural interchange with the people of the Amazon was an integral part of the expedition. He also realized that it was easier to start a fire with a cheap plastic lighter than with flint and steel.

Even though we're coated with deet the mosquitoes are swarming around us, and as the equatorial night drops fast I crawl into my hammock and close myself in. A symphony of insects performs, multilayered, shockingly loud. Thousands of mosquitoes tap against the netting, probing for an entrance. The cough-like whoops of howler monkeys echo in the distance. Then a low hiss builds and builds, until the temperature drops and the rain opens up like a jet taking off, drowning all other sound, enshrouding the night.

In the morning I put on my still-wet clothes from the previous day. Wrung-out is as dry as any of us ever gets, and Stafford tells me to look out for foot rot, staph-infected cuts, and all the other bacterial and fungal delights of the Amazon's petri-dish environment. In an uncaffeinated haze I remember that you are supposed to shake your boots out before putting them back on in the jungle. I tap one upside down and a cricket the size of a sparrow clambers out and hops away.

The Amazon has a keen sense of irony. Mention how easy it is to cross a log bridge, and you will do a gainer into a stream; praise the quality of the trail, and it will disappear into a swamp; comment on the fine weather, and a Wagnerian thunderstorm will ensue. Stafford has gotten used to the frequent mishaps and come to see them, afterward, as a kind of comic relief. One afternoon he left the map behind when we stopped for lunch. Mario, far faster than any of us and more certain of his direction, dashed off to retrieve it and returned at nightfall. Months earlier Stafford dropped his only machete during a river crossing and had to push on to the next village with his bare hands. Self-deprecation seems to be a key to his success so far, and he has the ability to take the expedition seriously and recognize its absurdities at the same time. Plunging up to our necks in a creek crossing, he mutters, "Bloody silly expedition," and soldiers on.

For days we continue slogging along the contours of the chart, different only in scale from the columns of leaf-cutter ants that march alongside us. It is exhausting, dirty work, and I am covered with mud, scratches, and bruises. The prospect of doing this with no clear end date would be daunting. Stafford stops periodically to check our progress with the GPS. Mario looks on politely, though he has no idea how to read a map and the GPS is an impenetrable mystery to him. Stafford defers to Mario's local knowledge but likes to double-check against modern technology. "I know with this I'd be able to make it without a local guide," says Stafford, "but it would be much slower, and much more work." The GPS shows that Mario has taken us almost exactly along the planned route.

It's disheartening to see indisputable data on how slow our progress has been. On a good trail, two or three miles an hour is reasonable, but in trackless jungle, scrambling over or under fallen trees, hacking through vines or wading through mud, forward movement can slow to an agonizing crawl. After struggling with the frustration of slow progress for much of the trip, Stafford has finally reached some sort of peace with it. In the slog through the Napo delta, he noticed that in chest-deep water his heavy pack became buoyant, and there was a "bizarre sort of serenity" as he made his way through the silent flooded forest. "For some reason my default mode is military, 'we've got to get there,'" Stafford explains to me. "Cho takes his time walking through water. Suddenly, I wasn't getting frustrated walking only 2.5 kilometers a day. It was tranquil, and I realized it's going to take as long as it takes."

Although Stafford has become accustomed to the physical hardships of the jungle, encounters with tribes remain Stafford's greatest challenge. Many villages speak unique dialects, using only rudimentary Spanish. There is a long history of exploitation of tribes by oil and gold prospectors, and thousands of indigenous and rural Peruvians were murdered during the years of insurgency by the Maoist Shining Path guerrillas. So it's for good reason that many indigenous communities harbor a deep suspicion of outsiders.

One of the most pervasive fears is that white people are *pela cara;* literally it means "face peeler," but the term has become a myth among many native communities that outsiders will steal their organs. "The last thing you want after an exhausting day of walking is to arrive someplace and have the whole community be scared of you," Stafford says, but he has learned how to stay calm, how to de-escalate tensions.

Once, upon entering a village back along the Apurímac, Stafford was immediately confronted by an angry mob of Indians. They poured water on him, shoved dirt in his mouth, and smeared his face with red paint. He was scared but did his best to stay calm. "I just shook hands with their chief, turned around, and walked out of the village," he recalls. Not long after that incident he and Cho were crossing a tributary in the pack rafts. Cho looked over his shoulder and saw that they were being followed by five canoes filled with furious Ashaninka Indians. The men were armed with bows and arrows and shotguns; the women carried machetes. "I was pretty sure we were going to die," says Stafford. Even Cho, normally unflappable, thought they were done for. They were surrounded, and the leaders of the tribe approached them, screaming, blind with rage. Stafford showed them their permits from the regional authorities, but nothing helped. The women seemed ready to hack them to pieces. Finally, speaking slowly and quietly and holding his hands open, he managed to get them to calm down. Andreas and Alfonso, the leaders of the tribe, ended up joining them as guides for six weeks. Stafford was astonished. "The people I was most afraid of on the entire expedition turned out to be the most kind, helpful, and loyal people I've met."

That experience has convinced Stafford that he'll be able to handle whatever situation arises downriver. But Brazil presents even greater risks. When Stafford applied for permits through a fixing agency in Manaus, he initially got no response. "When I finally reached them," he says, "they said they didn't respond because I was going to die. 'It's a suicide mission. The indigenous reserve on the other side of the border in Brazil is the fiercest in the Amazon basin. Colonial Brazilians don't even go there. You're white, don't speak Portuguese, and are wandering around with a video camera.'" All salient points, he thought, but decided he'd "just go in and be very friendly and very calm." He still believes that with the right guides and the right approach, he'll make it. "But I have yet to meet a Brazilian who thinks it's possible," he concedes. "The only people who say 'Yeah, you'll be fine' are your friends back home, who haven't a fucking clue."

While Stafford measures the risks rationally, Cho has a more mystical outlook. A deeply religious Christian, he believes that God is protecting them. Stafford is more fatalistic. "I am either going to make it, or I am going to die trying," he says in a way that is almost cocky, confident that he can manage the risks and come out the other end alive and victorious.

We stay in a Yawa village for a day, where I entertain the children with my Buster Keaton antics, smacking my head on five-foot-high door frames and falling out of hammocks. A boy in a dugout paddles us across the tributary Rio Apicuyu, loaded high with our gear. Drifting, watching toucans and scarlet macaws alight in the trees by the riverbank and huge iridescent blue morpho butterflies rising on the breeze, I am struck by the folly of Stafford's "bloody silly expedition." The Yawas paddle up and down the river in dugout canoes, slipping easily with the current wherever they wish. All the cultures in the Amazon make use of the thousands of miles of waterways. Walking the Amazon seems analogous to crossing the Sahara on snowshoes: you could do it, but it's certainly not the way the locals go. There's a reason nobody has ever done this before.

I bring this up to Stafford, and he laughs. "A friend of mine once said, 'I fucking love your expedition because it's pointless.' It's a real British mentality: it's fucking pointless, but we'll do it anyway." Like Livingstone and Scott before him, Stafford has completely bought into the stiff-upper-lip masochistic absurdity of his endeavor, and he's proud of it.

Sore and scraped up after three more days of hacking our way through maze-like jungle, we finally reach the next village. Porvenir is an idyllic scattering of thatch houses on stilts set on a bluff above the Rio Ampicuyu, another small tributary of the Amazon. From here we must temporarily leave the route of the expedition to rendezvous with Pete McBride, a photographer from Colorado. We spend five hours in a dugout canoe, motoring downstream to the ramshackle market town of Pevas, right on the Amazon itself, where we meet up with McBride, resupply our stocks of tuna and ramen noodles, and return to the spot where we'd left off.

This is one of the self-created regulations of the expedition:

whenever Stafford leaves the route, he sets a GPS marker so he can return to the exact spot and pick up where he left off. It's what makes the game of walking the Amazon fun, a stickler of a rule that presents all sorts of logistical challenges. There is, of course, nobody to enforce this except Stafford and Cho, but the idea of cutting corners is unfathomable to them. "I wouldn't bother suffering this much if I were going to cheat on the small things," says Stafford. "If we're going to do this, we're going to do it right."

Mario returns home to his family and village, and for the next leg of the journey we will travel with a guide named Bernobe Sancha, a thirty-eight-year-old Ocaina Indian. I wake up in the morning to find Bernobe standing perfectly still, perched on a root above the edge of the river, holding a machete. With a quick flick and a splash, he hacks downward. A fish, its head surgically cut in half, drifts up to the surface of the water. We gut it and split it for breakfast, five ways.

When we walk out through the fields behind Porvenir, I stumble across a well-tended little plot of coca bushes. We are only fifty miles south of the Colombian border, and a huge amount of drug trafficking passes through the region. Peru is the world's second-largest producer of coca, whose leaves are refined into paste before being trekked to drug labs across Colombia's border for further processing. Encounters with nervous traffickers, the vast majority of them poor Peruvians, will be a serious risk as Stafford and Cho approach the "Triangle of Death" at the Peru-Brazil-Colombia frontier. In Pevas I read an account of a Peruvian village that had been burned to the ground in a turf war between rival drug gangs. It was right along Stafford's planned route.

The jungle life is beginning to wear on me after ten days of trekking. As my willpower flags, my astonishment at Stafford's determination grows. My feet, soaked for twelve hours a day, look cadaverous. I long for water that doesn't taste like an iodized puddle. I am covered with ant bites, and my ankles are embedded with parasitic fleas. At one point Stafford stumbles into a swarm of wasps, and the four of us sprint in a panic back down the trail. Then, while crossing through waist-deep water, McBride looks down and shouts, "What the hell is that thing?" This is not something anybody wants to hear while standing in an Amazonian swamp.

The creature has a huge whiskered head like a catfish, but a bright red mouth and a tail that winds off behind a stump and breaks the water six feet away. It swims slowly toward McBride and then vanishes below the surface in the murk. Bernobe tries to explain in broken Spanish, repeating the word *anguila,* but none of us knows what it means. Only later do we realize that the thing was an enormous electric eel, which could have generated enough of a shock to knock us all unconscious, facedown in the water.

On the day McBride and I are to leave, we have to make our way to the bank of the Ampicuyu to meet with a boat down toward the Amazon. According to Stafford's GPS, the river is eight hundred yards away. We strike out toward it, hacking through vines and undergrowth, but after just a few yards there is nothing but flooded forest as far as I can see. The only way to the river is straight ahead. We are knee-deep, then waist-deep, and then the dry bag in my pack begins to float and the weight is lifted off my aching shoulders. Our footsteps are silent, and we glide around enormous root buttresses in the light-dappled water. The flooded forest is otherworldly, literally: an exact replica of the forest, the sky, and ourselves moving in reflection over the still black water. When it is too deep we load our bags in the pack rafts and push them through the water, swimming in our heavy boots, laughing, spiders and ants on every branch. The water is too murky to even see a hand below the surface—or an electric eel.

The flooded forest is the epitome of all childhood nightmares, and yet I'm not afraid. I now understand the realization Stafford came to while crossing the Napo delta: he learned to let himself float, to feel the tranquillity of the moment he was in. Stafford has a long way to go, perhaps eighteen more months, but you can't rush an expedition like this. It will take as long as it takes.

STEVEN RINELLA

Me, Myself, and Ribeye

FROM *Outside*

THE GRILL AT El Boliche Viejo steak house, in the foothills along northern Patagonia's Limay River, near Bariloche, looks like something made from the recycled parts of a medieval torture chamber. It's built of firebrick and heat-blackened iron, and the grate is adjusted by a hand-powered system of chains and sprockets that move with a fine-tuned clink. For the past seven years, this grill, or *parrilla,* has been under the jurisdiction of Rafael Huemchal. He's about forty years old, with a pudgy face and black hair that he keeps tucked beneath a cheap short-order cook's hat. He served a full ten years in the restaurant's back kitchen before ascending to his current position. The length of his apprenticeship suggests the national importance of his job, which bears the cool-sounding Argentinean name *asador.* That translates roughly as "grill man," though as I watched Rafael I thought of Dr. Frankenstein, who, if he'd wanted to assemble a cow instead of a human from miscellaneous body parts, could have come here and saved himself the hassle of digging around in old graveyards. Rafael regularly handles beef cuts from front legs, back legs, ribs, heads, necks, hearts, stomachs, intestines, kidneys, tongues, briskets, and diaphragms, and many of those were sizzling in front of us.

I'd been warned about this by my friend Diego Allolio. Born in Concordia, near Argentina's border with Uruguay, Diego, forty, co-owns Meridies, a Bariloche-based adventure travel company. The former rugby player often leads expeditions to such inhospitable places as 22,834-foot Aconcagua, the highest point in the Western Hemisphere. I had figured my humble quest to find the best steak in Argentina would be something he'd take lightly. If anything, I expected him to question my ability to adequately cover the culinary turf of a nation measuring more than a million square miles in nine days. Instead, he questioned my ability to cover the animal.

"Steak . . . ?" he asked. "In Argentina, we eat every part of the cow."

"I can handle it," I said. "Just take me where I need to go."

Diego tipped his head and looked at me in the same way I'd look at my six-year-old neighbor if she threatened to drink me under the table. I hadn't paid much attention to the gesture at first, but then Rafael gave me the exact same look upon hearing my purposes for coming to his restaurant. I could almost hear him thinking, "OK, little American, let's see what you're made of." He began placing each forkload of beef on the grill with a slapping movement that seemed to say, "Take that! . . . and that! . . . and that!"

Such aggression caught me off-guard. After all, I'd come to Argentina with the reverence of a Buddhist going to Tibet. If you were to add up my thoughts throughout the course of any given day, you'd see that I think about eating and cooking meat over other things by about three to one. I've tried everything from dog paws in Vietnam to antelope bladders in Montana, and I consider those line-drawn butcher's charts to be like fine art. I always figured I was an honorary Argentinean at heart. Residents of the country pack away 143 pounds of beef annually, much of it grilled on the *parrilla* (a word that can also refer to the restaurant or the grilled meat itself) and served with little more than a sprinkling of salt. That's almost fifty pounds more than burger-fanatic Americans drown in ketchup and mustard in the same period of time. No wonder former Argentinean president Carlos Menem offered this recommendation to the U.S. trade publication *Western Beef Producer:* "Tell your readers, 'Don't come to my country if they're vegetarian.'"

I'd been obsessed with Argentinean beef since my first visit to the country, eight years ago, when I spent a few days fly-fishing for trout in the arid and rocky foothills of the Patagonian Andes. At the end of my stay, something magical happened on a twelve-hour bus ride. I'd been sleeping for hours when I awoke to see that we'd stopped in a small town somewhere between Bariloche and Buenos Aires. I was drawn to a small curbside restaurant stand with smoke coming from a crude chimney. At the counter, I was served an unusual cut of meat that would forever alter my impressions of beef. It was long and narrow, almost like a wooden ruler, though it was well over an inch thick. It was obviously a strip of ribs, like what you'd get if you spaced two saws an inch apart and ran them down your side from armpit to hip. They weren't stewed and saucy and greasy like American-style ribs. Instead, they were steaky—there was lean meat and fat meat, charred meat and tender meat, and the saltiness seemed to come from inside the meat itself. I ate four strips, then savored the small hunks of bone as if they were meat-flavored Life Savers.

The experience left me banging my fist in frustration that I'd gone my whole life without tasting something so wonderful. For years I tried to replicate that meal, both at home and in Argentinean steak houses in the United States. I never came close. It was like a gastronomical version of an itch in the center of your back, right where it's impossible to reach.

But Rafael was probing the borders of my tolerance with the half cow he'd thrown on the grill. When the waiter poured me another glass of wine, I became emboldened and looked at Rafael.

"Bring it on," I said.

Luckily, I'd brought along my wife, Katie. She mistakenly assumed that this was some sort of fun couple's trip, but I was actually using her for her belly. My midwestern upbringing forbids me from leaving an unclean plate, and I figured that I might need backup to handle stray scraps.

If Katie and I ever seek marriage counseling, it will be over issues of foreign travel. Our styles are polar opposites. I like to keep things free and easy; Katie likes to plan. She thinks my method is lazy and leads to a lot of missed opportunities; I think of her method as a pair of strong, warty hands wrapped around the neck of spontaneity.

Because I was dragging her along on an adventure of my own devising, I agreed to bow to her desires. My efforts toward organization would have made a Secret Service man jealous. I read restaurant reviews going back twenty years. I talked to dozens of American and Argentinean beef connoisseurs. I even talked to people who didn't really know what they were talking about, because sometimes you can turn up surprising pieces of information like that.

What I learned is that locating the best steak in Argentina is like trying to pinpoint the whereabouts of Osama bin Laden. A cab-driver in Los Angeles told a colleague of my wife's that the best steaks come from the area around Bariloche. His opinion was in stark contrast with that of a friend of a colleague of mine, who suggested that the best steaks are more than a thousand miles north of there, near Iguazú Falls. He couldn't think of the name of the place, but he assured me that it was "on a main road near a bus station." Alberto Gonzalez, an Argentinean expat who owns one of my favorite restaurants in New York City, GustOrganics, explained that he couldn't in good conscience tell me about the best steak place. "Why not?" I asked.

"You would think I'm biased."

"Are you?"

"No, it truly is great. But it's owned by a friend."

"If you could tell me, what would you say?"

"I'd say, 'Happening. In Buenos Aires.'"

The testimonials suggested that I had to go just about everywhere. This was impossible, of course, so I settled on a plan to divide the country into three districts—central, south, and north, or Argentinean Beef Zones I, II, and III—and to conduct a whirlwind examination in each zone.

We started in Buenos Aires for the simple reason that that was where we landed, but, considering the history of Argentina, it was the perfect place to begin. Cattle were first introduced to Argentina in the northeast provinces by gold-and-silver-crazed Spaniards in the early 1500s. These early colonists didn't stay long, as they were harassed by natives and ran out of supplies. They abandoned many cattle when they retreated to Paraguay, and the animals turned feral and thrived on the verdant grasslands. When the Spanish finally returned, in 1580, to establish a permanent settlement in present-day Buenos Aires, they discovered a vastly multiplied and renewable export commodity that would enrich the city and provide the centerpiece of Buenos Aires cuisine for hundreds of years.

Katie and I planned to spend the next forty-eight hours eating steak for breakfast, lunch, and dinner. Our first stop was a hard-earned recommendation I'd pried out of Clint Peck, the director of the Beef Quality Assurance program at Montana State University, in Bozeman, which pursues a "commitment to quality within every segment of the beef industry." Peck frequently acts as a beef liaison between the U.S. and Argentina. When I brought up the subject of Argentinean steak, he offered some potent opinions.

"I've got a well-trained palate for beef," he said, "and some of the best steaks I've had have come out of Argentina. I'm not shy to say that."

"Anyplace in particular?" I asked.

"Estilo Campo," he said. "If your hotel concierge in Buenos Aires tells you differently, he's likely taking kickbacks."

"How do you cook the cow eyeballs?" I asked.

We'd just been seated at Estilo Campo, in Puerto Madero, a bustling neighborhood of shops and restaurants bordering a system of shipping canals. When we walked inside, the restaurant's overblown beef theme reminded me of a Chuck E. Cheese's for steak fanatics. There was cattle-related art and spits of roasted meat displayed behind glass windows that looked into the kitchens. The steak knives were essentially serrated machetes. Our waiter was dressed in baggy pants and a pressed shirt, which made him look like a cross between a traveling salesman and a gaucho.

He was confused by my question. "I don't understand," he said.

Nothing irritates me more than a waiter who doesn't know his own menu. I pointed to my copy and tapped the words OJO DE BIFE. "Right there, 'eye of cow'!"

His eyes lit up. "Beef ribeye. *Sí!*"

I played it cool by acting like I'd wanted that all along.

"Rare," I said. "Please."

Our attention turned to Katie. She's usually a very adventurous eater, but she was perusing the salads. I shot her the same glance I'll use if she ever admits marital infidelity and politely flipped her back to the meat listings.

She asked the waiter about the *bife de chorizo*. I recognized that from my beef studies. Unlike the Mexican or Spanish sausages that Americans are familiar with, it's actually a cut of beef similar to our sirloin strip.

He nodded, said, *"Excelente,"* and tucked his pad into his belt and disappeared. When he swooped back with our dishes, he placed on the table two slabs of beef that were big enough to pull up their own chairs and have a seat. The closest thing we had to a side dish was a shaker of salt. I thought about asking for a hunk of lettuce or a grilled zucchini, but international travel brings out a passivity in me that Katie finds infuriating. Instead, I did what any man would do: I dug in.

Right off, I recognized the mild saltiness that seemed to come from inside the meat. The fat was sweeter and more palatable than most American beef. The cut had a certain resistance to being chewed—not toughness, but a substance to it that was very pleasant. It tasted real, almost wild. I knew right off that this was the steak I'd been looking for all those years, but instead of feeling sated, I felt egged on. It was like finding a few quarters in the crack at the back of a couch. Rather than thanking good luck, you're compelled to dig deeper and deeper.

When you factor in a glass of wine, three glasses of water, and close to two whole steaks (to say I had to finish Katie's steak would overstate her role), you'll see that I left Estilo Campo weighing about three pounds more than when I went in. We waddled over to the famous Plaza de Mayo, where adoring thousands gathered in the 1950s to hear Eva Perón speak from the balconies overlooking a giant monument of national hero General Belgrano. I fantasized about how much steak I could eat if I were the size of that statue, then dozed off beneath a palm tree.

I awoke an hour later in a panic about missing our dinner reservation at Cabaña Las Lilas, a waterfront steak house recommended by *New York Times* food critic R. W. Apple Jr. as a restaurant worth the cost of a plane ticket. It's fair to say that his assessment is still drawing clients. The restaurant was sophisticated and packed with well-dressed international tourists. As best I could tell, we had seven people attending to our table, and the prim staff served our steaks with a level of care you'd expect at a Sotheby's antiques auction. Of course the meat was perfect, but the hefty bill almost mandated that it had to be.

The steaks I had for brunch the next morning were just as good, though they came without the high prices. A well-connected friend had recommended La Dorita de Enfrente, in the trendy Palermo district. After we ate, our wanderings were guided by our need to arrive for an early dinner with the second-generation co-owner of Happening, the place Alberto had recommended. The restaurant is located in the Costanera district, along the Río de la Plata. Katie and I waited at the bar for Fernando Brucco, forty, who met us wearing Italian sneakers and a wrinkled beige linen suit. I explained that I couldn't eat that much because we'd just tackled a couple of sumo-size steaks for brunch and another strange piece of meat for lunch. He advised me to drink more red wine, a commonly accepted Argentinean remedy for fullness.

As we ate a procession of amazing steaks, again and again I pressed Fernando about what makes the beef in Argentina so good. Finally he nodded at my half-finished ribs and said, "In Buenos Aires, about steak we do not talk so much. Not when we could be eating it."

I was reminded of his observation the next morning before we flew from Buenos Aires to Bariloche. There was a steak vendor across the street from the airport, working off a trailer-mounted grill. I ordered a steak from him, and he pulled the thin and strange-looking meat from a plastic shopping bag that was lying near the wheel well.

"Please tell me you're not going to eat that," said Katie.

I try not to talk with my mouth full, so I was unable to reply.

Diego Allolio, my friend and Bariloche-based mountain guide, had none of Fernando Brucco's reservations about discussing meat. He was driving Katie and me eastward out of Bariloche in his pickup. Lake Nahuel Huapí, the centerpiece and namesake of a vast national park, stretched away from us in three directions. Surrounded by snowcapped peaks, it was so absurdly beautiful you'd think it was sponsored by a postcard company. During our 830-mile flight from Buenos Aires that morning, I'd watched as the lush grasslands turned to arid desert and then began to rise toward these glacial valleys. As our plane dropped, we passed over the heads of hundreds of sheep and cattle and then landed in a small town dominated by Bavarian architecture dating back a hundred years. Now Diego was taking me to his favorite place to eat steak.

"No *parrilla* should be formal," he said. "Great meat is simple. It should be cheap." While Diego expressed some uneasiness about his government's often heavy-handed involvement in economic matters, his opinions on affordable meat have some political backbone. In 2005, a surge in beef exports led to a sharp increase in domestic prices. The price increase led to international attention and widespread inflation, the way increased oil prices can single-handedly drive inflation in the U.S. As a remedy, the federal government stepped in to stabilize beef prices in early 2006, which put the finest cuts at about one-half of U.S. prices.

I'd been eating steaks several times a day, and the weight of it had settled in my gut like a wad of lead the size of a racquet-ball. But as soon as we walked into El Boliche Viejo, I knew that to-night was not conducive to moderation. The medieval-looking grill was positioned in the room like the cross in a church, and Rafael Huemchal was piling on enough meat for a small banquet.

My sense of gastrointestinal dread was alleviated by the excitement of seeing a master at work. Rafael had next to him only a bowl of salt and a carbon carving knife. He didn't trim the meat of its connective tissues and silver skin. These, he explained, help retain the moisture of the cut and enhance flavor. Before cooking, he sprinkled the surfaces of the meat with a generous application of salt and let that soak in. The bars of the grill were made of quarter-inch angle iron with the troughs facing up and pitched at an angle in order to channel the fat and cooking juices away from the coals. This was imperative, Rafael explained, because one of the cardinal sins of *parrilla* cooking is to taint the charcoal flavor with the taste or smell of burned grease.

Another cardinal sin is to let the flame make contact with the meat. Alberto had explained to me that his countrymen can't help but laugh at American steak house commercials that feature flame-licked slabs of beef. Rafael kept the meat about ten inches above the heat source at all times. "This is not about speed," he said. He let the meat cook for an hour. Then, just before serving, he lowered the chains and dropped the grill to a position just above the charcoal. This was the moment when he put the signature Argentinean char on the steaks. The move represents one of the primary differences between Argentinean *parrilla* and your typical American barbecue, where meat is quickly "seared" the moment it's placed on the grill.

Thankfully, Katie was more interested in a local bottle of Malbec, so her palate had been lubricated for a starter of grilled thymus glands, kidneys, and stuffed sausages. The glands were succulent and rich, but I could hardly bring myself to try the kidneys, with their urine-like aftertaste. Katie dug right in. "Don't be a baby," she said.

I spent the next hour in a beef-induced trance. I'm a little hazy about what exactly happened, but I know that I consumed at least a few bites of every cut of beef on a cow. At some point Diego drove us back to our hotel; and then it was suddenly morning again and he was waiting outside our hotel in a pair of shorts. This time we headed down the Limay River into a narrow valley of grasslands and bizarre rock formations. We pulled off the road onto a narrow trail along the river; on the other side, a man climbed into a small skiff and motored over to pick us up. We weren't halfway across when I detected the now unmistakable odor of a fully loaded grill.

Diego's friend Jorge Pinto met us on the opposite bank. A lanky and eager guy with a bush hat held around his neck by a cord, Jorge runs the secluded and rustic fishing-and-rock-climbing lodge Valle Cantado, with his wife. One of their specialties is home-cooked *parrilla* served to small groups traveling downriver by boat. Jorge took us to look at the *quincho,* which is like a walk-in dome-shaped oven with a diameter of about fifty feet and a ventilation hole in the peak of the roof. It was well over one hundred degrees inside.

Within moments of arriving, I was cradling a glass of Malbec and looking down on several platters of perfectly prepared meat. As I ate, I swore I could taste the rivers, the hardwoods, and the mountains. Just when I wondered if it was possible to become paralyzed from overeating, Jorge suggested we climb into the hills behind his property to investigate a number of ancient cave dwellings. I commented to Katie that we should have waited to eat until after we'd climbed. Jorge overheard this and assured me that I could have more meat once we climbed down.

I figured I'd eaten about twenty pounds of beef in seven days, and for the first time in my life I was considering going on a vegan cleanse. I was hurting as we flew twelve hundred miles north of Bariloche to Salta, smack in the heart of Beef Zone III. Salta, a historic Spanish colonial city, lies near the northeast border with Bolivia; it's a rugged and hot place dominated by big ranches, dusty farmland, fast-moving flatbed trucks, and lanky dogs. I was traveling north of the city in the early-morning darkness with Agustín Arias, whose home, Estancia el Bordo de las Lanzas, produces beef, polo horses, tobacco, and a wide variety of organic crops.

We'd gotten up at 3 A.M. because Agustín had promised to show me a slaughterhouse, which was a couple of hours away. (Katie had bowed out and found herself a swimming pool and a bowl of fresh fruit.)

I was dozing against the window when Agustín awoke me with a proclamation: "There are two things that are important in Argentina," he said. "Soccer and beef."

"I think I heard that line from someone already," I said, "except the person said—"

Agustín interrupted. "Politics, labor strikes, polo . . . The first word doesn't matter. The second word—*beef*—that's what matters."

As the truck took a series of rolling bumps, I began to question the integrity of the steak I'd eaten from the plastic grocery sack near the airport. My stomach was making peculiar sounds. When I explained my concerns to Agustín, he suggested a remedy of red wine.

I expected the slaughterhouse to be somehow less advanced than the ones I've visited in the States, but in fact it was as modern and brisk and sanitized as anything I've ever seen. I followed one animal through the processing line. Its journey began with a blow to the head and ended as twenty knife-wielding workers took the steer apart as easily as someone undressing for bed. I looked at Agustín and made a joke about the unappetizing nature of the spectacle by patting my stomach.

"Yes," he said. "It makes me ready for dinner, too."

I made an embarrassing performance during a lunch of beef ribs, and then Agustín took me to visit a good buddy of his. We drove back south toward Salta, then followed a byzantine maze of double tracks and trails that wound their way higher and higher into the dry, brown hills. Just when I figured there couldn't possibly be anything back there, we rounded a corner and came across four gauchos separating a group of cows and calves in a cloud of dust. As we watched, the owner of the estancia, Francisco, pulled up alongside us. The first thing Francisco said to me was "Monday, Wednesday, and Friday, we eat meat. And we eat meat the day after those days, too."

In most respects, Francisco looks like your typical Wyoming rancher: four-door Ford diesel pickup, cowboy boots, a big gut that prevents his shirt from being fully tucked in. What set him apart was his red beret, which he wore with a haphazard fold above his ear. He has a 74,000-acre estancia and runs 4,000 head of cattle on it. The estancia has been in Francisco's family since the 1700s. Back then, they were raising the animals mostly for leather. Beef production didn't become the primary aim of the estancia until the advent of refrigeration, which allowed for the storage and distribution of fresh beef.

Francisco has not taken to trends in organic ranching. Rather, he's a follower of old traditions in organic ranching. When I asked if he uses antibiotics and hormones to facilitate faster growth, he responded as though I had asked him if it's socially acceptable to pinch your grandmother on the fanny. To do so would be a violation of cultural mores, he answered.

I found that Francisco doesn't employ the more egregious practices used by American ranchers. Many of Francisco's strategies are mandated by the economic realities of Argentina, where beef must be produced inexpensively. Instead of producing cattle with an eye toward high fat content, large body size, and quick growth, his aim is to raise healthy animals that can take care of themselves and live comfortably on the habitat without requiring constant attention from vets and gauchos. The calves must be small enough to pass through their mother's birth canal without human assistance. Rather than fattening cattle on grain for four months, which is typical in the United States, he puts his animals on grain for only five or six weeks before sending them to slaughter. It's just enough to add eighty pounds to the carcass, rather than the four hundred pounds common in the U.S. For the rest of their lives, Francisco's cattle run free-range in the meadows of his estancia.

Driving around with Francisco, I sometimes got the sense that we were watching a form of wildlife rather than livestock. His eyes brightened when he saw some animals through a distant gap in the trees. As we pulled up to Agustín's truck, Francisco seemed contemplative. "Everyone can produce beef. But in Argentina we have good grass, good estancias, and a good tradition. That's why Argentinean beef is the best."

That night, back at Agustín's, I thought of Francisco's statement as I poured Katie and myself yet another glass of red wine and watched one of Agustín's hired men prepare our meal on an outdoor *parrilla*. It was a process I'd seen half a dozen times or so by now, but still I reveled in the precision and uniformity of the task. There was the lighting of locally collected hardwood; the thoughtful adjustment of the grill; the sprinkling of salt, as careful as a beautician applying makeup; the long spell of patient waiting.

In America, we pretend that innovation and change are the hallmarks of great cuisine. We've even made game shows out of our desire to rethink every aspect of what goes into our mouths. There's always a new way to do this, a better way to do that. Hanging around in Argentina, though, I fell in love with the way people strive for a known and traditional goal. Not only do they know how to cook *parrilla;* they know that they know how. There's no apology, no second-guessing, and no need to mess with a winning system.

Forty-five minutes passed, and then an hour. The rib bones slowly turned the color of coffee with milk. The sausages lost their swollen, slightly medical look. The flank went from looking rubbery and impenetrable to something you could cut with a fork. It was slowly surrendering to the powers of heat and time, and once again my stomach was surrendering to the power of the *parrilla*. I'd waited eight years to eat this steak, and I took comfort that in eight more years I could come back and find it exactly the same.

DAVID   SEDARIS

Guy Walks into a Bar Car

FROM *The New Yorker*

IN THE GOLDEN AGE of American travel, the platforms of train stations were knee-deep in what looked like fog. You see it all the time in black-and-white movies, these low-lying eddies of silver. I always thought it was steam from the engines, but now I wonder if it didn't come from cigarettes. You could smoke everywhere back then: in the dining car, in your sleeping berth. Depending on your preference, it was either absolute heaven or absolute hell.

I know there was a smoking car on the Amtrak I took from Raleigh to Chicago in 1984, but seven years later it was gone. By then if you wanted a cigarette your only option was to head for the bar. It sounds all right in passing, romantic even— "the bar on the Lake Shore Limited"—but in fact it was rather depressing. Too bright, too loud, and full of alcoholics who commandeered the seats immediately after boarding and remained there, marinating like cheap kebabs, until they reached their destinations. At first, their voices might strike you as jolly: the warm tones of strangers becoming friends. Then the drinkers would get sloppy and repetitive, settling, finally, on that cross-eyed mush that passes for alcoholic sincerity.

On the train I took from New York to Chicago in early January of 1991, one of the drunks pulled down his pants and shook his bare bottom at the woman behind the bar. I was thirty-four, old enough to know better, yet I laughed along with everyone else. The trip was interminable—almost nineteen hours, not counting any delays— but nothing short of a derailment could have soured my good mood. I was off to see the boyfriend I'd left behind when I moved to New York. We'd known each other for six years, and though we'd broken up more times than either of us could count, there was the hope that this visit might reunite us. Then he'd join me for a fresh start in Manhattan, and all our problems would disappear.

It was best for both of us that it didn't work out that way, though of course I couldn't see it at the time. The trip designed to bring us back together tore us apart for good, and it was a considerably sorrier me that boarded the Limited back to New York. My train left Union Station in the early evening. The late-January sky was the color of pewter, and the ground beneath it—as flat as rolled-out dough—was glazed with slush. I watched as the city receded into the distance, and then I went to the bar car for a cigarette. Of the dozen or so drunks who'd staggered on board in Chicago, one in particular stood out. I've always had an eye for ruined-looking men, and that's what attracted me to this guy—I'll call him Johnny Ryan—the sense that he'd been kicked around. By the time he hit thirty, a hardness would likely settle about his mouth and eyes, but as it was—at twenty-nine—he was right on the edge, a screw-top bottle of wine the day before it turns to vinegar.

It must have been he who started the conversation, as I'd never have had the nerve. Under different circumstances, I might have stammered hello and run back to my seat, but my breakup convinced me that something major was about to happen. The chance of a lifetime was coming my way, and in order to accept it I needed to loosen up, to stop being so "rigid." That was what my former boyfriend had called me. He'd thrown in "judgmental" while he was at it, another of those synonyms for "no fun at all." The fact that it stung reaffirmed what I had always suspected: it was all true. No one was duller, more prudish and set in his ways, than I was.

Johnny didn't strike me as gay, but it was hard to tell with alcoholics. Like prisoners and shepherds, many of them didn't care whom they had sex with, the idea being that what happens in the dark stays in the dark. It's the next morning you have to worry about—the name-calling, the slamming of doors, the charge that you somehow cast a spell. I must have been desperate to think that such a person would lead me to a new life. Not that Johnny was bad company—it's just that the things we had in common were all so depressing. Unemployment, for instance. My last job had been as an elf at Macy's.

"Personal assistant" was how I phrased it, hoping he wouldn't ask for whom.

"Uh—Santa?"

His last job had involved hazardous chemicals. An accident at Thanksgiving had caused boils to rise on his back. A few months before that, a tankard of spilled benzene had burned all the hair off his arms and hands. This only made him more attractive. I imagined those smooth pink mitts of his opening the door to the rest of my life.

"So are you just going to stand here smoking all night?" he asked.

Normally, I waited until nine o'clock to start drinking, but "What the heck," I said. "I'll have a beer. Why not?" When a couple of seats opened up, Johnny and I took them. Across the narrow carriage, a black man with a bushy mustache pounded on the Formica tabletop. "So a nun goes into town," he said, "and sees a sign reading QUICKIES — TWENTY-FIVE DOLLARS. Not sure what it means, she walks back to the convent and pulls aside the mother superior. 'Excuse me,' she asks, 'but what's a quickie?'

"And the old lady goes, 'Twenty-five dollars. Just like in town.'"

As the car filled with laughter, Johnny lit a fresh cigarette. "Some comedian," he said. I don't know how we got onto the subject of gambling—perhaps I asked if he had a hobby.

"I'll bet on sporting events, on horses and greyhounds—hell, put two fleas on the table and I'll bet over which one can jump the highest. How about you?"

Gambling to me is what a telephone pole might be to a groundhog. He sees that it's there but doesn't for the life of him understand why. Friends have tried to explain the appeal, but still I don't get it. Why take chances with money?

Johnny had gone to Gamblers Anonymous, but the whining got on his nerves, and he quit after his third meeting. Now, he confessed, he was on his way to Atlantic City, where he hoped to clean up at the blackjack tables.

"All right," called the black man on the other side of the carriage. "I've got another one. What do you have if you have nuts on a wall?" He lit a cigarette and blew out the match. "Walnuts!"

A red-nosed woman in a decorative sweatshirt started to talk, but the black fellow told her that he wasn't done yet. "What do you have if you have nuts on your chest?" He waited a beat. "Chestnuts! What do you have when you have nuts on your chin?" He looked from face to face. "A dick in your mouth!"

"Now, that's good," Johnny said. "I'll have to remember that."

"I'll have to remind you," I told him, trembling a little at my forwardness. "I mean . . . I'm pretty good at holding on to jokes."

As the black man settled down, I asked Johnny about his family. It didn't surprise me that his mother and father were divorced. Each of them was fifty-four years old, and each was currently living with someone much younger. "My dad's girlfriend—fiancée, I guess I should call her—is no older than me," Johnny said. "Before losing my job, I had my own place, but now I'm living with them. Just, you know, until I get back on my feet."

I nodded.

"My mom, meanwhile, is a total mess," he said. "Total pothead, total motormouth, total perfect match for her asshole thirty-year-old boyfriend."

Nothing in this guy's life sounded normal to me. Take food: he could recall his mother rolling joints on the kitchen counter, but he couldn't remember her cooking a single meal, not even on holidays. For dinner, they'd eat take-out hamburgers or pizzas, sometimes a sandwich slapped together over the sink. Johnny didn't cook, either. Neither did his father or his future stepmother. I asked what was in their refrigerator, and he said, "Ketchup, beer, mixers—what else?" He had no problem referring to himself as an alcoholic. "It's just a fact," he said. "I have blue eyes and black hair, too. Big deal."

"Here's a clean one," the black man said. "A fried-egg sandwich walks into a bar and orders a drink. The bartender looks him up and down, then goes, 'Sorry, we don't serve food here.'"

"Oh, that's old," one of his fellow drunks said. "Not only that but it's supposed to be a hamburger, not a fried-egg sandwich."

"It's supposed to be *food* is what it's supposed to be," the black man told him. "As to what that food is, I'll make it whatever the hell I want to."

"Amen," Johnny said, and the black man gave him a thumbs-up.

His next joke went over much better. "What did the leper say to the prostitute? 'Keep the tip.'"

I pictured what looked like a mushroom cap resting in the palm of an outstretched hand. Then I covered my mouth and laughed so hard that beer trickled out of my nose. I was just mopping it up when the last call was announced, and everyone raced to the counter to stock up. Some of the drinkers would be at it until morning, when the bar reopened, while others would find their seats and sleep for a while before returning.

As for Johnny, he had a fifth of Smirnoff in his suitcase. I had two Valiums in mine, and, because I have never much cared for sedatives, the decision to share them came easily. An hour later, it was agreed that we needed to smoke some pot. Each of us was holding, so the only question was where to smoke it—and how to get there from the bar. Since taking the Valium, drinking six beers, and following them with straight vodka, walking had become a problem for me. I don't know what it took to bring down Johnny, but he wasn't even close yet. That's what comes with years of socking it away—you should be unconscious, but instead you're up and full of bright ideas. "I think I've got a place we can go to," he said.

I'm not sure why he chose the women's lounge rather than the men's. Perhaps it was closer, or maybe there was no men's lounge. One way or the other, even now, almost twenty years later, it shames me to think of it. The idea of holing up in a bathroom, of hogging the whole thing just so that you can hang out with someone who will never, under any circumstances, return your interest, makes me cringe. Especially given that this—the "dressing room" it was called—was Amtrak's one meager attempt to recapture some glamour. It amounted to a small chamber with a window—a space not much bigger than a closet. There was an area to sit while brushing your hair or applying makeup, and a mirror to look into while you did it. A second, inner door led to a sink and toilet, but we kept that shut and installed ourselves on the carpeted floor.

Johnny had brought our plastic cups from the bar, and, after settling in, he poured us each a drink. I felt boneless, as if I'd been filleted; yet still I managed to load the pipe and hold my lighter to the bowl. Looking up through the window, I could see the moon, which struck me, in my half-conscious state, as flat and unnaturally bright, a sort of glowing Pringle.

"Do you think we can turn that overhead light off?" I asked.

"No problem, chief."

It was he who brought up the subject of sex. One moment, I was asking if his mom gave him a discount on his drugs, and the next thing I knew he was telling me about this woman he'd recently had sex with. "A fatty," he called her. "A bloodsucker." Johnny also told me that the older he got the harder it was to get it up. "I'll be totally into it, and then it's, like, 'What the fuck?' You know?"

"Oh, definitely."

He poured more vodka into his plastic cup and swirled it around, as if it were a fine cognac that needed to breathe. "You get into a lot of fights?" he asked.

"Arguments?"

"No," he said. "I mean with your fists. You ever punch people?"

I relit the pipe and thought of the dustup my former boyfriend and I had had before I left. It was the first time since the fifth grade that I'd hit someone not directly related to me, and it left me feeling like a Grade A moron. This had a lot to do with my punch, which was actually more of a slap. To make it worse, I'd then slipped on the icy sidewalk and fallen into a bank of soft gray snow.

There was no need to answer Johnny's fistfight question. The subject had been raised for his benefit rather than mine, an excuse to bemoan the circumference of his biceps. Back when he was boxing, the one on the right had measured seventeen and a half inches. "Now it's less than fourteen," he told me. "I'm shrinking before my very fucking eyes."

"Well, can't you fatten it back up somehow?" I asked. "You're young. I mean, just how hard can it be to gain weight?"

"The problem isn't gaining weight, it's gaining it in the right place," Johnny said. "Two six-packs a day might swell my stomach, but it's not doing shit for my arms."

"Maybe you could lift the cans for a while before opening them," I offered. "That should count for something, shouldn't it?"

Johnny flattened his voice. "You're a regular comedian, aren't you? Keep it up and maybe you can open for that asshole in the bar." A minute of silence and then he relit the pipe, took a hit, and passed it my way. "Look at us," he said, and he let out a long sigh. "A couple of first-class fucking losers."

I wanted to defend myself, or at least point out that we were in *second* class, but then somebody knocked on the door. "Go away," Johnny said. "The bathroom's closed until tomorrow." A minute later, there came another knock, this one harder, and before we could respond a key turned and a conductor entered. It wouldn't have worked to deny anything: the room stunk of pot and cigarette smoke. There was the half-empty bottle of vodka, the plastic cups turned on their sides. Put a couple of lampshades on our heads and the picture would have been complete.

I suppose that the conductor could have made some trouble— confiscated our dope, had us arrested at the next stop—but instead he just told us to take a hike, no easy feat on a train. Johnny and I parted without saying good night, I staggering off to my seat, and he going, I assumed, to his. I saw him again the following morning, back in the bar car. Whatever spell had been cast the night before was broken, and he was just another alcoholic starting his day with a shot and a chaser. As I ordered a coffee, the black man told a joke about a witch with one breast.

"Give it a rest," the woman in the decorative sweatshirt said.

I smoked a few cigarettes and then returned to my seat, nursing what promised to be a two-day headache. While slumped against the window, trying unsuccessfully to sleep, I thought of a trip to Greece I'd taken in August of 1982. I was twenty-four that summer, and flew by myself from Raleigh to Athens. A few days after arriving, I was joined by my father, my brother, and my older sister, Lisa. The four of us traveled around the country, and when they went back to North Carolina I took a bus to the port city of Patras. From there I sailed to Brindisi, Italy, wondering all the while why I hadn't returned with the rest of my family. In theory it was wonderful—a European adventure. I was too self-conscious to enjoy it, though, too timid, and it stymied me that I couldn't speak the language.

A bilingual stranger helped me buy a train ticket to Rome, but on the return to Brindisi I had no one but myself to rely on. The man behind the counter offered me three options, and I guess I said yes to the one that meant "No seat for me, thank you. I would like to be packed as tightly as possible amongst people with no access to soap or running water."

It was a common request, at least among the young and foreign.

I heard French, Spanish, German, and a good many languages I couldn't quite identify. What was it that sounded like English played backward? Dutch? Swedish? If I found the crowd intimidating, it had more to do with my insecurity than with the way anyone treated me. I suppose the others seemed more deserving than I did, with their faded bandannas and goatskin bags sagging with wine. While I was counting the days until I could go back home, they seemed to have a real talent for living.

When I was a young man, my hair was dark brown and a lot thicker than it is now. I had one continuous eyebrow instead of two separate ones, and this made me look as if I sometimes rode a donkey. It sounds odd to say it—conceited, even—but I was cute that August when I was twenty-four. I wouldn't have said so at the time, but reviewing pictures taken by my father in Athens I think, That was me? Really? Looks-wise, that single month constituted my moment, a peak from which the descent was both swift and merciless.

It's only 350 miles from Rome to Brindisi, but, what with the constant stopping and starting, the train took forever. We left, I believe, at around 8:30 P.M., and for the first few hours everyone stood. Then we sat with our legs crossed, folding them in a little bit tighter when one person, and then another, decided to lie down. As my fellow passengers shifted position, I found myself pushed toward the corner, where I brushed up against a fellow named Bashir.

Lebanese, he said he was, en route to a small Italian university, where he planned to get a master's in engineering. Bashir's English was excellent, and in a matter of minutes we formed what passes between wayfarers in a foreign country as a kind of automatic friendship. More than a friendship, actually—a romance. Coloring everything was this train, its steady rumble as we passed through the dark Italian countryside. Bashir was—how to describe him? It was as if someone had coaxed the eyes out of Bambi and resettled them, half-asleep, into a human face. Nothing hard or ruined-looking there; in fact, it was just the opposite—angelic, you might call him, pretty.

What was it that he and I talked about so intently? Perhaps the thrill was that we *could* talk, that our tongues, flabby from lack of exercise, could flap and make sounds in their old familiar way. Three hours into our conversation, he invited me to get off the train in his college town and spend some time, as much as I liked, in the apartment that was waiting for him. It wasn't the offer you'd make to a backpacker but something closer to a proposal. "Be with me" was the way I interpreted it.

At the end of our car was a little room, no more than a broom closet, really, with a barred window in it. It must have been 4 A.M. when two disheveled Germans stepped out, and we moved in to take their place. As would later happen with Johnny Ryan, Bashir and I sat on the floor, the state of which clearly disgusted him. Apart from the fact that we were sober and were pressed so close that our shoulders touched, the biggest difference was that our attraction was mutual. The moment came when we should have kissed—you could practically hear the surging strings—but I was too shy to make the first move, and so, I guess, was he. Still, I could feel this thing between us, not just lust but a kind of immediate love, the sort that, like instant oatmeal, can be realized in a matter of minutes and is just as nutritious as the real thing. We'll kiss . . . now, I kept thinking. Then, OK . . . now. And on it went, more torturous by the second.

The sun was rising as we reached his destination, the houses and church spires of this strange city—a city I could make my own— silhouetted against the weak morning sky. "And so?" he asked. I don't remember my excuse, but it all came down to cowardice. For what, really, did I have to return to? A job pushing a wheelbarrow on Raleigh construction sites? A dumpy one-bedroom next to the IHOP?

Bashir got off with his three big suitcases and became a perennial lump in my throat, one that rises whenever I hear the word "Lebanon" or see its jittery outline on the evening news. Is that where you went back to? I wonder. Do you ever think of me? Are you even still alive?

Given the short amount of time we spent together, it's silly how often, and how tenderly, I think of him. All the way to Penn Station, hung over from my night with Johnny Ryan, I wondered what might have happened had I taken Bashir up on his offer. I imagined our apartment overlooking a square: the burbling fountain, the drawings of dams and bridges piled neatly on the desk.

When you're young, it's easy to believe that such an opportunity will come again, maybe even a better one. Instead of a Lebanese guy in Italy, it might be a Nigerian one in Belgium, or maybe a Pole in Turkey. You tell yourself that if you traveled alone to Europe this summer you could surely do the same thing next year and the year after that. Of course, you don't, though, and the next thing you know you're an aging, unemployed elf, so desperate for love that you spend your evening mooning over a straight alcoholic.

The closer we got to New York the more miserable I became. Then I thought of this guy my friend Lili and I had borrowed a ladder from a few months earlier, someone named Hugh. I'd never really trusted people who went directly from one relationship to the next, so after my train pulled into Penn Station, and after I'd taken the subway home, I'd wait a few hours, or maybe even a full day, before dialing his number and asking if he'd like to hear a joke.

PATRICK SYMMES

The Filthy, Fecund Secret
of Emilia-Romagna

FROM *Condé Nast Traveler*

THE SOIL IN THE ARDA VALLEY was, in the first days of
September, already furrowed for a second crop. Everywhere we
looked, right beside the roaring A1 or at some forgotten crossroads
amid collapsing farmhouses, machines had plucked the harvest
and turned the ground. Emilia-Romagna, the flat northern heart-
land of Italian farming, was combed into neat rows. Everywhere we
paused, we stared in disbelief. Finally, outside the supermarket in
Lugagnano Val d'Arda, I stepped in among the clods.

If you've ever gardened, you know the feeling I had. The dirt
— millions of years of silt, washed down from the Alps and Apennines and deposited into this great bowl by the flooding of the Po
River — lay meters deep. It is a rich brown humus, fine, dense,
almost chocolaty. This stuff — mere dirt — is the building block of
the wealth, strife, and food of the Po Valley, the great plain at the
heart of Italian agriculture.

The story of Emilia-Romagna is the story of that soil, which grows
the grass that feeds the cows that flavor the milk that makes the
Parmesan cheese taste so good just down the road in Parma. This
is the soil that sprouts the corn and wheat that fatten the pigs that
become the ham that becomes *prosciutto di Parma*. This is the brown
muck, fantastically productive, that grows the Trebbiano grapes,
cooked down into the aged vinegar *balsamico di Modena*, in the town
of that name, just another half hour along the A1. And beyond
that, right down the curve of the immense plain — the largest flat

place in Italy—all the products of this soil have been gathered into Bologna, one of Italy's great, innovative trading cities, whose nimble-minded gourmets invented much of what passes for Italian food around the globe. Ravioli? Tagliatelle? Lasagna? Polenta? Tortellini? Half of all pasta shapes? All from Emilia-Romagna. If your mouth is not watering, stop reading here.

The soil next to the supermarket in Lugagnano wasn't just brown and rich: it was practically alive, a tightly packed silt that the machines had turned up into chunks the size of dinner plates. I prodded one with my foot. "The size of dinner plates," I said to my wife, awed.

"Bigger," she corrected. Some of the pieces were the size of serving platters.

If you want to know how Emilia-Romagna has conquered the world, one table at a time, you need only look down.

We had rented a stone house in Castelletto, an obscure village high up in the Arda Valley. It proved to be a steep hamlet of stone houses, many empty, and about forty year-round residents, mostly old women. Ours was the only rental property in Castelletto, found online. It had good views, modern everything, and it rattled in the fierce mountain winds.

Our son, Max—a precious bundle, aged fourteen months—attempted his first steps in Castelletto's empty playground. We took our first steps too: awkward greetings in Italian, and a quick scamper to the valley's most famous site, the fortress town of Castell'Arquato. I struggled up the medieval keep with Max on my back, and we surveyed the views up the Arda—an ugly dam, and then the gentle Apennines, sharing a border with Tuscany. In the other direction was the great flat plain of the Po River.

Our goal was to go local in every sense: language, cooking, daily life. By staying in this small town for a week, we could wander far and wide through Emilia-Romagna but always come back to a single point—depth in Italy rather than breadth. We gathered fallen apples from our yard and fed the baby apple mush that had traveled only a few yards in its life. I studied Italian. We walked, cooked, and made slow but encouraging progress in befriending the town's elderly doyennes, who were enthralled by my son's head of Irish hair. *Il bimbo rosso,* they called him: the red baby. *Che bello.* The village was dying, demographically, but EU money had paved even the smallest roads, flavored the local tomatoes with farming subsidies, and put seven sheep and an Audi in the same yard. The houses were in good repair—the children and grandchildren returned on weekends for the essential rituals of Italian family. Rural life was sustained on this high-fat diet of state support, provincial support, supranational subsidies, and an enthusiastic public willing to pay for good, local, traditional foods.

We followed our landlord's tip farther up the Arda Valley to Cà Ciancia, an *agriturismo,* or farmhouse that takes in guests—an embodiment of the last of these trends. We parked against giant hoops of hay and walked past a small barn full of cows, pigs, and rabbits. In the kitchen—half a dozen local women roasting and knifing— these ingredients were cooked and served a few yards from where they were born. In both dining rooms huge collective meals were in progress, a dozen people at one table, eighteen at the next. The food—truffled anolini, pork loin with crisp potatoes—can only be described by my wife's abrupt declaration, just halfway through, that "this is the greatest meal of my life."

Food has to come from somewhere. Emilia-Romagna has beauty in it, but also more hog processors than ruins, more grain silos than medieval towers (and they have a lot of medieval towers). In the Po Valley, "what you see is what you smell," Bill Buford, author of *Heat,* a tale of learning to cook Italian, explained to me. That can mean foodie bouquets of simmering sauce, rich cheese, and roasted chestnuts, but, Buford noted honestly, "even the fog smells like pig poo."

Ask an Italian where the best food comes from, and he will mention his mother, and then his home region. But if pushed, many will admit, as one Roman told me, "Of course, there is Emilia-Romagna." Why here? Good dirt, to be sure, but also rotten politics that created concentrated Renaissance wealth, and aristocratic rulers like the Estes, a clan that rivaled the Medici, sprinkled castles throughout Emilia-Romagna and practically invented the culture of banqueting and conspicuous consumption.

Then there is what the British explorer Richard Burton, writing in 1876, called *sveltezza d'ingenio*—the mental agility, the inventiveness—that is key to the region. Design and industry are fused in local brands like Ferrari, Ducati, and Lamborghini. Reggio Emilia, a quiet university city in the west, perpetually jousts with nearby Parma for the highest per capita income in Italy.

Yet Emilia-Romagna is a kind of lost region for foreigners, known, if at all, for its gemlike cities—Parma, Modena, Bologna, Ferrara, Ravenna—rather than its awkward hyphenated name, rooted in the ancient disputes of the Gauls and the Romans and pronounced with an almost silent *g*. The various cities have been rivals throughout history, pitted against each other like pawns in war and peace, swapped and traded among dukes, emperors, and popes. Naturally resistant to agglomeration, they have preserved and cultivated styles, habits, food specialties, and personalities that are independent of one another (the Parmese are reserved, the Modenese vivacious, and the Bolognese consider themselves the best lovers in Italy, or so the story goes).

As an identity, Emilia-Romagna exists chiefly on maps, which show it as a series of highways and train lines connecting outside places that are more important—Milan in the west to Florence in the south to Venice in the north. Forty million tourists a year come to this nation—two for every three Italians—but typically they just pass through Emilia-Romagna in transit.

So it is overlooked.

Fine. More for us.

What foreigners want from Italy changes over time, as we saw the next day. Having left Castelletto at the crack of noon, we toured Fontanellato, one of the many castles studded through the region by rival dukes, protecting their wealth and status with fairy-tale battlements and moats better suited to fishing than holding off a French army. A church wedding here fascinated us, the young men all in funereal black, the women erupting in purple and red organza, everything scented with Catholic incense. But after a few missed turns we arrived at nearby Colorno, whose vast Farnese palace has been divided into a psychiatric hospital in one wing and one of Italy's most ambitious cooking schools in the other. Called Alma, it was opened in 2004 to train hundreds of international students a year as Italian-speaking evangelists of an Italian cuisine held to the highest standards.

One of the school's star chefs, Paolo Amadori, briskly gainsaid the claims that Emilia-Romagna has the best food in Italy. ("Let them talk," he said of food writers. "We don't make any distinctions.") Italian cuisine as a whole was not respected enough. Amadori cited the "Michelin gap," the way restaurants in a single French city hold more Michelin stars than are awarded in all of Italy. "Bottom line, unfortunately, is that Italian cuisine was exported from Italy by nonprofessionals," Amadori said. He meant the poor emigrants who flooded out of Italy, taking a cuisine of hunger built on the ingredients of poverty that was intended to satisfy need, not Michelin. Italian food suffered from what he called "the *nonna* problem."

"They still think the momma should be in the restaurant," he told me, in his chef's whites and toque. "We have had only twenty years of professionalism fighting against a hundred years of the *nonna*, the grandmother. Why are we always talking about the *nonna?*"

A bold stand to attack the grandmothers. In Parma the next day, we saw the arguments for professionalism. The city is a model of affluent northern Italian efficiency, and in the streets—like in all Emilia-Romagna cities, the layout is octagonal, following the shape of a castle designed to deflect cannonballs—we saw only Italians here, as in so much of the region.

Granted, there are greater things in Italy than in Parma alone. But for a first-time visitor like me, this was more than enough. Even for my wife, a jaded connoisseur of European beauty, the constant surprises—Renaissance frescoes, Byzantine mosaics, free Wi-Fi in the Parma town square—made Italy enthralling all over again. Later I would see Florence, the magic Italy, the famous Italy, with everything that Emilia-Romagna had to offer but done on steroids, at much greater scale and at infinitely higher cost, and with greater glory. Yet I would also see Florence amid roaring buses, be elbowed off the tiny sidewalks by beaming Russians, and have my pockets cleaned out by the exorbitant fees for museums and meals that came with free jostling. In Parma, by contrast, we had our own little Italy almost to ourselves. We ate a marvelous meal—practically alone—at La Greppia, on the edge of the city center. This was a restaurant advanced by Mario Batali, the New York–based chef, who had built his career on the pasta secrets he learned from three years in Emilia-Romagna kitchens.

La Greppia lived up to Batali's hype and Amadori's standards. Our lunch, made without a *nonna* in sight, featured Parma's gifts to the world: *prosciutto di Parma,* porcini from the Apennines, fresh, soft tagliatelle like long strips of butter, and what a Baedeker Guide would call excellent cheese. The famous Parmigiano Reggiano appeared three ways, first whipped into a curious and liberating *spuma di parmigiano,* like a savory ice-cream appetizer, an oddity that no grandmother would attempt and only a machine could produce. Then there was Parmigiano shaved liberally onto ribbons of pasta, and finally it appeared in fat chunks, pried from half a wheel by a waiter taken with our grinning child. Max sat through the meal in his high chair, eating Parma from each tiny hand. This habit now costs me $16.99 a pound.

Parmese say you eat twice: first at the table, then by talking about it. The food traditions here are among the oldest and most continuous in Europe, giving people enough time to try and reject every adornment, leaving a plateau of quality, a rare combination of inventiveness and simplicity.

If there is one place in Europe you can tour without a car, it is Emilia-Romagna. Even the second-class Eurostar train is utterly clean, quiet, and stress-free, linking the major cities in a straight line (by October, it should be possible to travel from Milan to Florence, right through Emilia-Romagna, in less than a hundred minutes). Secondary cities, like Ferrara, are served by regional trains, slower and covered with graffiti, but nonetheless reliable and cheap, and filled with the real life of Italy: students, immigrants, even dogs, who can ride if they have their own ticket. This is how we came into Modena, on a twenty-five-minute local run. We plopped Max in his stroller and hoofed it into the center of town, gradually falling into silence. The teenagers leaving a local high school were dressed like Nautica models, their scooters the fanciest available; every building was in a nearly idealized state of repair; and in this, the hometown of Luciano Pavarotti, small shops sold sheet music and instruments to lines of enthusiastic customers.

The Giusti family has run a *salumeria,* a meat shop, since 1605, and had roots in vinegar production before then. Originally, the store sold both pork and duck. "The duck was for the Jews, the pork was for the Catholics," the current owner, Matteo Morandi, told me as he showed me around. The store was still bustling in the Italian way—with a fantastic array of wines, high-end cheeses, and meats—but locked down under shorter hours than a Swiss bank. Starting almost seventy years ago, at fifteen, Matteo's father, Adriano, had come to work here as a shop boy for the Giustis. He eventually bought the *salumeria,* and in 1989 opened Hosteria Giusti, a restaurant that, with just four tables, is among the most coveted in Emilia-Romagna. The place is accessible through a tiny passage in the back of the store that winds past the kitchen to tables in the old storage room where hams had hung to cure (the hooks are still driven deep into the overhead beams). We ate a symphony of al dente pasta and milk-fed veal.

The meal ended with a stunningly simple dish: *gnocco fritto,* or pillows of fried dough topped with a few intense drops of sixty-year-old balsamic vinegar. The *balsamico* was so thick that it had to be coaxed from the bottle. The question of what constitutes true balsamic vinegar is nearly impossible to answer. Many balsamics are produced around Modena with unregulated titles like "authentic," "original," and "genuine," but these can be made from Trebbiano grapes in a few days, adulterated with caramel for color, sugar for sweetening, and flour for thickening. The addition of one spoonful of truly aged vinegar is enough to earn the label "aged." These industrially made vinegars are serviceable—Italians routinely use them to lightly flavor a salad dressing—but the truest, artisanal balsamics are produced under the title *tradizionale,* from nothing but a reduction of grapes and time. With a dozen years and up to seven changes of oak or other wood barrels, they take on a nearly black coloring, a thick texture, and an intense, fruity flavor that mark the best balsamics. Those aged more than twelve years earn the title *vecchio; stravecchio* covers the rare brands stored for twenty-five years or more.

The great appeal of these complex, winelike vinegars—from *vin aigre,* or "bitter wine" in French—is the way they naturally accompany a diet heavy in fats, from olive oil to glistening slabs of Parma ham. The *tradizionale* are not mixed into dressings but are highlighted as a prime feature of the meal—dripped onto the finest cheeses or fried vegetables, used to stain vanilla ice cream or risotto on the plate, sprinkled on sweet strawberries with ground pepper to work strange alchemy.

It may seem odd that such a meal was accompanied by a wine that is mocked by snobs. This is Lambrusco, Emilia-Romagna's curious sparkling red, served chilled in violation of every known rule of American connoisseurship. In America, Lambrusco is trailed by a disastrous association with the 1970s, when sales of sparkling red became anathema to a rising gourmet culture. But it is a light and refreshing drink that seems to cut through the richness of Italian food in the same way that balsamic vinegar is an antidote to the fat. A bottle can be a kind of guilty pleasure, all the sweeter for the disapproval of the erudite.

After the meal, I asked Matteo what I asked everyone: Why here? Why is Emilia-Romagna the center of the food universe?

"It's because of the pasta," he said. "Every region in Italy is proud of its cuisine. But we have the tradition of pasta. It's continuous, unbroken."

Then I asked him if Italian food has a "*nonna* problem," if the cuisine is too closely based on images of grandmothers stirring the sauce.

"But that's our whole idea!" he burst out. Speaking loudly and slowly, to compensate for my bad Italian, he said that *of course* Italian food should be based on what *grandmothers* were cooking. "The cuisine is *of the casa*," he told me. "We make *our mothers'* food." His own mother—the *nonna* to his three children—was in the kitchen right now, he pointed out. I popped over a few feet from where we sat in the alley; there was *nonna*, frying the little pillows of dough I had topped with *stravecchio*.

Score one for the grandmothers.

Like a good detective story, Ferrara benefits from what is missing: the dog didn't bark and the tourists didn't come. Of those 40 million annual visitors to Italy, I literally did not see another during five days in Ferrara. Boasting an idealized layout, and claiming to be Europe's first planned city, Ferrara lies on the northeasternmost plain of Emilia-Romagna, alternately bathed in summer heat and winter fog, and ignored by all but the most discerning travelers—chiefly Italians seeking some authentic piece of their own nation that has not been squeezed through a tourism machine.

Ferrara benefits from the quiet: although it is common in Emilia-Romagna for cities to ban traffic in their central zones, in Ferrara the bent alleys of the entire core are pedestrian-friendly. The clattering of wheels over cobblestones and the polite tinkle of bicycle bells may be the loudest sounds you encounter here. For us, wielding a small baby through the region, Ferrara offered a secure and confident respite, where our son could practice his walking freely, at no risk greater than a bombardment of kisses from neighborhood *nonnas*. (When my wife took him walking outside the hotel at six-thirty in the morning, I could track their progress by the faint cries of *"Bambino bellissimo!"* and *"Che bello!"*)

Since Roman times, a road—the Via Emilia—has run straight through Parma, Modena, and Bologna, to Rimini, but Ferrara lies off this access. Ferrara's relative isolation led to stagnation and noble rot; in 1786, Goethe called the city "lovely great depopulated" Ferrara.

Colomba, the owner of a sleepy and delicious trattoria, told me, "Eighteen hundred, 1900—those were abandoned times here. Only in the last five years has tourism picked up." A Lebanese chef, raised in Nigeria and trained in Italy, he had the kind of mixed heritage often concealed behind Italy's classic façade. He was cooking pastas with *ragù alla bolognese* and featherweight gnocchi in sage butter. Ferrara was once a center of Jewish life in Italy, and we sampled heritage dishes here like smoked eggplant and goose with grapefruit. The lack of industry, modernity, and population pressure has preserved the urban core more perfectly than in nearly any other large city in Italy, leaving a *centro storico* of gently curved pedestrian streets.

Ferrara is a humid city in the plains: hot, frequented by mosquitoes, where the women wave Chinese fans to stay cool. I made a rare nocturnal foray, slipping out on a sleeping wife and baby to walk the streets at 11 P.M. Lovely depopulated Ferrara was suddenly coursing with life, the plazas packed with hordes of beer-drinking young people. While eating pizza I made a naive, if profound, discovery about Italians. Everyone was hugging and kissing, slapping backs, the men holding hands, people in rapt conversations still checking cell phones and looking over their shoulders to miss no opportunity with another person. Personality and human relations lie at the core of Italian identity. I watched in amazement as an Italian gallant, clearly on a first date, abandoned his voluptuous companion to race into the street, hug an acquaintance, log some face time with him, engage in a passionate push-me, pull-you argument with the pedestrian, and work hard at persuading his friend of something—and not return to his lady friend for a full fifteen minutes. Personality is an art form to Italians, the purpose of life.

Here is how you make fresh pasta dough: mix flour and eggs together. That's it. There are some useful techniques and tricks, and you can call this dough *sfoglia* if you like, with a good Italian accent. But that is all that lies at the very heart of the secret of Italy's greatest regional cuisine. In Emilia-Romagna in general and in Bologna in particular, the genius of the table is simply fresh pasta. Once you get something right, the only advance comes from simplifying it, and Bologna is the place that gets things right. The city is known by a series of nicknames that shed some light on its history: Bologna the Fat, for its wealth, especially at the table; and Bologna the Red, originally for the dominant color scheme of its buildings and later for its politics. The city remains a Communist Party stronghold, even as it is known as a city with the finest clothes, the best food, and the most beautiful homes in Italy. Medieval arches and porticoes line twenty-five miles of city blocks, and although there are some conspicuous tourist attractions here, like a pair of brick towers from the Middle Ages, the city is more "real" than Venice or Florence, oriented toward regular people and home to 100,000 students and some of the best food markets in the country.

I had a chance to put my high theory of cuisine to the test here —two chances, actually. Determined to have at my fingertips the secrets of Emilia-Romagna, I signed up for a couple of cooking classes. One, conducted in the kitchen of a Bologna bed-and-breakfast called Casa Ilaria, was patronized by several young English couples who had, thanks to the bargains available for European air travel, flown to Bologna for the weekend. This class took a few hours and was taught by Ilaria herself, a relaxed and informal teacher who worked us through the mixing of *sfoglia* dough and the technical challenge of rolling out and cutting the result into wide tagliatelle, while assembling a traditional *ragù alla bolognese* and creating a tiramisu for dessert. Ilaria was in the *nonna* school: Like any Italian home cook, she used *soffritto*—the base of minced onion, celery, and carrots—that came from the supermarket freezer section. Her tips were all practical, like flavoring the sauce with "the wine that's open, red or white," and "pasta feels the weather, so keep some flour back until you see the mix." I left feeling, How easy!

The other class was an altogether more serious affair, a week-long culinary tour of Emilia-Romagna and Tuscany led by noted foodie Mary Beth Clark, which I joined for a single day. We began at dawn beside Bologna's famous statue of Neptune, where Mary Beth pointed to some mysterious white stones embedded in a wall —signs of the original marketplace that thrived here in medieval times, when illiterate servants had to measure out their orders for bolts of cloth and roofing tiles against these standardized forms. We traipsed across the plaza for some early-morning shopping among the cheese and egg vendors, the makers of fresh pastas and cured meats. Then we crossed a few blocks to enter one of the city's most reserved and secretive institutions, the Club Bologna, in a sixteenth-century palazzo. (Trained among Bologna chefs, Mary Beth is the rare female member of this private entity.)

Forget the *nonnas*. We were greeted by a butler, served coffee by uniformed staff, and issued aprons and recipe collections for what would be a whirlwind effort to cook our way through a dozen classic dishes of the region. Assembling in the club's kitchen, guided by Mary Beth and the club's own chefs, we started with the same dishes I had done the night before: fresh pasta dough and a *ragù alla bolognese*. This is the sauce that conquered the world, at least in theory. Genuine *ragù alla bolognese* is a thick, almost dry sauce made with pork and beef that are coarsely chopped, a little tomato, and no garlic or herbs (salt is also little used, since it is present in so many local ingredients, like Parmesan cheese and prosciutto). True Bolognese sauce is used in baked lasagna, or as dressing on broad pastas that can support the meat, like tagliatelle. A Bolognese would sooner go out for Chinese than eat spaghetti alla bolognese, since the thin noodles leave a pile of meat behind in the bowl. In true meat-obsessed Bologna fashion, we also worked up a roast tenderloin and classic *polpetini* meatballs made with veal.

Mary Beth's theory was impeccable, her process professional enough to please even the doctrinaire chefs at Alma. She minced her own *soffritto* rather than using the stuff from the freezer section; she urged us to "harmonize" the *ragù alla bolognese* by using only the same vintage of wine we would be serving with the meal. A true purist, she even declined to put Parmesan cheese on the dish, which Bolognese regard as an unnecessary improvement. And she confirmed my base instinct about Po Valley soil by noting to the class that "if you understand geography, you understand what forms the people, the way they look, and pardon me, the way they smell."

Among the guests was an amiable gray-haired Italian-born man traveling with his Australian wife. He often served as a kind of translator during the cooking, joking and grinning, but I was struck at one point when a shadow passed over his face. He had been talking to the elderly lady rolling out the pasta dough, and I caught a phrase in their rapid exchange that puzzled me: *figli della lupa*. With my dictionary Italian, I misunderstood this to mean "children of the wolf." Clearly it had nothing to do with cooking. I finally forced it out of him. These two gray-hairs, who lived continents apart for almost their whole lives, had found an instant point of common grief in their origins. What he had told the woman was, "We are both Children of the She-Wolf," a reference to Mussolini's Fascist version of the Boy Scouts, the Figli della Lupa. Here was a jolting connection to the old Italy of poverty and dread, recalled at leisure in a luxurious social club, in the relaxed terminus of long lives.

Emilia-Romagna offers plenty of reminders of this history, too. Although Mussolini was actually born here (in Forlì), the region was an anti-Fascist stronghold, and Bologna was the only city in Italy to liberate itself before Allied troops arrived. Northern Italy paid a steep price for this stubborn independence: In Bologna, Ravenna, and Modena, I had seen plaques listing the partisans who died at the hands of the Nazis, and in Ferrara there are plaques remembering the Jews deported to the death camps. Allied bombing and desperate, last-stand fighting by the Germans flattened some towns in the region. This history, combined with the incredible cruelty of the ruling medieval and Renaissance aristocrats, seemed like an incentive to live well while you could. We are all children of the wolf.

The Adriatic Coast has retreated from Ravenna. We blew down the A1 from Ferrara and reached the onetime capital of the Byzantine

Empire by midmorning. This drive took us through the eastern-most parts of Emilia-Romagna, flat and ugly in a way that only a foodie could love. ("Everything smells of pig shit," the author Bill Buford had said of Romagna, sighing with pleasure. "It's pig shit when you wake up, pig shit when you go to sleep, pig shit all day.") Anyone addicted to the Italian table knows what that stink pro-duces, so buck up and breathe deep.

Romagna has more to offer than pig poo, fortunately. Our day was spent touring some of the world's greatest mosaic work, found in Byzantine churches and tombs dating back to the sixth century. I'd seen Roman and Byzantine mosaics in Syria, Turkey, and Leba-non. But the art of stone tiling reached its zenith here, in glittering works of gold and blue that put even Hagia Sophia in Istanbul to shame. In Ravenna, we devoured the famous portraiture in stone of the Basilica di Sant'Apollinare Nuovo and the tiny but stun-ning mausoleum of Galla Placidia. Then we finished the day with a sprint into the Romagna marshlands, where the very oldest mosa-ics lie inside the Abbey of Pomposa. There, in cool shade, I was distracted by the frescoes overhead illustrating Christ's life until I heard a suspicious squeak. I looked down but too late.

Bambino alert. Max was speed-crawling under a velvet rope, mak-ing his way onto the oldest mosaic in Italy. It is a section of flooring from 535 C.E., a closed archaeological site. Old stones were sud-denly causing me a heart attack. Max four-pointed his way into the center, sat down, and, looking around in satisfaction, said, "Hup-hup-hup." He was drooling on treasures from the first millen-nium.

In America you might be arrested for this. In Emilia-Romagna they have a different attitude. A gray-haired docent dismissed all of my concerns using three languages (if you count sign language).

"*Kinder* OK," he said, and waved a hand.

SIMON WINCHESTER

Take Nothing, Leave Nothing

FROM *Lapham's Quarterly*

SEVENTEEN HUNDRED MILES from what is customarily called civilization—in this case, the western shore of the Republic of South Africa—lies a tiny British-run volcanic island populated by fewer than three hundred people who lay claim to living in the most isolated permanent habitation in the world.

I am presently sitting five cables off this island, Tristan da Cunha, wallowing on the swells on a small boat that is hove-to just off the mole at the entrance to the harbor of Edinburgh of the Seven Seas, the island's capital and only settlement. But while my fellow passengers will soon be landing—once the easterly gale blows itself out and the seas die down to an acceptable level—and so are excitedly preparing themselves to enjoy the fascinations that Edinburgh has in store (a visit to the fields where the islanders grow potatoes being the main advertised attraction), I will not be joining them.

For I have been sternly and staunchly forbidden to land. The Island Council of this half-forgotten outpost of the remaining British Empire has for the last quarter century declared me a Banned Person. I am welcome on Tristan neither today nor, indeed, as was succinctly put to me in a diplomatic telegram last year, "ever."

It would be idle to suggest that I have been terribly incommoded. Though some may suspect sour grapes, I have to confess that there is little of great charm to Tristan. Such as it possesses derives almost entirely from its status: there is a very large hand-painted sign in the Edinburgh square saying WELCOME TO THE REMOTEST ISLAND, and once our visitors have had themselves photographed beside it, have exchanged pleasantries with various

islanders over warm English beer at the rather underdecorated Albatross Pub, have studied the piles of canned pork sausages and
sugar-rich candies on sale in the cinder-block shop, and have made
the obligatory two-mile pilgrimage (on the island's only road) to
the fields where the potatoes grow, most will be eager to return to
their waiting cruise ship, to wonder as the island fades away astern,
why on earth anyone would wish to live there.

The latest census says that 275 people do. They belong to just
seven eternally intermarrying families. Two of the families are the
descendants of the civilian support staff of a military garrison that
Britain established on the island in 1815 to help ward off any
French loyalists who might try to rescue Napoleon from St. Helena, fifteen hundred miles to the north. An Italian ship was later
wrecked on the island, bringing with it two further surnames. Two
more family names came down from passing American whalers
and one from a similarly wandering Dutchman, expanding a gene
pool which remains to this day severely limited—and is said to be
responsible for the curious similarity of the islanders' appearances,
and the numerous cases of asthma, *retinitis pigmentosa,* and other
genetically influenced ailments that afflict the population.

Utter isolation—just a scattering of supply ships and randomly
appearing cruise liners happen by each year; there is no airfield
—instills a healthy self-reliance into what is in any case a very singular culture. The men fish for lobster (a pair of which appear on
the island's coat of arms), tinker with their boat engines, tend the
herd of cattle and flock of sheep, dig the vegetable patches; the
women knit (large woolen sweaters called "*ganzeys,*" socks to be put
inside sea boots called "ammunitions"), perform most of the island
paperwork, organize regular morale-lifting celebrations.

The older islanders incorporate nineteenth-century "thees" and
"thous" into their speech—on hearing such chatter it seems perfectly reasonable that only sixty years ago all trade was performed
by barter: to send a letter to England cost five potatoes. And though
satellites have had their recent effect, it seems understandable, too,
that until thirty years ago all contact with the outside world was by
Morse code—fitful, unreliable, and subject to the vagaries of the
ionosphere.

But London keeps its eye on this far corner of the empire. Two
British diplomats preside—colonial figures hardly cut from the

same cloth as the old viceroys of India or governors of Nigeria or Hong Kong. The senior man is usually on the verge of retirement, having enjoyed rather too little distinction in his career, or else sporting a stated fascination with bird watching, since there is a local and much-celebrated albatross. His assistant is invariably an eager youngster—on this occasion an ambitious young woman who was leaving after six months for a long-sought and career-boosting posting outside Kandahar. There is usually rather little for the pair to do: the only signed order currently posted on the island's official notice board refers to a power cut due for two hours the following Tuesday.

Once in a long while, though, there is a crisis. The event for which Tristan is perhaps best remembered was the eruption of its volcano in 1961, and the evacuation of the entire population. The 264 islanders—the population size has remained very stable for the last half century—were brought to England and put up in a disused army barracks in Hampshire. But the supposed delights of Western civilization—cars, elevators, cinemas, none of which the islanders had ever seen before—did not seduce them into staying: two years later all but fourteen went home. They rebuilt their ruined town and settled back to their uncomplicated routines of fishing for lobsters and knitting *ganzeys*. The *Daily Mirror* of the time said, admiringly, that by doing so the islanders had delivered to all smug Britons a much-deserved and contemptuous slap.

I first went to the island in 1983, then again a little later. I was welcomed, though warily: the self-reliance of the islanders is matched by a fierce devotion to self-protection and privacy. They knew I was a writer: they warned me that anything I might publish would be read and analyzed for years to come. And though nothing untoward occurred while I was visiting (my time ashore I spent fully impressed with the idea of leaving only footprints and taking only snapshots) it was shortly after that second trip that I quite inadvertently committed the indiscretion which resulted in my lifetime prohibition.

At first blush it all sounds to have been innocent indeed. It stems from a somewhat bizarre British government decision, taken during World War II, to reclassify some of its more remote island possessions as ships. Tristan was transmuted into HMS *Atlantic Isle,* and its role was to patrol (from its rock-hewn state of immobility) for any German U-boats that might be lurking in the southern Atlantic. To compound the fantasy a small party of sailors was posted there to man the ship—one of them a young and apparently romantically minded lieutenant and littérateur manqué named Derrick Booy.

In the grand tradition that has long intertwined nice girls and sailors, Lieutenant Booy fell for one of the island's prettiest, a slip of a lass then named Emily Hagan. He stayed only eighteen months on the island, and once the war was over he wrote a memoir, published in 1957. In it he made many tender mentions of Miss Hagan, and though his writings leave little doubt as to his own feelings, they are somewhat ambiguous as to the degree to which his ardor was reciprocated.

Two paragraphs stood out as most pertinent. One recorded the pair's first meeting:

> The night air was an enveloping golden presence as we stood at the break in the wall. I was conscious of bare, rounded arms and the fragrance of thickly clustered hair. The lingering day was full of noises. As the sky darkened to a deep, umbrageous blue, speckled with starlight, and the village was swallowed by darkness at the foot of the mountain, from somewhere in that blackness came the throaty plaint of an old sheep, like a voice from the mountain. From that other obscurity, silver-gleaming below the cliffs, came the muttered irony of the surf. The girl waited only a few minutes before her full lips breathed "Goodnight," and she slipped toward the house. "Shall I come to see you again?" I called softly. She may or may not have answered "Yes." If she did, it was probably from politeness.

And the other notes the mechanics of their eventual parting, recorded after Lieutenant Booy had boarded the whaler that would take him out to his waiting navy ship, and away.

> The watchers on the beach were all very still, the women sitting again in their gaily dressed rows, as if waiting primly to be photographed. None of them waved or cheered. They just sat watching. All looked very much alike, young and old. But there was one at the end of a row, in a white dress with a red kerchief, bright-red over smooth, dark hair. She sat perfectly still, staring back until she became a white blur. Then her head went down, and the woman behind her—a large one in widow's black—put a hand on her shoulder.

Whatever her feelings for the jolly Jack tar, ten years later Emily Hagan was married to Kenneth Rogers, an islander who had been employed as a mess boy by the visiting naval party, and who after the war worked both as the island's baker and a butcher. By the time I got to Tristan he was in his sixties, working as a part-time assistant barman at the Albatross. But the very moment I fetched up outside his tiny thatched cottage, notebook in hand, he knew exactly what I wanted. "To see our H'em'ly, I suppose," he said, glumly. He knew just why. He didn't want to let me see her. He placed himself four-square behind his garden gate, keeping it firmly latched.

He gave me a stern lecture, all the more touching by being couched in his elegant and ancient English. He said he wished I would purge from my mind all that I had read in the "navy man's" book. The revelations, he said, had "hurt us all. It was all a long, long time ago, and we'd just as soon forget it." He was courteous, kindly, firm. And two days later, just before I left the island for good, he came down the harbor to see me off. "Remember," he said, *"whatever you write will last for years; we back on the island will pore over it and analyze it a thousand times. Be careful what you write—for our own sakes."*

But I have to confess that, when it came to writing, I ignored him. I began work on a book about all of the remaining outposts of the British Empire—for my visit to Tristan was but part of two long years of wanderings that took me from Pitcairn to Diego Garcia, from Bermuda to the Falkland Islands, from Hong Kong to Gibraltar, and to all those other weather-beaten relics of Imperial Britannia. When I came to the Tristan chapter, I decided that I would in fact tell the story of Emily Hagan and Derrick Booy, in full.

It would be a very small part of a story about a very small island in an overlooked corner of the world. But as a story it was a good one—especially if I quoted from his book Derrick Booy's two rather overwrought paragraphs. My rationale for doing so was simple: everything had already been made public; everything was in the prints; and in any case the story, told in an exquisitely gentle fashion, was just a near-beer account of a wartime love affair which, by all accounts, had been tender, unconsummated, and quite possibly entirely imagined. I thought that back on a Tristan which now seemed a very, very long way away, old Kenneth Rogers was being just too, too sensitive: the story was the thing, that was all there was to it. So I wrote the book; it was duly published. The reviews were kindly, the sales modest—and I thought little more of it.

Except that twelve years passed, and then out of the blue in 1998 I was invited onto a cruise ship on passage through the Southern Ocean. I had been asked to go along to talk to the passengers about various places I had visited: the Antarctic, South Georgia, Gough Island, Inaccessible, Nightingale—and Tristan. I did as I was bidden, without incident for the first two weeks of the voyage. Then on a Friday morning, during a half gale just north of the Antarctic convergence, I gave my talk about the history of Tristan. We arrived the following evening, and when we were comfortably at anchor off the Edinburgh mole, we were boarded, somewhat surprisingly, by a very large imperial policeman. He had a brief announcement to make: everyone would be permitted onto the island the following morning, but regrettably not—the ship's passenger manifest had been radioed ahead—Mr. Winchester.

I had, he explained sternly, betrayed an island secret. I had been warned; I had actually been implored. But I had gone ahead, and now the islanders were every bit as hurt and upset as Kenneth Rogers had forewarned. The constable was implacable, immovable. And so the passengers, most of them greatly amused, filed past me down to the gangway, boarded their Zodiacs, and were swept off behind the riprap into Calshot Harbor—named for the village in Hampshire to where the islanders had been evacuated in 1961—and off to see the sights of Edinburgh. When they returned an hour or so later they shook their heads as one: *why would anyone want to live there?* And then they puzzled over my exclusion: *it's not as though you had killed someone.*

Another invitation, from a second cruise line, dropped through the mailbox in the spring of 2008: it was for a voyage due to begin in the austral autumn of 2009, in March. This time, anticipating problems, I wired ahead. I asked the British chief resident envoy to Tristan, David Morley (whose career path had previously included postings to such out-of-the-way legations as Kaduna, Mbabane, and Port Stanley), if I was still banned. Surely not, I said I supposed.

Twenty-four years had passed. Emily and Kenneth Rogers were now both dead. Surely by now I had purged my contempt?

Weeks passed until his telegram of reply. Sadly no, he finally reported. The Island Council had met, had formally considered the request, and had voted that "you will not be able to land on this occasion or, indeed, ever."

And so with that knowledge I boarded the MY *Corinthian II* (in Ushuaia, in southern Patagonia, a town where I had once spent three months in prison on spying charges during the Falklands War, but which by contrast still welcomes me warmly each time I happen by), and off we sailed, along the familiar sub-Antarctic milk run. I delivered without incident my lectures about the Falklands, on South Georgia, on the history of the Atlantic—and eventually, about Tristan da Cunha. And it was then that I told the passengers that I would not be going with them, and explained why.

By now I had built up something of a rapport with the passengers, and a gasp went up. Most seemed quite incredulous. Nearly all were American. Many happened to be lawyers. These last were especially exasperated on my behalf. Over dinner later they insisted that I sue. Freedom of speech, they chorused. Moreover— Tristan is British, and you are British: it isn't even an immigration question. It is a simple assault on free speech. A village in Yorkshire, said one attorney who had spent time there, would not legally be able to ban someone from visiting because he had written that the village was ugly, or the inhabitants were unpleasant, or that the publican was having an affair with the vicar's wife. So sue! Go to the Tristan High Court! The St. Helena High Court! The House of Lords! You'll be bound to win. No problem!

I let the passengers press past me once again on their way down onto the gangway, and I watched with some melancholy as they filed into the Zodiacs. I stood on the bridge with the lugubrious German captain and borrowed his binoculars to watch the tourists make their way to the Albatross, to the slopes of the volcano, to the church, to the potato fields. And then I went back to my cabin, and for the next few irritating hours pondered my fate and thought about travel in general, and about such weighty matters as the sayings of Blaise Pascal, who once infamously wrote that all of mankind's ills stemmed from his inability to remain peacefully at home in his living room. Then as dusk was falling, I emerged back onto the deck to greet the returning scrum.

And I found that I had in those few hours become both contrite, and a convert. Pascal, I concluded, had a point. I was now in fact quite certain that, whatever high principle might be involved, the islanders of Tristan were in fact quite right and I, as a clumsily meandering and utterly thoughtless outsider, was very, very wrong indeed.

For though I sedulously followed the rule of taking nothing and leaving nothing, it suddenly seemed to me that my very being on the island, and my later decision to record my impressions of that visit and the impressions of earlier visitors, had resulted in a series of entirely unintended and unanticipated consequences—consequences that were as inimical to the islanders' contentment as if I had plundered or polluted there.

I had no understanding whatsoever that by repeating that naval officer's memoir, I could hurt the feelings of anyone. To my clumsy, unthinking, touristic mind, the notion seemed quite absurd. To be sure, old Kenneth Rogers had explained it to me kindly—but I had chosen to ignore his warning, to dismiss his assertion of feeling. I had failed, even for one second, to consider what he and his fellow islanders might think—because I held to an unspoken assumption that as a visitor from the sophisticated outside, I knew better, and that I had something of a prescriptive right to do with him and his like, more or less as I pleased. (Repeating it here, a second time, as a didactic exercise, seems unlikely to compound the felony: even as he told of the renewed ban, the island constable who boarded our vessel assured me that few of the younger islanders now minded, and only a very small number even remembered. "And if it were up to me, I'd let you back.")

Then came a cascade of similar memories, from earlier journeys. The woman from San Diego whom I met in a truly remote Amazon village, buying up everything she could see—a volcano-size pile of old chairs and tables and statuettes assembled on raffia mats in the village square, the villagers looking on in eager anticipation of their good fortune from the sale of their castoffs—but who promptly walked out on the deal when told that the village had no facility for taking her Visa card. The Microsoft billionaire who arrived on Namibia's Skeleton Coast with five helicopters full of bodyguards, and demanded that all available local lions be collected in one oasis so that he could see and picture them. The Texan who insisted on being pictured beside his golf club's pennant on every Arctic and Antarctic stop he made, then teeing off and driving one ball—such a *little* ball, he would sweetly insist—into the sea.

We have an unceasing capacity to make ourselves nuisances, basically. Students of tourism science can and do construct elaborate theories from physics, of course, invoking such wizards as Heisenberg and the Hawthorne effect and the status of Schrödinger's cat to explain the complex interactions between our status as tourist-observers and the changes we prompt in the peoples and places we go off to observe. But at its base is the simple fact that in so many instances, we simply behave abroad in manners we would never permit at home: we impose, we interfere, we condescend, we breach codes, we reveal secrets. And by doing so we leave behind much more than footfalls. We leave bruised feelings, bad taste, hurt, long memories.

Attractive-sounding mantras about footprints and photographs won't fully resolve the problem. The only real solution, however impractical and improbable, is to hearken to Pascal's much-scorned adage, to resolve to resist the blandishments of the brochure, and stay away. Certainly the people of Tristan da Cunha would have been happier had I stayed back—and who would deny the rights of the people of Tristan, just as ourselves, to be left happy, and at peace?

Except that in the specific case of Tristan da Cunha, it is probably too late. The island has recently appointed a government tourist officer, and the community's leadership has recently come formally to accept—rather later than most other places—that catering to the visiting curious is quite a reliable way of making what, back in the barter days of sixty years ago, most Tristanians knew little about—money. Tourism for the islanders, it was argued in Council, has the advantage of being less hazardous a road to riches than rowing out to catch lobsters, and a good deal more profitable than spending the long evenings knitting sweaters.

It has taken them some time, but now the most remote island in the world seems to have come fully round to opening its arms to the world's immense traveling community, just as the people of Paris and Bangkok and Lima and London have done before them. That community is still swelling exponentially, and alarmingly: the 45 million Chinese who toured the world last year, for example, are expected by Beijing to reach 100 million by 2020.

The 275 islanders far off in the South Atlantic may share the hope that among those thousands who eventually throng to have their picture taken beside the famous Edinburgh signboard, there will be few tourists as thoughtless as I. But they shouldn't count on it.

Contributors' Notes

Notable Travel Writing of 2009

Contributors' Notes

Henry Alford is the author of three works of nonfiction — *How to Live*, about the wisdom of the elderly; *Big Kiss*, which won a Thurber Prize for American Humor; and *Municipal Bondage*, a humor collection. A regular contributor to the *New York Times*, he has also written for *The New Yorker* and *Vanity Fair*.

Tom Bissell was born in Escanaba, Michigan, in 1974. He is the author of *Chasing the Sea*, a travel narrative; *God Lives in St. Petersburg*, a story collection; *The Father of All Things*, a hybrid work of history and memoir about his father and the Vietnam War; and *Extra Lives*, a work of video game criticism. "Looking for Judas," which is drawn from his travel narrative about the tombs of the twelve apostles, marks his fourth appearance in *Best American Travel Writing*. He lives in Portland, Oregon.

Colby Buzzell is an Operation Iraqi Freedom combat veteran, as well as the author of the book *My War: Killing Time in Iraq*. In 2004, Buzzell was profiled in *Esquire* magazine's "Best and Brightest" issue and has since contributed frequently. He lives in San Francisco.

Avi Davis is a writer, musician, amateur farmer, and photographic archivist who lives and teaches in Mexico City. He has contributed to the *New York Moon*, *Tennessee Mountain Defender*, and *Greenpoint Gazette*, among other publications. More of his writing can be found at the blog "Shreds and Clippings."

Michael Finkel lives with his family in western Montana.

Ian Frazier is the author of *Great Plains, The Fish's Eye, On the Rez,* and *Family,* as well as *Coyote v. Acme* and *Lamentations of the Father.* A frequent contributor to *The New Yorker,* he lives in Montclair, New Jersey.

Ted Genoways is the author of two books of poetry and the nonfiction book *Walt Whitman and the Civil War.* His travel writing and reporting have appeared in *Harper's Magazine, Outside,* and *Mother Jones,* where he is a contributing writer. As editor of the *Virginia Quarterly Review,* he has won four National Magazine Awards and edited six pieces selected for *Best American Travel Writing,* including Tom Bissell's essay in this volume. His trip to Suriname with his father was supported by a grant from the Pulitzer Center on Crisis Reporting.

J. C. Hallman is the author of several books of nonfiction, including *The Chess Artist* and *The Devil Is a Gentleman,* and a short story collection, *The Hospital for Bad Poets.* "A House Is a Machine to Live In" appears in his book *In Utopia: Six Kinds of Eden and the Search for a Better Paradise.* He can be reached through his Web site, jchallman.com.

Peter Hessler, a native of Missouri, went to China in 1996 as a Peace Corps volunteer. For two years he taught English in Fuling, a small city on the Yangtze River, not far from the Three Gorges region; this experience is described in his first book, *River Town.* After finishing the Peace Corps, Hessler moved to Beijing, where he eventually became a staff writer for *The New Yorker* and a contributing writer for *National Geographic.* All told, he lived in China for more than a decade, writing a trilogy of nonfiction books: *River Town, Oracle Bones,* and *Country Driving.* In 2007, Hessler moved to southwestern Colorado, where he lives outside the town of Ridgway. His wife, Leslie T. Chang, is also a writer and a wanderer. They expect to move overseas again in 2011.

Christopher Hitchens is a columnist for *Vanity Fair* and the author of the memoir *Hitch-22,* as well as the book *Imperial Spoils,* about the Parthenon Marbles.

Garrison Keillor is an American author, storyteller, and humorist, and the host and writer of *A Prairie Home Companion* and *The Writer's Almanac* heard on National Public Radio stations across the country. He was born in Anoka, Minnesota, and raised in a family belonging to a Plymouth Brethren congregation. Keillor has written many magazine articles and is the author of more than a dozen books, including *Lake Wobegon Days, The Book of Guys, Love Me,* and *Homegrown Democrat.*

Peter LaSalle is the author of a novel, *Strange Sunlight,* and three story collections: *The Graves of Famous Writers, Hockey Sur Glace,* and *Tell Borges if You See Him: Tales of Contemporary Somnambulism.* His fiction has appeared in many anthologies, including *Best American Short Stories* and *Prize Stories: The O. Henry Awards.* In 2005, he received the Award for Distinguished Prose from the *Antioch Review.* He divides his time between Austin, Texas, and Narragansett, in his native Rhode Island, while continuing to travel as much as he can to read favorite authors in the places where their work is set.

Peter Jon Lindberg is editor at large of *Travel + Leisure,* where he covers food and drink, music, cultural trends, architecture and design, the hotel industry, and the curious business of travel. He is a graduate of Harvard University, where he was managing editor of the Let's Go travel guide series. His writing has been featured in *New York, Food & Wine, Men's Journal, Details, Glamour,* and the *New York Times.* In 2005, he was named a Travel Journalist of the Year by the Society of American Travel Writers (SATW) and was a finalist for a James Beard Foundation Award for food writing. His essay "In Defense of Tourism" won an SATW Gold Award and was nominated for a National Magazine Award. He lives in Brooklyn, New York, with his wife, *Travel + Leisure* features editor Niloufar Motamed.

Susan Orlean was born in Cleveland and has lived in Ann Arbor, Michigan; Portland, Oregon; Boston; New York City; Los Angeles; and, currently, the Hudson River Valley of New York State. She has been a staff writer for *The New Yorker* since 1992 and has contributed to *Esquire, Vogue, Rolling Stone, Smithsonian,* and the *New York Times Magazine.* Her seven books include *The Orchid Thief, The Bullfighter Checks Her Makeup,* and *My Kind of Place.* She is currently writing a cultural biography of the dog actor Rin Tin Tin.

David Owen has been a staff writer for *The New Yorker* since 1991. Previously, he was a contributing editor at the *Atlantic Monthly* and, prior to that, a senior writer at *Harper's Magazine.* He is also a contributing editor at *Golf Digest.* He is the author of more than a dozen books, including *High School,* about the four months he spent pretending to be a high school student; *None of the Above,* an exposé of the standardized-testing industry; and *The Man Who Invented Saturday Morning,* a collection of his pieces from *Harper's* and the *Atlantic.*

George Packer is a staff writer for *The New Yorker* and the author of *The Assassins' Gate: America in Iraq,* which received several prizes and was named one of the ten best books of 2005 by the *New York Times Book Review.* He is also the author of two novels, *The Half Man* and *Central Square,* and two works of nonfiction, *The Village of Waiting* and *Blood of the Liberals,* which won the 2001 Robert F. Kennedy Book Award. He is the editor of *The Fight Is for Democracy: Winning the War of Ideas in America and the World* and a two-volume edition of George Orwell's essays. His play *Betrayed,* based on a *New Yorker* article, won the 2008 Lucille Lortel Award for best off-Broadway play. His most recent book, *Interesting Times: Writings from a Turbulent Decade,* was published in the fall of 2009.

Matthew Power came across the idea to follow Ed Stafford on his epic trans-Amazonian walk by typing "insane expedition" into Google. If all goes according to plan, Stafford will complete his nearly three-year expedition by the time this anthology goes to press. Power is a contributing editor at *Harper's Magazine,* and his writing has also appeared in the *New York Times Magazine, Men's Journal, National Geographic Adventure, Outside, Wired, GQ, Discover,* the *Virginia Quarterly Review, Granta, Mother Jones,* and *Slate.* He has been anthologized in *Best American Spiritual Writing* and *Best American Travel Writing* and is a 2010 Knight-Wallace Fellow at the University of Michigan. He grew up in Vermont and lives in Brooklyn, New York.

Steven Rinella is the author of *The Scavenger's Guide to Haute Cuisine* and *American Buffalo: In Search of a Lost Icon.* His writing has appeared in many publications, including *Outside, Field & Stream, Men's Journal,* the *New York Times, Glamour,* and *Bowhunter.*

David Sedaris is the author of the books *Dress Your Family in Corduroy and Denim, Me Talk Pretty One Day, Naked, Holidays on Ice, Barrel Fever,* and *When You Are Engulfed in Flames.* He is a regular contributor to *The New Yorker* and National Public Radio's *This American Life.* His latest collection, *Squirrel Seeks Chipmunk: A Modest Bestiary,* will be published in October 2010.

Patrick Symmes, a New York City–based writer, is a longtime contributor to *Condé Nast Traveler* and a contributing editor at *Outside.* After two decades reporting in South America, Cuba, China, and remote corners of the ocean, he recently made his first trip to Italy.

Simon Winchester's new book, *Atlantic: The Biography of an Ocean,* will be published in the United States in November 2010. He lives in New York and the Berkshires.

Notable Travel Writing of 2009

SELECTED BY JASON WILSON

MATTHEW AIKINS
   The Master of Spin Boldak. *Harper's Magazine,* December.
DAVID AMSDEN
   The Lost Art of Getting Lost. *GQ,* July.
LESLIE ANTHONY
   No Zen on a Powder Day. *Skiing,* February/March.
NEGAR AZIMI
   Dubai Is for Flamingos. *Harper's Magazine,* June.

LUKE BARR
   At Home in Provence. *Travel + Leisure,* April.
KIMBERLY BEEKMAN
   El Otro Lado (The Other Side). *Ski,* March/April.
MELINDA GEROSA BELLOWS
   In Search of Magic. *National Geographic Traveler,* November/December.
KATHERINE BOO
   Opening Night. *The New Yorker,* February 23.

SUSAN CONLEY
   China Flu Blues. *New York Times Magazine,* November 29.
TED CONOVER
   Slipping from Shangri-la. *Virginia Quarterly Review,* Spring.

ROBERT DRAPER
   Shattered Somalia. *National Geographic,* September.
DANIEL DUANE
   My Father's Mountain. *Men's Journal,* September.
CANDACE DYER
   Greetings from Helen. *Atlanta,* September.

DAVID FARLEY
   On the Perils of Travel Writing. *WorldHum,* July 6.

J. MALCOLM GARCIA
   Call of the Narcocorrido. *Virginia Quarterly Review,* Fall.
   Who's in Power? *McSweeney's,* Panorama edition.
A. A. GILL
   The Out-of-Towners. *Vanity Fair,* January.
HERBERT GOLD
   The Messiah Returned to Haiti, but It Didn't Help. *Hudson Review,* Autumn.

JONATHAN HARR
   Lives of the Saints. *The New Yorker,* January 5.
LEIGH ANN HENION
   The Dangerous Spring. *Washington Post Magazine,* March 29.

PICO IYER
   Nowhere Need Be Foreign. *Lapham's Quarterly,* Summer.

VERLYN KLINKENBORG
   Northern Light. *National Geographic,* June.
CAROLYN KORMANN
   Last Days of the Glacier. *Virginia Quarterly Review,* Spring.

JOHN LANCASTER
   Study Abroad. *The Smart Set,* June 26.
PETER LASALLE
   Plasticize Your Documents: With G. Flaubert in Carthage. *Another Chicago Magazine,* no. 46.
PETER LAUFER
   Calexico: Bordering on a State of Mind. *Southern Review,* Autumn.

FRANCES MAYES
   Under the Polish Sun. *Smithsonian,* September.
BUCKY MCMAHON
   Relocation! Relocation! Relocation! *GQ,* December.
JON MOOALLEM
   Raiders of the Lost R2. *Harper's Magazine,* March.
JASON MOTLAGH
   Sixty Hours of Terror. *Virginia Quarterly Review,* November.

SHOBA NARAYAN
   My Life as a Geisha. *Condé Nast Traveler,* October.

ROBERT YOUNG PELTON
   The New War for Hearts and Minds. *Men's Journal,* February.
TONY PERROTTET
   Hellfire Holidays. *Slate,* December 14–18.
MARC PERUZZI
   Teton Passing Lane. *Mountain Sports + Living,* Winter.

ROLF POTTS
  Where No Travel Writer Has Gone Before. *WorldHum*, November 16.
WILLIAM POWERS
  Freewheelin' Liberia. *Washington Post*, July 19.
FRANCINE PROSE
  Serene Japan. *Smithsonian*, September.

DAVID ROMPF
  In Mr. Hiyoshi's Building. *Memoir (and)*, Fall/Winter.
WITOLD RYBCZYNSKI
  Words Apart. *The American Scholar*, Summer.

DAVID SEDARIS
  Laugh, Kookaburra. *The New Yorker*, August 24.
GARY SHETYENGART
  A Winter's Tale. *Travel + Leisure*, December.
SETH STEVENSON
  The Young Couple and the Sea. *Slate*, October 19–23.
EMILY STONE
  The Chapín. *The Smart Set*, September 11.
ROB STORY
  Welcome to Switaly. *Skiing*, January.
GINGER STRAND AND JAMES WALLENSTEIN
  In Pursuit of the Wild Cohiba. *The Believer*, October.
PATRICK SYMMES
  Between the Devil and the Deep Blue Sea. *Outside*, September.
  Hugo's World. *Outside*, April.

JEFFREY TAYLER
  Cycling India's Wildest Highway. *WorldHum*, February 23.
  Face-off on the Congo. *WorldHum*, June 1.
PAUL THEROUX
  The Long Way Home. *Smithsonian*, September.
JUNE THOMAS
  Men at Work. *Slate*, January 26–30.

CHRISTOPHER VOURLIAS
  At Home in . . . Zanzibar. *Washington Post*, October 11.

MICHAEL J. WHITE
  One Night in Villa. *New York Times Magazine*, May 31.